All rights reserved. First published 2019.

All characters and places in this publication are fictitious and any re is purely coincidental.

# AUTHOR'S NOTE

The main problem with writing about another country, is that the inhabitants invariably speak a different language. In my book, we encounter three different categories of Spaniard. Firstly, those with almost perfect English. Carlos the Spanish teacher, for example, and Rafi the estate agent. For them, I have reported their conversations verbatim.

Secondly, we meet those locals attempting to learn English. 'Plees we go bar of old queens thees night, take beer!' Once again, what appears in these pages, is how it came out. More or less!

Finally, we are introduced to the *Village People*. No, not six camp singers from the mid-seventies, waving their arms above their heads, to the tune of Y.M.C.A. Great song, danced to it many-a-time, at weddings. But sadly, native Americans, cops, bikers, builders, soldiers and cowboys do not feature in this volume. No, when I say *Village People*, I mean the people of the village, the neighbours, the older generation generally, who speak not a word of English. For them, I have attempted to translate, as best I can, which was not easy at times, especially at Andalucian pace, and volume!

Hopefully, all will become clear, as the book progresses. So read on, and enjoy! I hope you get as much pleasure from following our adventures, as we did 'living the dream'!

John Austin Richards, Andalucia, Spain.

## PROLOGUE. STORM CLOUDS APPROACHING...

A park bench, south Bristol, in the drizzle. The grey half-light of dawn, angry, stressed, sleep deprived, after driving through the night from the Calais ferry, permitted an hour's rest only, in the various so-called 'services' on the M4 west of London, then chased out of the reserved parking area outside Chrissie's mother's flat by an over-zealous parking warden. Waterproof jackets on. Well this is August, after all. Chrissie smiles sweetly, remarkable self-control after the night we have had. 'I wonder what is happening right now, back home?' she ponders. 'I bet Isabel will be out sweeping the street. Loli will be on her patio, clearing her throat. Fernando will be blowing his nose, like the Queen Mary leaving Southampton. The dustman will be towing his rubber bin up the hill. Cruzojo will be peeping through his blinds. Susanna will be polishing her windows with that white dog. Campo Pete will have his Elvis records on, Leopard-skin woman and auntie Vera will be gossiping, and sexy-eyes Jose the Pan will be missing me, I hope! And, of course, the sun will be out!'

Home? Did she say home? She *did* say home. Our Spanish home. But for how much longer, I wonder? I glance up at the sky, which is the colour of a tramp's underwear, although not as dark as the stormy black clouds surely looming just over the horizon. Metaphorical clouds, for now, but they are there.

*Brexit.*

We followed the referendum campaign in our online newspaper and on the internet, of course, and I did actually predict, to our incredulous Spanish friends, that Britain would vote to leave the European Union. And now it has happened. So what will it mean for us? Will we need visas to visit Spain, or permission to stay, or be forced to return to Britain for a part of each year? What about healthcare, driving licences, our personal pensions, our state pensions in future? Will we face hostility, over Gibraltar, from the locals? Already, sterling has devalued by around ten per-cent, making everything correspondingly more expensive for us over there. And although the UK will not actually leave for another couple of years, a considerable number of expats with ongoing health problems are openly talking about getting out while the going is good, before house prices devalue, and to re-establish their NHS entitlements.

No idea, of course. Might be a storm in a teacup, a fuss about nothing. But what will become of our hopes and dreams, in the land of sunsets, and olives?

## CHAPTER 1. A (SAD) LIFE ON THE OCEAN WAVES.

No, I was not woken by the hairy Ukrainian lorry driver snoring away in the next seat, in the somewhat optimistically titled 'Executive Sleeping Lounge', even though this fellow could snort for his country, like a field of pigs who have decided to get together for a grunting contest, in the middle of a thunderstorm. Nor was my beauty-sleep disturbed by the three female Romanian asbestos miners coughing and hacking away at the back of the room, in the manner of a pack of asthmatic Labradors, every now and again sending an eddy of stale cigarette smoke wafting down in my direction. And on the rare occasions when my new Eastern European friends fell silent, a baby started grizzling. I don't suppose the infant cared either way, but seriously? A trip like this? Why didn't the parents go to Center Parks, or Butlin's?

Before this I had gone to the restaurant in search of sustenance, where the roast lamb looked good, which goes to prove that appearances can be deceptive. Mind you the surly Soviet-era server behind the counter didn't help, 'Would Sir like chips and tomato sauce with his lamb?' No I bloody well wouldn't, you have potatoes with lamb, roast and boiled, but being a foreigner he doesn't grasp that concept, so there are chips, and they are not even proper chips, or rice. I opt for the latter, and anaemic looking veg, which I now know to have been the wrong choice, then ask him what sauce he would recommend? 'Gravy' he replied, ladling it all over the plate. Actually, describing this as 'lamb' undoubtedly contravenes all sorts of Trading Standards legislation, more like 'mutton done up as', rather like the woman opposite me in the dining area who is surely twenty-five years too old for those tight white jeans and stilettos, hair in the classic 'Croydon Facelift' ponytail, and a cleavage which they could have used down on the car deck earlier, for parking the motorbikes. £9.75 they wanted for one gristly slice of old ram, (the meat, I mean, not the woman) which could probably have limped back to my table on its own. Doing my best to force it down, to mask the taste of the mutton, to take my mind off the glutinous gravy-encrusted rice, I was drinking mini-sized bottles of French red wine, 'Old Farmyard' it was called if my schoolboy French served me correctly, and boy was that an accurate description, essence of rooster with a hint of dung, and a smidgen of sweaty old Gallic farmer thrown in for good measure. Actually I doubt it was actually wine at all, more like a 'wine-flavoured beverage', bottom of the barrel stuff which the French thought they could foist on the Brits, at three times the price for this small measure, as what I pay for a whole bottle of good stuff in Spain, where strangely enough this boat is headed. Truly they should have paid me the £9.75. Plus danger-money.

Around this time I began to seriously regret reading the *Sunday Times* travel section, a few months ago. *'New bargain-price ferry service to northern Spain'* the headline ran, although I am willing to bet the journalist was not bedding down on a seat, from a 1970's Ford Zephyr, in a cloud of Benson & Hedges fumes, amid a symphony of lungs, windpipes and whining ankle-biters. No, he was without doubt ensconced in a cosy cabin on the top deck, room service, sheet turned down, mint on the pillow, first off the car deck tomorrow. Elderly sheep was not on his menu, that's a sure fact. Or Bisto on his rice.

And no, I was not woken by the tunes playing in my head, an annoying selection by the Bee-Gees, thoughtfully provided by the tribute act in the bar earlier, three middle-aged blokes with high voices and sunglasses, 'Ah, ah, ah, ah, stayin' alive, stayin' alive.' *Yeah thanks for that guys.* Slumping dejectedly in a chair at the back of the bar, nursing a pint of overpriced, under-strength, lager-flavoured water, as far from the 'entertainment' as possible, but sadly still within earshot, I spotted a copy of *The Sun*, and in a moment of madness which I now bitterly regret, picked it up, for want of anything better to do, intending to wile away a few sad lonely minutes flicking through the pictures. 'Oi, that's mine!' complained a voice behind me, 'but you can read it if you like.' Turning to face the objector, I was stunned to find myself gazing into the eyes of Elton John, circa 1986, complete with ginger hair and orange sunglasses. Who knew that *Rocket Man* travelled by car ferry, across the Bay of Biscay, and was a fan of Page Three?

For a couple of seconds I was rendered speechless. Uncanny, he even has Elton's voice, what little I have heard, on TV. *Surely, it cannot be him?* Smiling, my new acquaintance slipped his hand into his pocket, and handed me a business card, bearing the legend *'John Roberts, UK-Spain-UK Removals. No job too small'*, which only served to add to my confusion. So why is a removals guy dressing up as Elton John? Is this some grotesque wind-up? Is this part of the entertainment? Are Ant and Dec, or heaven forbid, Noel Edmonds, about to spring out from behind a pillar? This nightmare on the high seas is rapidly going downhill, if that were possible. Not that there are hills out here, but you know what I mean.

Suddenly, Elton, aka John Roberts, snatched the card from my hand, turned it over, and quickly handed it back. *'Bobby John'* the reverse side read, *'Britain's best Elton John tribute act.'* And he started to sing. *'I remember when rock was young, me and Suzie had so much fun...'* And he was good, very good. So what the hell? We only pass this way once, hopefully. I decided to join in. I often get lairy, after a couple of water-flavoured lagers. Especially if they cost £6. *'Holding hands and skimming stones, had an old gold Chevy and a place of my own!'*

John/Bobby/Elton clapped me on the back, grinning widely. 'Hey, nice voice!' he exaggerated. 'So, do you know Gea, John ?' he enquired. *John? He knows my name? This MUST be a wind-up, right? Am I being stalked? Is my wife having me followed? How is this possible? I mean, it's been a tough day already, the ride down to Portsmouth in the pouring rain, wringing about a gallon of greasy gutter-water from my leathers in the ferry terminal and trying, and spectacularly failing, to dry them under a pathetic fifty-watt hand-dryer, changing into some dry-ish clothes on the car-deck in front of assorted caravanners, Romanian truckers and a bunch of Saaf-London mods on ancient Lambrettas, complete with parkas and tiger-tails, searching optimistically for the 'Executive Sleeping Lounge', the old ram, the essence of farmer, the Bee-Gees, and finally Elton John. All I need now, to complete the perfect day, is for Noel Edmonds to appear.*

My new friend sensed my confusion. 'You know, where this boat is going. Gea-John. Ever been there, have you?'

*Ah yes. The famous Gijon. A ferry-port in northern Spain, apparently. Although it is clear that, of the two of us, only I know the Spanish pronunciation to be 'Hee-HHON' , with the throaty, phlegm-encrusted second syllable. HHON. And the only reason I am aware of this, is because I caused a massive hullabaloo at the conversation group, at Santa Marta library, when I announced I had booked a ferry from England to Gea-John. Gijon. I mean, any English-speaker would, wouldn't they? Tears were rolling down faces, tissues produced, thighs slapped, noses blown, and a visit from Marie the librarian, to threaten us with expulsion. Although when appraised of the reason for the merriment, she too dissolved into paroxysms of laughter. Come on. Hee-HHON? Who knew?*

'No, this is my first, and last, voyage on this route!' I confirmed. 'I mean, I've gone Dover to Calais before, and I wish I'd done that this trip. Taken a couple of days in France, wild camping, eating in little bistros, MacDonald's even would have been preferable to this rip-off, along the back roads, instead of feeling like I am imprisoned in this hell-hole. Seriously, I sailed from Weymouth to the Channel Islands on the *Sealink* in about 1976, and that ferry was more modern than this one.'

'So what sort of bike are you riding?' Elton giggled. *Bike? BIKE? How on earth does he know I'm riding a bike? This guy is seriously spooking me out. First it was John, now it's a bike. This HAS to be a wind-up, right? Ant and Dec are behind the next pillar, for sure.*

Nevertheless, I smiled sweetly, in case there was a camera trained on me from around the corner. 'How do you know I am riding a bike?'

Elton sniggered again. 'Er, it's on your tee-shirt. *Live to ride, ride to live.* UNLESS YOU'RE A SEX MANIAC!'

At that precise split second, the 'Bee-Gees' were winding up their act, and 'Barry Gibb', the lead singer, was asking the audience for any suggestions for the big encore. Cue complete silence. Until Elton's voice came booming out across the dance-floor. 'UNLESS YOU ARE A SEX MANIAC!'

To be fair, 'Barry' dealt with what he must have regarded as drunken barracking, with true professionalism. 'That's not one of our songs!' he laughed. 'Sounds like a Tom Jones number! So we're gonna do 'How Deep is Your Love.' Thank you for being a great audience. Good night, and God Bless.'

Meanwhile Elton and I were creased up with laughter. 'Christ! I forget how loud my voice is! It's cos I'm a professional entertainer, see? So what's your name? You can call me Bobby.'

'Sorry' I sniffed, wiping tears from my eyes. 'It's been a hell of a day, all told. I'm John, I ride a Harley, an old one, a twelve-hundred.'

'So, on your own, are you John?' he observed. *Yeah, yeah, so I am a complete 'Johnny No-Mates'. But then, so is he, although I guess he actually is on a delivery job, or a gig in Spain, or both. A conjurer is coming on-stage now, penguin suit, comb-over, although mercifully there is no Debbie McGee lookalike, complete with a flock of doves, and a white rabbit. I was wrong earlier. Life has just got a whole lot worse. 'Paul Daniels' has just turned up.*

I took a sip of my beery water, and grimaced. 'My wife and I moved to Andalucia last year. Bought a house, settled in. Then we took our English right-hand-drive car back to the UK last month, left it in our daughter's barn. My bike has been in storage at my mate's bike shop for a year, he did a service and MOT for me and now I am riding it down to Spain. My wife is flying back this week.'

'I ship bikes' he cheerily confirmed. '£245, or £275 for bigger ones. Door to door. So how much did you pay for this trip?'

*I hate a wise-ass. Especially wise-asses who tell you stuff when it is too late. Mind you, he does have a point. Right now, I would happily have paid twice that to have avoided watching a magician produce a five-pound note from his ear.* 'Oh, about the same' I lied.

'Yeah, plus petrol, food on the boat, somewhere to stay tomorrow night on your way down' he kindly reminded me.

'Well, you've got me there, Bobby' I smiled, through gritted teeth. 'Wish I'd known about you earlier.'

'And I charge £100 a cubic metre, for ordinary stuff, furniture, boxes, anything really' he continued. 'Do you know how big a cubic metre is, John?'

*What is this, 'Mastermind'? Or 'Who Wants to be a Millionaire'? Can I phone a friend?* 'Well, when I was at school, a cubic metre was a metre, cubed. So a metre wide, a metre deep, and a metre high.' I resisted adding a sarcastic comment, just in case Magnus What's-his-name was lurking somewhere.

'Correct. So do you know how big two cubic metres is?'

I narrowed my eyes and gave him a stare. 'Are you sure you are not a Chris Tarrant tribute act, as well as Elton John? Can I ask the audience? Or go fifty-fifty? No, actually I know this one, Chris. Two cubic metres is two of what I described in my last answer. So two metres wide, by one metre deep, and one high. Have I won a million? Gimme the money!'

Bobby was laughing. 'Not a million, but I'm gonna buy you a pint! Do you like Guinness? That stuff you are drinking is watered down, but the Guinness is pukka.'

*Do I like Guinness? Been my drink since about 1968, Bobby. Or any real ale. Taunton cider. Not in the same glass obviously. Sadly, there is no real ale on this old tug, and Taunton cider is now brewed in somewhere like Beijing, so go on, twist my arm. Anything to take my attention away from Paul Daniels, who has now invited an hysterically giggling woman onto the stage, although whether he is about to saw her in half, or make her disappear, is not clear. Either would be good, Paul, if you can manage it.*

Bobby came staggering back clutching two glasses of the black stuff, although whether it was the effect of the rolling waves, or because he was rolling drunk, was impossible to say. 'Sorry to wind you up about cubic metres, mate, especially on your holiday' he giggled, slopping Guinness over the table, 'but you wouldn't believe the arguments I have had, with people who think that two cubic metres is two by two by two. They are expecting to pay £200, and when I tell them that they have eight metres, and that it's gonna be eight hundred quid, they blow a fuse!'

*Holiday? Well it was a holiday, with my wife Chrissie, camping in Spain and France on the way over, staying a few days with her mother, touring Devon and*

*Cornwall, visiting our daughters for some quality time, meeting our former colleagues. Until I picked up the bike, since when my backside has been more or less permanently damp. A fortnight in Siberia would have been preferable to the M27 in August. And what can I say about his customers being unable to multiply two by two by two? Surely banging out 'Candle in the Wind' is easier?*

'Anyway, what is your favourite Elton John song?' he enquired, whipping out a smart-phone. 'We can have a look at my website, watch me singing it!'

*There's a a way to pass an hour, on a ferry. I'd rather swim back to Spain, quite honestly. Two middle-aged blokes staring at a smart-phone, watching someone pretending to be Elton John. Right, payback time! I'll give him cubic metres. My turn, now!* 'Tiny Dancer' I replied, without hesitation.

He grimaced. 'Don't do that one. Choose another.'

*Aha, got you, sunshine!* 'OK, Blues for Baby and Me', from *Don't Shoot Me I'm Only the Piano Player*.' And I started to sing. 'The Greyhound is swaying, the radio playing, some blues for baby and me!'

'Hey, great voice' he lied again. 'But I don't do that one, either. Choose another.'

*Love it! On a roll now!* 'Right, 'Skyline Pigeon', from the same album? Great song!'

'Don't do that one. Choose another.'

'Love Lies Bleeding', from *Yellow Brick Road?*'

He slammed the phone onto the table, narrowly missing the puddle of Guinness, and fixed me with a glare. 'Look, I'm a tribute act, right? So I only do the singles, not the album tracks. SO CHOOSE AN EASY ONE!'

At that moment, 'Paul Daniels' was persuading the giggling, blindfolded woman to select a playing card, from a pack he was holding up. And once again, Elton's voice boomed out across that stage. 'SO CHOOSE AN EASY ONE!'

'But not the ace of spades!' laughed 'Paul'. 'That one is in my back pocket!'

Bobby and I were rolling around laughing. 'You'll get yourself kicked off the ship, if you carry on like that!' I reminded him. *Actually, not a bad idea. Maybe he can get us both kicked off. Cast adrift in the Atlantic would be preferable to facing another plate of gristly sheep.*

He waved his arm dismissively. 'Ah, don't worry, I know all these entertainment guys, work with them all the time. Actually, I'm doing a gig on here next week, on the way back.'

I almost choked on my Guinness. *So he is not actually* 'Britain's best Elton John tribute act.' *More like* 'The Only Elton John Tribute Act On This Refugee From A Russian Scrap-Yard, In The Bay Of Biscay.' *Probably not enough room on the business-card for that, but it would surely contravene less trading standards legislation.*

'So not 'Pinky' from *Caribou*?' I continued.

'NO!'

Or 'Tower of Babel' from *Captain Fantastic*?

NO! NO!

I sat back in my chair. Puffed out my cheeks. *I am not saying 'Candle in the Wind.' Everyone requests that, I bet. OK, put him out of his misery.* 'Well, it should be 'Your Song', but seeing we are travelling to Spain, even though there are probably no 'red tail lights' on the back of this old wreck, I choose 'Daniel.'

'No problem John! We can watch both!' he replied, tapping his screen. *Me and my big mouth. But still, watching someone pretending to be Elton John has to be better than the Executive Sleeping Lounge, doesn't it. Not much in it, admittedly, but marginally, surely? Although hang on a minute! We are in the middle of the sea. And although it's pitch dark outside, I am willing to bet there are no mobile phone masts out here. My low-tech clamshell stopped working just after we passed the Isle of Wight. What a bummer. No signal!*

The little blue wheel was spinning on his screen. 'I'll just get us two more, Bobby, while that is downloading' I cheerfully offered. 'Same again?' Suddenly, my eyes came to rest on a printed sign, lopsidedly fixed to a pillar next to the bar. 'Free Wi-Fi Zone.' *Deep joy. Daniel is actually travelling tonight on this* tug. Ah well, watch the video, drink this one, make an excuse, swift stroll around the deck, then off to my executive seat. Never, never, NEVER again will I waste a day of my life on this blatant, ill-mannered attempt at separating the maximum amount of money from a captive audience.

Bobby meanwhile was waving me to hurry up. His screen fired into life, and there he was, behind the piano, tapping out those famous chords, that unforgettable melody. And he was utterly sensational, visually and musically identical to the real thing. Actually, he was more like Elton John, than the man himself. He started singing along to the video, and I simply had to join in. 'They say Spain is pretty, though I've never been...' One or two people on nearby tables were giving us funny looks, although after they day I'd had, I was past caring. Meanwhile 'Paul' was winding up his act, with giggling woman, sadly still in one piece, holding a giant rubber duck. *Missed that part of his act, thankfully.* 'OK, big round of applause for Julie here, thank you for being a great audience, and have a safe trip when we get to Spain tomorrow. Oh, and I almost forgot. I have one last piece of magic for you! I saved the best to last. Ladies and gentlemen, magicked all the way from Caesar's Palace, Las Vegas, the one and only, Rocket Man himself, MISTER ELTON JOHN!'

'The bloody swine!' Bobby growled under his breath, then quick as a flash, took on his stage persona, standing and waving, beaming smile, at his stunned audience. Who for a few seconds, seemed unsure what to do. You could sense what they were thinking, *no surely not? Can it really be him?* Then someone near us started clapping, and suddenly, people were coming over. One wanted a selfie, another an autograph, and a woman who probably have known better planted a sloppy kiss on his lips. *So this is what it's like to be famous. But surely, nobody seriously believes that a superstar is travelling on a third-rate ferry? Are people really that dim? OK, I can understand someone thinking that two by two by two equals two, but Sir Elton?*

Just then a woman came weaving her way across the swaying ballroom, my age maybe, possibly a year or two younger, slim, dark, well-dressed, but instead of crowding around Bobby, she slid in next to me. 'You're him, aren't you!' she smiled, breathlessly. *Well honestly, what do I say to that? I want to burst out laughing, but she seems really sweet, and I don't want to appear* rude, although clearly she is mistaking me for someone else. I mean, I have a terrible memory for faces, but I really have no idea who she is.

'Yes, I am me!' I grinned, playing for time. *Someone we met in Spain? Surely I would have remembered, despite rapidly approaching senility. Must be someone from years ago?*

She shifted in closer. 'You're Bernie, aren't you? I've been watching you with your friend!'

*Bernie? Who the hell is Bernie? Right now I can only think of two Bernies. Bernie the Bolt, from the 1960's TV game-show 'The Golden Shot', and Berni Inns, the steakhouse chain from the same era. And right now I could murder prawn cocktail, rump steak, Black-forest gateaux and a bottle of Mateus Rose. Even chicken-in-a-basket would be preferable to the slops I have just endured.*

'Sorry, my name is John' I apologised.

She smiled conspiratorially, resting her hand seductively on my arm.' OK, I know you are Bernie Taupin, but your secret is safe with me! I won't tell anyone!'

*Bernie Taupin, Elton's lyricist? Is she utterly and completely mad? All right, they say we all resemble someone famous. When I was a little boy, my mother claimed I was the double of Prince Charles, minus the ears hopefully, then as a young man my auntie swore I was a dead ringer for Bobby Ewing, from the US blockbuster 'Dallas'. My dad meanwhile found it amusing that I allegedly bore a strong resemblance to Jim Bergerac, of the BBC TV Jersey-based detective series. So if you are in Spain one day and bump into an amalgam of those three, say hello. Without stroking my skin if possible. But Bernie Taupin? Nothing like him. They used to put his photo on the early album sleeves. Different shaped nose. Different shaped face in fact.*

Meanwhile, Bobbie's smart-phone was still playing a selection of his 'greatest hits'. 'Your Song'. My new acquaintance was wiping away a tear, and completely ignoring my denials. 'Oh these are such beautiful words! 'Yours are the sweetest eyes I've ever seen.' That tune melts my heart every time I hear it!' And she leaned in, brushed her lips against my ear, and whispered 'hope to see you later', before sashaying across the dance-floor and disappearing into the crowd around the bar.

*Oh. My. God. So THIS is what it's like to be famous. Nobody ever gave my ears a lick, even back in the day when I was the spitting image of TV-stars, with Royal connections. Nearly had one bitten off in a scrum once, in entirely different circumstances, of course. My fault, for grabbing him by the jock-strap. But now, with everything rapidly going South? This HAS to be a wind-up.* I glanced furtively round to make sure nobody had overheard the last part of the exchange, to find Bobby leering suggestively. 'Looks like you're fixed up for the night, you dirty old dog!'

'Christ no, Bobby!' I spluttered, angrily. 'What do you take me for? I'm a happily married man. My wife would kill me! And you're a fine one to talk, surrounded by simpering women. What is wrong with these people?'

'Tell you what, mate' he grinned, puffing out his chest, 'it's always like this, when I am on tour. I reckon I get lucky at least twice a week.'

*OH PLEASE! Will someone shoot me now. Put me out of my misery. It's not as if he is good-looking. Certainly not Jim Bergerac, that's for damn sure.* I bury my face in my hands, but cannot dispel the thought of Bobby getting jiggy from my mind. *Right. Decision made. I am off to bed. Or the Ford Zephyr seat. Why didn't I leave the damned, cursed Harley in England. Two-and-a-half hours on Ryanair, and I would have been home, instead of cooped up with these lunatics.* Expertly downing the remains of my pint, I gripped my new friend by the hand. 'Time for some shut-eye, hope to see you in the morning' I lied, and avoiding any amorous fans who might have been lurking near the bar, I shuffled off in search of the Executive Sleeping Lounge.

Back behind the Iron Curtain it is clear I am getting no sleep next to old Vladimir, so I gather up my stuff and head to the front of the room, where I brush away a pile of last week's dog-ends, and avoiding a large, squelchy damp patch, which I sincerely hope is stale lager, I bed down on the floor, kicking off my espadrilles, and plumping up my fleece into a pillow shape. The trouble is, the ship's engines seem to be right below me and the floor is vibrating, making me feel like a nymphomaniac on a tumble dryer, and the light fittings are rattling in time, tapping out a tune by the Bee-Gees, but whether from Grease or Saturday Night Fever I cannot say. Unless of course we are directly above Bobby's cabin, and that is his headboard I can hear rattling, in time with 'Saturday Night's All-right For Fighting.' Who Knows? Eventually I must have drifted off to sleep for at least a minute as I am dreaming I am locked in a pig-sty, with the heating turned up, and all the ventilation blocked. I wake with a start and find I have been sleeping with my face resting on an espadrille. God, the stench is appalling, like a cross between a dead hyena and burning rubber. Yes, I was woken by the smell of my own footwear.

It is at this time that I start to bitterly regret not forking out the extra hundred Euros for a cabin, but they do not do singles, and the thought of bunking down with a Freddie Mercury lookalike from Milton Keynes was too awful to contemplate although a night of rampant bum-fun would surely have been preferable to this hell-hole. Just then I feel the overwhelming urge to break wind. I do my best to ignore the sensation on the grounds of health and safety, but what the hell, everyone else is making a noise except me, so I decide to go for it. Maybe I could trump the first verse of 'God Save the Queen' to prove to the Ruskies, and any Frenchmen present, that Britannia truly does rule the waves, parp parp parp parrrrp, parp parp, but decide instead for one long blast, like the ship's hooter. I cannot give it 100% for fear of being prematurely reacquainted with the old ram, but even at 75% it is a truly impressive effort, but guess what? Yep, old Vlad just keeps right on snoring. I do however hear some stifled giggles from the back of the room, and a voice calls out 'Have that one on me, your highness.'


The executive sleeping lounge in the cold grey light of dawn is a dreadful sight, like a scene from the Crimean war. Bodies are strewn about who certainly weren't here when I came to bed last night, one bloke is face down like a stiff in an American cop series, but without the chalk outline, and another has slumped down the wall and is sleeping sitting up. His jeans seem to have acquired a damp patch too. I am absolutely bursting for a wee, so gathering up my stuff and slipping on my espadrilles, which have cooled down to room temperature now, I head to the toilets. There is however a large sticky puddle below the urinals and stepping in that, in my already poisonous footwear, is not an option, so I splash some tepid water on my face and attempt to straighten my spine, which resembles Richard the Third. Glancing down into the sink I spot an impressive collection of tomato skins and diced carrots, the hand dryer is not working, and my reflection in the mirror reminds me of someone who has spent the last forty years living on Waterloo station. My mouth feels like I have slept with someone else's false teeth in, my tongue resembles a pack of Poundland sandpaper, and there is a bit of grey fluff stuck to my nose which might once have been part of the insole of an espadrille. I simply have to clean my teeth so I turn the tap on full to disperse the assorted spew in the sink, and water fountains out onto the crotch of my jeans to complete the Waterloo tramp look. Stifling a rising gag, I reckon I have about ten seconds until I pebble-dash my shirt, so I limp out on deck and find myself at the back of the ship. There is not a soul about so throwing back my head I proceed to vomit what seems like about two gallons of wine-flavoured beverage and lagery water, with a hint of Guinness, into the Bay of Biscay. God, the relief is indescribable and I rest my head on the railing to catch my breath, allowing the fresh sea breeze to soothe my shattered torso. I then notice, through bleary eyes, that the deck below juts out farther than mine, and that directly below me is a partitioned off area with tables laid with snowy white cloths and expensive looking cutlery, clearly the first-class dining terrace. Probably reserved for *Sunday Times* journalists. I sincerely hope so. It must have rained in the night as some of the table cloths are wet, which is strange as my deck is bone dry. Just then a smart waiter comes crashing out to the dining area, glares angrily at the damp linen, and glances up furiously, checking for rain, or whoever has honked over the tables he has carefully laid. Quickly I snap my head back and rush back inside the ship hoping to mingle with the crowds who are on their way to breakfast, so I decide to take a look, more in hope than anticipation.

The scene that greets me in the dining room is reminiscent of the Little Chef on the A303 circa 1979, the fried eggs are congealed together and have brown frilly bits round them, the bacon looks char-grilled and the sausages of such low quality as to be almost guaranteed to contain traces of horse. The continental option is no better, sweating squares of vivid yellow processed cheese sit next to quivering pink oblongs of a ham-like substance which again could well have been a Grand National runner from a previous century. The miniature boxes of Corn Flakes bear the legend 'Best Before' which possibly they were, but at £3.99 there is no way I am about to find out, and the jugs of milk look so thin and watery that I am guessing it has never passed through a cow, but merely a dairy-flavoured beverage. I am about to grab a coffee-flavoured drink and head out on deck, praying that the next three hours pass quickly so I can get off this joyless version of a 1960's holiday camp, when suddenly a familiar voice rings out behind me. 'Don't bother with that crap, mate! Come with me, down to the lorry-drivers' canteen. Get a full-Monty for a fiver down there!'

Twisting my stiff neck and pulverised spine, I regard my new friend with my only functioning eye. 'Lorry-drivers? Did you say lorry-drivers? I've just spent the night with about a hundred hairy-arsed lorry-drivers. Why in the name of all things holy would I want to eat breakfast with them? If I never see another lorry-freaking-driver this side of Kingdom Come, I will be a happy man. Bugger-off, Bobby!'

He guffaws loudly, attracting the attention of a few passengers in matching deck-wear, stripy nautical tops, chinos in various pastel shades, and boating shoes, who wisely give us a wide berth. Particularly me. He slips his arm round my shoulder. 'You look like shit, by the way! I'm guessing you didn't get lucky last night!'

*Lucky? I feel like I have been trampled by a herd of buffalo, then gnawed by rats. The only aspect of my current existence remotely approaching 'lucky' is that in a few hours I will be cruising through the Spanish sunshine, crossing the Picos de Europa, which I assume are mountains of some description, and heading south towards home, this maritime misery far behind me.*

Suddenly he recoils. 'Christ! You smell like shit an' all! Don't they have showers and toilets up there in the sleeping lounge?!'

I cannot help a wry chuckle. I have perked up, slightly, at the thought of a full-Monty for a fiver. Even if I have to consume it surrounded by lorry-drivers. Perhaps I can close my other eye. 'Yeah, they do, but they've recently been pebble-dashed. But not by pebbles.'

He roars with laughter. 'Come on, let's get you cleaned up downstairs, and stuff a couple of massive, greasy fry-ups down our guts.'

*Sounds like a plan, Bobby!*

Soon, mercifully, the coastline of Spain appears through the heat-haze, we head down to the car-deck, and say our fond goodbyes. I have his business card in my pocket, and fully intend contacting him about the two cubic metres of personal possessions in the loft of our UK house, following the next change of tenants. Which will be the year after next, hopefully. I will miss the fellow, but a little of Bobby goes a long way. Trust me on this one, should you ever have cause to contact *'John Roberts, UK-Spain-UK Removals. No job too small'*, just don't ask him to sing. OK? And try not to think about him getting jiggy…….


I'm not sure who was the more surprised, me or the wasp, but the bastard stung me anyway. Having negotiated a forest of cars, a sea of caravans, an ocean of lorries, half a dozen Saaf-London Mods on puny Lambrettas and the delights of the Hee-HHON ring-road, here I am, minding my own business, cruising along in the warm early-evening Spanish sunshine. After pining for a whole year, I finally have my beloved Harley back, full service and MOT, and raring to go. Gone are damp backsides on the M27 and the dubious, greasy delights of the 'Little Thief' on the Okehampton by-pass. I am heading south across the sun-drenched heart of Spain to our Andalucian home. Empty roads beckon. Plus an absence of fog, and drizzle.

And now this has to happen, miles from anywhere. Hurts like begorra too, I can tell you. I was hit on the arm by a stray dart whilst playing for the Rose and Crown against a bunch of myopic pensioners from the Red Cow in about 1976, and it wasn't half this painful. And to add insult to injury, the stripy swine is hanging on, stuck in the fleshy bit inside my wrist, wiggling his back legs like Winnie the Pooh trying to escape from Rabbit's burrow. And a Spanish wasp, too. Aren't European insects supposed to be worse than the British variety? An English wasp would play fair, sting you once, politely, then die, but Johnny Foreigner here seems intent on injecting me with everything he has. Of course, in the UK I would be dressed in leathers, and gauntlet gloves, barely a square inch of flesh exposed to the elements, and wildlife. But here? Leathers? No chance. Tee-shirt, jeans, and little finger-less mitts.

My instinct is to knock the beggar off, but don't want to end up in a ditch, so gingerly I pull over, kill the engine, prop the bike on the stand, and swear. Loudly. I flick the offending creature away, revealing the remains of the sting sticking up proudly from my skin. About half a dozen veins in that area too, but by a miracle he appears to have missed them all. Still, aren't you supposed to suck the poison out? Didn't I see that in a John Wayne film once? Or was that a snake bite? Can't remember, but what harm could it do? Rather be safe than sorry. Pursing my lips, I take a tentative lick, then decide to go all out, like Davy Crockett, and give it an almighty suck. Which reveals an angry red hole, but praise be, no sting. Result. I wasn't a Wolf Cub for nothing, you know.

Sadly, I have no first aid kit, or any of the other paraphernalia one is supposed to carry abroad. A red triangle, a hi-viz vest, a GB sticker, a breathalyser kit, a piece of sticky plastic to deflect the headlight beam, a green insurance card, a set of light-bulbs or one of those things for getting the stones out of horses hooves. OK so I made one of those up. I do however have a Chinese tent, sleeping bag, pegs, mallet and a pillow, all of which I intend using tonight, wild camping in the Picos de Europa, which are those huge gray things on the far horizon, I assume. Man in tune with nature. And, in the unlikely event of inclement weather, a ridiculous notion given that I am five hundred miles south of the M27, a rubber-backed pair of over-trousers and hooded jacket in a fetching shade of camouflage, £20 all-in from the Army Surplus Stores. My favourite shop. Sorted. Nothing to eat, mind you, but that is the beauty of Spain. Every filling-station has freshly-baked bread by the yard, and *chorizo* by the foot, all for less than the price of a minuscule bottle of water at the Little Thief, so I ain't going hungry. I reckon the nine-quid I spent on gristly ram last night in the Bay of Biscay would last me three days out here in wild Spain. No five-a-day of course, but who cares? I'm riding a Harley, not flower-arranging.

For the uninitiated, the left hand on a motorbike controls the clutch, so on a normal ride, once up and running, this hand is largely redundant. Apart from gripping the handlebar, of course. No, it is the right which controls the twist-grip for the accelerator, plus the front brake. And which wrist bears the imprint of my attacker? Yep. Anyway, what is the worst that could happen to me out here in the wilds? Death obviously, the poison runs up my arm and I turn into a writhing, frothing heap in the gutter. Unlikely, but haven't I read about people dying from insect stings? Not a great option. Or what about my wrist swelling so badly that I am unable to operate the bike, and having to camp here at the roadside? Wouldn't be the end of the world would it, there is a patch of meadow over there to pitch the tent, no yards of bread or feet of *chorizo*, obviously, but I'm sure my fat will sustain me through the night. On the other hand, Loli, Isabel and Fernando might drive by, I can just picture Loli rolling down her window, thrusting out her head, and hollering something like 'what you doing, neighbour?' Unlikely, given that they live five hundred miles away, but maybe they fancied a weekend in Gea-John. You just never know. 'Expect the unexpected' is my motto since moving to this country.

But what about this scenario? Didn't I read that insects, and wasps in particular, in their death throes give off a distress signal? Don't elephants do the same thing, when one member of the herd is attacked, the rest gather round for protection? So what if every bumblebee this side of Madrid is, right now, zoning in on me? A mighty swarm, weapons at the ready, like the Luftwaffe crossing the channel, radar locked onto my throbbing wrist? And actually I can hear them coming, a high-pitched drone, an angry buzzing, slowly but surely, malevolently, inevitability, focused solely on my destruction. And the hideous noise is getting louder. In a panic, I cast around for some sort of refuge, but there is nothing, no building or tree, behind which I can shelter. Suddenly, around the bend, come half a dozen Saaf London Mods on puny Lambrettas, grinning widely at the stranded Harley, parkas and tiger-tails flapping in the breeze, feeble engines buzzing, straining against the gradient. *And the final guy gives me the finger as he passes regally by.* The bastards. The final humiliation, being overtaken by a bunch of weedy skinheads. The worst that could possibly have happened, just has. Including dying, quite frankly.

Right, back in the saddle, fire up the beast, and back out on that road again. Show those shaven-headed louts what a real motorbike sounds like. My engine is bigger than all six of theirs. This kind of stuff matters, to us blokes undergoing mid-life crises. Wrong! The first few spots of rain cause me no concern, although the sky ahead has gone an ominous shade of black, and the Picos have disappeared in the gathering gloom. I am not troubled by the first flash of lightning, either. Aren't I supposed to be protected from electrocution by the rubber tyres? Didn't I learn about the Faraday Cage principle in school?

Or was that a car? Forget now. Anyway, I am still standing on the roadside, so the first fork of lightning in my direction and I am toast. Suddenly, the heavens open, and I am scrabbling about trying to locate my Army Surplus Stores wet weather gear. Too late, I am already soaked to the skin, but at least my rubberized PVC will prevent me getting any wetter, if that were possible. There is so much water running down the hill that it wouldn't surprise me to find a grey-haired old bloke, a queue of animals lined up two-by-two, and a large home-made boat, around the next bend. THIS IS NOT SUPPOSED TO BE HAPPENING. THIS IS SPAIN, NOT THE M27. I am unsure what to do next, although if I stand here much longer I will be swept away. Hee-HHON is twenty miles behind me, so do I head back there, or do I press on? And without a map, one of the other things I omitted to bring, I really have no idea what lies ahead. A village with a small hotel would be good, given that laughably, camping is going to be out of the question. The rain might conceivably go off, but the ground is going to be like a quagmire, for about the next year.

Right, onwards. Into the unknown. My twelve-hundred CC's (are you listening, Lambretta riders?) cough reluctantly into life, and gingerly I guide my way through the surf, ten miles per hour, headlight on full, crouched over the tank in a vain attempt to prevent seepage. Not working, is it? My Army Surplus boots are rapidly filling up, and I feel as if I am sitting in a stone-cold bath. This is dangerous, quite honestly, hypothermia will be setting in any time now, but mile after mile pass without any habitation whatsoever, not even a bridge, a bus shelter, a ruined barn, to get out of this cursed deluge. Not a light, a house or any form of human habitation, apart from a few maniac lorry drivers coming in the opposite direction, kicking up a huge wave-wash every time they pass. Shivering with cold, I am beginning to think I will never make landfall, when mercifully, up ahead is a light. Two lights. A building. A large building in fact. An illuminated sign. Not a mirage, surely? Not a cruel trick of the mind. No. A few scattered houses, a village, and a hotel, a big, beautiful hotel. A big, beautiful French hotel, in fact, one of those chains, which momentarily causes me to wrestle with my conscience. Having spent the last twenty-six hours entombed and being royally ripped-off on a French ferry, I swore I would never patronize another Gallic business, for at least a few years. Teach them a lesson, eh? But quite honestly in my present predicament I would share a bed with the Devil.

To hell with principles. And I don't care how much it costs, either, I am going in. And if the beer is twenty quid a pint, I am having one.

Parking outside the entrance, I ease my stiffened bones out of the saddle, and slosh my way into reception. Beaming my finest smile at the girl behind the desk, it is time to dust off my best schoolboy French. 'Avez-vous un chambre, si vous plais?'

The young Spaniard giggles. 'Are you English? This is Spain, not France. Are you lost?' Hiding my face in embarrassment, I nod my head vigorously. *Yes I am lost, I am shivering with cold, I need half an hour under a scolding shower, I need some beer, and some food, any food, twelve hours sleep, and I don't care if I have to share a bed with a little red fellow with a pronged fork and a pointy tail.* I don't tell her that, obviously. I think she can guess. But do you know what? I did actually get all of the above. A King-sized bed, too, although whether there was a little red fellow under the sheets I have no idea, as I was asleep before my head hit the pillow.....


Two days later I emerge from a long road tunnel into the province of Andalucia, and the *Despenarperros* national park. No idea what that means, something to do with dogs presumably, although hopefully the 'despen' bit doesn't mean 'desperate', or 'wild'. Less than fifty miles to go, now, after a momentous journey, not a single cloud in the sky following that first night, leaving me suntanned, wind-blown and poached. Could probably do with a change of diet too, crusty bread and *chorizo* by the yard gets a bit samey, I have found. Looking forward to seeing Chrissie of course, what day is it, Sunday I think, so she should be home by now. Just the one concern really, will the bike fit inside the house? Is the street wide enough to manoeuvre it inside? Will the double front doors actually open far enough? I think so, I hope so, as if not, I have absolutely no idea what I will do. You step down into the hall, so before we left Spain in August I made a ramp from some old planks of wood I found in the street. Will the ramp work? Again, not a clue.

Our town, in common with many others in this part of Spain, is built on the side of a mountain, and the narrow, cobbled streets in the historic part are a maze of zig-zags. Streets which are now echoing to the rolling, rumbling, throaty sound of the Harley. Music to the ears. (Are you listening, Lambretta riders!?) As I traverse the final few hundred yards, heads pop out of doors, people are waving, and shouting, not that I can hear them of course. Blimey, a Harley is louder than a Spaniard shouting. Who knew? As I pull up outside our place, a reception committee forms. Loli, naturally, Isabel, Fernando, Juan the dustman, Mercedes waddles down, Leopard-Skin woman, Auntie Vera. And Chrissie, of course. Everyone seems to be shouting at once, in typical Spanish fashion, so I reel off a list of the places I have been. Hee-HHON, Ley-on, Salamanca and Toledo. Plus a ferry, sadly. Pulling off my helmet and sunglasses, Loli is consumed with laughter. 'Neighbour, you look like a panda!' *Well you should have seen me a few days ago, Mrs. More like a big wet fish.*

Chrissie opens both doors, and places the ramp over the step. Now I could really do without an audience for this delicate operation, but we both know there is less than a zero chance of that happening. I daresay this is the first time anyone has tried to reverse a Harley into a cottage in this dusty old street, and competition for a ringside view is fierce, I can tell you. The Englishman could end up looking a complete fool, and I suspect they realise this, and none of them are going to miss it for the world. Right, here goes. Sitting astride the bike, with my back to the front doors, pushing with both feet, backwards and forwards half a dozen times, until gradually, gradually I disappear regally down the ramp, and into the hall. Loud cheers erupt from the street, and to a man, and woman, every single neighbour pokes their head inside, just to make sure. Phew! More luck than judgement, somewhat ungainly the first time, but I will get better with practice. What matters is that I am home, back in the land of Sunsets, and Olives!

**CHAPTER 2.  BACK IN SPAIN-THE MADNESS CONTINUES...**

Monday morning, early September, my first complete day back, breakfast on the patio, enjoying my second mug of black coffee, feet up, glancing through my morning paper on the Kindle. My favourite time of day, apart from evenings on the patio with a glass of wine, watching the sunset, obviously. Following our break in the UK, featuring full and frank discussions, we are ready to pick up again on our lives here in Spain, with several small adjustments required. Nothing major, just tweaks here and there mainly. Besides, England was not that great, to be honest. After a year of eating full-flavoured Spanish food, the menu in Wetherspoon's seemed strangely bland. Clearly our palates have changed. My all-time favourites, pork pies, scotch eggs and pasties, had lost their appeal. Fish and chips left us bloated. The second walnut inside the Walnut Whip had disappeared. Wagon Wheels had shrunk even further. And don't even get me started on the weather. Got my pint in the Rose & Crown, mind you, which was excellent, as always, so there were some plus points, but on the whole, weighing it all up, Sunny Spain won out, for the time being, at least.

So what changes in particular? Well, more time for ourselves, basically. The last few months before our holiday had been completely manic, me working with Del-Boy, and Chrissie with her English students. Del always insisted on putting-in full days, so much so that I was not getting home until late afternoons, not what I signed up for. And with him not owning a car, it fell to me to collect him in the mornings, from his cottage at the top of the town, up numerous hairpin bends, and deliver him home in the evenings. Meanwhile, my car was being used as a builders van, with Chrissie constantly giving me grief about the whiff of sweaty builders she felt she could discern, when we went out for a drive at the weekend. And barely a week went by without a phone call from a Spaniard seeking English lessons. We didn't advertise, it was simply word of mouth. 'You speak Eengliss with my cow-seen Maria, plees I take classes Eengliss with you?' Of course, with the trusty Volvo now taking a well-earned retirement in our daughter's barn, the issue of the builders transport has gone away. There is zero chance of me lugging sacks of cement on the back of a motorbike. So Del will have to accept jobs within walking distance, together with the fact that his trusty oppo will be knocking off at lunchtime. I still need to have this conversation with him, but that is how it's going to be in future. And no more new pupils, at least until the numbers thin out a bit.

With these happy thoughts, I pour my third mug, and contemplate the first day of the rest of our lives. Today is the first Spanish/English conversation group at the library following the summer break, and I am planning to go early and peruse the small but impressive rock CD collection there. Just about the most upsetting aspect of moving here was having to get rid of my extensive collection of original sixties and seventies singles and LP's. The Beatles, Stones, Kinks, Manfred's, Hollies, later graduating to Cream, Jethro Tull, Yes, Zeppelin, Purple, Sabbath and the like. All sold, on eBay, and at car-boots. Broke my heart, but having taken the decision to only bring what would fit in the back of the Volvo, there was no other option. I managed to digitalise most of the collection of course, where it now resides happily on four inches of plastic known as an I-Pod, although I noted that our library has several Hendrix and Janis Joplin CD's, among others, which I can record, and transfer, apparently, having been shown which buttons to press by my trusty former-secretary, Amy. Just not the same though, is it? The delights of the gate-fold *Sergeant Pepper* album, with those inserts, compared to an image on a little screen. Truly, I could weep.

Suddenly, my reverie is shattered by a loud knocking on the front door. Chrissie jumps to her feet, knowing how much I hate being interrupted at the crack of dawn. It's barely nine o' clock, for heaven's sake. She raises her hands in a placating gesture. 'Stay there, stay there! I will go.'

Then, almost immediately, comes a burst of Spanish shouting, from the back of the house. Loli. The crazy neighbour. The rottweiler. The all-seeing-eye. 'Neighbour! There are English people, at your front door!' *How is this possible? The knock on our door was less that five seconds ago. How can she have got from hearing the knock, thrusting her head out the front, spotting our 'English' visitors, although they could conceivably be from Outer Mongolia, shutting her door, sprinting through to the back, and hollering across our patio. Seriously, Linford Christie would have struggled in that amount of time. And Loli limps like a three-legged badger. Just not possible, but it's just happened.* Not for the first time, or the twentieth, I marvel at the enigma that is our *vecina*.

'Yes, thank you, Loli, Cristina is going.' *There. That should shut her up. Or not.*

'But neighbour, there are English people! At your front door!'

*Well so what? It doesn't take two of us to answer a door. Unless the Queen of Sheba has decided to pop over for a few days of sunshine. Which I am unable to translate into Spanish.* 'Yes thank you Loli, Cristina is coming now.' *Now please go away.* I can hear British voices in our hallway, and Chrissie emerges onto the patio with a couple, whom she introduces. Babs and Andy, from Oxfordshire. A few years younger than us, her petite, brunette and bubbly, he taller and stick-thin, both dressed for a day on the beach, in shorts, tee-shirts, and flip-flops. *No wonder Loli knew they were English.* I rise, smiling, and offer my hand. 'The coffee is freshly made, if you would like to join us.' And I gesture to the patio chairs.

Babs takes up the narrative. 'Well thank you, but, er, we don't have much time. We are meeting an estate agent-woman at ten, looking at some houses, and last night we stayed here at the hotel in town. We were looking round after dinner, stumbled upon your street, and saw a house for sale sign. Number forty-one. *Se vende*. That's right, isn't it? *Se vende?* For sale? We didn't want to knock on the door that time of night, gone nine it was, so we came back this morning, and a grey-haired old woman came out, babbling away in Spanish she was, couldn't understand a damn word of course, we were pointing to her house, she was still rattling on, then she was saying 'Eengliss' and pointing up the street, in this direction, she must have known we were English, God knows how she knew that, then she took my hand and traced a five and a five, pointed this way, so here we are.'

Andy checks his watch, with the two of them still standing there. 'We were wondering if you might, you know, come down there with us and translate, if you can speak Spanish that is? Only we don't have much time, see.'

*Not going too well, is it, this 'more time for ourselves' plan? I've only been back a day. And quite honestly he could have phrased his request more politely. Still, I have some time this morning, before seeking out Jimi and Janis, so why not? They must be talking about 'Auntie Vera' as we christened her when we first arrived, Antonia to her friends, neighbour of Leopard-skin woman. We were devastated to hear she was selling up, as our days are brightened considerably by the pair of them, even though we only understand a fraction of what they are telling us as we pass by, but smiles and laughter are always the order of the day. Antonia is only moving to the other end of the street to live with her son,* up by the hairpin bend, so we will still see her from time to time, but it won't be the same. Everything changes, as they say.

And I wonder if Babs and Andy have been warned what to expect, house-hunting, Spanish-style? The homely aroma of fresh-baked bread, or percolating coffee, will not waft past their nostrils, that's for damned sure. We were greeted by a dead-man's breakfast, and the imprint of his corpse in the bed, at our first viewing. No such horrors will greet them in Antonia's, hopefully, unless Pirate Pete crept into her bedroom last night, un-noticed, and croaked, but still, her house is like a cross between a church and a shrine, complete with a life-size statue of the Virgin Mary lurking in the corner. You don't get that in Henley-on-Thames, as far as I'm aware. So, should I warn them? Andy is checking his watch again, clearly in a hurry, a habit he is going to need to lose if he ever wants to move to this country, unless he intends winding up as a gibbering wreck. Nah. Let them find out the hard way….

'Right, let me splash some water on my face' I smile, 'and we can get down there.' Emerging from the bathroom, I can see Chrissie gesturing surreptitiously in a *tell them about the Virgin Mary* way, or she might just have something in her eye, or wind, who knows, and who cares quite frankly, as Andy steals another glance at his watch, so I open the front door, to be confronted by Loli. 'GOING DOWN TO LOOK AT ANTONIA'S HOUSE, NEIGHBOUR?' she hollers, on the off-chance that anyone this side of Granada was unaware of my plans, which I only formed within the last minute. We have long suspected she has our house bugged, but how she translates our indoor conversations into her native tongue is beyond us, or MI6.

Nodding serenely, but wishing secretly I could have our crazy neighbour committed, or tranquilised at the very least, the three of us head down the street, to be confronted by another welcoming committee consisting of Ferret-woman, Leopard-skin-woman, Pirate Pete and of course, Auntie Vera herself. 'Is there an asylum, or some sort of institution, near here?' Babs whispers. 'We only arrived in Malaga yesterday, drove straight up here, but everyone seems, you know, completely barking mad. Why are they all just staring at us? Don't they have anything to do?' *Wish I had time to explain Babs, but your husband has just checked his watch again, and you do look like you've stepped of the set* of 'Baywatch', fifty miles from the nearest beach, but we are here now, so in we go.

Antonia apologies profusely. 'Sorry I don't speak any English, and your friends don't understand Spanish, so I sent them up to you! Pasa, pasa!' Which means 'come in', I am guessing. Gesturing for my new acquaintances to follow the little old Spanish lady inside, I turn and wink at Leopard-skin woman, and step over the threshold. This is going to be good. York Minster has a gift shop, but I am willing to bet there are fewer religious artifacts per square foot in their emporium, than there are in this house. With big heavy curtains across the front door, and the windows shuttered, I lurch into the gloom and almost collide with Babs, who has stopped dead, in sheer utter amazement. 'Bloody hell, is this a church?' she whispers, under her breath.

When I was a boy I always wondered at the meaning of the song 'When the Saints Go Marching In.' Marching in where, precisely? And now, fifty years later, I know where. Antonia's house, Castle Street, Santa Marta, Andalucia, Spain. Over twenty of them, at least, ranging in size from a couple of inches to over a foot, on every available surface, a dresser, side tables, shelves, with religious pictures adorning every wall. I have been in here a few times and it always takes me by surprise, so what our new friends must be thinking I have no idea. Catching Babs' eye, I nod my head imperceptibly in the direction of the Virgin Mary, standing regally behind them in the far corner. She follows my glance, then screams spectacularly as she focuses on the figure, grabs Andy who has also spotted the image, and the pair of them lurch drunkenly into me, almost scattering a dozen figures in their wake. By a miracle, I manage to retain my footing, and Antonia's saintly collection remains unscathed, although I receive a painful kink in my spine for my trouble. Babs is clutching her heart and has gone a deathly shade of white, while Andy utters the 'Eff-word' under his breath. What our elderly neighbour is thinking I cannot begin to imagine, although a burst of Anglo Saxon is beyond her translation skills, I am praying. 'There are not usually saints in British houses' I smile, by way of explanation, a statement Antonia seems completely unable to come to terms with, although at that moment the peace is further shattered by a loud burst of machine-gun Spanish as Leopard-skin Woman pokes her head through the door, having no doubt been alerted by the commotion. Babs again jumps spectacularly, then turns to me, ashen-faced, beseechingly, as if all this is somehow all my fault. *Yeah well, at least she isn't looking at a dead man's egg and bacon.*

The remainder of the viewing passes in somewhat of a haze, particularly for our new British acquaintances, who seem totally shell shocked by the experience. Lounge, kitchen, bathroom, bedrooms and outside space are all inspected in a state of complete unreality before we find ourselves once again confronted by the Virgin Mary, and the burning question. How much is Antonia asking for this cathedral, with a small house attached? Time to show Andy that, yes, I can actually speak Spanish. More or less. 'Quanto questa, la casa?'

The little old Spaniard smiles sweetly. 'Quattro.'

*Quattro? Four? Surely not. Four thousand euros? Spanish numbers I find confusing, but surely 'forty' is 'quarenta'? So what else can 'quattro' be? No way is she asking forty grand for this, so it must be four. And if it is, I am off home right now, scrape together every single euro in the house, be back in two minutes with the deposit, then max out our credit cards and return by nightfall with the balance. Tell Babs and Andy she is asking thirty.* Andy senses, perhaps, my confusion. 'How much did she say?'

I take a deep breath. *Annoying, aren't they, consciences?* 'Er, not sure, exactly.' I turn to our neighbour. 'Quattro?'

'Si.'

*Bloody hell. My ship has just come in, after all these years. Has to be worth at least twenty, even with Westminster Abbey thrown in. Winter in the Caribbean beckons.* 'Quattro meel?' Four thousand?

'Auntie Vera' throws back her head and roars with laughter. 'Neighbour! Not meel, mee-lee-onay!'

*Mee-lee-onay? Millions? Surely that is impossible. Something has gone badly wrong with my Spanish translation, although enquiring the prices of things is an everyday occurrence and surely I should have mastered it by now? Apparently not. Four million?* I narrow my eyes and shake my head, indicating I have maybe misunderstood. 'Quattro mee-lee-onay?'

Our lovable neighbour smiles patiently, takes my hand, and traces a four, followed by six zeros, confirmation she is indeed asking four million for this unremarkable lump of Spanish real estate. My senses are reeling. Maybe the saints, and the Virgin Mary, are included in the price. Perhaps they are priceless artifacts from a bygone millennium, even though they look identical to the ones on sale in the Chinese bazaar in town.

'I thought you said you could speak Spanish' whispers Andy, accusingly.

I turn my head and focus my best Paddington Bear stare in his general direction. 'She is saying four million is the price' I growl, which elicits incredulous gasps from the Oxford contingent, hopefully shutting them up whilst I get to the bottom of this riddle. I focus again on Antonia. 'Euros?'

This time she screams with delight, convulsing into laughter. 'Neighbour, not Euros, pesetas!'

*PESETAS? WHAT? For a few seconds I am too stunned to speak. Pesetas? How long ago did Spain join the Eurozone? Has to be a decade. There are no pesetas here, apart from a few old coins we found hiding in the bottoms of drawers in our house. We have lived here for just over a year and the word 'peseta' has never once come up in any aspect of our existence. So why is she quoting pesetas now? OK she is elderly, maybe she still thinks in the old money. I know I do, and Britain lost shillings and pence in 1970 or thereabouts. 'FIFTEEN BOB FOR A MARS BAR?' was one of my utterances on our recent UK visit. But a house is not an item of confectionery, and I would never use 'bobs' to a foreigner, although many of the 'Village People' here are particularly unworldly, rarely venturing outside the province, let alone the country. Maybe she thinks we understand. So is there a parallel currency in operation here? Is this maybe a tax fiddle? Does she have a huge stash of pesetas under her bed, or buried in the garden? I guess we will never know. But I can at least attempt to discover how much four million might be.* 'How much is that in Euros?'

Antonia is now sitting down, no doubt recovering from the shock to the system this visit by English people has been. She shrugs, and grins. 'Don't know!'

Well that solves that then. 'OK, I am going to the library later, I can ask them there about it.'

The look of utter horror on her face is a picture. 'JONNEE NO! DON'T SAY ANYTHING ABOUT MY HOUSE IN THE LIBRARY!'

Well obviously I wasn't intending to be specific, just mentioning that a little old lady was selling her house for four million pesetas, and did anyone have any idea how much that might be in real money. So maybe it IS a tax fiddle, with her not wanting the authorities to find out? Perhaps she already has the hole dug, although I have to say I didn't see anything suspicious in the garden. Perhaps she has it covered with sticks and leaves, like a Pooh Trap For Heffalumps, intending to slink silently down there in the dead of night with her sack of swag.

Andy checks his watch for the umpteenth time. 'Right, we have to get going, thanks for your help', and he turns to Antonia. 'Muchas gracias'.

'They are going to look at some other houses now', I explain to our bewildered-looking neighbour, and we stumble gratefully out into the daylight, where by some miracle the crowd has dispersed. Phew! No Spanish Inquisition required. As we stroll back to our place, where Babs and Andy will carry straight on for their meeting with the estate agent, I whisper that I will enquire at the library, in general terms, about the pesetas. 'Pop back tonight if you like, we can have a drink on the terrace, have a catch-up.'

'So how much do you think that place is worth?' Babs enquires, 'give us some idea what to expect with the others we be looking at.'

I puff out my cheeks. 'Wouldn't be surprised if it was twenty-five grand'.

Andy giggles. 'Would that be groats, florins, guineas, or Euros?' and he shakes my hand, Babs pecks me on the cheek, and they amble off up the hill to their meeting.

*Right, I need a sit-down, recount the extraordinary tale to Chrissie, grab my laptop, and seek out the company of Jimi and Janice. There is still time, if I get a move on.*

Wrong! Chrissie is full of her latest discovery. 'There are dozens of artists' canvasses down by the bin, just dumped there' she explains breathlessly. 'Proper professional canvasses, like you see in art shops, stretched out over wooden frames. Some have been painted on, some are blank, but they must be worth a fortune.'

I greet this news with less than enthusiasm. I cannot draw for toffee. I am all right slapping up a coat of gloss, and I did get GCSE Art in school, but that was for ceramics, not painting. 'What, thinking of starting a new hobby, are you?' I chuckle. 'Thought you had enough on your plate with the garden?'

'Not me you plonker' comes the reply. 'I thought our artist friend might like them.'

'Artist friend? What artist friend?' I have absolutely no idea to whom she is referring. Totally baffled.

She smiles sweetly. Always loves these little battles of the sexes, does my wife, contests she invariably wins. 'Phil, the chicken-man?'

*Blimey, I'd forgotten the father of John, Paul George and Ringo, formerly known as Bossy, Flossie, Bessie and Jessie. Spanish 'ens, who turned out to be geezers. I vaguely recall, one drunken evening last year, after being plied with strong cheese and malt whisky, being shown round his 'studio', an attic room containing brooding, disturbing depictions of women in various states of undress. 'Do you shell many of theeshe?' I recall slurring. 'None yet, but don'cha worry, mate, I will' he optimistically predicted, gazing deeply into my eyes, arms round my shoulders for balance.*

'Go down the bin quickly, before someone else nabs them, and see what you reckon,' Chrissie continues, 'give him a call if you think he would like them.'

*Not gonna happen, is it, Hendrix and Joplin? And this time for myself is going well, too.* Shooting my wife a hunted look, I grab my phone and head down to the refuse, where indeed several dozen canvasses have been thrown in a haphazard heap. Some have already been started, modern, cubist representations, not to my taste, but Phil can always paint over them, I believe. Didn't Michelangelo do the same thing? There is also a large frame picturing a golden retriever sitting on a path somewhere, the unknown artist has captured perfectly his wide doggy grin, tongue lolling, his ruff glowing in the sunshine. The only problem is the scale of the background, it is too small to my admittedly untutored eye. The dog resembles a Jumbo jet coming into land. Wouldn't like to come face to face with the creature on a dark night, that's for damn sure. Still, the eye of the beholder and all that. I whip out my phone and call the Londoner, who seems supremely keen on the haul, and he promises to be right with me.

I suppose I had better shift the paintings away from the bin slightly, first come first served of course, so I need to claim them as mine. Incredible what people will throw away. Much of it complete rubbish, old beds and sofas, crappy chipboard furniture. But just before our holiday we picked up two canvas deck chairs, almost new condition, together with a five-gallon wooden wine barrel, complete with stand. I cut a hole in the top, Chrissie planted it up, and it now resides on our 'El Sombrero' patio, where it gives off a wonderful alcoholic aroma, as well as a floral display. The best of both worlds. And these canvasses, I have no idea how much they cost new, but at say a fiver each there is over a hundred Euros worth here. Or a thousand pesetas if your name is Antonia. There are too many to carry them back to my place, so I start to shift them a few yards away, when suddenly a tortured, squealing sound rents the air behind me. Startled, I turn to see a diminutive, hairy figure on a bicycle hurtling down the hill, gripping his brakes in a vain attempt to bring the ancient conveyance to a halt. Boggle-eyed, he steers majestically around the bend, and finally comes to a breathless halt on the uphill section. 'Blimey Phil, you need to get your brakes adjusted!' I laugh, 'and best of luck carrying two dozen paintings on that bike!'

'Nah worries mate, I was just up the hill when ya called' he puffs, mopping sweat from his brow, and eyeing his prizes. 'These look great though, ta ever so much, can we shift them to your house, then I can come back with the car?' Indeed we can, and by another miracle we manage to transport the goodies to our place without attracting the attentions of the local populace. Not a single Spanish housewife is sweeping or mopping the street, which must be a first in this dusty old town. Ten minutes later he returns with his battered Ford Escort, we load the frames into the back, and after more grateful thanks, and the promise of a 'little nip', which I fully intend holding him to, he chugs off up the street.

*Right. Half ten. If I really get a serious move on, I can copy the two CD's to my laptop before the conversation class begins at eleven.* Wrong! 'Neighbour!

What you doing?' Juan, 'The Dustman', dragging his rubber bin behind him, puffing up the hill for his morning break. 'Morrow loco!' he cries. Indeed. Juan is a lovely man, always keeps us abreast of local events, but the problem is his teeth, or rather the lack of them. Which makes deciphering his utterances all the more difficult. 'Loco' is crazy of course, so clearly something crazy is happening, but 'morrow'? Not a clue. 'Tomorrow' is he saying? No, can't be, everyone knows the Spanish for 'tomorrow.' Manana. Man-yanna. The most popular word in the dictionary. Usually with Juan I have to wing it, and I have to say I usually get there in the end, but today I am stumped. 'Your friends house' he continues, no doubt sensing the hesitation in my reply. 'Your friends house, the street below, *puerta rotada*.' Broken door? Blimey, but whose door? 'Gracias, ya boy' I tell him, which means I am on my way, apparently.

Chrissie to the rescue again. 'What about Janie and Nigel?' Oh hell, I forgot about Janie and Nigel, they have a holiday cottage on the hairpin below us, had it for a few years, and manage to get across for a week or so at a time, as they are both still working. Luckily we have their key, to keep an eye on the place, which I have singularly failed to do, but I only got back yesterday. That is my excuse and I am sticking to it, so grabbing my phone and Nigel's key, I head rapidly down the zig-zag, to their house, unsure of what I might find.

As I near the bend, I can suddenly hear metallic clanging, irregular banging, certainly not a tune by the Bee-Gees, or Elton John. No, someone is beating the hell out something. As I approach Nigel's, all becomes clear. A wild looking man is hitting an aluminium soup ladle against the wrought iron around the window of the next-door cottage, as you do. A tall man, same height as me but smaller about, mid-thirties maybe but difficult to tell exactly under a mane of shaggy hair and unkempt beard, clothes he has clearly been sleeping in for a month or more, and shoes with his filthy toes poking through. He turns towards me, waving the ladle menacingly, and bellows 'ROO-SEE-YA!' Quite. My thoughts entirely. Is he shouting 'Russia'? Does he think I am from the Former Soviet Union? Is this the famous *morrow loco*? Certainly seems that way. Determined not to appear intimidated, but equally keen not to be beaten over the head with a kitchen implement, I fish Nigel's key out of my pocket, craning my neck to confirm that someone has indeed broken open the wooden door of the next house. 'Inglaterra' I smile politely but firmly, and unlocking the door, I disappear inside, bolting it securely behind me. And blow out my cheeks. As my heart rate returns to normal, I take a tour of the house, checking for signs of intruders, but thankfully all seems well. OK, dilemma. Do I tell Nigel someone has broken in next door. I don't want to worry him unduly, but I feel he should be aware of the situation. *Difficult one.*

There is a bit of history attached to that house next door, which Janie and Nigel refer to as 'Miguel's' after the old man who used to live there. He sadly died a few years ago, following which his family, who lived in a different part of Spain, simply locked the house and effectively abandoned it to the elements. The brutal heat of summer has left the masonry cracking and paintwork peeling, contributing to the general air of dilapidation.

And does someone need to contact the police? I am unaware of the position here but presumably breaking and entering, or squatting, or whatever you want to call it, is against the law wherever you are? Glancing out of the window, I can see crazy man in the street trying to ignite a gas cylinder with a cigarette lighter, a physical impossibility without the regulator attached, but something needs to be done, before he blows us all to Kingdom Come. I need to get to the library, take advice from the locals and hopefully get one of them to contact the Old Bill. After I've phoned Nigel. Decision made.

He greets the news with less than enthusiasm. 'Oh bloody hell, no. That damned Miguel's, I've been worried about something like this for a long time, going to rack and ruin, depreciating the value of our place. Janie will have a fit, I know. Can I ask you a big favour? The wall in the back garden, between us and Miguel's, is falling down, can you have a look, and if you have time, get it rebuilt, whatever it takes? I'll transfer some money today, if you need it.

I totally understand how he feels, living over a thousand miles away. Our bungalow in the UK, whilst managed by highly competent letting agents, remains a nagging doubt in the back of my mind. 'Look, don't worry' I hopefully reassure him, 'everything is secure here, I will keep popping down and if Crazy Man spots me going in and out maybe he will think your place is occupied. I will look at the wall now and call you tonight with an update, and we can talk about money then, OK?'

*Easy for me to say, but what if Crazy Man is out there right now? What if there are garden implements in Miguel's? A soup ladle I might just about be able to avoid, but a damn great spade?* Unlocking Nigel's back door, I pop my head out quickly, but all seems quiet. Maybe Crazy Man is taking a nap, after all his exertions. Perhaps he has popped out for food, who knows? On this side of the street, the gardens are accessed up a flight of steps. 'Uphill houses' I call them, as opposed to ours which is a 'downhill house.' The consequences of living on the side of a mountain. On our side we have the extensive views out over the town, and the olive fields beyond, plus of course the spectacular sunsets. This side, they only have a huge great mountain to look at, very pretty in its own way, but I know which I prefer. Edging up the steps, I spy the garden wall, which in typical Spanish fashion is indeed falling down. Three feet thick, made from two parallel courses of stone, the middle filled with any old junk, soil, rubble, small rocks. The whole thing is then capped off with cement, which over the years cracks, letting in the winter rains, causing the whole wall to burst open. A lack of basic maintenance, we had a similar problem in our garden, but our damage was a couple of square feet only, simple enough to repair. This damage is maybe eight feet long however, although the remedy is the same. Mortar in a couple of courses of stones, leave it to go off overnight, then next morning fill in behind with the rubble. Another couple of courses, let them set, and so on until I eventually reach the top. Cap the whole lot off with some of those yard-long bricks they sell here, mortar it over, and job done. A week's work easily, but actually less than an hour or so each morning.

In Nigel's scullery is a small set of steps, so as silently as possible I prop them against the undamaged section of wall, and climb up for a better look, my first view down into Miguel's patio. And what a truly depressing sight it is, cold and damp and totally uninviting, even though it is probably over thirty degrees in the sunshine today. If the front of the house was bad, the rear is ten times worse. Just about everything that could possibly crack and flake, is. Gutters and down-pipes hanging off, rusty ironwork, weeds sprouting from just about everywhere. There is a first-floor bathroom extension, clearly a 1970's add-on, providing a covered patio area outside the back door, similar to ours, although whereas we have repaired, tiled and painted, walls decorated with plants and pictures, Miguel's resembles a back-street chippy which has been condemned on health grounds. And scary somehow, although that might be my imagination running away with me, on account of who or what might be lurking inside.

At the top of the steps up from the back door is a garden area, which could one day be made into a pleasant setting, but which right now looks as if it has been used for military exercises. Tank traps, bomb craters, plus the rubble from the collapsed wall. This Miguel fellow was clearly not a gardener. Suddenly, I spot what appears to be a snake, nestling in a clump of dried, dead grass. Now had this been a rat I would have been back into Nigel's, with the door firmly bolted, in record time. Snakes I am just about OK with, although I do adjust my position from sitting, to kneeling, in case said reptile decides to go walk-about. Or slither-about I suppose. Strange-looking creature to be honest, about a foot long, stubby nose leading to a pointed tail. And strange colours too. I thought snakes were diamond-patterned, not that I am an expert mind you, but this one is various shades of chocolate brown, darker at the head, and milky at the tail. Clearly a Spanish snake as it seems to be asleep, even though it's not siesta time for another few hours.

*Right, Hendrix and Joplin will have to wait for another day.* Down the library now, via the builders merchant to order the materials for tomorrow morning. Looking forward to meeting up with our local friends too, and learning a bit more of the language, although what the Spanish is for 'what is a morrow loco, how much is four million pesetas, and by the way who wants to accompany me to the police station?' I have absolutely no idea. The class is underway by the time I arrive, although the room is in uproar due to the sensational news that Alicia has been kicked off the course. Crazy, lovable Alicia, always arrived half an hour late, causing massive disruption to the group, dressed in hooker-chic with ankle boots, fishnet tights, a leather mini-skirt and a low-cut blouse. Not a great look for a woman approaching sixty, at an English lesson. And she always managed to squeeze her way in next to me, for some unknown reason, a fact which Chrissie always managed to remark upon. Her place has been allocated to a young man called Amador, mid-twenties, and very camp. Camper that a field of bell-tents at a Boy Scout jamboree in fact, but great fun, excellent English, although he does tend to end each sentence in a high voice. 'My name is Amador, I have twenty-six years, and I live Santa MARTAA' he explains by way of introduction. 'Pleased to meet you JONEEE!' Not a problem for me of course, and at least I won't have Chrissie glaring at me for the entire lesson in future...

The other members are the same as before the summer recess, Teri, mid twenties, Rafi early thirties, Marie late thirties, and the guys Jose and Juan, mid and late twenties respectively. All of them highly educated and qualified, and sadly looking for work in the total car-crash that is the Spanish economy. Such a crying waste of talent. Juan is the economist of the group, so I address my query about the pesetas to him, without mentioning any names, obviously. 'Ahh thees es Antonia in you street, she is my haunt, sister my father, she selling her house.' *Well that went well, didn't it? Auntie Vera's tax-dodge exposed to the four winds.* 'Many ancient person in Espain no trust the Euro' he continues, 'the goberment they fixy the peseta to Euro, at one million to six thousand. So four million peseta es twenty-four thousand Euro.' I am almost expecting him to shout 'SIMPLES' like the Meerkat at the end of Coronation Street, but thankfully he has never had to endure British television soap operas.

Marie chimes in to the conversation. 'Much peoples here think pesetas, if you see in supermarket, prices show in Euro, and pesetas. Ver small on label.' *Oh yes, of course! I have seen this, '400 pta', written in small figures after the Euro price. I thought it referred to Club-card points...*

So next question, about the 'morrow loco'. Teri explains. 'Moro is bad word for Moroc person, many old people still say thees word, but today it shows no respect. You must not to say thees to head of Moroc peoples.'

'Face?' Chrissie suggests.

'Hoder!' Terri cries, 'face, yees, sorree, I forget my Eengliss over summer! I must to start my classes of Eengliss with you, Cristina!' Indeed she does.

Rafi however is concerned about Crazy Man. 'You say thees person, how you say, break-in, to house of Miguel? My house close to thees. We must to go to house of polices-mans, after the class. You come now, plees!' It is approaching one PM, the class is breaking up anyway, so off we head, up the cobbled street, to the house of polices-mans. On the way, I ensure she is fully briefed about the soup ladle, the gas bottle, and the effect on the value of Janie and

Nigel's house. Not to mention, as a serious issue, the effect on the elderly people in the street, with this lunatic on the loose. Plus of course, the danger to the Englishman who has to repair the garden wall in the morning. I referred to the local boys in blue as the 'Old Bill' earlier. Actually I should amend that to the 'very, very, extremely ancient Bill', given that most of them seem to be well past retirement age. You rarely see an old Bobby in Britain, do you? In fact many might say you rarely encounter ANY age of Bobby there. Here however, there appears to be a surplus of the whiskery old gentlemen, given that the concept of early retirement is unheard of, although whether they are capable of actually apprehending any suspects I seriously doubt. We are about to find out, I imagine.

Entering the house of polices-mans, there he is, the venerable old copper, propped up behind his desk, newspaper open to the sporting pages, half-eaten sandwich on one side, mug of coffee on the other, a crappy Spanish soap-opera playing on the flat-screen TV on the opposite wall. This could be a scene from a nursing-home, quite frankly. Is he actually still alive? If he is, he certainly won't be chasing any villains this side of the grave. Rafi coughs theatrically. Not a flicker. She seems unsure what to do next, but I am not having it. What am I paying my rates for? Not that we've actually paid any rates yet, but it's the principle, isn't it? Lives could be at stake here. Mine, specifically, in the morning. 'HOLA!' I bellow. The effect is spectacular. Rafi and Chrissie burst out laughing, and Dixon of Dock Green's grandfather snaps back his head, like he's just seen a ghost, or St Peter. He seems to be unsure precisely where he is, perhaps he is expecting a nurse to pop in and change his bed-pan, or his medication. Slowly his rheumy eyes come into focus, and wiping a line of drool from his gums, he regards us for the first time. Clicking his false teeth into place, he utters a single word.

'Que?'

I turn away and stuff my knuckles in my mouth, shaking with subterranean mirth. 'Fawlty Towers', isn't it? Manuel, the Spanish waiter. 'SI? QUE? WHAT?' Thankfully, Rafi seems unaware of any John Cleese sitcoms, and so launches into her speech. I'm not sure of the Spanish for 'soup ladle' but I do catch 'butano', so she is relating the tale of the gas bottle. Old Father Time seems resolutely unmoved however, his eyes repeatedly switch back to the TV, and all too soon, Rafi is directing us outside, without him having taken a single note. Maybe he has one of those sponge-like memories, able to absorb every minute detail of a conversation? Sponge-like brain, more like it.

Outside in the street, our eyes adjusting to the blinding sunshine, Rafi relates the brief conversation. 'Thee polices-mans he say me, ahh do not worry, thees man he only want hot house, he will not be problem for you.'

*A HOT HOUSE? Did he mistake Crazy Man for a tropical plant? Beyond belief, what an utter and complete waste of time. This is partly Rafi's translation of course. What she clearly meant to tell us was that the vagrant was only looking for somewhere warm to stay, despite it still being over twenty degrees at night here. Poor chap must be freezing. Maybe the banging I could hear this morning was his teeth chattering, not the ladle clanging on the wrought iron?*

Shaking my head in disbelief, we thank Rafi for her help, she veers off into the street behind Miguel's and home, and we head directly for our sunbeds under the fig tree. I am exhausted, in severe need of a lie-down. Easing backwards onto my pillow, I gaze across at my wife who is contentedly flicking through her Kindle. 'If this was the first day of the rest of my life, can I change my mind? Can I get a refund? Is there a fourteen-day cooling-off period? Surely mixing cement for Del-Boy was easier than this? And we still have Babs and Andy coming back tonight to discover what four million pesetas is, and I need to phone Nigel about his wall.'

Chrissie slams her device into her lap. 'For pity's sake will you stop moaning. You've only been back a day, just lie there and shut u....'

Too late. I am already fast asleep.


The following morning, after a restless, tortured night, featuring exploding gas bottles, soup ladles and chocolate-coloured Spanish snakes writhing away everywhere, I am somewhat bleary-eyed, to say the least. Still, all is calm. Loli's medication is clearly kicking-in. And the sun is out. Hopefully, the second day of the rest of my life will be slightly more tranquil than the first. Fingers crossed. As I pour my second mug, I smile sweetly at my wife. 'I have the bricks and mortar arriving at Miguel's this morning. Would you fancy coming down and helping me unload? Please?'

She regards me unenthusiastically. 'Ooo, let me think. Can a girl resist the sight of Dirty Diego the Dumper Driver picking his nose, adjusting his crotch, clearing his throat and gobbing disgustingly across the pavement? Who could fail to be aroused as he grabs my breasts whilst handing me a sack of cement? You really shouldn't put temptation on my way like this, there was me thinking I might have the boring task of tidying my rose garden this morning, and now you are enticing me with the manly charms of Dirty Die…..'

'All right all right, I get the message! I take it that's a no? I just thought you might like to share the delights of the rest of our lives? You know, what we agreed? On that beach in France? Remember?'

She narrows her eyes. 'No, that was the rest of *your* life you were talking about, the rest of *my* life is perfectly fine, thank you very much. The rest of *my* life needs no input from you. You go and get on with the rest of *your* life, and if that involves having *your* breasts caressed by a disgusting old Spaniard, remember it was *your* decision.'

I am shaking with laughter. She can be extremely droll over the breakfast table, Chrissie. At least, I think it was humour…..

Part of my nightmare-tinged sleep last night involved the soup ladle, and more specifically, the other utensils which formed part of the Prestige stainless-steel kitchen set which was extremely popular as a wedding present in the 1970's. We were given one as I recall, the bracket on the wall, and five or six implements which hung from it. What were they? A slotted spoon? Give you a nasty slap, one of those. A fish slice, or 'that thing for scraping up fried eggs'. Ditto. A potato-masher? A Painful whack on the back of the head. But the one giving me the biggest heebie-jeebies is that damn great fork, eighteen inches long, with two huge prongs. Easily penetrate my layer of fat, one of those. Still, maybe Miguel was not much of a cook. What was the fork used for anyway? Holding down the roast beef whilst carving? Dunno, a bit of stewing steak was all we could afford, back in the day. The fork certainly remained unused, in our house. And do Spaniards eat roast beef? Don't think so. You never see signs outside pubs advertising 'Roast beef and all the trimmings.' So maybe the

Spanish Prestige stainless-steel kitchen set didn't actually feature the dirty great fork. Perhaps it only contained flippy, tapassy little implements. I hope so anyway, getting pronged by Crazy Man is not on my agenda this, or any, morning.

Grabbing my phone, in case of emergencies, and Nigel's keys, I make a huge play of leaving the house. 'Right, just off to meet Diego, and run the gauntlet in Miguel's garden. Wish me luck, will you, I am just going outside and may be some while!'

My dearest barely raises her eyes. 'Well you're not off to the bloody Antarctic, are you? You're only going a hundred yards. Just get on with it and stop being such a drama queen!' *See what I mean? Extremely droll...*

There is no sign of life at Miguel's as I approach, so I slip inside Nigel's and close the door. I am hoping to perform my tasks as silently as possible, to avoid rousing Crazy Man, obviously, but also not alerting the neighbours, if that is possible in this country, as technically I will be trespassing, in Miguel's garden. Mind you, the Ancient Bill were not concerned at blatant breaking and entering, but you never know. This is not my country, so I am keen to escape the attention of the local constabulary. I figure that the wall is jointly owned, and that as Miguel's is unoccupied, I am simply carrying out running repairs, to avoid further damage. That will form the basis of my defence anyway, should I fall foul of any laws. I intend mixing the mortar in Nigel's garden, steps up to the wall, down the other side, bed in two courses of rocks, back up over the wall and away.

The chug-chug of Diego's vintage dumper heralds his approach, and with it goes any semblance of a quiet morning. 'WHAT YOU DOING, NEIGHBOUR?' *Oh no, just what I need, Pirate Pete bellowing out. Fan-flipping-tastic.* I start waving my arms in a 'please be quiet' kind of way, but it is hopeless of course. 'I am doing a bit of work in my friend's garden' I whisper, which is technically true of course. 'WELL DON'T WAKE UP THE MORROW LOCO!' he hollers. I run my hands across my face, and smile, through gritted teeth. What I could do with a Prestige stainless-steel potato-masher, right now. Up clatters Diego, and I wave him back into his driving seat, hopefully to avoid his groin, his phlegm, and being grabbed in the whatnots. I can manage the unloading, perfectly well, thank you. I pay the man, off he trundles, and still no sign of life from next door. I might possibly have got away with it.

Right, up on the wall, and check out the local wildlife, before committing myself. Incredibly, the snake is still in the same place as yesterday. Not moved an inch. Is it dead? Is it an ex-snake? Certainly appears that way. Perhaps that explains the colour? I am somewhat short-sighted, and don't have my glasses with me, but maybe I can risk slipping over the wall, lob a stone at the reptile, and see what happens, so gingerly, keeping a wary eye on Hissing Sid, and Manuel's back door, I step down into the wilderness. And almost vomit. OH. MY. GOD. It is not a snake, it is a length of poo. A foot-long turd. My throat is gagging as I stare in disbelief at this humongous faeces. Who, or what, has been shitting in Miguel's garden? Not an animal surely, far too big for a dog, and I should know, having retrieved plenty from behind my beloved retriever, Nelson, over the years. I almost stumbled over some elephant dung in India once, round as a football and all grassy. And last time I checked, there were no jumbos tramping about in wildest Andalucia. So not an animal. But how could it be human? The garden is completely enclosed, with no possible public access, and besides, wouldn't there be, ahem, a few sheets of Andrex lying around also? A mystery, but I make a mental note to add a quid or two to my hourly rate, when I send Nigel his bill. Health and safety danger money.

There is some loose earth handy so using my spade I do my best to cover the offending pile, and lob a large rock on top to avoid stumbling in it, as I regularly used to manage when working amid Del-Boy's eight dogs. *OK, pick out a dozen or so suitable rocks, get the mortar mixed, flop it down and get the hell out of Dodge.* Wrong! 'ROO-SEE-YA!' Stumbling up the steps to the garden, folded newspaper under his arm, unbuttoning his trousers, comes Crazy Man. *OH NO. OH PLEASE NO. THIS CANNOT BE HAPPENING. Is he coming up to perform his ablutions?* He reaches the top of the steps, and we stand, facing each other, like two gunslingers in a Western. Problem is I don't even have a Prestige stainless-steel potato-masher, let alone a six-gun. Luckily he is similarly unarmed, apart from the newspaper, and I cannot recall anyone dying from injuries sustained being whacked by the Daily Mirror, or whatever the Spanish equivalent is. Suddenly, he throws back his head. WAAAARRRRRRRRRGH! *Yeah, whatever mate, but this ain't your garden, and I'm here to do a job of work.* Still, I hold up my hands placatingly, 'I am repairing the wall' I smile, gesturing at the pile of stones.

Crazy Man seems suitably appeased, but what happens next? Is he going to just, er, perform? Should I look discreetly the other way. Sadly I have forgotten to bring my guide to etiquette, not that I imagine there is any advice about what to do when a tramp wants to take a dump in someone's garden. I decide to withdraw gracefully, so back up the steps, over the wall, and down into Nigel's, locking the door behind me. In the kitchen I pour myself a large glass of water, and gulp it straight down. So how long do I give it? Five minutes, ten? I do actually feel overwhelmingly sorry for the poor man. Clearly he has massive personal issues but surely there are places available here where he can get professional help, and medication? Although, perhaps, he is here illegally, and unable to access the local heath-care system? I don't suppose I will ever know, which is possibly the saddest aspect of all.

Janie and Nigel have a roof patio in their cottage, so I head up there, pull out a folding chair, intending to give Crazy Man a quarter-hour or so, but in the warm autumn sunshine I am soon drifting off to sleep, and I haven't actually done anything yet this morning, work-wise….suddenly I am woken by the tinkling of my phone. Nigel, wanting to know how the repairs to the wall are going. 'Well actually, mate….' and I recount the story so far, apart from the bit about me reclining in his best patio chair, of course. And about my hourly rate mysteriously increasing….

 From the roof terrace I can see down into Miguel's garden, which now seems deserted, so back downstairs, out in the sunshine, mix the mortar, over the wall, no 'snakes' or bits of 'El Daily Mirror' visible, perhaps he couldn't, er, go, after all that, doubt whether I could have either, to be honest, flop down the mortar, position the first two rows of rocks, check they are straight, but frankly who cares after all this, back over the wall, lock the back door, out the front, secure the house, and back home, all in record time, and without the imprint of any Prestige stainless-steel implements in my scull.   WHEW! Fig tree, sunbed, out for the count.

The following morning is Wednesday, which can mean only one thing; boiled eggs and toast cut into soldiers, for breakfast. Always been a boiled egg fan, but never really had the time in the mornings, when I was working. Now, following early-retirement, this is part of my midweek ritual. Sipping a second coffee, watching the morning sun slanting through the olive trees, all is at peace with my world.

Or not. 'NEIGHBOUR!' *Oh please no, not again. Crazy Loli, hollering about something trivial. I hope she is not going to make a habit of disturbing my mornings, following our return to Spain.* Reluctantly, I drag my body to the patio railings and peer over. 'NEIGHBOUR! MORROW LOCO. CAR SELL!' *Not the faintest idea. Morrow loco something.* I smile my appreciation at this useless nugget, and slump back in my chair. Hang on a minute. Car Sell? Did she say car sell? Is Crazy Man selling his car? Does he even have a car? This is beyond my comprehension. The bloke is barely coherent. He is not fit to be left in charge of a gas bottle, let alone a CAR? What manner of vehicle could he possibly own anyway? An image of a wheezing, ancient conveyance flashes through my mind, the front riddled with bullet-holes, the rear destroyed by high explosives.

Chrissie meanwhile has been in the kitchen making a fresh pot of coffee. She emerges onto the patio. 'What was she bellowing about?'

I shake my head in disbelief. 'Crazy man is selling his car, apparently. I know it sounds impossible but that is what she said.'

My wife bangs the coffee pot down on the side table, then folds her arms and fires me a glare. She might only be five-feet nothing, but she has this glaring stance off pat. Particularly at me. 'Tell me again what she said?' she commands.

I exhale dramatically. '*Morrow loco, car sell*. That was it.'

Her glare becomes even more withering, if that were possible. 'You blathering idiot. You steaming, blathering idiot. Those are English words. Car. Sell. Did you think Loli took an intensive English course, during the night? Learning her past tenses in her sleep?'

I am aghast, and bury my face in my hands, in a vain attempt to conceal my embarrassment. 'All right, all right, yeah yeah yeah. Look, it's only just gone nine. My brain still thinks it is midnight.' And I begin to chuckle.

She is not finished with me yet, however. 'I am getting seriously worried about you. I think you should see a doctor, before your condition gets any worse.' *Oh yeah, I can just imagine that conversation with a Spanish quack. 'I am a steaming, blathering idiot, Doc. Best of luck looking up those symptoms in your medical text-book!'*

The pressure is relentless. 'So what does 'car sell' mean in Spanish then, do we know?'

'Not a clue' I wince, 'because I didn't do Spanish 'O' Level in 1969, DID I?' *Some relaxing morning this is turning out to be.*

'Well I'll tell you what it means, shall I? It means 'prison'. Crazy man is in prison.'

Jumping up, I poke my head over the patio to find Loli still there, so I cross my wrists in a handcuff gesture. 'Car sell?'

'Yes neighbour, prison, last night!' and she waves her arm in the general direction of the house of polices-mans.

*Blimey. Prison. I wonder what he did? Perhaps old sponge-brains Ancient-Bill actually took some action. Maybe the other neighbours complained? Or possibly a gas bottle went bang?*

The glaring is not over yet, however. 'So crazy man is locked up. Which means you can stop banging on about stainless-steel kitchen implements and gigantic turds. Maybe you can get down Miguel's and do some actual WORK? Get that thrice-damned wall finished? So you can get back here and get the swimming pool patio actually completed, so that maybe I can have a dip, this side of CHRISTMAS?'

Ah yes, the swimming pool patio. Where once were horrible, tumbledown animal sheds in the garden, now stands a beautiful area, full of hardcore, which only needs a layer of sand on the top, and then tiling. Tony and Jo have a stand-up pool for sale, about three metres across, OK so not a 'Hi-Di-Hi- style'

Olympic-sized pool, but enough for a dip, and a splash round. And no need for a building permit, either.

I stand to attention, and salute. 'Yes ma'am, certainly ma'am, I will flog my aching body down to Miguel's right now, and get the wall done. If you wouldn't mind shifting a bit of that hardcore in the garden, you will have somewhere to bury my CORPSE!' And the pair of us roll about laughing.

At Miguel's all is quiet, a quick peek over the wall reveals no more surprises, and lo and behold my mortar of yesterday has set perfectly, so without further ado I start shoveling the rubble into the space behind my newly laid stonework. If I can crack on here, get the next course of stones into place, then maybe, yes, I can get back home and put an hour or so into our new patio. I would quite like a dip before Christmas, too.

Wrong! 'Heffe!' Who is that? I cannot see a soul in either direction, up or down the street. Again comes the shout, 'heffe!' A male voice, but where? Glancing frantically around, I suddenly spot a man leaning out from the patio of one of the cottages in the zigzag above, maybe twenty feet up. I say man, but it could actually be one of those gargoyles you see stuck on the side of cathedrals, which has been there for about a thousand years. A visage of ghastly proportions, nothing about his features is symmetrical. Boggle-eyed, one looking at me, possibly, one pointing to the sky, his nose follows a circuitous course, even his lips are on the slant. He certainly hit every branch on the way down, when he fell out of the ugly tree. Still, he has news to impart, about Crazy Man, probably. 'Morrow loco, last night!' he cries, indicating a shoe wedged in the gap in his patio fencing. Surely not? Crazy man was climbing up there? Why? For what purpose? And is that actually one of his shoes, wedged in the chain-link? Need my glasses to be sure, but it certainly looks like one, I can just make out the hole in the toe area. Tramp footwear, for sure.

Gargoyle-man is still gabbling away, I am struggling to follow his conversation on account of his lips barely meeting, but he is pointing from his fence, to his neighbours, and the house after that, with barely a foot-hold visible. Did Crazy Man really climb across those fences? Is he actually part-chimpanzee? Mister Ugly then indicates the opposite direction, towards the top of Miguel's garden, where there is what appears to be a ruined grain-store, with a rickety lean-to at the front, and makes a diving or falling gesture. *'Ky-eedo!'* Ah, I know this word. It means 'fell'. And closer inspection reveals a gaping hole in the lean-to roof. So let me get this right. While we were sitting peacefully on our terrace, sipping a glass or two of red, Crazy took a nocturnal stroll, as you do, across some patios, twenty feet up, got his foot stuck in the fence and fell through a roof. And got himself arrested into the bargain. There's a night-out with a difference. Maybe I could organize some stag-parties from the UK, cheap flights to Malaga, a load of Spanish beer. Beats vomiting into the Danube, surely? Next year we'll be millionaires, as Del-Boy Trotter might have said.

Right, the morning is slipping away, as per usual. Waving my thanks to Gargoyle, I select a few more suitable stones, mix up the mortar, and flop them into place. Really starting to look like something now. Not sure what precisely, but it looks like something. I'm sure Nigel will be highly delighted. Locking up and heading home, striding down the street is a stranger, small, wiry, with wild, ginger hair, so not a Spaniard, presumably. 'I reck you, don't I?' he enquires, pleasantly. An Irishman, by the sound of him. 'You remember, down the ironmongers, Ronan's me name? Translated for me, ye did.' Not a clue, quite honestly, but before I can comment either way he launches into a monologue, all delivered in that wonderful 'stream of consciousness' style. 'Now was I telling you I bumped into this Cockney feller yesterday, Phil, wonderful artist so. We had a couple like, then went back to his place, for a couple more, and hasn't he got a studio, up in his attic? Twenty or more paintings, all in various stages, like, a lot of it modern stuff ye know, squares and circles, but there was a lovely painting of a Retriever dog, two foot by eighteen inches maybe. Now when I was a wain we had a Retriever, Bobby he was called, and every year we used to go up to Connemara for holliers like, and Phil's painting looks just like Bobby sitting on a path in the mountains up there. So I says to himself, would ye be looking to sell the painting like, and he says yeah, I painted it for some British people last year, but they didn't come back, so yeah I need to sell it, get me time and materials back, so. And I says to him what are ye looking for, and he says well something this size would usually be tree hundred Euro, with all the details of his fur and that, and the mountains, but seeing yer a good fellow I can let ye have it for two-fifty, like.'

*OK. Moral dilemma time. I know for a fact Phil didn't paint that picture, as Chrissie found it in the street, and I loaded into the back of his car not two days ago. So do I tell Ronan, and risk falling out with Phil, and both of them, possibly? Phil is lying through his teeth, which is between him and his maker, and I'm not worried he is making a fast buck. Wish I'd thought of it myself, actually. But it all seems, I dunno, a bit dishonest. Then again, if Ronan saw the painting in a shop, would it be any different in principle? He is happy with the price, so what's the problem? Dilemma solved. I'm keeping shtum.*

'So have you actually paid Phil yet?' I enquire, for no particular reason.

'Ah no, I only had a fifty on me, like, so I will go down the bank in the morning, get the rest of the grade, and pay yer man. Then all I need to decide is whether I take the painting home to me house in Ireland, like, or keep it here in me wee cottage in the mountains of Spain.'

'Bit big for your hand-luggage on Pad.. er Ryanair, isn't it?' I smile. I was going to use the term favoured by most British expats here, *Paddyair*, but don't want to cause any offence.

'Ah that Micheal O'Leary now' he fumes, 'fecking villain, so, and a terrible gobshite!' *So no love lost there, then, between compatriots!* 'Maybe yer right, it will be too big for me bag, an' I don't want to pay that bastard anything I don't have to! Anyway, come up me house over the weekend, I can show you me painting, sure you're dying to see it!' *Too late. Seen it already.....*


After briefing Nigel that night on the antics of Crazy Man, I get another call from him on Thursday morning, just after breakfast. 'Right, Janie and me have been talking and we'd like you to put a bar across the front door of Miguel's, and brick up the back door. The whole situation is causing us so much stress, we always worried about dossers in there after the old man died, but now it's actually happened and it is just unbearable, being so far away.'

*Hmmmm. I wondered when this was coming. I do feel for them of course, but it will be me in the firing line, should it all kick off with the polices mans.* 'I'm sorry mate, but I really can't do that, as it's not your house, or mine, and everybody knows I have been working down there, and if there are any comebacks, It's my neck on the block.'

I can sense the disappointment surging down the line. 'Well couldn't you just sneak in the back door, bolt it from the inside, then quietly brick up the back door, completely seal it up?'

'Sorry Nigel, if it were your house I would do that in a flash, but you know it's impossible to anything 'quietly' here, all the neighbours know, Fag-Ash Lil, Pirate Pete, Dora the Explorers granny, Mr Ugly over the back, grey-woman, sexy neighbour, …'

'WHO?' he cries, momentarily forgetting his anguish, 'there are no sexy neighbours round there!'

'The woman over the back, always wandering about in her nightie' I giggle. 'I don't know what anyone is called down your end of the street' I confirm, 'that is why I give them all nicknames!'

Suddenly, I can feel my wife's eyes, boring holes in the back of my head. *Oh no, done it again. Dropped myself truly and completely in it.*

'Anyway, never mind all that' I hastily continue, 'the point is they all know I'm down there, and I'm really sorry but I cannot take the risk.'

But Nigel is not letting go. 'Neighbours in nighties eh? Remind me to scrutinize your work carefully when we come over next! And I will be looking in great detail at your bill, when you send it!'

'Tell you what' I chuckle, 'that wall is perfect. OK so the sides go in and out a bit, and the top looks like the Loch Ness Monster's back, but it will be the best thousand quid you will ever spend!'

I can hear the spluttering and strangled oaths from over fifteen-hundred miles away. 'Right, you're fired!' comes the reply, but we both know he doesn't mean it.….

*Right. Time to get down there. Final couple of courses of stones.* Wrong! I am unable to move, as Chrissie has the neck of my tee-shirt from behind, and is gradually twisting, choking the life out of me. 'So. Sexy neighbour? Nighties?

All this time you've been pretending to dodge this alleged Crazy Man, who I don't believe actually exists, you have really been down there perving. Remember what you said yesterday about burying your corpse under the patio? Well consider it done, Sonny Jim. Plans are in place. The last day of the rest of *your* life is nigh!' *Like I said, so droll is Mrs Richards…*

Down the street, nursing a tender thorax, someone appears to be waiting for me outside Miguel's. A bloke, my height, but younger, and smaller about. Smart casual clothes, polished shoes, styled hair, clean-shaven, but strangely familiar somehow. I feel I know him from somewhere, but without my glasses I cannot quite see……. 'ROO-SEE-YA!'

NOOOOOOOOOO! This cannot be happening. Younger brother of Crazy Man? Or. Is. It. The. Same. Bloke? Astounding, the change. A spot of midnight mountaineering, bust up a roof, and look what happens. A complete makeover. Eat your hearts out, Trinny and Susannah. And why not, I ask myself. Hopefully he got a full English, this morning, before they let him go. And some medication. Just two burning questions however. Is he still dossing at Chez Miguel? And has he had a number-two this morning? I feel I deserve answers. Seriously though, I truly hope they have found him somewhere safe to stay, and that he can maybe turn his life around.

I smile and wave, unlocking Nigel's door and securing it firmly behind me. *Right, get this done quickly, back home, and spread out some sand over our new patio area. Level it off, maybe earn myself a stay of execution. If there is time, lay out a few tiles, make it look as if something is really happening, and who knows, get my sentence commuted.*

No problems with Crazy Man today, no unwelcome deposits in the garden, so in half an hour I am back home. Hopefully, finally, the nightmare for Janie and Nigel will be over. Wouldn't it be great if my next report was one hundred per-cent positive? I regard my pile of sand, fetch my spade from 'El Woodshed', and scatter a couple of shovel-fulls across the hardcore. Suddenly, I am overcome by fatigue. Not sure why really, as this week's activities have not been particularly strenuous, maybe just the mental strain of it all. Wears you out doesn't it, the fear of being pronged by a Prestige stainless-steel kitchen implement?  Whatever, I need to close my eyes for a few minutes, Chrissie is with Teri her student this morning so won't be home for over an hour, so I flop down onto my 'beach', wriggling my hips to get comfy, and in seconds I am away to the Land of Nod.

In my dreams I can hear voices. Female voices. 'Oh look, what do we have here, Teri? A British workman. Fast asleep. Doesn't he look peaceful, poor chap, he has been working really hard and is just taking a few minutes rest. Shall I make him a quick cup of tea, before I BEAT HIS BRAINS OUT WITH THIS SHOVEL?'

Teri meanwhile is rolling with laughter. 'Jonneee, you are Espaniss man now, sleeping when working!'

*Oh no, done it again, haven't I? Dropped off and dropped myself right in it, literally.* Grinning sheepishly, I attempt to struggle to my feet, but Chrissie still has the shovel, hovering menacingly a few feet from my head. 'No, no, don't move, stay there in that declivity, I can just throw a few shovel-fulls over you, save me digging that hole to bury your CORPSE!'

*When will I ever get something right....?*


The following morning Nigel calls for his regular update. *If he is asking me to brick anything up again I am going to get a bit cross, and my hourly rate might have to mysteriously increase, too.* 'OK, listen up!' he cries cheerfully. 'Big news. Janie and I have decided to try to buy Miguel's, if you can possibly find out the owners, maybe get a phone number, so we can ask our Spanish lawyer to negotiate with them. We don't have an unlimited budget, obviously, but realistically how much can that place be worth? And hopefully we can get it dead cheap, after all the problems with Crazy Man.' *Hmmmm. That is one solution, certainly. A bit drastic perhaps, and a complete money-pit as far as I can tell, but a solution nevertheless.*

Very strange, to us Brits, this concept of just locking up a house and walking away. In the UK, when a relative dies, just about the first thing the family do is get the house on the market, but with a property worth say a quarter-million, pounds obviously, not pesetas, entirely understandable. Here, inheritance laws mean the whole family benefits, so with maybe twenty relatives and a house worth under ten grand, as this one surely is, the prospect is far less enticing.

Anyway, if that is what they want to do, who am I to stand in their way. 'What I will do is ask Rafi if she knows any of the family, she lives in the street behind, she might even be a distant relative, everyone seems to be related some way or another in this town. If not she will surely know someone. I will give her your phone number and you can take it from there. OK?' Nigel professes himself delighted, and the rest of my day passes in tranquil fashion, for a change. I even manage to get some sand laid on our new patio.

*The calm before the storm.*

Saturday morning comes another call from England. Nigel, bubbling over with excitement. 'We've done it! Bought Miguel's! Agreed the price! How much do you think?'

*What can I say? Personally, I wouldn't give twenty pence for the old ruin.* 'Oh, I don't know, ten thousand possibly?' *I mean pesetas, clearly, although only I know that.*

'Four!' he cries, barely able to contain himself. 'Four thousand! What do you think of that? Result, eh?'

'Result indeed' I confirm. 'Miguel's family are giving you four thousand Euros to take the place off their hands. You are very lucky!'

'CHEEKY SWINE!' he bellows. 'So you don't want any of the work, renovating the place, then?' *Oh deep joy. I am going to be down there for the rest of my life, because that's how long transforming that hovel into something habitable is likely to take, assuming I reach my three-score-and-ten.*

But Nigel refuses to be offended for long. 'They were asking six, but I think ours was the only offer on the table.' *No idea why that was, Nigel. I would have thought people would be queuing up. Fighting to get their hands on the place. Gazumping, the whole shooting match.* 'We are coming over in a few weeks to sign the papers, but the deposit is paid, which means you can get on with securing the front, and bricking up the back. His family have agreed you can do that.' *Wondered when this was coming, frankly. But I did say I wouldn't do it unless he bought the place, not that in a million years I thought they actually would....* 'So first thing Monday morning, if that is OK with you? Get it secure? Please? So you, er, need to get down the builders and order the bricks this morning, before they close? Please?'

'Yeah yeah, I'm actually walking down the builders right now!' I lie, with a healthy dose of sarcasm. *Bless him though, he is so excited. Not every day you become the proud owner of a ruin, is it? And whoopee, another visit from Dirty Diego on Monday morning. Isn't the rest of my life going so spectacularly well?*

The weekend passes without incident. Crazy Man seems to have disappeared, as fast as he came. So Monday morning, breakfast on the patio, and Chrissie is sniffing the air. A human bloodhound, she is. 'Can you smell burning?' she enquires. 'Smells like a bonfire, somewhere.'

I take a deep breath, but my olfactory powers are not that great, to be honest. Explains a lot, probably. Some old farmer burning up some olive twigs, I imagine. 'Anyway, never mind that, I have Dirty Diego coming again this morning with the bricks for Miguel's, do you fancy giving.....right OK, obviously not!' Cannot say I blame her, all things considered.

Walking down to Janie and Nigel's newly-acquired wreck, I spot a larger-than-usual collection of neighbours hanging around outside. Nothing particularly unusual about that of course. If 'Standing Around Gossiping' were an Olympic sport, Spain would have the gold medal, for sure. And probably the silver and bronze too. Is this a welcoming committee? Is there a ribbon to cut? Will there be Champagne, or more likely that cheap Spanish rot-gut, Cava? And actually I can now smell wood-smoke. Is there a barbecue? Sausages with fried onions? Only just finished my breakfast of course, but I always have room for a sausage with fried onions, in a crusty bap. One of my life-rules.

The first person to greet me is Pirate Pete. His cataract operation was a complete success apparently, so he no longer needs to wear the eye-patch, but to us he will always be 'Pirate Pete'. 'Where you going neighbour?'

I explain I am heading to Miguel's, to secure the front and back doors.

'No you're not!'

*Eh? Has he misunderstood? Or, more likely, is my Spanish not that good.* 'Yes, out friends have bought the house, so I am going inside to....'

'No, you're not!'

*What is wrong with the bloke?* 'Por que?' Why?

'Because the house is on fire, neighbour!' and he gestures to the top floor, from which thick, acrid smoke is billowing. No flames, thankfully, yet.

OH. MY. GOD! MIGUEL'S IS ON FIRE. For a few seconds, I am lost for words, and have no idea what to do. Complete panic.

Pirate Pete comes to my rescue, nudging me in the ribs. 'Don't worry neighbour, look, the *bomberos* are coming!' Sure enough, in the street below is parked a fire-engine, and here comes an elderly firefighter, strolling leisurely up the steps, dragging a length of hose behind him. He is joined by a younger colleague, but not that much younger, and the pair of them, combined age of well over a hundred, step through Miguel's front door, which already appears to be open, and disappear inside.

Quick as a flash, leaving a trail of chattering Spaniards in my wake, I dash into Nigel's and start feeling the party walls. Ground floor, first floor, and top floor. All stone cold, thankfully. Out onto the roof terrace, no flames thank goodness, and the smoke does seem much less than just a few minutes ago, but I need to call Nigel, right now, and impart the bad news. Which is greeted by stunned silence, followed by wailing, shouting, and understandably in the circumstances, swearing. 'NO, NO, NO! HOW CAN THIS BE HAPPENING?' Following which there is a large crash, and the line goes dead. Has he collapsed? Fainted? He is supposed to be a retired fireman for heaven's sake. Aren't they meant to be calm under pressure? Unflappable? Mind you, usually they put out fires in other peoples' property, not one they have just scraped together the deposit to buy, only three days ago. I wonder if he got the place insured? Better not ask that one. Suddenly my phone chirps into life. 'Sorry mate, dropped the phone! How bad is the damage, can you see?'

I adopt my reassuring voice. 'Well, the party walls were cold, and I cannot see any flames, from up here on your roof patio... and the fire brigade are just leaving, actually. They are just rolling up the hose, and heading off back down the steps.'

The relief is palpable. His heart rate, and breathing, return to normal. Mine too, actually. 'Maybe only a small blaze in the chimney, hopefully?' comes the reply.

I am slightly puzzled, given that I cannot see a chimney pot. 'Chimney? There is no chimney up here.'

'Yes there is! he cries indignantly. 'There is a huge walk-in chimney, in the back kitchen, beautiful wooden moldings both sides, and around the mantle-piece, together with a painting of the Last Supper above, all encased in glass. It is the showpiece of the whole house, Miguel was so proud of it.'

I take a deep breath. 'Well I tell you what, I have never been inside the place, obviously, but I know what a chimney looks like, I am on your top terrace gazing down on Miguel's roof, and there is not a chimney in sight. Dick Van Dyke would be of no use whatsoever up here, singing Chim-Chim-Cheree!. This roof is pot-less, and flue-less.'

Silence on the line for a few seconds. 'OK, I trust what you are saying, of course. So that means the stack was taken down at some stage, and the hole tiled over. Probably the flue was capped off. So if Crazy Man lit a fire in the grate, there would be nowhere for the smoke to go, and no draught to ignite the flames, apart from small, localised damage. This is good news! I am feeling better already! So can you, er, get in there and check out the damage? Please? Soon as ….'

Suddenly comes a loud, urgent banging on the front door. 'Hang on a minute' I interrupt, peering over the terrace into the street, 'someone is trying to beat your front door down! I better see who it is, and call you back as soon as I can get in there.' Hurrying downstairs, I fling open the front door to be confronted by what appears to by a madman, waving a huge length of wood above his head. Must be a yard long, three inches wide, and he appears intent on embedding it into my scull. Jeez, what is it about this end of the road? Bonkers, the lot of them. Deftly, I step back, before he can take aim, and slam the door firmly shut. No idea who he is, middle-aged maybe, casually dressed so not an official of any sort, not that I got that good a good look you understand, being more than keen to protect my nut from a beating. He is hollering and banging again, but no way, Jose, I am not going out there until you calm down, or go away. I am just an innocent bystander after all.

The ranting continues for a few more seconds, then silence. Has he cleared off, or just trying to trick me, so that if I pop my head out, he can slice it clean off? Trouble is, I am trapped here. Suddenly, mercifully, help is at hand. I can hear the chug-chug of Dirty Diego the Dumper Driver, coming round the hairpin bend. Blessed relief. Never before have I been so glad to see the filthy old Spaniard. He can scratch his balls all he likes, clear his throat to his heart's content. Expectorate until nightfall. He is my saviour. My hero. My guardian angel. Surely, no harm will come to me with Diego on hand as a witness, not that his eyesight seems all that great behind thick pebble glasses. But an observer nevertheless.

Waiting until the wheezing conveyance has come to rest outside Miguel's, I take a tentative peek through the window, to see my hero conversing happily with Ranting-Man. Who is still brandishing the wood, but at least he appears to have calmed down. The pair of them appear acquainted, so I open the door and call out a greeting, keeping hold of the handle however in case it all kicks off again! 'Heffe, I got your bricks!' cries Diego, 'and Pedro here has some wood to secure Manuel's door!' *Wood to sec……….Oh madre mia.* I feel a bit of a lemon, but maybe if Pedro, whom I have no idea actually is, or what it has to do with him, hadn't waved said wood above his head like a screaming banshee, we might have got off to a better start. Grinning sheepishly, I advance towards the greasy builders truck, still keeping a wary eye on this Pedro fellow, in case the story about securing the door is just a ruse, and he still intends giving me a quick whack. Besides, I can do better then a wormy old length of timber, if we really are securing the door. An iron bar in fact, a yard long, half inch thick, four inches wide. Found it in Miguel's garden, rusty as a sailors bell-bottoms but still more than adequate for keeping crazy people out of Nigel and Janie's recent purchase, unless they happen to possess an angle-grinder, or dynamite. And by the greatest good fortune, said length of steel comes complete with four holes drilled at convenient locations, meaning I simply have to drill corresponding holes in Miguel's double doors, whack in four coach bolts and we will have better security than the Tower of London. Without any ravens, obviously. Which is a good thing actually. I usually find ravens a right nuisance, when bricking up the back door of a filthy Spanish doss-house.

Right. Unload Diego's bricks, the yard-long variety especially designed for Spanish doss-houses, three sacks of the magic plaster, yesso, which goes off like iron after about two minutes, and my saviour chugs away, leaving me alone with Pedro. *But I have an iron bar, matey, so don't try anything with your yard of Spanish plywood.* Out with my trusty drill, four holes in the doors, two in each, and I mime holding the bar against the doors and inserting the coach-bolts, basically as I don't know the Spanish for holding the bar against the doors and inserting the coach-bolts. Clutching the nuts and washers, I step inside Miguel's for the first time, Pedro closes me inside, and I am alone in the smoky darkness. Let's hope Crazy Man is not at home, eh?

Luckily, the back door is open, throwing a murky light over the whole depressing scene, puddles all over the tiled floor, no doubt left by the recently departed fire brigade. Shame they didn't give the whole house a decent hose down, actually. I hear the clunk of the iron bar against the outside of the doors, and lo and behold the four coach bolts appear, as if by magic. Threading on the washers and nuts, and producing a spanner from my back pocket, I tighten each nut in turn and that is it; no-one is coming through here until Nigel and Janie get over to sort out this unholy mess.

Right. Quick look round, assess the damage, get the back door bricked up and get on with the rest of my life, which seems to be slipping away at a rapid rate of knots. The first room contains a solitary, woodworm-infested dining chair, although the worms appear to have long since departed for tastier pastures new. Into the back room, and as predicted by Nigel, is the seat of the fire, the huge walk-in chimney. Once no doubt a highly impressive period piece, now a sad, charred, soaking, soggy mess. I dare say it will dry out in time, and some of the moldings might be salvageable, but the glass covering the depiction of the Last Supper is blackened and cracked, and some of the Apostles have singed feet, never a good look I feel. Such a crying shame, I have never seen anything remotely like this outside of a stately home, and certainly not in a ratty old Spanish cottage.

The remainder of the 'kitchen' consists of one free-standing unit, although the prospect of preparing a meal on this virus-ridden specimen is beyond unthinkable. Curious, this local custom of the moveable kitchen. This one still has its four original legs, always a good thing, considering I have seen them standing on bricks, but why don't they, I dunno, bolt them to the wall? Perhaps they take their kitchens with them when they move, although personally I wouldn't be caught dead with this evil collection of chipboard and plywood in the back of a removals van. Bobby 'Elton John' Roberts wouldn't touch it, for sure. Even the local woodworms have given it a wide berth. In the corner is what might have been described as a 'sink' in the seventeenth century, white, originally, possibly, but now a rainbow-like spectrum of stains rarely seen outside of a path-lab.

Mentally making a note to add a further couple of quid to my hourly rate, on account of the very real risk of catching a fatal disease, I head up to the first floor, and the famous bricked-up French Doors. I vividly recall Janie and Nigel relating the story behind this bizarre decision. Towards the end of his life, when he got doddery on his pins, Miguel's family were understandably concerned about him exiting the doors and crashing off the Juliet balcony to meet an untimely end in the street below. But rather than, say, fixing the doors so they couldn't open fully, they instead opted to entomb the poor old man in a darkened room. The thought-processes behind this are unimaginable. 'Sorry grandad, we're worried about you having an accident, so we're going to brick you up.' The logic beggars belief.

Stumbling through to the back room, where at least a chink of light is visible through the dust and wood-smoke, the breast wall where the chimney once was is showing signs of cracking, no doubt from the flames, but nothing drastic, certainly nothing a competent DIY-er couldn't fettle. Or me, apparently, in the absence of such a person. Then through to the 'bathroom', a seventies add-on, which appears not to have benefited from a wipe round with a drop of Ajax liquid ever since. Trust me on this one, you don't want to know. But what the hell, it's my book. So, a skid-mark encrusted collection of beige porcelain. No wonder Crazy Man preferred crapping in the garden. One good thing however; no self-respecting rat would be found lurking in this hell-hole.

Up to the top floor, and a rather pleasant surprise, the best room of the whole house, which is not saying much admittedly, but a beamed ceiling and a small window overlooking the street. OK so the plaster between the beams is cracked and blackened, but with a little effort this could be very pleasant, a fact not lost on Crazy Man as what appears to be his roach-singed sleeping bag is thrown in one corner. Into the final room at the back, and yet another surprise, one which has me rocking with silent mirth. A mattress, rather yellow and old, with patches of even yellower stains, and a black tyre mark right the way down the middle. A big tyre too, from a van, or a four-by-four. So what can have happened here? Clearly nobody has driven a van through the top room of the cottage, so I imagine the mattress was 'acquired' from the street. Maybe someone left it out by the bin, it toppled over in the wind perhaps, some half-blind Spaniard came along in a beat-up Land Rover and drove across it, following which Miguel, or Crazy Man, discovered it lying forlornly in the road and decided it would be a worthy addition to their sleeping arrangements. Something like that, anyway. Before I retired, the concept of a mattress bearing the imprint of a tyre would have been beyond my comprehension. You don't find anything like that in Beds R Us, do you? Here, however, it seems somehow utterly normal. How has my life come to this?

One thing I must remember however is to warn Janie to bring some rubber gloves with her when they come over to take possession of the house, as she is rather precious about her fingernails I recall. Maybe she should acquire a Haz-mat suit too, in view of the various contaminants, lurking inside her new purchase. Best of luck getting that through security, at Luton airport.

Right. The back door. Time to start bricklaying. There will be no skill involved in this action. Nope, flop some yesso on the ground and on the wall both sides of the door, and whack down a brick. Repeat with the next brick, and so on until the door opening disappears from view. The main thing to remember is that I am outside whilst performing this action, to avoid entombing myself. And to make sure I take all my tools with me, obviously. Simples, to quote that Meerkat. The only thing to bear in mind about yesso is not to mix too much at a time. So three or four handfuls only. Add water, slap it on, lay the brick, and wait a couple of minutes. And so on. In less than an hour, the doorway has disappeared, replaced by solid wall. And short of a sledgehammer, no-one is entering this house again. Blimey, what a day! Gathering my tools, I hop over the newly-repaired garden wall, through Nigel's back door, out the front into the street, where thankfully the crowds have dispersed. The only evidence that the momentous events of the last week have actually happened is a soup ladle, tossed casually, forlornly, on the ground next to the bin. Home. Sunbed. Asleep in seconds.

That evening in bed, drifting off to sleep after a relaxing dinner on the patio, a few glasses of red, and Classic FM on the internet, I am suddenly catapulted awake. 'Oh my God! What have I done? How could have I forgotten? What a disaster!'

I can hear Chrissie thrashing around in the darkness. 'What the hell is wrong now? Can't a girl get any sleep around here?'

I am rubbing my head in desperation. 'How could I have done that? How could I have forgotten? Must have been all the excitement, all the stress. I just can't believe it!'

Chrissie fumbles for the bedside lamp. 'You're scaring me now. What have you done?'

In the half-light I turn towards her, face in my hands. 'I have bricked up Crazy Man's sleeping bag!'


Three weeks later we are out for the evening with Janie and Nigel, together with Rafi and her husband Pablo. Our British friends are treating us all to a slap-up meal as a thank-you for all our hard work. Nigel raises his glass. 'I just wanted to say how grateful we both are for everything you have done for us recently. We signed the papers yesterday, picked up the keys from the lawyer today, so Miguel's is now officially ours! Mind you, some joker has bolted a dirty great iron bar across the front door, and bricked up the back, DIDN'T THEY, MR RICHARDS?'

I narrow my eyes and give him my best, mock, Paddington Bear stare. 'Only as instructed, Mr Pollard. Only as instructed!.' We are all rolling around laughing. Even Pablo seems to have cottoned on. Or perhaps he is a Paddington fan, who knows. 'Besides' I continue, 'you are probably best off leaving that house sealed up for about a hundred years, give the Bubonic plague inside chance to die down!' Janie however is keen to get inside, start cleaning up. Fair enough I suppose, but personally I would give it at least a hundred years. 'OK, so you need a bloke with an angle grinder to come out and open the place up, luckily I know someone who will do this for thirty euros!'

'Oh who is that then?' she smiles, 'anyone we know?'

'Yes. Me!'

After the merriment has died down, Nigel turns slightly more serious. 'Er John, we wondered if you noticed, when you were checking over Miguel's after the fire, if there were any paintings in there?'

*Paintings? Uh-oh. I can imagine a small hole opening up in front of me.* 'Paintings?'

'Yes, Miguel was quite a famous artist, you know. He exhibited in a number of galleries locally, not Nationally or anything like that, but he was extremely well-known in this part of Andalucia. His paintings used to sell for three or four hundred each.' *The hole is getting wider.* 'He had an artist's studio on the top floor of the house, he invited us in there once, not to our taste really as it was mostly modern stuff, but we did commission a painting of our dog, the last time we saw the old fellow. *It's a tank-trap now.* We gave him a photo of Benji, our retriever, and he agreed to copy the picture. It was a lovely image, Benji was sitting on a path in the Lake District, typical doggy pose, you know, mouth open, tongue lolling, big grin on his face. Anyway, the next time we came over Miguel was dead, the house abandoned, so we never got to see the painting of Benji, or even if he'd finished it. And there must have been twenty or more paintings in there at one time, worth five-grand at least. We were hoping, you know, to have sold them to go towards the cost or renovating the house. So, did you see any paintings in there, John?'

*Gaping chasm, now, isn't it? Into which I am about to plunge, head first.* And out the corner of my eye I can see Chrissie starting to fidget, nervously. The penny has finally dropped. It was Crazy Man, clearly, who dumped the pictures into the street, that first morning. So the strict answer to Nigel's question is

'No, there weren't any paintings in Miguel's.' *They were in the street*. But splitting hairs, isn't it? Right, moral dilemma time. Do I just deny the whole thing? No, I hate telling lies, and besides, we only did what we thought was right, letting Phil have the cursed pictures. So do Nigel and Janie know him? Actually I don't think so. *But they might know Ronan*. Imagine them getting an invite to his place, and spotting Benji hanging serenely above his mantlepiece...

I puff out my cheeks. Take a deep breath. 'Well, what happened was........'

## CHAPTER 3. MEET 'VIC THE FISH'.

'Jonneee! I have much beautiful feeesh for you thees day! Prices lower, yees, much bargain!' I am with our friendly local fishmonger, Victor, known to us of course as 'Vic the Fish', late twenties, tall, slim, wire-framed spectacles, and a serious air. He reminds me of a librarian, or scientist, rather than an expert in all matters seafood. Yet a true *aficionado* he is. Not only does he tip me off regarding the daily specials, he offers advice on how each dish should be prepared, even which wine might be served with it. Plus he is an expert salesman. Bearing in mind Chrissie is a 'fishetarian', we blow a serious hole in our weekly food budget with Vic, but he is worth it, if only for the entertainment value. Like many young Spaniards, Victor is keen to learn English, so our weekly encounter amounts to a free lesson for him. I get the bargains, he gets the English class. A fair exchange, in my view. One of the highlights of my domestic week.

And his fish counter is truly a work of art. Not for him a few fillets slapped on some half-melted ice. Oh no. Today, for instance, his display features an array of marine creatures, all of which appear to be swimming, placed in an upright position on a thick bed of ice. Pride of place goes to a huge, scary, steel-gray fish, over four feet long, face like a mother-in-law, mouth open, displaying a vicious array of razor-sharp teeth, a mini *Jaws*, or a German battleship, butting through the Channel on a Mad March Day. A truly scary prospect to encounter whilst bathing in the sea, which is why I always keep my feet on the sand when I am taking a dip. You just never know what is down there, do you?

Next to the monster, paddling happily along in his wake, are some smaller, easily recognised species. A few mackerel, to one side, some rainbow trout the other. Then come the flat-fish. Nothing I particularly recognise, no spotty plaice for instance, but three different varieties, none of which thankfully are covered in breadcrumbs, truly an abomination I believe. Towards the back are some cod fillets, thick and meaty, plus a number of salmon cutlets which I am imagining are already grilling away nicely in our Andalucian Aga. A squeeze of lemon juice, a sprinkle of sea-salt, and a pinch of black pepper. I am salivating at the prospect.

Further across, in shallower waters perhaps, are the shellfish. A huge pile of mussels, complete with barnacles, razor-clams, a few periwinkles, king prawns and a lobster, amongst others. The whole display resembles a giant flotilla, reminiscent of Navy Days, or Sir Francis Chichester returning triumphantly to Plymouth Sound in 1967. Must have taken Victor ages to prepare, and it will almost be a pity if someone comes along to buy anything, and disturbs the arrangement, a highly likely scenario actually, given his sales skills, and patter.

I open my arms, grinning widely at the fishmonger. 'Victor, that is a beautiful display. And not a hint of plastic packaging in sight!' He smiles bashfully, then turns more serious. *OK, the sales pitch is about to begin…*

'Thees day I have for you booey!' he cries. 'Delicioso. Booey!' And he kisses the tips of his fingers, like a Frenchman.

*Booey? Surely not? We followed four booeys round the streets of the town last June, at 'La Romeria', an orgy of eating and drinking, spotty dresses, covered wagons, an all-night party and the image of a saint thrown in for good measure. Booeys. Oxen, in English. Huge, placid creatures, four legs, not fins. Turf, not surf. Not seafood, for sure.* 'Booey?' I puzzle, frowning. 'Moooo!?'

Victor roars with laughter. 'Sorreee, I mean booey del mar, of course. I confusing you. My Eengliss ver bad!'

*Booey del mar? Ox of the sea?. Is he serious? What manner of creature could be an ox of the sea? My mind is spinning, running riot. A whale? One of those sea-cows we saw in Florida years ago, when the kids were small? Manatees they were called I seem to remember? Surely not. The Spanish will eat almost anything of course, we were offered, and flatly refused, sparrows in red wine sauce in the bar the other night. But a Manatee? They are protected anyway, aren't they?* 'Sorry Victor' I chuckle, 'I have no idea what a booey del mar is. Do you have one, you can show me please?'

'Of course, wait one minute plees!' and he disappears through the plastic curtains, into the cold-store behind. He has me on the hook, he no doubt feels, not reeled me in yet, but he can sense a sale. But that's what he thinks. Doesn't sound very nice, does it, ox of the sea? Then again, take that German battleship. Probably tastes incredible, filleted. But eating the mother-in-law?

So what size is this ox of the sea anyway? If it really is cow, or who knows, ox-like, will he have the whole thing back there? Won't he need to chop it up into smaller pieces, like in a butchers? Not a clue, but I am about to find out as here he comes, backing through the plastic, something in his hands but certainly not bovine dimensions. Then he turns with a flourish and places a crab on the counter. An ordinary crab, like you get in Cornwall or Devon, or many other seaside destinations in the UK. As served in that little place on Brixham harbour, mayonnaise, chopped onion and herbs, with brown bread. Sensational. *'Fresh from the boat, straight down your throat!'* as the little blackboard on the quayside proclaims, with just a hint of Westcountry humour. A British crab, not one of those spidery things they have in France, orangey-red in colour, about a foot wide, but about as un-ox-like as I could possibly imagine. He is grinning widely. 'Jonneee, booey del mar! How you say booey del mar en Eengliss?'

'Crab.'

He reacts with horror. 'Jonneee no! Booey del mar ees beautiful, not crap! Why you say thees?'

I cannot help a chuckle. Poor fellow looks so serious. 'No, crab, with a 'b'. Not crap with a 'p'. C.r.a.b. Crap is something completely different.' *For a second I am back in Miguel's garden.*

He runs his hand across his face. 'HODER! My Eengliss ver bad! So do you eating crap in you countree? HODER! Crab! Sorree!'

*Once or twice, Victor, once or twice!* My mind is still reeling with how something resembling a pie-crust could, in Spanish, equate to a farm animal. I mean, ever seen pincers on the front of an ox, have you? Pincers with dirty great elastic bands on them...*NO NO NO! The thing is still alive!* I step back, waving the startled purveyor of crustaceans away. Call me hypocritical, but I cannot stand seeing things alive, before I start eating them. I mean, if I order a plate of lamb chops in a restaurant, I don't want to watch them gambolling across a field beforehand, do I? The same with Ringo the Rooster, stuffed and plucked, in Phil and Jackie's kitchen last spring. I built his chicken coop for heaven's sake. No way could could I have him for Sunday lunch. But how can I explain this? Impossible, really. Best just say I don't like eating crap. Sorry, crab.

It seems however as if Victor has got the message. Placing the ox of the sea next to the prawns on his tableau, he snaps on a pair of white rubber gloves, and with a flourish extracts a salmon cutlet, which he lovingly proffers. 'Sall-mon. Womans sall-mon.' Right. He has me baffled again. Womans salmon? Would that be 'salmon for women' possibly, or did this piece of seafood come from a female version of the species? Sensing my confusion again, he lifts his apron to one side, stretches out his fingers, and runs his hand up and down his groin area. OH. MY. GOD. I cannot believe that just happened. And an elderly woman who has crept silently, unseen, into the shop, looks on aghast as her fishmonger mimics a vagina.

For a few seconds I am rendered speechless, then rub my hands across my face. 'So you are telling me this piece of fish was female?'

'HODER! Yees. Female! Womans sall-mon!'

*Well that clears it up nicely. Why would I care? Why would it matter if it were male, female, or ambidextrous? What possible reason could Victor have for imparting this particular nugget of information? The thing swam across the Atlantic, presumably, found it's way up the same river where it was born, so they say, leaped over a few weirs, did the dirty with a member of the opposite sex, got caught in a massive net and ended up sliced and diced on Victor's counter. So are the mans sall-mon easier to catch, and therefore cheaper? Is that what this is all about? Do the bloke salmon hang around chatting about the football, and sex, then whoosh! In with the net and scoop the lot of them up? Are the female of the species more wily, difficult to nab, and therefore more expensive? Wouldn't surprise me. And is Victor trying to stiff me for an extra couple of quid, pretending this is a woman cutlet? Any more of this and I am off down the supermarket for a box of fishfingers, and who cares if they are covered in breadcrumbs? Or female.*

Right, I need to get to the bottom of this, if only for the sake of my sanity. Who said moving to Spain would be easy? Buy a house and lie around in the sunshine all day. That is what just about everyone said, on our recent visit to the UK. They don't realise we have all this to put up with, clearly. 'So tell me Victor, what is the difference between male and female salmon? Apart from the obvious?' And I point vaguely, but discreetly, in the direction of my lower half.

My Spanish friend regards me with utter bewilderment. 'Jonneee! You not know thees? The flavour of womans sall-mon is dulce, how you say, sweeter! Man sall-mon fuerte!' And he flexes his arm muscle, and pumps his fist. *Well blow me down. Who knew? Been a consumer of salmon since I was a boy, from a tin in those days, of course, but the red stuff, not the cheap pink rubbish, with the bits of skin. Tea-time, on a Saturday. And when we were courting, Chrissie's mother used to prepare us a packed lunch on a Sunday, for days out in my trusty Ford Anglia. Salmon and tomato rolls. One of the reasons I married the woman. (Only joking, darling!) Anyway, me and salmon, of whatever sex, go back a long way.* 'So Jonneee, how you say 'womans sall-mon' in Eengliss?'

I cannot help a crafty chuckle. 'Salmon'.

'So how you say mans sall-mon in Eengliss?'

*Right matey, time to get you back. Mans sall-mon indeed.* I stare at him, deadpan. 'John West.'

'Jonneee, no! John West not mans sall-mon! John West he boy-cow. I see he on films Americano.' And he draws two imaginary six-guns from his holsters, and shoots me dead. 'The hell I will! You joke me, Jonneee, John West he boy-cow!' The little old lady meanwhile has given up. She barks a few choice sentences in our direction although whether she means *you are a pair of lunatics*, or *I'm just off to the post office*, I am unable to say.

Adopting my best John Wayne voice, and stance, I mimic a passable impression of a boy-cow. 'Say pardner, do ya have any man sall-mon, for this hungry pilgrim?'

My friend rapidly cottons on. 'Jonneee, you want I show you mans sall-mon?' I nod in the affirmative, so he turns on his heels, and disappears once again into the cold store. And returns, two seconds later. 'Jonneee, I show mans sall-mon later, you want now I show you gold-feeesh?'

*Did he just say goldfish? Surely not.* 'Goldfish?'

'Yees, gold-feeesh, delicioso!' And he does the Frenchman thing again, with his fingers, and vanishes. *Have I passed into some parallel universe here? Goldfish? They eat goldfish in this country? Wouldn't surprise me, to be honest, with this lot. Sparrows, ox of the sea? So why not goldfish?* In my mind I am transported back over fifty years, to my first ever pet, the day the funfair came to town. Dad won me a tiny goldfish, about two inches long, in a polythene bag. Whether it was hoopla, or knocking over a target I cannot remember, but I proudly clutched my puny prize on my sweaty knee, all the way home on the bus, silently cursing the driver every time he went over a bump. Mother, predictably, went mad, 'we have nowhere to keep a goldfish, Raymond!' but after ten minutes rummaging around in the back of the dresser, she emerged with an ancient glass punchbowl, a relic from Christmases gone by, which was where 'Goldie' spent his first night. So no way on God's green earth I am eating one of his descendants. Anyway, you would need about three to even make up a tapas, wouldn't you? Although I suppose Victor is about to emerge with something slightly longer, like one of those Koi you see lurking in the murky depths of ponds, or boating lakes? And how long to they take to grow to about a foot, anyway? Years, I imagine. I always thought they looked as tough as old boots, to be honest.

And here he comes, carrying a silver specimen, about a foot long, plump and rounded, rather like a bass. But SILVER. Not a hint of gold anywhere to be seen, around the eyes, the fins, the tail. *Is this payback time for John West?* 'VICTOR, THAT FISH IS SILVER!' I bellow, starting to get rather cross, now. 'You said goldfish. That fish is not gold. And actually', I continue, wagging my finger in a very un-British way, 'I recognise that, we have had it before. It is called a Dorada. A SILVER Dorada!'

He smiles serenely. 'Jonneee, yees! You are correct. Ees Dorada! But in Espanees, translate Dorada as gold-feeesh!'

*BUT IT'S NOT A BLOODY GOLDFISH! It's the silveryest fish I have seen in my entire life. What an utterly, completely ridiculous country this is. Sea-ox. Goldfish.* I shake my head, and puff out my cheeks, in exasperation. 'Jonneee! Ess Espain!' *Don't I know it...*

He carefully places his silver goldfish on the ice, and disappears out the back again, calling 'mans sall-mon' over his shoulder. *Cannot wait. I only came in for a nice bit of cod.* This time, there is a lot of crashing and banging, the sounds of rummaging, huffing and puffing, and general melee. Several other old women have entered the shop now, so I smile and shrug my shoulders in a non-committal way, unaware of the Spanish for 'Victor's just gone to fetch a mans sall-mon.' I fact it sounds as if he is catching the thing, or possibly it is catching him, the noise he is making. What can it be, a slightly bigger cutlet possibly, being male? Suddenly, he staggers against the curtain, his back arched against a huge weight, and he lurches through the doorway with the biggest fish I have ever seen, in the flesh, in my entire life. His arms are surely a yard apart, and there must be eighteen inches of marine creature hanging out either side, a huge ugly head to the left, a massive flappy tail to the right. A veritable tree-trunk, with scales, and gills. I mean, we went to Sea World with the girls, years ago, and met 'Shamu' the orca, although whales are mammals, aren't they? And dolphins? But this mans sall-mon is gigantic. Boggle-eyed, with a bead of perspiration trickling down his face, despite emerging from a cold-store, our crazy fishmonger hefts the mighty leviathan higher up his torso, then with a final grunt, heaves it on to the other end of the counter, to rapturous applause from half a dozen locals, no doubt attracted by the hullabaloo, and their uncanny knack of sniffing out a spectacle.

Our friend produces a towel from beneath the counter, and mops his sweaty countenance. 'So, Jonneee, do you like booey, womans sall-mon, gold-fees or mans sall-mon?

*Gone right off the whole seafood thing, to be quite honest. Still, after all his efforts it would be rude to just walk away, wouldn't it?* I smile sheepishly. 'Got a nice bit of cod?'

That evening, we are with Janie and Nigel for their final evening of their holiday, if it be so described, before their flight home tomorrow. Tapas and wine, on their terrace. They finally managed to gain access to Miguel's, as some kindly soul came down with his angle grinder and cut away the iron bar across the front door, free of charge. *Saint, aren't I?* New bolts inside, top and bottom, a hefty deadlock, wood all repaired, even the holes where the coach bolts went have been filled, the doors sanded down, and two coats of thick varnish. Looks fantastic, amazing what they have achieved, in only a few days. Just a shame about the rest of the house. Wisely, they have left the back door in its bricked-up state, in case any of the locals decide to go midnight walkabout, twenty feet up, along Mister Ugly's chain-link, before crashing through the roof of the lean-to, not that there's much left to crash through, to be honest. And Crazy Man? Disappeared from the face of the earth. Whether he is still banged-up, following the fire, we have no idea, and frankly I for one will not be enquiring, at the house of polices mans.

Janie, meanwhile, is bubbling over with news. 'Guess what, we paid that Ronan a visit last night!' *Oh blimey, am I in the dog-house again?*

Chrissie meanwhile is dying to find out what happened. 'So how did that go? Get your painting of Benji back, did you?'

Nigel takes up the story. 'Did you actually study the painting of Benji, before GIVING IT AWAY TO THAT THEIVING COCKNEY?' *See, told you I was in the dog-house!*

We are all laughing now. We know, or rather hope, he is only joking. We are both nodding, 'yes, we did!' giggles Chrissie.

'So what did you think?' Janie smiles. 'Come on, honest answers, please!'

My wife is trying to be diplomatic. 'Well, the actual dog was very good, I thought, but the background was, er, wrong somehow, made him look slightly too big, really.'

'SLIGHTLY TOO BIG?' Nigel splutters, 'HE WAS THE SIZE OF A BLOODY TRACTOR!'

'More like a seven-four-seven, I thought!' I chip in.

For a few seconds we are all rendered incapable of speaking, then Janie regains her composure. 'We had a lucky escape, actually, Miguel must have completely lost his touch in the last few months of his life. We went into Ronan's front room, and there is Benji, all ten-foot-six of him, propped up on the mantelpiece. I mean, we didn't go up there with the intent of causing any trouble, grassing up the Londoner, but I actually had a copy of the original photo we gave Miguel, on my phone, in case it all kicked off. Two hundred, or thereabouts, Miguel quoted us, which we were happy with, but when we saw the final result on the Irishman's wall, which he paid two-fifty for, well we could barely stop ourselves bursting out laughing!'

I slip into my serious-face suddenly. 'Well I reckon you are being extremely unfair on Miguel, you know.' Silence round the table for a few seconds. They know something is coming, they are just not sure what. 'Michelangelo. Heard of him, have you? Used to paint ceilings, a few years ago? He had a lot in common with Miguel, I'll have you know.' Eyes narrow. 'Miguel couldn't paint dogs, you say? Well Michelangelo couldn't paint cats, either.'

Nigel, taking a sip of wine, almost chokes, and dissolves into a fit of coughing. 'You steaming idiot. I almost got wine down the front of me shirt! Anyway, time for a reckoning up, for what we owe you for all your hard work!' My ears prick up. I can save my Michelangelo pussy joke for some other time. 'Right, ninety-five euros for the wall, you said, including the bricks?' I nod my assent. 'Then fifty for the door bricking-up, and all the bits? Call it one-fifty all-in. And then, we reckon we owe you the two hundred we would have paid for the painting, so call it three-fifty in total.'

It is me who is spluttering now. 'No no no! You don't owe me anything for the painting, that is ridiculous. I cannot possibly accept that.'

Our friend holds up both hands. 'I have spoken. WE have spoken. Janie and I both agree, you worked over and beyond the call down there, what with the crazy fellow, and the poo, and everything else. We owe you three-fifty, and that is all there is to say about it.'

I am flabbergasted, quite honestly. What an amazing gesture. They are such lovely people. I am truly moved. I blink away a tear. 'Well, I still don't agree, there really is no need for that, yes it was a difficult job in many ways, although I can laugh about it now of course. But thank you both very, very much. From us both.' And I reach across the table and touch Chrissie's open hand.

Nigel hasn't finished yet, however. 'OK, so that is three-fifty we owe you, so if we deduct that from the five grand you owe us, for the paintings you gave away to the Cockney, I reckon you owe us...' and he counts his fingers..' four thousand, six hundred and fifty euros. We'll take a cheque, if you don't have the cash on you.' And he sits back in his chair, arms folded. Complete silence round the table. Apart from the sound of me swallowing hard. Janie is looking down, Nigel has something in his eye, and Chrissie stares in complete disbelief. Another few seconds pass in acute, excruciating silence, before my wife's mouth starts turning up at the corners, Janie's shoulders take on a life of their own, and Nigel bursts into uncontrolled laughter. 'GOT YOU SUNSHINE!' he bellows, got you back for all that perving you did, at our neighbour! I have waited weeks for this moment, but it was worth every second! Every single second!'

The three of them are splitting their sides. I jab an accusatory finger in Chrissie's direction. 'You knew about this, didn't you? You were in on it all along. Well I reckon the whole lot of you are utter and complete BAAAST.......'

**CHAPTER 4. DYING, SPANISH STYLE.**

A few days later, we arrive home following our evening *paseo* to find a larger-than-usual collection of Spaniards standing around in the street, apparently doing nothing. If 'Standing around in the street, apparently doing nothing' were an Olympic sport...well you know the rest. It's just that there are more than there would usually be, on any given night. And not all from our bit, either. Fag-Ash Lil, Dora the Explorers Granny and Grey-Woman all live down the bottom, so have no real need to come up this end, especially at this time of night. So what is going on? Is it a Neighbourhood Watch meeting, possibly? Don't think they have that in Spain, actually. Anyway, nothing to do with us, they will disperse eventually. We smile and call out a few *Buenas-Noches* as appropriate, and head towards our front door.

Just then Loli steps out from the crowd. 'Carmelli, neighbour!' she calls out, at half her usual volume, which would probably still be considered a holler in the UK. *What about Carmelli, the dear old lady who lives just a few doors down from us, on the opposite side?* Frail, wrinkled and walks with a stick, in her eighties at least, Carmelli loves sitting outside her front door of an evening, watching the world go by, and we always stop for a chat as we pass, winging it as we usually do, but we generally manage to get there in the end. Earlier this year, we were given a huge sack of almonds by Jose at the library, so we set about dividing them between the neighbours. Carmelli got her share of course, but was muttering something we couldn't understand, so contrary to all advice, we nodded in the affirmative. Several nights later, grinning widely, she gave us a bag of something. Shelled almonds. She'd spent two days hammering away and was giving us about half back. 'Got any more?' she laughed. Apparently she loved shelling almonds, therapeutic or something like that, she said. Considering that using nutcrackers is just about the worst aspect of Christmas for me, Carmelli found herself gainfully employed over the summer. Payment in nuts, of course!

'Carmelli, yes?' Chrissie ponders.

'She's dead!' comes the somewhat abrupt reply.

*Oh no. How terribly sad. Poor Carmelli. Such a lovely lady, always smiling. We only met her less than a year ago of course, but our days will be the poorer for her passing.*

'When was this?' Chrissie enquires.

'Oh, about twenty minutes ago.' our neighbour casually imparts. 'She fell backwards off her chair and hit her head. There she is, look.' And she gestures towards Carmelli's front door, where, through the milling Spaniards, we can just about make out an overturned chair, two feet sticking straight up, and a body lying flat out in the doorway.

OH. MY. GOD. I am stunned. Chrissie's hands have flown to her face, and we are both rooted to the spot, in sheer, utter disbelief. What are these people DOING? This is outrageous. The poor woman is lying stone dead and people are gathered around just gawping. I literally cannot believe this is happening. I lean against the wall, cover my face with my hands, head spinning. We are in someone else's country of course, as we constantly have to remind ourselves, but surely in any culture this is a grotesque lack of respect? Kids are running about, cycling up and down the street, for pity's sake. I assume a doctor or paramedic will need to come and pronounce life extinct, so the body cannot be moved until then, but surely someone could have covered her with a sheet, shepherded the onlookers away, put an end to this loathsome sideshow? People will always gravitate to a disaster of course, simple human nature, but her daughter and son-in-law live opposite. Couldn't he have come out and taken charge?

I turn to Chrissie. 'Come on, home.' I whisper, 'I cannot stand here with these ghouls.'

Suddenly, matters take a turn for the worse, if that were possible. Down the street marches Marie. Crazy Marie, utterly, barking mad. Around our age, bleached blonde hair which is constantly in curlers, a pink housecoat, slippers and a silver charm-bracelet around her wrist, which is tinkling in time with her strides. Her usual daywear, in fact. Ignoring the other neighbours, she steps right up next to Chrissie, grabs her arm, and tries to pull her towards Carmelli's house. 'Come on, we have to go inside, get a good seat!'

WHAT? The look on my wife's face is one of utter horror. Has someone just died here? Is there a body lying in the doorway? Or are we watching the latest box-set on Netflix? Chrissie is struggling to free her arm but Marie is having none of it. 'Yes, we must stay with the body all night.' Why on earth would anyone want us in there, with the body? We are not family, and we have only lived here for a year. We are not Spanish, can barely speak the language, and besides, just about the whole street is related, we believe. Surely there are better qualified people for this task?

At that moment, Loli pipes up. 'Look neighbour, here are the family', and down the street come four middle-aged people, two men, two women, other sons/daughters, and their spouses, no doubt. The crowd parts like the Red Sea, and the 'children' step around the stricken corpse, and head inside. I am writhing with embarrassment, and none of this debacle is actually my fault. Maybe this is entirely normal here, the family certainly didn't seem to bat an eyelid, but I cannot, in my wildest nightmares, imagine receiving this devastating news, and arriving at the house to find a disorderly crowd jostling for ringside seats.

Marie meanwhile still has Chrissie firmly in her grip, so short of physically tearing the madwoman off, there is little I can do. We are stuck here. Although one thing is for certain. No way is my wife maintaining a candle-lit vigil, tonight, or any other.

Loli seems to have appointed herself as commentator. 'Here come the ambulance, and police, neighbour!' Sure enough, at the bottom of the street, blue lights are flashing. As far as they can possibly get of course, given the bottleneck that is our road. They will have to walk the rest of the way. And here he comes, the very, very extremely Ancient Bill, strolling casually up the cobblestones, accompanied by two paramedics of slightly younger vintage, but only slightly, carrying a stretcher between them, although whether this is for Carmelli, or in case Ancient-Bill suddenly drops dead, is impossible to say. As they approach, Fernando pushes his way through the motley throng. 'Hey Paco! *Que pasa?* Did you see the football last night?'

Paco rests his end of the burden against a wall. 'Nando, you old dog! Yes, we were lucky! That Sergio Ramos is a right donkey!'

*Er hello? Is anyone actually doing any work here? You know, the body?* Although Paco is correct. That Ramos is indeed a right donkey.

Meanwhile Ancient-Bill stoops over our deceased neighbour. 'Yes, she is dead!' he proclaims. 'Right, who wants to come in first? Kids?' And pushing, jostling as they do, half a dozen little ones fight their way inside. Completely. And. Utterly. Unbelievable.

At that moment, a number of things happen simultaneously. The ambulancemen stoop down to recover the body, a massive scrum forms around the front door of Carmelli's cottage, Marie bursts into tears, and Chrissie is finally able to free herself from the madwoman's clutches. We nip deftly towards our house, turning as we enter to witness a scene I could never have imagined in a thousand years. Two paramedics, with loaded stretcher, wrestling their way inside the house, through a mass of unruly Spaniards.

Pouring myself a beer, I slump into my patio chair to reflect on the last half-hour of our lives in this impossibly crazy country. Quite frankly I found it hugely distasteful. Then again, those are my personal values, what right have I, as a guest, to apply those to another culture? People here are far more down-to-earth, qualities we have so far found hugely endearing. But tonight? I don't know. I will need to sleep on it, I guess. And never mind that, what has happened to Chrissie? Where has she disappeared to? I head upstairs to find her peering around the wooden shutter of the bedroom window, gawping at the scenes below. 'Why are you doing that, being very British, peeping out like a little mouse?' I query, with a hint of sarcasm. 'You turned down the chance of a ring-side seat earlier. If you want to know what is going on, why not take a chair outside like all the others?'

My wife waves a hand dismissively. 'Shhhhhhhh! The Civil Guards are coming!'

*The 'Guardia Civil'. The slightly-more important-and slightly-younger-polices-mans. Well woopy-do.* 'You are just as bad as the rest of them' I cry, accusingly. 'Come on downstairs, pour yourself a drink. I am starting dinner now.'

She turns to face me. 'Well let me know when it's on the table. I'm staying here! Right?'


The following morning, breakfast on the patio, and yet more interruptions. 'NEIGHBOUR!' *Why didn't we stay in England?* I peer out over the edge and greet the vastly annoying woman. 'Funeral of Carmelli, ten-thirty' she proclaims. *Yes, but what date?*

'Cuando?' I enquire. When?

'I told you neighbour, ten-thirty!'

I wave my appreciation at this piece of half-information. No doubt it will be three weeks hence, plenty of time to find out the date from a saner source.

Chrissie returns with a fresh pot of coffee. 'Did she say the funeral was half-ten? Blimey, better get a move-on, then, find myself something to wear. Which gem from your extensive collection do you think you might select?'

*Oh very droll.* 'Well who cares? It isn't for another fortnight, probably, and besides, you have plenty to wear in that humungous collection of yours. Sit down, you are making me dizzy.'

She regards me without affection. 'You really and truly are a complete, steaming nincompoop, aren't you. I am phoning the doctor, right now. You know very well that funerals in Spain are always the following day! And don't bury your face in your hands like that', she continues, mercilessly, 'I don't want to hear any more of that 'my brain thinks it's midnight' crap, for God's sake get a grip!' And she storms off, banging the front door behind her.

*Blimey. Has she left me? Surely not? She has that humungous great wardrobe to clear out, first. But she is correct, I really must get a grip.* I am of course aware of the local custom of having the funeral on the day following the unhappy demise. I should have realised it would be today, but as my brain still thinks it is midnight……

Ten seconds later, she is back. 'Right, I've just seen the death notice stuck on Carmelli's door, the funeral is at ten-thirty, at St Mary's. So I'm gonna sort through my HUMUNGOUS wardrobe for some dark clothing, and I suggest you do the same, when you finish your coffee, of course. Won't take you long, will it!' And giggling, she disappears again. Ah yes, the death notices. In the absence of the tradition of a local newspaper here, every time someone dies there is an A4 sized sheet of paper, fringed in black, usually with the image of a saint, outlining the name of the deceased, their age and location, together with who the family are, and the details of the funeral arrangements, pinned to the front door of the dearly departed, and at various locations round the town. All I can say is that the local printers must work around the clock, to assemble the information, print the things, and get them posted. Good business to be in, all things considered.

At ten twenty-eight, soberly dressed, we arrive outside St Mary's, to be greeted by the usual Spanish chaos. *And the hearse is already there. Oh, I'm going to love this!* Stroking my chin theatrically, I turn to my wife. 'Now who was it who claimed the funeral was due to start at half-ten? And what is this here, this extremely long vehicle with windows in the back? Could it be a hearse by any chance? A hearse with no coffin inside. And this is Spain remember, so they cannot possibly be early. They have started already. So who couldn't translate the time properly?'

Which earns me a painful dig in the ribs, plus her best Mrs Paddington Bear stare. 'Actually, I think you will find it was our SPANISH neighbour Loli, who said it was ten-thirty? But of course you don't remember that, do you, as your minuscule brain was still thinking it was midnight?'

*Never won one yet, in almost forty years.* Before the exchange can become even more deadly, a figure in a vest-top and jeans is pushing his way through the melee. 'Cristina! Jonneee! How lovely to see YOOOU!' Amador, the newbie from the library group. 'Where you go, een black CLOTHES?' Chrissie explains. 'Me ALSO! CARMELLI. My HAUNT! Sorree, haunt of my FATHERS!'

WHAT? Dressed like that? Surely not? We only met him a few weeks ago, so we cannot really say anything, but a tank top at his great-aunts funeral? Although, looking round, very few have made much of an effort to dig out their black clothing, which is strange in a country where 'Sunday Best' is very much a national pastime. Curious.

'Thees way plees, we go in CHUR!' Yeah, easier said than done, my friend, as the door is completely blocked by a typical Andalucian ruck, the cause of which soon becomes apparent. A coffin. Carmelli's coffin, presumably, placed on a wheeled frame, and stuck in the middle of the entrance porch. Truly, it is as if the bearers have thought 'now where could we leave this to cause maximum disruption?' Still, this is Spain, as they say. There will be plenty of time. It's not as if this will be a typical British 'sausage machine' funeral, inside the chapel, favourite song, quick address by someone who didn't know the dearly departed, a hymn which no-one knows the tune of, another favourite song, then out, just as the next crowd of mourners are lining up outside. Although the speed at which some of the mourners are passing the coffin is less than rapid. It would be a wild exaggeration to describe it as 'snails pace' to be honest. Kissing, caressing, a few tears, and that is before they've even got to the wooden box. At this rate, it will be time for my funeral, before we get seated.

Still, gives us time for a spot of people watching. And they are all here, the neighbours. Loli, Isabel and brother Fernando, squeezing his ample stomach into a pew, Leopard-skin woman with Auntie Vera, joined at the hip as usual, Pirate Pete, grinning at all and sundry, making the most of his restored vision, crazy Marie, rattling her jewellery, cross-eyed Cruz-ojo, gazing every which way. Even Ferret-woman has slunk into a seat at the back. The only one missing appears to be Juan 'The Dustman', last seen sweeping up a pile of dog-ends from outside the bar.

The next hundred years pass quickly and eventually we are able to take our seats, Amador inside, Chrissie next to him and me on the outside, in case I need to make a run for it. Not sure what to expect here today of course, but we got ourselves trapped at the back of an evening Mass once, and it felt like a life sentence. Without warning, it appears as if something might be about to happen. A priest appears, then a gentle trundling announces the passage of the coffin-on-wheels, a smartly-dressed funeral director on each corner. I am trying to be British and direct my gaze to the front, although just about everyone else are craning their necks to see what is happening, when a voice in my ear whispers 'Gold-feeesh.' Somewhat startled, to say the least, I turn to be confronted by 'Vic the Fish', in undertaker gear, positioned at the back corner of the cortege, who smiles and winks as he passes. Blimey, is he moonlighting? Has he left his job as a fishmonger? Do we have to rename him 'Vic the Coffin'? Who knows, but presumably we will find out, over tea and cakes, and a beer or two hopefully, when this is finally over.

The next hundred years drag a bit, I have to say, but eventually we emerge, blinking, stretching, and in the case of some of the mourners, coughing and windpipe-clearing, into the warm sunshine. Amador grabs my arm. 'OK, see you next WEEK!'

I stare at him, uncomprehending. 'Sorry, aren't you coming to the wake? And where is it , by the way?'

Our friend appears mystified. 'Sorree, I no understand YOOOU!'

'The wake, Carmelli's wake.'

Total bafflement. 'NO! My haunt she not awake, my haunt she die, she with Cassoo, NOW!'

Chrissie takes over the narrative, although I am beginning to get the distinct impression we are not getting tea, cakes or a couple of beers, as the mourners seem to be dispersing to the four winds. 'A wake is a small get-together after a funeral, in the family home maybe, or often nowadays in the pub, to celebrate the life of the person who has died. It could be just a quiet affair, but sometimes it can turn into a bit of a party!'

'OH MY GAAAAD! You EENGLISS! You have party, in PUB? OH MY GAAAAD! My haunt she die, yester-DAY! OH MY GAAAAD!' *Nope, we ain't getting tea, cakes and beer this day.* What a miserable lot they are. Although, on reflection, the difference is that Carmelli only passed yesterday, maybe the family are too grief-stricken to want to be buttering rolls. I just assumed that, bearing in mind the Spanish seem to need no excuse whatsoever to sit under a parasol quaffing beer and munching tapas, there might just be a quiet do? Apparently not.

But we cannot just leave it like this surely. I place my hand round his shoulders. 'Tell you what, why don't we go into this cafe here, have a coffee, and you can tell us all about your haunt. Sorry, your aunt. She was a lovely lady, we enjoyed talking to her, so what do you say?'

Amador brightens visibly at the prospect. *Maybe we will have just a small wake, after all. And of course, there will be tapas!*

Down the street to the nearest bar, and who should be propping it up but Del-Boy. Who seems to have been here for a while. Not three sheets to the wind, possibly, but several, without question. 'Wotcha! Oose ya mate?' Chrissie quietly introduces a shell-shocked Amador, and explains we have just been to his aunt's funeral, and have popped in for a quick coffee. 'Sorry to 'ear that' the chirpy Cockney consoles the startled Spaniard, from about six inches away, 'what ya needs is a coupla beers. ROBERTO! FOUR BEERS, OVER 'ERE!'

Amador turns to me, and whispers tremulously 'is this what it is be awake, een EENGLAND?' Quite possibly it is, my friend, quite possibly it is. Say what you like about Del, however, and many do, he is a convivial host. If anyone can coax Amador out of his grief, it is him.

Emerging, a number of hours later, into the bright afternoon sunshine, I grip Del warmly by the hand, and off he then totters, down the street, in the opposite direction to his house, in search of who knows what, but like a randy tom cat, bless him, he will eventually find his way home. Amador, meanwhile, is leaning on me for support. *Can't hold their beer, Spaniards.* 'Cristina, Jonneee' he slurs, 'thank you moocho. I want I be Eenglees-man! I want I die in Eengland! I want party like THEES!' And off he weaves.

Chrissie and I head for home, and the fig tree in the garden. Been a sad but good day, all in all. Educating the locals to celebrate a funeral correctly is going to be a long old job. But someone's got to do it, right?

## CHAPTER 5. WHO LET THE WATER OUT?

Finally, after what seems like an age, the new pool patio is ready. Rome wasn't built in a day, of course, and neither was our patio, although personally I believe the constructors of the Eternal City had it easy. They didn't have Loli, Isabel and Fernando to deal with, did they? And who knew Loli was an expert in building paved outdoor areas? Just about every morning, came a running commentary. 'Neighbour, building a wall with bricks, are you?' 'Neighbour, laying hardcore?' 'Neighbour, doing the tiling?' Stating the bleeding obvious, quite honestly. In the UK, such questions would be met with a healthy dose of British sarcasm. *'Tiles? Ooh, I wondered what these boxes of ceramic things were.'* And they all do it, the locals, I listen to them sometimes, talking amongst themselves, in this town built on a mountainside. Exit your front door, you can go one of two ways. Uphill, or downhill. *Arriba, or a-back-o.* 'Going a-back-o, neighbour?' *No actually I'm going arriba, but walking backwards.* Or sometimes I wish that, when Chrissie and I leave the house together, she would go one way, and I the other, like that Scottish song. 'You'll take the high road, and I'll take the low road..' 'You go arriba, and I'll go a-back-o..' That would fox them, wouldn't it?  Often, when Chrissie is carrying a plate of sandwiches down to our hideaway under the fig tree, Loli will call out 'having your lunch, neighbour?' Stating the bleeding obvious, which were it an Olympic sport….

Actually, I do feel somewhat sorry for our neighbours. No doubt when the old couple lived in our house, *Jose Ocana Pastor*, or 'Joe Shepherd' to use our Anglicised nickname, he and his wife, being Spanish, would no doubt be happy to stand around all morning doing nothing, gossiping, stating the bleeding obvious. We don't do that of course. We can't do that actually, not possessing the language skills for one thing, but we are simply not wired up that way either, being Brits. Gotta get on, and all that. Even in these balmy days of early retirement, we do what needs doing in the morning, and relax in the afternoons, otherwise our patios and outside spaces will not be finished before one of us croaks. Rome might not have been built in a day, but Spain has taken about five thousand years, and it ain't finished yet, the speed this lot move.

Mind you, Loli does have one advantage over the rest of the villagers; she gets first dibs at what the crazy English are up to, which no doubt gives her massive bragging rights when it comes to gossiping in the street. 'What do you think they did today? Had their lunch under the fig tree!' 'Today he was building a patio. I told him he was doing it wrong, but he wouldn't listen!' All her Christmases came at once, the day we moved in.

And I have to tell you, this Joe Shepherd character wasn't much of a builder. Take his ramshackle collection of animal sheds, which once stood on the area where our new swimming pool is hopefully going to reside, for example. An eyesore and a death-trap, all rolled into one, a seemingly random, unrelated collection of tree-trunks, corrugated asbestos, and tin sheets. Back in the summer, adopting my usual 'bull in a china-shop' method of demolition, I did actually come very close to croaking, which would no doubt have delighted my pension provider, but was certainly not on my agenda, I can tell you. If you visit a cathedral in the UK, the elderly guide will proudly point out the 'keystone', the central point which holds up the whole roof. You don't tend to encounter that feature on one of Joe Shepherd's collection of tree-trunks, corrugated asbestos, and tin sheets, to be honest. In hindsight, booting away the worm-infested length of plank was a bad idea, causing as it did the whole roof to collapse on my head in a choking cloud of dust and a stream of strangled oaths. Boggle-eyed, staggering, bent almost double, bearing the weight of the entire structure on my neck, in real danger of ending up a whimpering, gibbering, grime-encrusted corpse, around the side of his house came a stomach, followed what seemed like several hours later by Fernando. My rescuer! My hero! My salvation! No doubt he will leap the wall, like Superman on a mission, although hopefully without the tights, and shoulder my burden. We can then, together, lower this noxious structure gently to the ground, hug, and go for a pint. Nope. What did the corpulent Spaniard actually do? Resting his gut on the garden wall, he uttered those immortal words, which have since gone down in the annals of history, at least in this house. 'I will have those tin sheets, neighbour, if you don't want them.'

And take Isabel, the only 'sane' one of the family. Although that is stretching a point, to be honest. The sweeper. The brush queen. The pursuer of specks of dust, invisible to the naked eyes of mere mortals. Scratch scratch, rustle rustle, swish swish, coming down the garden path. My fear of certain rodents is legendary, and lying in one of Joe Shepherd's filth-encrusted dungeons has my senses on high alert for what might be lurking silently, awaiting the chance to attach itself to my nose. And the damn woman gets me every time, scratch, rustle, swish, causing me to leap spectacularly to my feet, only to find the smiling face of Isabel peering over the wall. 'Having a rest, neighbour?' I swear I have ground several millimetres of enamel from my teeth, since moving to this country.

So here we are. The day has arrived. Blowing up the pool day. With air, I hasten to add, not explosives. Our new pool, sourced from Tony and Jo, who have upgraded to a bigger, free-standing, tubular-framed, heavy duty rubber version, from Carrefour. 'Don't know why you didn't get one of those free-standing, tubular-framed, heavy duty rubber ones they sell in Carrefour, that thing looks like a kiddies paddling pool', Chrissie complained, when I returned with my prize after a morning's labour at their house, levelling the ground in their garden, for their new pool. *Because those cost a hundred and fifty euros, that's why*. OK, I'll give her that, it does resemble a kiddies paddling pool, but much bigger, ten feet across, and four feet deep. A kiddies paddling pool, for big kids. Like me. Plus it comes with an electric pump, to suck out all the dust which will no doubt accumulate on the water, after Isabel has done her worst. Bargain.

I have delayed inflation until Loli and Isabel have gone shopping, so that hopefully I can get it half-filled with water before the Spanish Inquisition commences. And what could be simpler? Utilising lung-power to pump-up the giant rubber ring, followed by half an hour lying down, gasping painfully, like a freshly-caught mans sall-mon on Victor's fish counter, then out with the hose, straighten out the creases as it fills, sit back and enjoy. I will be getting wet, this afternoon, for sure. This is going to be so good. One especially pleasing aspect of my construction is a pool changing-room, complete with a plug socket, and soft electric lighting to illuminate the whole scene in a tranquil glow, for nocturnal bathing. All right, a forty-watt bulb, OK? Meanwhile, Chrissie has dug out some towels, and our bathing costumes. As soon as there is about an inch in the bottom, I am going in!

Or not. 'I got my bikini out, neighbour!' There's a chilling thought, Loli's quivering flesh on display. Like a Christmas turkey, before it goes into the oven, I imagine, a thought I quickly dismiss from my mind. The three of them are younger than us, by a good ten years we reckon, but it would not be conceited to state that they certainly don't look it. Although non-smokers, they all cough like Siberian salt-miners, with a similar pallor, not the merest hint of a tan, and the athletic ability of retired cart-horses. Much talk is made of the so-called Mediterranean diet, but there ain't much evidence of it in this neck of the woods, I can tell you. Loli and her siblings appear as if they've spent their entire lives feasting on saturated fats, with a side-order of fries.

Chrissie strides jauntily down the steps, to check on the progress. 'Who's a lucky fella, then? Loli in a swimsuit! Down, boy!'

I narrow my eyes. 'Not so fast, Mrs. I reckon that at right this minute, Fernando will be squeezing into his budgie-smugglers. As Del-Boy Trotter might have said, that will knock you band…..'

'AAAARRRRRRHHHHHHHH! NOOOOOOOOO! WILL YOU SHUT UP?' My wife is dancing on the spot, flapping her arms, and retching. *Well she started it, right?*

Meanwhile, twenty feet up on her kitchen patio, our tormentor mistakes our jollity for excitement. *If only she knew…* 'Neighbour, do you have any sand left, make a small beach? Where are the toffee apples, and the cotton candy? What about the donkeys? And the fish and chips, at the end of the pier?' *WHAT?* This is extraordinary. Where on earth did Loli learn about the British seaside? We are certain she has us bugged, but this is just not possible. She told us once she has only been to the *Costas* less than half a dozen times in her life. And there are certainly no toffee apples or candy-floss down there. Donkeys there are none. Or piers. And as for fish n chips, Jose at the library summed it up best. 'Yees in Espain we eat feeesh, of course, and cheeps occasionally. But not on the same plate, or from newspaper!' So there you have it. The Spanish think we are a bunch of savages. But what do they know? I tell you this, when I get to Heaven, providing there is a pier with a chip shop on the end, I will be happy to remain there for all eternity. Or even longer.

Suddenly, annoying-woman is waving something over her patio railing, a book of some sort. 'Neighbour, English book of my nephew! I have been reading about a day at the beach!' Of course, why didn't I remember the famous English textbook, given to most junior-school kids here? We were shown one at the library once, which contained illustrated explanations of typical British activities, including 'A day at the beach.' Fair enough, sounded like a traditional seaside visit to me. What was stranger however were some of the activities listed under the section 'A typical Sunday in Britain.' *Taking your dog to the pub* was one, no problem there, done it myself countless times. But *cheese-rolling?* Charging down a steep grassy hill in pursuit of a wheel of Cheddar? The Spaniards at the conversation group simply refused to believe my denials that I had ever partaken of this ridiculous activity. It was in the text book, so that was that. I can just picture the scenario; *'Coming for a pint, Jonno?' 'I am, yeah, but just let me catch this lump of Double-Gloucester, a minute. Hold me dog and me chips, will you?'*

Right. The water level is coming up. Time to christen the pool. Wrong 'Neighbour! Kay-so!' Yep. She has the page open showing the cheese-rolling. I smile through gritted teeth. *No, different part of the country, Loli. London, probably, sounds like it anyway. I'll get Del to explain it to you one day. I get my kay-so at the cheese shop like most sane people.* I wave gaily and disappear into the changing-room, resisting the temptation to bang my head against the newly-plastered walls, emerging thirty seconds later in my swim-shorts. *No budgie-smugglers in this house, Fernando.* I still have the audience, of course, there is zero chance of Loli going away until she has committed the entire scene to memory. I can envisage the brownie points stacking up. She will have massive bragging-rights in the street this night, and for many more to come, I imagine. But who cares? This is the early-retirement dream, right? Taken us over a year of hard work to get this far, turning this sloping Spanish shambles into something resembling a garden, and there is still another level to finish yet. But right now, I feel a frisson of satisfaction. Chrissie is under the fig tree already, having deduced that an audience of one is sufficient for the time being. 'Right, I'm going in!'

'Well hurry up, I want a go too!' comes the reply. Into the water, ooohhh, a bit nippy to be honest, needs a few hours sunlight on it I am guessing. Only a couple of feet deep, but I slosh backwards and immerse my entire torso.

'That water is too cold, neighbour!'

She is wrong there, it is not too cold, it is absolutely bloody freezing. I stand hastily up, and beat my chest with both fists. Loli no doubt thinks I am doing Tarzan impressions, but really I am attempting to re-start my heart. I smile serenely, through chattering teeth. 'This is no problem! I am English!'

The Wild Witch of the West cackles, through her gappy teeth. 'You certainly are, neighbour, you certainly are!'

A quick change into shorts and tee-shirt, and a jog down the garden path, to get my circulation going again. Chrissie is meanwhile raring to go. 'I'd give it five minutes, if I were you' I smile, 'give the audience a chance to clear off. Really, we are going to need to get a parasol up there, to give us a bit of privacy.'

My wife sniggers. 'What, worried she was perving at you? Her dream-boat, in a pair of cheap Primark trunks? Bit of a sex-symbol, are we?'

I cannot resist a wry chuckle. 'All of that, yes, but also I now know how the sea-lions at the zoo must have felt. Honestly, it was like being a circus animal. It's a wonder she didn't lob me a fish!'

My wife still finds this amusing. 'Our pool is just a novelty, what are you worrying about? They will soon get tired of gawping at us. Why waste money on a parasol? Just forget it, OK?'

*If you say so, dearest, if you say so.* Up the path she treks, and after a few minutes I hear the sound of splashing, followed by strangulated gasps. A few minutes later she is back. 'We are going to the caravan this weekend, yes? Right, that giant Carrefour just off the motorway near Malaga? In there, and get a parasol. No messing, just get one!'

*Oh sometimes life can be so sweet.* 'Just a few seconds ago you were telling me not to waste our money on a parasol. What can possibly have changed your mind, I wonder? Of course, if you really want one, maybe YOU could pay for it!'

Which earns me a glare. 'Fernando. The great, hairy, silver-back gorilla. Perving at me the the entire time I was in that pool.'

'Was he wearing his Speedo's, could you see?'

Which earns me a whack with her pillow. 'Friday. Malaga. Carrefour. Parasol. Lie down on that sunbed, and go to sleep, RIGHT NOW!'

*Oh yeah! So good!*

I wake during the middle of the night to the sound of rainfall. Strange, Juan the dustman didn't say anything about inclement weather today, amateur forecaster as he is. We are still sleeping in the 'summer kitchen' apartment on the lower ground floor by the back door, so as I need a tinkle I head upstairs, passing the window overlooking the street on the way. Curious, the cobblestones are dry. OH NO, don't say we have a water-leak, somewhere? Switching on just about every light in the house, I carefully check for drips and seepage, of which there are none. Maybe it was just a dream? Creeping back downstairs, Chrissie is wide awake, of course. 'Is it raining?'

That settles it. We have a burst. The only other place with water is outside the back door, on the covered *El Sombrero* patio, where there is a laundry area, old and new, washing machine and ancient stone sink with corrugated sides, for beating the clothes in days of old. But not a drop anywhere. 'Try the swimming pool?' comes the voice from inside, 'I told you to get a heavy-dut……' OH MY GOD! THE POOL! Sprinting down the steps, throwing on the whole forty-watts, I am greeted by a pathetic heap of damp rubber, and about a thousand gallons of pool-water cascading down the mountainside. Utter despair. The dream only lasted twelve hours. What could possibly have happened? Clawed by cats? Chewed by other creatures of the night? Has Crazy Man made a return, attacked it with a Prestige stainless-steel kitchen implement, for, I don't know, bricking up his sleeping bag?

Suddenly, silhouetted in the restful glow of forty watts, I notice the air valve on the rubber-ring bit has been opened. How could this possibly have happened? Sabotage? Did I forget to seal up the little nozzle and press it firmly home? Impossible, I have blown-up countless rubber-ducks, arm-bands and Li-lo's over the years. Did I simply forget, in all the excitement, and Loli's bellowing? Who knows, and quite frankly it's the middle of the night. Closing the valve, which is a bit like that horsey, stable-door thing, I head back up to bed.

'So what happened to your precious pool, then?'

*Not nice is it, sarcasm at three in the morning?* 'I think Fernando, dressed in a pink spandex mankini, performed a swallow-dive, with three-and-a-half turns, plus pike, off his patio, and burst the bloody thing! Happy now?'

Suddenly the mattress is shaking, although whether with subterranean laughter, or if she is being sick, I cannot say, as I am asleep already…

Next morning, following breakfast on the terrace, the approaching reverberation of spectacular throat-clearing can mean only one thing. *Neighbour, look at your pool…* 'Neighbour! Your pool. The tide has gone out!' *What can I say? We think your brother went skinny-dipping last night, and popped it? Hardly.* Shaving another few microns from my dental enamel, I smile widely, as if vanishing pool-water were an everyday occurrence in the lives of British ex-pats. *Nothing to see here, Loli. Now kindly move along….*

Plus, of course, I have Chrissie on my case. 'So are we having a dip, today, by any chance?'

*Not nice is it, sarcasm during my third mug.* 'Well, I have it all figured out, actually.'

'Figured it out? How? It was pitch dark last night, and you haven't even been down there this morning.'

I flash her my best self-satisfied man-smile. 'I figured it out during the night, if you must know.'

'During the night? You were asleep before your head hit the pillow, snoring away like that sea-lion you referenced yesterday. I was going to throw you a fish, actually, but I didn't have one to hand.'

'It's what us guys do best! It's what I do best. Fixing things. Solutions to problems, working it all out. Why my head is so big, stuffed full with brains. Problem-solving brains.'

Which earns me my first whack of the morning, with a patio-chair cushion. 'OK Mister huge-brain, what is the problem, and what is your solution? I can't wait to hear this, agog as I am. I don't think my teeny-weeny woman-brain can absorb your gigantic man-brain thought-processes, but let's hear it, anyway.'

*This is only going to end one way, for me, isn't it? Badly. I have stuffed-up, yet again, although maybe, just maybe, I can get away with it. Gonna cost me, for sure, whatever happens. Right, here goes.* 'Well, did you notice, yesterday, when you were getting perved at, the pool had a deep-end, and a shallow-end? Not by much, admittedly, but at the bottom of the patio it was deeper than the top? Well, ye canna change the laws of physics, Jim. It's the slope on the patio, see? I had to build a slight slope on the patio, so that rain could run off, plus any escaping water, so there is always going to be a deep-end on the pool. And the water pressure on the rubber ring bit is just too great, it forces the valve open, so the pool deflates.'

She considers these nuggets for a few seconds. 'So your gigantic man-brain has identified the problem. What solutions has it come up with?' And she cups her hand to her ear.

*Not nice is it, sarcasm when I am offering solutions. Trying my best, aren't I?* 'Well, apparently, Carrefour sell a free-standing, tubular-framed, heavy duty rubber version. So I have just heard. We have to call in there tomorrow, don't we, to get a parasol, to stop Mister Budgie-Smuggler leering at you? So maybe we could think about buying a free-stand…'

Which earns me my second whack of the morning, with a patio-chair cushion. *Didn't get away with it, did I?*



**CHAPTER 6. PAYING THE RATES, SPANISH-STYLE.**


A few days later we arrive home to find a yellow printed form stuffed into our mail-box. A curious feature of life here is that very few houses have letter boxes cut into their front doors. No idea why. Cannot trust a Spaniard to saw straight, possibly? Quite likely, actually, considering some of the DIY disasters on display, as we wend our way around the town. Instead we have these metal post-boxes, flap at the top and a key to open the front, fixed to the walls of the houses, many clearly without the benefit of a spirit-level. The inability of the local populace to drill two horizontal holes is shocking, quite honestly. At least ours is level. Had a good eye, did old Joe Shepherd.

So what is this yellow slip? Looks official, bearing as it does the town crest at the top. Can only herald bad news, one way or the other. Someone is after us, and clearly not to wish us a merry Christmas, in mid-October. The form seems to be part of a carbonated set, as some of the words are printed, and some handwritten, although in what language is impossible to say. Hieroglyphics, possibly? Are there Ancient Egyptians in this part of Spain? As always in these situations, we have a network of friends, and translators, at the library, and by a stroke of good fortune there is a conversation class today. Sadly, the senior financial guru, Juan, seems to be running late, and Jose and Teri appear completely baffled. Rafi however detects a glimmer of sense in this missive. 'Who Jose Ocana Pastor, plees? Thees message for he.' We explain that 'Joe Shepherd' was the previous owner, and that we bought the house just over a year ago. 'Then you must to pay you ee-bee. How you say ee-bee in Eengliss, plees?'

Ee-bee? The only expression I can think of is 'heebie-jeebies', which describes perfectly my feelings regarding this mysterious communication. Marie meanwhile has been checking the dictionary. 'Taxis' she exclaims. Not a clue. There is usually a motley collection of licensed conveyances gathered outside the bus station, but we have certainly never taken one. Some of the other neighbours, yes, on account of them having no lungs to speak of, but us? Never. So is this incomprehensible yellow document a taxi account, possibly? Has crafty old Joe Shepherd been blagging free jaunts around the town, or who knows, trips to the seaside, and 'accidentally' omitting to notify the authorities of his new address? Over my dead body am I paying that, although quite what the Spanish translation of that might be I have no idea. But what the hell. We are here to learn, are we not?

'Arriba mi cuerpo!' I announce, which causes wild hilarity, and they seem to get the message, hopefully. Fortunately at that moment Juan strides in, and takes charge of this complete chaos. Relieving Rafi of the pesky slip, he studies it carefully for about ten seconds, then whacks it down on the desk. 'Ee-bee' he announces. *Yeah we all knew that bit, thank you very much.* 'Tax.' he continues, 'tax of you house. Every year you must to pay tax of you house to a-junty-mento. You pay tax to a-junty-mento plees thees year?' *Not as far as I know. Tax of you house? Rates? Community charge? Poll tax, or whatever they call it now? Daylight robbery, whatever name it goes by. Eighteen hundred quid we were paying, before we emigrated. So is that what all this is about? And a-junty-mento? We haven't paid any form of ee-bee to any mento, certainly not a junty one.* 'A-junty-mento?'

Rafi senses my confusion. 'Hall of town, you say in Eengliss, near to chur of Santa Maria, and house of polices-mans.' She wags her finger severely at Juan. 'Cristina and Jonneee not to go hall of town to pay they ee-bee. For to pay thees they must to go office at *La Fuente Marbella*, office with *banderas*.'

Amador meanwhile has just arrived, catching the tail-end of Rafi's speech. 'BANDERAS! Oh my GAAD. Antonio Banderas, he so SEXY!' *All this for one manky bit of paper.* But Amador is in full-flow now. 'Oh my GAAD, last week die my haunt, after funeral Cristina and Jonneee take me PISSY! With they Eengliss friend CRAZY! I no understand one word they friend SAY. Oh my

GAAD! We get PISSY!' *Well clearly he did understand one word Del taught him.* 'After funeral Eengliss persons get PISSY! I love you COUNTREE! Oh my GAAD!'

Not one single Spaniard present has the foggiest idea what the newest member of the group is talking about, and some are clearly beginning to regret kicking Alicia out. Maria meanwhile still has hold of the dictionary. 'Sorree, I no see thees word pissy. Explain me plees?'

'Yees, in Eengliss, drink much beers, get PISSY!'

Teri however remains totally baffled. 'You say me last week died your haunt, and after funeral you went *drinking? Are you insane?*'

Chrissie rapidly takes up the reins, before a fight breaks out, and explains that, yes indeed, there is a tradition in Britain for a respectful get-together after a funeral, where friends and relatives of the deceased might partake of tea and cakes, and that on occasion these events can indeed involve the consumption of alcoholic beverages, in small quantities. Or you can get completely rat-arsed, the choice is yours. But please to bear in mind that funerals in Britain are often three weeks after the death, and not the following day as they are here. Which summed it up perfectly, I thought. *Mind you, Amador and Del were completely rat-arsed that day.*

'Flags.' Maria is still flicking through her Spanish/English tome. 'Banderas. Flags, in Eengliss.'

*Oh yes, the flags, of course, I get it now, I think.* In all this confusion about getting pissy, we had gone completely of the subject of our scrappy bit of paper. 'So we need to pay our house tax for the year, and to do this we must go to the office of the town council, which is that old stone building with the flags outside, near the Marbella fountain? Correct?' Spanish heads nod around the table. I grip the crumpled message with thumb and forefinger, and hold it disdainfully aloft. 'And how am I supposed to know how much I have to pay?'

Juan snatches it back. 'No, thees not you beel,' he cries, waving it viciously at no-one in particular, 'this you moolta!' *Well that clears it up perfectly.*

Maria is still in translation mode. 'Fine.' *Actually it's not fine though, is it, shoving this undecipherable scribble by a left-handed octopus, which contains* naff-all information as to amounts and due dates, into our mail box? Don't they have a printer in this town? And it didn't even come in the post, someone just shoved it into the box. AND IT'S IN THE WRONG BLOODY NAME. Old Joey Shepherd could be dead, for all we know. And if he is, I guarantee his family didn't get pissy after his funeral. But I digress. 'No, it isn't fine.' There, that should do it.

Juan still seems agitated. 'No no, yees, thees moolta, es fine, es penalty. You no to pay you houses-tax, you must to pay penalty. Moolta!'

Chrissie and I stare at each other, dumbfounded. WHAT? He has to be kidding, right? We have been fined, for not paying something we haven't received a bill for? *Arriba right over mi cuerpo,* as they say in Andalucia. Such an infuriating contrast, living in this country. Only last night, on our evening *paseo,* we were remarking on the pavement cafe-culture here, tables and chairs occupied by large family groups, all generations together enjoying the warm evening sunshine, and so utterly enchanting, especially when compared to the stress-inducing nightmare of the M27, in the rain. And now this. Down to earth with a colossal bang. Clearly, we knew there would be some form of houses-tax here, and have been expecting a demand to drop into our box in the fullness of time. I referred to it a few weeks ago, when complaining about the apparent inability of the local constabulary to evict Crazy-Man. But for the town hall to issue the communication to the previous owner? Surely they were notified we had moved in? Didn't Pedro our lawyer do this? Basic stuff, surely, and I can feel my blood, not exactly boiling yet, but on a low heat, certainly. Simmering.

I need to be careful here, as none of this debacle is the fault of our good friends around the table, a fact not lost on Chrissie who, smiling sweetly, showing remarkable calm under the circumstances, takes up the narrative. 'Does anyone know approximately how much our actual bill is likely to be, and the fine also?'

'My house similar to you' Rafi observes, 'and we pay eighty euros, so I think possibly you will be similar?' The others nod in agreement. 'And I not sure but maybe the moolta is ten por-cento?' One or two shrugs, but no outright dissenters. *OK, eighty euros a month? I can cope with that. Less than half what we paying in the UK, that's for sure. So ten months, say, eight hundred in total, plus a ten per-cent surcharge for something which wasn't our fault? That's a bit naughty, stiffing us for another eighty. OK, ignorance of the law and all that, but it's taken the shine off my day, I can tell you. Bubbling up, I am. A sign my long-suffering spouse recognises.*

'So when do we need to pay this eight-hundred, plus the fine of eighty?

Rafi is waving her arms around. 'I sorree, my Eengliss ver bad, I say eighty, not eight-hundred. Ochenta euros.'

Chrissie places a reassuring hand on our friend's arm. 'Your English is very good, Rafi, it is us who don't understand! But eighty euros a month, for ten months, is eight hundred ...'

There are wild gasps, and excitable Spanish shouting, around the table. Followed by uncontrolled laughter. 'Eighty euros por an-yo, a jeer!' splutters Juan, wiping away a tear. A YEAR? Did he just say a jeer, I mean a year? Eighty euros a year? OH MY GAAD, as Amador might have said. Someone has switched off my gas, and I am returning rapidly to room temperature. But hang on just a cotton pickin' minute, to paraphrase Deputy Dawg, before I start punching the air, and performing acrobatics. I have to get this nailed down, right now.

'You are telling us our houses-tax is likely to be around eighty euros, a year?' I whisper, as my throat has gone dry suddenly. Five Spanish heads nod and grin in agreement, and Chrissie is almost in tears. *I love this country, did you know that? What an utterly unbelievable place this is. If I haven't yet convinced you to buy a house here, do so, right now. Get on the internet, before the best ones are gone. I want to give them all a big wet slobbery kiss. And the Lord and Lady Mayor as well.* 'Shall I tell you how much we used to pay in England?' I croak, hoarsely. 'One thousand, eight hundred pounds, a year.'

The stunned silence is punctured by Amador, predictably. 'TWO THOUSAND EUROS? OH MY GAAD! You no SERIOUS! What thees words you friend Derreee teach me, at Eengliss party, funeral my haunt? Fox ME! OH MY GAAD!' Oh my gaad indeed. Eighty Euros. Seventy quid or thereabouts, for which we get three massive, professional firework displays, with music and lasers, the saints days and processions, free productions at the theatre, the flamenco, brass-band and classical music concerts, and so much more. I feel I have died and gone to heaven, a fact which has not gone un-noticed by Amador, who is checking his watch. 'Yees, the pub OPEN! Come ON! We take much BEERS! We get PISSY!'

Indeed. Why not. Absolutely. I feel like dancing, and a beer certainly to ease my tonsils, which are on the arid side, to be sure. Seventeen-hundred smackers in my pocket, as good as. Just one small clarification, however. 'Yes, we would like to invite you all to the bar after this, but just one question.' Silence falls around the table, an unusual event certainly, in this noisy country. I grab the creased, grubby, yellow paper, which if not virtually unreadable before, certainly is now. 'So can I go to the office with the flags tomorrow, and pay this?'

Juan smiles. 'I can go with you, if you want, but plees no forget your knee.'

*Well good job you reminded me, my friend, I was going to unscrew my whole leg, actually, and hop down there. I do this, from time to time.* Grinning, I point to the joint between my shin and thigh. 'Knee?'

The poor fellow is confused, momentarily. 'Yees, no, yees, sorree, no Rhodesia!'

*Rhodesia? Been Zimbabwe for about thirty-odd years, hasn't it? Ian Smith, UDI, Mugabe and all that. The capital was Salisbury, as I recall, although not the dreamy spire as depicted by John Constable.* 'Rhodesia? The country?'

This is the wonderful thing about these conversation groups. No-one has the slightest clue what is happening, or what anyone else is talking about, but we get there in the end. Most of the time. 'No, yees, no, Rhodesia ees knee in Espaniss, I no say you Rhodesia, knee, I mean you knee plastico.' And he wipes away a bead of perspiration.

He thinks I have a replacement knee? Not me, matey. I spent enough years having seven shades of all things holy kicked out of me, during the rugby season, and never a broken bone to show for it. In fact, I've had far more head injuries in this country, bashing my nut on ludicrously low door lintels, built for five-foot Spaniards.

Marie is performing sterling service on the dictionary, this morning. 'Tar-hetta. Card. Espaniss card plastico.' Indeed we have our various UK bank cards, plus the one issued on this side of the Bay of Biscay, the Spanish health card, entitling us to full access to doctors and hospitals, which Juan himself helped us obtain, last year. Trouble is, and this might also be a problem getting drinks for the assembled locals later, I rarely carry my wallet, on the grounds I am too absent-minded, and likely to leave it somewhere. Too many bangs on the head, see? Luckily, Chrissie is rooting around in her bag, locates said bill-fold and fishes out the green tar-hetta, which she passes to our friend. He holds it up, indicating, in the bottom corner, the legend *N.I.E*, followed by some random letters and numbers.

'Look! You knee!' *Well blow me down.* Actually he has Chrissie's card, and quite what that was doing in my wallet will be a conversation for later, but mine is identical, presumably, apart from the names of course. And the knees, one assumes. We have a pair of Spanish knees. *Who knew?* But he has not finished yet, it appears. 'Thees not you knee, you have other tar-hetta plastico, plees?'

I regard our friend with a puzzled frown. At this rate, the pubs will be shut, and Amador will have to wait for another occasion to get pissy. 'You just said this was a knee, N.I.E in English, so do we have another number, are you saying? Two knees?' *The tax might only be seventy quid here, but I am beginning to realise why. This must be what it was like paying your rates in the Middle Ages. In groats, or swans.*

I swear I can read his mind. *Why the hell did I want to learn English, anyway? Why didn't I just stay home playing Candy Crush?* 'Yees, no, here in Espain you must to have tar-hetta knee, with you knee!' *Well we haven't, all right, so that is that. And who could possibly care less?* There is the knee number, stamped on the medical card, so whoever produced the thing, with their Spanish *Letraset*, or one of those hand-held embossing tools you could get in England in the sixties which printed a strip of sticky-back tape with your name on, which you could put inside your wellingtons in school, but which always peeled off in the first shower of rain, must have had a record of it. Bit like your NI number in the UK, isn't it. Mine has a 'Y' in it, but if you offered me a million quid I could not name one other single numeral. And why would I care? In the unlikely event of anyone wanting to know it, I could dig out an old P60, possibly, and there it would be.

I glance at Chrissie, and roll my eyes. 'Hang on a minute' she ponders, tapping her head with a finger. 'Don't we have those bits of paper at home, from that *heffe* bloke, with an official stamp? You remember Pedro the lawyer gave them to us, with the house deeds?' *Nope. Slept since then, my dearest.* I flash her my best *why the hell didn't you say that ten minutes ago in case one of us died* stares, but before she can frame a suitably ribald reply there is a sharp intake of breath from around the table. *What? Have we transgressed? And do you lot actually want a celebratory drink, or what?* I know what I am having, one of those *cubo's*, five bottles of beer, in an ice bucket, with tapas, for three euros.

'A paper knee?' wonders Teri. *Ah yes, I remember now, two A4 sheets which describe me as 'Austin John Richards', and Chrissie's as 'Anne Richards Christina'. Pedro obtained them when we opened our bank account, and they have been shoved in with the house deeds, ever since.*

'You no have plastic knee?' Rafi worries. 'What happen if polices-mans ask to see you edente-fee-kathy-on?'

Identification? Is that what this is all about? ID cards? Plastic knees? Must be. But it's time to get down the pub. That cubo is calling, the seventeen-hundred is burning a hole in my pocket, and I could crawl faster than any copper in this town could run, so who cares?

And a mellow time was had by all, the summer-wine, buckets of beer and tapas galore were dutifully consumed. And only one of us got pissy. DIDN'T YOU, AMADOR?


The next morning we present ourselves, knees intact, outside the tax office, at the crack of dawn, or about half-nine in early-retirement-speak. No sign of Antonio Banderas, however, which is actually a good thing as far as I'm concerned, not having any of his records on my iPod... The usual Spanish hullabaloo is in evidence, although as we enter the building, through the foyer and into a larger room beyond, there are only two old men, brandishing yellow slips just like ours, two male staff sitting at desks pointedly doing nothing, and a harassed-looking receptionist who appears to be in charge of four large cardboard boxes, into which hundreds of green A4-sized forms have been stuffed. Clearly the paper-less office hasn't arrived in this locale yet. And how can five people possibly make so much noise? Seems impossible, doesn't it? But every cloud and all that, because everyone looks up, as they always do here, whether it be shop, bank, post-office or any other public building, and wishes us a cheery *buena-dia*. There is always time to wish a stranger 'good morning' in Spain, and I have to say I find it delightful.

The two old boys seem highly amused about something. Us, it appears. They are waving their slips, and pointing at ours, which Chrissie has produced from her bag. Like the walk of shame isn't it, us non-payers, we've all been caught, and fined. *Mooltad*, if you like. Suddenly, the front door bursts open and in crash three old ladies, side by side like a four-foot-ten Pontypool Front Row, and suddenly it is getting crowded. Here we are, crushed into this little corner, whereas the room is huge. The Spanish don't mind this of course, they love to squash together in tight groups, and seem to have no concept of personal space, whereas us Brits like to stretch out a bit. I can peer over their heads of course but I can see Chrissie becoming agitated as she is surrounded by jabbering locals, at eye level. I indicate for her to give me the yellow slip then wait in the foyer until our turn arrives, which it hopefully will, some time soon. One of the old ladies spots this and starts bellowing. '*Bastardos! Lad-Ronnies!*' Indeed. I know this word, *Lad-Ronnies*, which has nothing to do with a boy called Ronald, as it happens. No, it means 'thieves'. And the reason I am aware of this is because the locals use it to describe any politician or person in power, on the assumption that the whole lot of them are corrupt. Furthermore, the word is similar, to my untutored ears at least, to *Lad-Rios*, the name for 'bricks'. And on one memorable occasion, I went to the builders merchant and ordered a hundred *Lad-Ronnies.* They still talk about it to this day, at the builders yard, where for ever-more I will be known as the Englishman who ordered one hundred thieves.

So who are these particular *Lad-Ronnies* and *Bastardos*? Each old woman is clutching a screwed-up yellow slip, and the comments appear to be directed at the office staff. Who seem to be entirely unfazed, I have to say. Perhaps being called a bastard and a thief is an everyday occurrence, in the Spanish tax office. And the old woman is not muttering under her breath, that's for sure.

Eventually, it is our turn. I smile at harassed-woman, wave the yellow slip, and trot out my rehearsed speech. *Quiero pagar mi ee-bee*. There. What about that, then? The perfect way to inform a woman in the tax office you would like to pay some tax. Or not. She seems confused about something. Maybe she is mystified I haven't referred to her as a bastard or a thief, who knows? She peers at the writing on the slip, which after all came from her office so surely she is familiar with it, opens her mouth as if to speak, changes her mind, narrows her eyes and gazes at us as if we have just arrived from Mars, then licks her index finger and starts flicking through the first box of papers. Can't be that difficult a job, can it? Presumably the forms are filed alphabetically, by street, or by taxpayer, but she is rifling away like crazy, getting nowhere. More wetting of fingers and on to box two, without success, another intense scrutiny of the screwed-up yellow missive, then on to box three. Just as I am beginning to form the impression she might not be the sharpest tool in the box, she actually confirms it. 'These forms were a different colour green, last year.' Which has to be the second-most stupid thing anyone has ever said to me, in my lifetime. Want to know the actual stupidest thing? Just wait a few moments. It is coming. I mean, who cares if the forms are sky-blue pink with unicorns in each corner? *They are all the same shade of green.* They could be carved on to tablets from the time of Moses, for all the difference it makes.

I am not sure what to say next. Chrissie meanwhile has turned away as she is unable to keep a straight face, and I am struggling. Harassed-woman presses on to box four, and then, triumphantly, extracts a green slip, identical to the rest of course, but a different shade to last year, apparently, and with a flourish, places it reverently on the desk. And emits those immortal lines. 'Are you Jose Ocana Pastor?' *Am I Jose Oca....* I am a blue-eyed, blond-haired (all right, all right, with the merest hint of grey, OK?) fair-skinned, ruddy-faced, six-foot Anglo-Saxon. I could hail from nowhere else on earth. I bear less resemblance to the local population than Mickey Mouse does to Mount Everest. I could never consider committing a crime in this country as the identification line-up in the police station would be a farce. Seven swarthy Spaniards and me. 'There he is, officer.'

'No.' Come on, what else *can* I say? Describing this woman as 'thick' would be a gross injustice to thick people everywhere. I would like to have been a fly on the wall at her job interview, actually. Can you imagine what the other candidates were like? And I cannot wait to discover what she makes of our knees. Just imagine her deciphering *Austin John Richards and Anne Richards Christina*. Not sure I have that long left to live, actually, and I am rapidly losing the will. Why didn't we stay in Britain, when we had the chance? I would happily pay eighteen-hundred quid to get away from this complete absence of brains.

Chrissie fishes out our knees from her bag and places them on the desk. Not sure that was a great idea, actually, judging by the reaction. We might as well have produced Martian ID, to be honest, for all the good it does. Must be the paper, obviously. Confused the hell out of the educated Spaniards at the library, imagine what is going on inside this woman's head. Very little. The cogs are turning, but not meshing up with anything. Right, that is it, I admit defeat, surrender, white flag. Ask Juan or one of the others to come with us, tomorrow. 'We will return with our Spanish friend' I smile, painfully. Give her the chance to pull a sickie, hopefully. I am out of here.

Stumbling into the bright sunshine, we are laughing hysterically, leaning precariously on the old stone walls for support, attracting curious glances from passers-by. Eventually Chrissie is able to stand unaided, and grabs me by the arm. 'Come on Jose Ocana Pastor, let's get you home, you must be worn out, you poor old chap!'


The following morning, clutching the yellow slip, our knees, and the deeds to the house, which Marie advised us to bring, we rendezvous with our dear friend at the same ungodly hour as yesterday, to find a complete absence of anyone calling anyone else a bastard or a thief. Silence. Perhaps we have been beamed back up to Mars. The two office blokes are still there, doing nothing, but harassed-woman looks even more harassed, despite there being no customers. Probably spent a restless night, having nightmares about our return. Briefing her last night on the phone regarding our experiences of the Spanish tax system that morning, we merely recounted there were one or two difficulties, not that we thought harassed-woman was thicker than the entire contents of a brick factory. She might conceivably be a friend or relative, in this little town. Let her make her own conclusions regarding her abilities. Marie immediately takes charge, and fairly soon it becomes clear from the dialogue, which we can just about follow, that she shares our opinion. The woman is making a phone call, calling for help from superior I imagine, and hope, when our friend turns to us, and in a low whisper confides 'she is plug.' *Surely not? Plug from the Bash Street Kids?* I am immediately transported back to the world of my boyhood, and tales of Fatty, Smiffy, Spotty, Danny and Wilf, not forgetting Teacher of course. And it's not as if harassed-woman has sticky-out ears, and protruding teeth. *Bit harsh really, Marie?* 'Yes, she is plug, we say here in Espain. Some person got job for she.'

A plug-in! Chrissie and I are both laughing, conjuring up images of Dennis the Menace, and Biffo the Bear. 'A *shoe-in*, we say in English!' I giggle. Harassed-woman ends her call, and more arguing continues, and I can tell by Marie's demeanour that she is getting crosser by the minute. She turns to us, completely blanking Plug, 'she say me, thees womans, that you must to pay *moolta*, I say she, no no you Eengliss not know regulation, but she estupid.'

Chrissie, as always, is keen to deflect any conflict. 'How much is the fine, the *moolta,* please?'

'Four euros.'

My wife smiles. Our friend is trying her best, we don't want to undermine what she is trying to achieve, but surely we all have better things to be doing with our morning? 'Well look, four euros is nothing, let us pay it and forget all about it. Please don't worry, we can just pay them what we owe, and all go for a coffee?'

She is not having it however. 'Yees, four euros will pay for the coffee! No no, these persons are thieves, you not to pay four euros. I not accept thees!'

Wondered when we'd get round to the *Lad-Ronnies*. No-one has called anyone else a *bastardo* yet, however, which is always something of a disappointment in any tax office. More heated argument ensues, when suddenly our translator snatches our papers from the desk. 'We go upstairs, see bossy of she. Follow me please!' And she strides from the room, leaving the poor woman open-mouthed, and us struggling to catch up. I cannot help a backwards glance however. She tried her best, did Plug, with the limited means available. And the forms *were* a different shade of green this year. *'Muchas gracias!'* She won't forget the day an Englishman called Jose Ocana Pastor paid her a visit, that's for sure.

Up the stairs, breathlessly, and into an identical room as the one below. Three staff, two male, one female, and a woman, who looks vaguely familiar, striding about in the middle. Suddenly, there is total commotion. 'Cristina! How are you!' And striding-woman has my wife in a bear-hug, and bafflingly, I get the same treatment. *Who the hell IS this?* Whoever it is, she is now dancing, and waving her arms around. *In the tax office.* 'Granny smokes, Granny drinks, Granny dances!' The office staff, plus Marie, look completely and utterly stunned. And I am rather bewildered, I don't mind admitting.

Luckily, my wife possesses almost total recall. Rather like an elephant, she never forgets, usually to my detriment. 'Conchi! I am very well! How is your daughter Ana getting on in Coventry?' *Conchi? Ana? Coventry?* Usually in these situations, and they happen more often than I care to admit, I just bluff, smile, go along with the conversation, and when the people move off down the street, ask 'who the hell was that?' Chrissie meanwhile is in full flow, and very often she will drop a few hints, to give me a chance to catch up. 'That was a wonderful fiesta in your village last Spring, and didn't we look fantastic in our flamenco dresses at *La Romeria*?' Got it. Conchi is the mayor of the village where our friends Tony and Jo live, we met her last spring at the 'Dancing on the Hillside' fiesta, where I got chocolate sauce down my trousers, was trodden on by an old woman, and a bullfighter narrowly missed having his man-pieces removed. And again she was one of a group of women in spotty dresses who paraded round the town, where Chrissie was asked to join in. We also met the daughter who was going off to study English in the UK this summer.

'So what are you doing here in this office?' cries the mayor. My wife explains we are attempting to pay our *ee-bee*, but not having much luck, having incurred a *moolta*, so we have asked our good friend Marie to help us out. Horrified, Conchi spins on her heels and barks a rapid-fire broadside of Spanish at the senior of the two men, who is cowering behind his desk like a little whipped puppy. 'Antonio here will complete all the paperwork, and of course there will be no *moolta!* I must go now, I am sure everything will be perfect for you, but any problems give me a call.' And she glares witheringly at puppy-man, who has subsided even further into his chair. 'And when you come to the village next, please call me!' And she spins on her heels, kisses the three of us, and marches regally from the office. Blimey, that was some performance, and she's not even the mayor of our town, just some dusty old *pueblo* in the back end of beyond.

For a second or two nobody seems to know what to do next, then puppy-man catapults into life, chairs scraping as he selects three, dusting them off with his shirt-sleeve as he bids us to join him round the desk, then gallops off, returning several seconds later with a laptop, which he plugs in and fires into life. Marie meanwhile is rocking with laughter, 'Cristina, how you do that? You incredible! I never see nothing like thees. *La alcada,* she free-end you?' But Chrissie didn't actually *do* anything, did she? We just walked into the room, and it happened. As it does so often here. The Spanish have that knack of making us feel like honoured guests, but hey, if it gets us off the *moolta,* bring it on. We have gone from being a confounded nuisance yesterday to royalty today, and it certainly feels good. I bet old Joey Shepherd never had his rates sorted out by the mayor, even if she is the mayor of somewhere else, that's for sure. 'Expect the unexpected' has just happened again.

Puppy-man Antonio is tapping furiously away on his laptop, all the while keeping up a running commentary for our friend, who then translates for our benefit. 'So, *ee-bee* is to pay in Abril and Octubre each jeer, you bought you house in Octubre the last jeer, but Jose Ocana Pastor he pay *ee-bee* the last jeer, so you need pay Abril and Octubre thees jeer only.'

What a blooming nice chap that Joe Shepherd is. I would buy him a pint, if I knew what he looked like, or indeed if he is still alive. 'So how much do we actually owe now, please?'

More consultations. 'Antonio say me ees forty-one euros for Abril and the same for Octubre. So eighty two euros in total. There was to be a *moolta* for

Abril because you pay later but Conchi *La Alcada* say must to cancel *moolta* as she free-end you.'

I feel sheer utter relief coursing through my veins. I know the library gang said it would be around this amount, but to hear it from the horses mouth, or the puppy's mouth in this case, is cause for wild celebration. Wild celebration every day, bearing in mind what we are saving. *No wonder Del is always drunk….* We have brought the cash with us, sorry *Chrissie* has brought the cash with *her*, as I simply cannot be trusted not to leave it somewhere, on the assumption that if they don't send printed bills through the post, they are unlikely to have a cashless payment system, and my wife starts to rummage through her bag for my wallet. Finally, we might actually be able to get this done and forget all about *ee-bee* until next Abril. Wrong!

'Antonio he say me, are you in you house, now?' I narrow my eyes and frown at Chrissie, who in turn frowns at Marie, who narrows her eyes and frowns at no-one in particular. Puppy-man meanwhile is waiting expectantly for a reply. From anyone, presumably. *Is this whole thing a dream? Is there some sort of parallel universe-thing going on here? Will I actually wake up and find a rates demand for five-grand on the mat, and be tipped into bankruptcy?*

Chrissie is the first to regain the power of speech. 'Er, no, we are here, we are not in our house, at the moment.'

Another brief con-flab with puppy. 'Antonio say me, are you in you house at middle-day, thees day?' *Mid-day? Probably, although right now I am rapidly losing all sense of time, or place. Get this paid, coffee with our friend, lunch under the fig-tree, so yes, home by mid-day, easily. But what does that have to do with paying the rates?*

'Why?'

'Antonio he say me, Paco he go you house at middle-day.'

'Who is Paco?'

Marie turns and gestures towards the other member of staff, still seated behind his desk, who seems not to have done a stroke of anything this morning, let alone work.

'Why?'

'Antonio he say me, Paco he go you house, give paper to you.'

'Why, what paper?'

'Ees paper, so you come here tomorrow, pay you ee-bee.'

That is it. I have lost it. Sadly we are seated in the middle of the room, so there are no walls within reach, against which I can bang my head. Are they seriously suggesting we go home, open the door to Paco at middle-day, who is seated not ten feet from us at this precise moment, then waste another morning coming to this loonie-bin tomorrow? Do you know what? They actually are.

My blood is frothing, a symptom my wife recognises. 'Can we not pay this now, today? she smiles.

Another brief consultation. 'No, Antonio say me, papers not ready yet. Paco come you house, with papers, middle-day.'

I am about to shove my chair violently back and leap through the nearest window, regardless of whether or not it is open, when suddenly I have a brain-wave. Doesn't happen often, I have to tell you, but boy, when my brains start waving, look out. I turn to Chrissie. 'Do you have my phone in your bag? Can I have it please? I am going to call Conchie, right now!'

The effect is spectacular, like tossing a hand-grenade into the room. Puppy is tapping violently on his keyboard, while Paco sprints to the corner, where an ancient printer is spluttering into life. *Blimey, they actually have technology here? All they need is a fax machine and they will be right up to date, with the twentieth century.* Within seconds, our paperwork is ready. Puppy is on his feet, gesturing us to follow into the adjacent room. 'You go' I chuckle, 'you have the money. I have done my bit!'

Marie is full of praise, while I bask in the limelight. 'Jonneee! How you do thees? Never I see Espanee peoples move rapido!'

Minutes later the three of us are in the adjacent cafe, Chrissie clutching a hand-written receipt for eighty-two euros, wiping tears from her eyes. 'So tell me' she giggles, 'what are you doing with Conchie's number in your phone?'

The Cheshire Cat couldn't possibly grin any wider than I am right now. 'You know very well I don't have her number. I couldn't even remember who she was, half an hour ago. It was a bluff. A giant, Spanish bluff!' And the pair of us dissolve into more laughter.

Sipping her coffee, Marie looks puzzled. 'Bloof? Giant Espanee bloof? What thees, plees?'

I am still on cloud nine. 'Friends in high places' I smile, squeezing her arm. 'We have friends in high places!'

**CHAPTER 7. BUYING A CAR, SPANISH-STYLE.**

Autumn is upon us, and with it the turning of the year. The intense heat of high summer is past, and whilst the days are still pleasantly warm, it can go off chilly at nights now, and the evenings are drawing in. If there were any leaves to turn brown, no doubt they would have already done so, but the olive trees, and the scrubby pines which are the only other form of vegetation, are evergreen, so our vista from the patio is largely unchanged. The main difference is that the spectacular sunsets have moved slightly to the left, plus the sad fact I have had to dig out my slippers, a sure sign that winter is around the corner. Going barefoot is one of life's pleasures here, but all good things and all that, and besides, it won't be long until spring, hopefully.

Having taken our UK-registered car back in August, we have been relying on the Harley to get us out and about at weekends, exploring the surrounding towns and villages, and trips to the beach, but with winter on the horizon and the prospect of a few rainy days, we need a form of transport which avoids us getting wet. A car, in other words. Nothing beats the wind-in-your-face sensation on a bike of course, and there will be days when we can still get out for a ride, hopefully, but we need to be pragmatic. Four wheels.

Which presents a number of problems not usually encountered in the UK. The language barrier being the main one, obviously. Telephone calls are extremely difficult for us, it is much easier conversing, or attempting to converse, face-to-face. On the other hand, Phil the artist has a Spanish car, and he barely speaks a word. How did he manage that, I enquired. 'There's these English fellers selling Spanish cars, mate, they got websites an' all that, one lives down Malaga way, we got ours there, juss 'ave a look, see what they got, an' give 'em a ring. No need to speak the lingo, and they do all the paperwork.' Indeed. And what a revelation that website was. 'Wrecks & Bangers dot-com' it should have been called, and nothing under a thousand euros. And surely dealing solely with British people somewhat defeats the object, the joys even, of living in a foreign country? I mean, paying our council tax took three mornings of our lives, and was a complete farce from start to finish, but what an experience when all said and done. So no, we will not be getting our next mode of transport via an expat website.

We put out a few feelers at the library group of course, *buscando coche barato*, which I sincerely hope doesn't translate as 'I am looking for an *expensive* car', and Jose kindly volunteered to act as intermediary and translator on our behalf. So that is the language barrier sorted, and hopefully we can add to our Spanish vocabulary along the way. All we have to do now is to find something suitable. Easier said than done, as many local cars here have surely travelled through a war-zone, at some stage in their lives. I am not talking about a few dings, dents or scrapes here, such as might be incurred in the supermarket car-park, but serious collision damage. Whole bumpers held on by gaffer-tape. Missing headlights. Huge jagged abrasions along the entire side of the vehicle. Aside from clearly-new cars, most of those in our budget look as if they have been taken outside and given a severe kicking. Punishment beatings, with iron bars. Knee-cappings and the like. Presumably they have insurance here, but doesn't anyone ever make a claim? Get the damage repaired? Or are they content to drive around in something which might actually fall to pieces at any minute? Jose provided the answer. 'People here get money from insurance, and do repairs they-self.' *Repairs?* Can whacking a bit of sticky tape on a headlight be classed as a *repair?* Don't they have things like 'approved garages' here, or 'insurance assessors'? Presumably not. Still, avoiding these death-traps should be relatively easy. We will not be considering any vehicles featuring adhesive strips on the bodywork.

I think that much of the damage to these severely battered cars is caused by the way many Spanish park, which in my view can only be described as being without any respect or consideration for other road-users, or pedestrians, whatsoever. Double-parking is normal, triple is not uncommon, they park on pavements, even zebra-crossings, and it is one aspect of life here I truly dislike. They shoe-horn their vehicles into the tiniest spaces, on occasions literally shunting cars already parked a few inches, to squeeze into the space. Many of the apartment blocks in the new part of town have communal underground parking garages, all of which display the circular 'no parking' sign with a red cross on a blue background, which when we first came here I found extremely strange. Why? It is clearly a garage, surely no-one is going to block it, are they? Wrong! They do, regularly, which is why you often hear the sound of irritable honking drifting on the breeze, from irate drivers who have been blocked in, or out. 'Vic the Fish' told me only a few weeks ago that he had returned home one evening to find his garage entrance blocked by some inconsiderate moron, meaning that Vic was unable to go anywhere, and was stuck in the street. At that moment the ancient old-bill came around the corner and proceeded to severely berate Vic, demanding to see his license and insurance, during which time the offending driver returned and simply drove away, without any sanction from the cops whatsoever. Unbelievable.

One day recently I did have cause to smile, however. Walking to the bank past the six-way junction known as the 'Old Fountain', I passed the usual Spanish melee, with cars parked in every conceivable space, delivery lorries blocking entrances, pavements and crossings, vehicles blocked in, waiting to get out, others trying to squeeze in, mums on the school run, spectators shouting advice, and incredibly, one car completely blocking the street while the driver conducted a leisurely chat with a pedestrian, seemingly oblivious to the stream of traffic backed up behind him, all honking furiously. Incredible. And there is a perfectly good car park a hundred yards down the street, but no, these selfish individuals have to park right outside the shop or office they need to visit, and they don't care about the utter chaos they are causing. Exiting the bank a few minutes later, imagine my delight to see the police arriving on the scene. The *Guardia Civil* too, not the ancient local lot. This is going to be good. There must be at least a dozen infringements taking place right now, and the cops are going to have a field day. And so am I, watching the tickets being written, fixed to windscreens, just as the miscreants come dashing back, imploring the Bobbies to tear up the tickets.

Selecting a park bench with the best view, I watched, in anticipation, as the two coppers extracted themselves slowly from their vehicle, which incidentally was parked on the pavement as barely a square inch of road was available, stretched luxuriously, pulled their jackets from the back seat, fitted their cloth caps unhurriedly to their heads, gazed expectantly across the square, and began a leisurely consultation. What were they saying? *You go over that side, start nicking that lot, while I nab these on this side?* No. With a friendly wave at a few passers-by, they sauntered into the cafe. Distraught, I was. What a let-down.

Another problem is the complete lack of information provided with the cars you see parked up with a 'for sale' sign on the windscreen. A phone number only. No price, nothing about the service history, mileage, how long the MOT is, how many previous owners, the kind of information you would expect to see on a car in the UK. Why? I cannot think of a single reason not to provide as much information as possible, if you do actually want to sell the thing. What a waste of everyone's time to phone up, only to find they are asking some ridiculous price. And you don't seem to be able to tell the age of the vehicle from the number-plate, as you can in the UK. The value of a fifty-five-plate Ford Fiesta in Britain, for example, is not going to vary by more than a hundred pounds or so, is it? Here, you could be enquiring about something with an age-range of five years or more. Even the used-car garages dotted around the town don't display prices. Truly bizarre. There is one called 'Cars From One-Thousand Euros', but not a single price-sticker on any of them. Waste of time. It is one of my life-rules that if a vendor of anything cannot be bothered to display the price, than I cannot be bothered to look at it. Call me 'Victor Meldrew' if you will, and Chrissie certainly does, but there you go. Grumpy old man R me!

So. Battered old wrecks with no prices. What to do? Luckily, Jose has the solution. 'You should to look on *Meel Anoon-seeos*. Ees website with many things for sale, for all Espain, but you can to focus you looky at Andalucia, even Santa Marta I think. Thee website will have all information on cars for sale, *re-viz-e-onny, ee-tee-oobie,* thees things mas important. How you say *re-viz-e-*

*onny* in Eengliss plees?' *Not the foggiest, obviously.* Sounds a bit like 'revision' to me, but I have been wrong before...

'Can you explain what re-viz-whatever actually is please? Is it a part on a car?'

Jose smiles patiently at my ignorance. '*Re-viz-e-onny* is where take you car to *consessionario*, he look you *assy-etty*.'

*Not my assy-etty he isn't, that's for damn sure.* Hang on a minute, *assy-etty* is the word they use for olive oil, isn't it? Do cars run on olive oil here? I mean, in the UK people have converted their diesels to run on chip-shop fat, haven't they? And Santa Marta is awash with olive oil. There must be half a dozen factories in the town alone, apart from the ones in the little villages. And there was me thinking they were drizzling it on their salads.

'Assy-etty?'

Jose is clearly beginning to regret volunteering for this job. But he is practicing his English, isn't he? Expressed a desire to work in the UK, seeing as how there is sod-all here for qualified engineers. 'Yees, you must to put *assy-etty* in you *mow-tor*, or you *mow-tor* go boof!' *Engine oil? They use the same word for olive oil and Castrol GTX? Who knew?*

'I think you are talking about having the car serviced, as we say in the UK. They change the *engine* oil, filter and various other things. Put a stamp in the little book which comes with the car. A service, as we say.'

Jose seems puzzled, however. 'You say me at Chreesmas in chur you have service in Eengland?'

'Very good! Quite correct, you have a church service, and you service your car. We also expect good service in a shop, or bar, for example.' See what I mean? English lessons. Far more use to him, if he ever goes to the UK, than chasing a lump of cheese down a hill, for sure. 'So what is this ee-tee thing, then?'

'Ee-tee-oobie. Ees where you take you car for exam, make sure you car segur, how you say, safety?'

An MOT? They have MOT's here? Could have fooled me. How often do they have them, once a decade? I can just imagine a Spanish MOT. 'Is you car safety?' 'Yees.' 'OK you have passed! See you in two-thousand-and-twenty-five!' Oh my gaad, as Amador might have said. 'So how do you spell this *ee-tee-oobie,* please?'

Neither of us has a pen or paper, so Jose takes my hand and traces the letters I.T.V. *Of course!* Suddenly, everything drops into place. When we first came to Spain, we kept noticing road signs saying *ITV.* Just that, nothing else. No clue as to whether or not *Coronation Street* was being filmed on location in Andalucia. Ken Barlow having a tapas, followed by a siesta. So we followed a sign one day, and were amazed to be directed to a garage, full of cars, people milling around, the usual Spanish anarchy. What a let-down. No sign of Elsie Tanner anywhere.

So we have some research to do this weekend, searching *Meel Anoon-seeos.* And what are we looking for exactly? Well, as proud owners of a £350 Volvo currently enjoying an extended break in the UK, we clearly are not worried about having something up-to-date, all the bells and whistles, and latest gizmos. Had our fair share of new cars over the years, been there, done that. No, we are seeking a vehicle to match our lifestyle. Slightly old-fashioned, something to convey us from A to B, in safety of course, but in style? Nah. Under a grand or thereabouts, long *ee-tee-oobie,* history of *re-viz-e-onny* if possible, low mileage, or whatever they call 'mileage' in this land of kilometres, an absence of shrapnel and definitely no duck-tape. Gathered round the laptop that evening, it proves simplicity itself to narrow down the search to the town and surrounds, in our price bracket, revealing a surprising number of choices. The adverts are completely in Spanish of course but many of the descriptions are easy to follow. There is one however which proves beyond our powers of translation. *No gasta nada*. Not a clue. I am on clicking duties, so Chrissie is in charge of translations. A few flicks through her trusty dictionary, (see what I mean about slightly old-fashioned?) a few puzzled frowns, followed by her answer. 'Don't use nothing.' *Would be nice, wouldn't it, a car that don't use nothing, but I am guessing it translates as 'economic'?*

We only need something small, and on the second page is a Renault, dark blue, don't use nothing apparently but there is no mention of the *ee-tee-oobie* whatsoever. The owner probably forgot I imagine, and the photos are somewhat blurred so it is difficult to tell if there is any evidence of strife on the paintwork, but one to put on the 'possible' list certainly.

The following page however reveals what appears to be a gem. A little white *SEAT*, albeit from a different century, but which nevertheless matches all of our criteria. The bodywork looks perfect too, unless of course they have just given it a quick coat of Dulux Brilliant White gloss, but one to enquire about, for sure. A quick call to Jose confirms he is free the following morning to make a few phone calls before the conversation class, so with anticipation building we embark on our regular Sunday evening walk, round the city walls, past the castle, to a church perched dramatically on the side of the cliff, with spectacular views over the surrounding countryside. Santa Marta, like many towns and villages in this part of Spain, was built on high ground, no doubt to observe advancing invaders, and we love to watch the sun slipping slowly behind the olive groves, and the lights twinkling in the other villages silhouetted against the western sky. Our route home is always interesting too, down precipitous cobbled pathways and streets, a warren of zig-zags and white cottages clinging precariously to the hillside, requiring total concentration to avoid a painful tumble.

Rounding one particularly acute bend, we are astonished to see a little white car perched at an impossible angle. *THE SEAT!* It is the same one for sure, as I recognise part of the registration number, JW, which were my grandfather's initials. What were the chances of that? An omen, surely. In real-life it seems to be even better than the photos, and if it drives as good as it looks, we might have found our first Spanish car. Just a shame it is impossible to tell where the owner might live, any one of a dozen or so cottages might be it, or none at all, a different street maybe. Anyway, it is getting too dark to see, almost, so excitedly we head home and pray no-one else buys it overnight.

Meeting up with Jose the following morning, we ask him to phone about the Renault first, as actually it is newer than the SEAT, and we want to make enquires about the both, if only for the experience. The vendor answers his call, we are more or less able to follow Jose's questions about the *re-viz-e-onny* and *ee-tee-oobie*, when suddenly his voice drops and he ends the call. Something not right, for sure. 'Thees man he say me, car not have *ee-tee-oobie*.

I say he why, and he say not to worry as not necessary to have *ee-tee-oobie* in the village.'

'So did the ITV simply expire, and he didn't bother to renew it?'

'What thees *expire* plees?'

'Sorry Jose! Did it run-out?'

'What thees *run-out* plees?'

'Expire. To finish. To end. To run-out.'

'Ah sorree! No, he say me, have car much years but not have *ee-tee-oobie* never!'

'So is this usual here for people to drive round without ITV's?'

'Si. Yees, in the small villages, yees.'

Blimey. Explains a lot, really, your car is written-off, but as long as it still runs, who cares? Explains all these death-traps driving about. But hang on a minute. If the car is not technically legal, wouldn't the insurance company just wriggle-out of paying, in the event of an accident? A sobering thought.

'OK Jose, we have this second car we really like the look of, a *SEAT*, we actually saw it last night in the street, the *Meel Anoon-seeos* advert said the ITV was until August, which is good, so maybe you could arrange for us to have a test-drive please?' Our friend does, and arranges a meeting for one PM, after the conversation group. Chrissie gives a little skip of excitement, and squeezes my hand. 'Vamos a mirar un coche!'

Indeed we are going to look at a car, and Jose is coming with us. And there it is, sparkling white at the kerbside! And standing next to it, a large middle-aged man with a dark, swarthy complexion. Our friend is completely taken aback. 'Oh my gaad, is a gypsy, no to buy car from he!'

No, it is Valentine!' I giggle.

Jose is astonished. 'You know thees man?' I do indeed. I know him very well as it happens. Valentine is a neighbour of Del-Boy, and often popped out for a chat when we were working on my Cockney mate's house, last winter. Del has known him for years, they have done bits of business together, and Valentine will often knock on his door of an evening bearing a number of litres of beer, which they will then consume amid the squalor of what passes for a sitting room *chez*-Del. Thus mollified, I introduce the two fellows, and a number of minutes pass in the usual Spanish fashion, big hearty handshakes, a back-slap for me and a bear-hug for Chrissie. *Right, what do we do now?* It is years since I last bought a car. I am no mechanic of course but I know how they work, and I smile inwardly as I recall my father's advice about peering at an engine. *'If it looks like oily knitting, give it a miss!'* I needn't have worried, however, Valentine lifts the bonnet methodically, like a little old lady extracting half a dozen eggs from her basket, revealing the motor, not sparkling having just been wiped off for the occasion, but exactly what you would expect for a machine dating from the late twentieth century. So far so good.

'Could you ask if we can take the car for a drive, please?' Jose does, a short conversation ensues, but it seems the news is not good.

'He say me sorree, but he no have *seguros*. How you say *seguros* in Eengliss plees?'

We know this one of course, having arranged insurance on the house last year. 'Insurance. He has no insurance on this car?' And I wag my finger at Valentine in a mock telling-off gesture.

He throws back his head and bellows with laughter, waving his arms dismissively. 'Not important. There is no need for insurance, in the village!'

For pity's sake! What is it with this place, and these drivers? Does no-one observe the law around here? And Valentine works for the council. We often see him driving around in a dumper truck. Shouldn't he be setting an example? I can just picture the headline in the local paper. *'Council digger-driver fined for having no car insurance.'* Lose his job, surely? And what are the ancient old-Bill doing about it? Oh well, scrub that last bit. We know what the ancient old-Bill are doing. Sat in the nick with their feet up, eating sandwiches and watching TV. Daft question. The thing is however, we really need a test-drive, I am not prepared to buy it without one, so either we find a solution, or we walk away, which would be a huge disappointment.

It appears we are worrying about mere trifles however. The situation has resolved itself, apparently. Stuff the insurance, as they say in Santa Marta. Valentine pulls back the front seat, Chrissie and Jose climb into the back, I slip into the passenger side, our swarthy friend behind the wheel, and away we go, across the cobbled square, past the *police station,* and out towards the dual-carriageway on the main road. The car performs perfectly, I even get to drive for a short period (*weren't me officer, it were the fat bloke*) and before long we are back in the town. Right. Time to haggle. Never felt comfortable doing that to be honest, but when in Rome and all that, and besides, the tyres look as if they will need replacing in a few thousand miles. I fix Valentine with my best telling-off look again. 'Take off a hundred for the tyres and we have a deal!'

He roars with laughter again, and turns to examine the rubber, caressing the tread like he is applying talc to a baby's bottom. 'Nothing wrong with the tyres!' he cries, in a voice which would surely attract every copper south of Madrid, if they happened to be awake, that is. Actually, considering people here don't bother with MOT's or insurance, it wouldn't surprise me to learn that they run their tyres down to the canvas. These are nowhere near that of course but I am not letting this go. Jose meanwhile is nattering away about the neumaticos, and eventually turns to me and confirms that Valentine has agreed to knock off fifty. Seems fair, ask for tuppence, take a penny as my grandad JW used to say. We have a deal, and a little white *SEAT*.

'So what happens now, Jose? I need to dash to the bank before they close, to get the cash out. Do we meet up with Valentine later to sign the log-book and pay the money?'

'What ees log book plees?'

'Sorry Jose, the log-book is the registration document.'

'What ees registration document plees?'

*Blimey. No insurance or MOT's, bald tyres and no log-books. What's the betting there is no road tax, either?* 'The paperwork for the car?'

'No, what we must to do is visit to Hester.'

*Hester? Is this Valentine's wife? Does she keep the paperwork, and the money?* OK. I am a bloke, right? I know that Valentine supports Real Madrid. His favourite beer is San Miguel. He can assemble a motorcycle gearbox. He can shout *OLE!* when he belches. But does he have a wife, or children? Not a clue. The subject has never arisen.

Jose senses my confusion. 'Hester must to give you *permisso de circulo.*' Permission to what? To circle? Am I buying a little white *SEAT*, or a Jumbo Jet? Am I expected to join a holding-pattern at thirty-thousand feet above Heathrow? 'Yees, we go see Hester at six in the afternoon, thees day. I meet you here, at six minus quarter?'

Been a long old morning, hasn't it? And we still have the joys of extracting some cash from the bank. Still, I am really excited, and I can tell Chrissie is too. Our first Spanish car. See Hester, sign the log-book or get circling permission, pay over the money, and maybe out for a little spin tonight. Right. Bank, fig tree, asleep.

At six minus quarter I assemble again with Jose, Chrissie having strangely concluded she has better things to do, to find he has brought his car this time. Clearly we are driving to see Hester? If she is Valentine's wife, don't they live in that jumble of streets on the side of the cliff? Where it is almost impossible to drive, unless you have a little white *SEAT*, of course? And a strange name, Hester, in these parts, where just about everyone seems to be called Anna, Maria, Jose or Antonio. A very small pool of names, in Spain, which can get mighty confusing at times, I can tell you. We know Big-Anna, Little-Anna, Teacher-Anna, Crazy-Anna and Anna-Who-Lives-Opposite-Ronan, and I am sure there are a few more lurking around somewhere. Jose drives almost to the edge of town, then parks up outside a rank of shops, where Valentine is waiting outside an office with the name *Gestor* above the door. *Hmmmm.* Through the window I can see a young woman sitting behind a desk, dealing with a couple of scruffy-looking blokes. 'Is that Hester, Jose?' I enquire.

'Yees, thees Hester, but she name Anna.' Fair enough, another Anna to add to the list. Hester-Anna. So who is this woman? Clearly not Valentine's wife. What is her function? The three of us file into the office, everyone then bids everyone else good evening, and we sit down to wait our turn. Eventually, after the scruffy blokes have exhausted their quota of about a million questions, it is our turn. Jose, Valentine and Hester-Anna all start talking excitedly at once, the way Spanish people occasionally do, when suddenly Hester-Anna turns to me. 'You knee?'

Oh for Pete's sake. Not my bloody knees again. Is this my knee knee, or my Rhodesia knee she is talking about? I turn beseechingly to Jose. 'What does she want my knee for?'

'You no have you knee? Where your knee plees?'

'At home.'

'Why you not have you knee with you person?'

What can I say? *Because we are British, and are simply not used to this ridiculous notion of carrying our flipping knees around in our pockets?* Not really, a bit rude actually. We are in someone else's country, and have to respect their customs. But still, we don't carry i.d. do we? I smile sheepishly, in an *oh silly me, I seem to have forgotten it* way, then turn to Jose. 'Do I have to go back home, to collect my knee?'

'Ah not worry. We drive to you house.'

Ten minutes later, perspiring freely, because Jose understandably didn't want to drive up our street, so I had to walk, in thirty degrees, we are back at Hester-Anna's office. Valentine is still waiting patently, but it appears we have lost our place to the two scruffy blokes again, who have clearly realised they were several questions short of their quota. Eventually they leave, reluctantly, and we are back in front of her desk. I hand her my knee, which she studies patiently, especially the Austin John Richards bit. '*Nombre*?'

'Si.' That is indeed my name, *but not necessarily in the right order*, to paraphrase Eric Morecambe.

Jose is unimpressed, however. 'Sorree, she ask you nombre. You name.'

I am missing something here, clearly, but no idea what. 'Yes, those are my names, John Austin Richards. They made a slight mistake on the form.' And I shrug in a *sorry but what can you do?* fashion.

'No, she need you *nombre*, and you *apple-eedo*.'

Nope. Me neither. Luckily, Valentine has been scrolling through his smart-phone. '*Apple-eedo*. Sooor-name.'

Got it. Christian name and surname. Why didn't they say that in the first place? Hester-Anna is not satisfied with something else, it appears. 'No *direction*.' *Me neither, actually. Utterly and completely lost.*

Jose snatches my crumpled document. 'You knee, it not show you *direction*. You address. Why you knee no show you address?'

*You know what, I've been wondering the same thing myself. Keeps me awake at nights, it does. NOT!* But what the heck. 'My *direction* is Castle Street, number fifty-five', I smile, using the Spanish method of putting the house number after the street name. *Right. I'm getting thirsty. Can we please get whatever we have to do done, and move on?* Apparently not. Hester-Anna is still not satisfied. '*Esky-toora*?'

Ah, I know this one. *Esky-toora*. The house deeds. Stuffed in the back of the drawer with our knees, usually....Oh. She. Cannot. Be. Serious? Yep. She is. I have to go home AGAIN and get my Esky-toora. I am struggling to remain calm. 'Jose, I've just given her my address, what is the problem, doesn't she believe me?'

Jose grins, but has the grace to look embarrassed. 'Yees, no, sorree, you might be lad-ronny. Criminal. She must to see document with you *direction* address.'

*I'll give him criminal. People driving around with no insurance or MOT's.* I take a deep breath, and smile, widely. No point getting annoyed, they have their systems here, and we have to fit in. But honestly? 'Are we driving?'

Arriving back at the office for the third time, I am absolutely dripping. I have the deeds, the plans, every damned thing I could find in the back of the drawer. If this doesn't do it, I am off. Thankfully however, it seems it does. Five minutes of frantic typing pass quickly, and eventually I have a sheaf of printed documents to sign. Jose rifles through them, and emerges with one particular form. 'Thees ees permisso de circulo temporary' he confirms. 'Ees much important you keep thees documento in the car, in case polices-mans want to see. In two weeks Hester-Anna will call you, when you permisso de circulo arrive from office of traffico, you must to come here and collect thees.' I have to come here AGAIN? At this rate I will have to add Hester-Anna to our Christmas-card list.

Still. Finally. We are done. The car is mine. Wrong! She has not finished with me yet. 'Fifty-five euros plees.'

WHAT? I turn to our friend, with a *what the hell is that all about* look. 'Yees, you must to pay twenty-five euros to traffico to translate car to you name, and thirty euros for she.'

I slump theatrically on the desk. *What was that about a lad-ronny?* Shall I tell her? Yeah, why not? I've paid for her time after all. 'In my country, you write your address on the form, sign it, and put it in the post. GRATIS!'

Cue hilarity around the table. But Hester-Anna has the last laugh. 'In you countree I not have job!'

Right. Pay the lady, pay Valentine, get the keys, hug Jose, grab my paperwork, and call Chrissie. 'Meet me in that street where we used to leave the Volvo, in five minutes, if you like. We can go for a spin.'

'A spin? It'll be dark soon! Are you like Johnny Cash, collecting the car, '*one piece at a time*?'

And here it is, our first Spanish vehicle, standing proudly at the kerb, glowing in the evening sunshine. Waving at the others, I automatically open the right-hand door, to find no steering-wheel. *Gonna take some getting used-to, this left-hand-drive malarkey.* Jose and Valentine are crying with laughter, so to cover my acute embarrassment I wave my arms dramatically. 'Some *Lad-ronny bastardo* has stolen the wheel!' Switching sides, I take a few minutes to familiarise myself with the controls and gear stick, none of which are in the right place, then gently, like the little old lady with the basket of eggs, I pull away up the street. And it is so easy. No problem at all. Approaching the meeting point with Chrissie, I indicate, then suddenly BANG! Complete panic. I haven't hit anything, but I have lost all forward motion. The engine is still running but the gears have disappeared somewhere. Luckily this is a slight downhill stretch so I am able to pull into the kerb and switch off the engine, heart in my mouth and a sick feeling in my stomach. I've only travelled half a mile, and now this. Has Valentine stitched me up? Surely not, the thing was running fine yesterday. In desperation, I exit the car and am frantically looking around, just as Chrissie comes strolling around the corner.

'Lost something have you?' she giggles, then spots the look on my face. 'Blimey, you've gone white! What on earth has happened?'

I am almost crying. 'The car went bang. The engine is still going, but the clutch has fallen off, or the gearbox, or something like that. Oh my God, what are we gonna do?' And I drop to my knees and start peering underneath.

'Well what do clutches look like? And gears?'

'I don't bloody know' I snap. 'Clutches are like dinner plates, I think, and gears are like, well, gears, with teeth.' I crane my neck then roll on the ground. 'But I can't see any....'

'And what are potholes like?'

'Eh?'

'Potholes, you know. Holes in the road about a foot deep. About a yard wide. Please tell me you didn't drive into that, IN OUR NEW CAR?'

I am still scrabbling around in the gutter. 'What pothole?' I struggle to my knees, peering round the back of the car in the direction my exasperated wife is pointing. 'Blimey, look at that pothole.' I didn't, surely? Although, in my defence, I was struggling with the controls, everything on the wrong side, trying desperately not to hit anything. And I did, it seems.

'So why don't you get back in the car, start the engine, and check if there are any clutches and gears, then?' she hisses.

My heart is still racing, however. 'I can't. I'm too jittery, too stressed. Just leave the car here, and come back tomorrow.'

She barges me out of the way, wrenches the door open, shifts her seat forwards, starts the engine, clips on her seat-belt, and with a quick check of the mirror, pulls smartly away, leaving me standing, feeling like a lemon, on the pavement. *Oh well, looks like I'm walking home, then. Could do with the exercise, actually.*

Suddenly, around the block, comes a little white *SEAT*. She pulls over, rolls down her window, and in her best Cockney-Del voice, calls out 'awright, darlin'. Fancy a ride, nah wot I mean? 'Op in, will ya!' *One of these days I'll get it right…..*


## CHAPTER 8. WHERE DID ME ROOF GO?

'Was that lightning I saw then, over in those mountains?' I am driving from Malaga airport to Santa Marta with Jake, who has a holiday cottage in the town, together with his mate Andy. 'A few days, lying in the sun, drinking beer!' Andy had giggled, rubbing his tired eyes, lobbing his bag in the boot outside the terminal.

'Yeah, I saw that too' chips in Jake, from the front seat. 'That's our direction, roughly, isn't it?'

*Don't want to worry them, but it was exactly our direction. Maybe it won't come to anything…* 'That kind of direction, but a lot further away, I think' I cheerfully lie.

Ten miles further down the road and the weather has taken a decided turn for the worse. Ahead and to our right the sky is inky-black, and huge jagged forks of lightning are illuminating the scraggy peaks of the mountains and rocky valleys with an awe-inspiring display of the power of nature. Then the rain starts, a few huge drops on the windscreen at first, thunder-spots as my Nan used to call them, from the back seat of the family Austin 1300, but within twenty seconds the skies have opened, I have the wipers on double, headlights on full and have reduced my speed by half. Visibility is down to about fifty yards and the little car is being buffeted by massive gusts of wind. 'Jeez, whatever is this, Jakey?' comes the cry from the back, although we can barely hear him due to the rain hammering on my immaculate paintwork. 'You promised me wall-to-wall sunshine, but this is worse than bloody Manchester!'

'Rubbish!' comes the predictable reply. 'You don't get olive trees in Manchester, do you?'

'Olive trees? What olive trees?' This is true, the olives have disappeared, everything has disappeared. All we can see out of the windows is rain, mist, fog, and the occasional terrifying flash.

'Anyway don't worry' Jake continues, 'it will clear up in a few minutes!' *Clear up?* If anything, the rain is getting harder, I am down to third gear, crawling along, as in places I can barely make out the road ahead.

Another ten miles however and it seems Jake's prediction was correct. The sky is clearing, the rain has stopped, and by the time we reach the Santa Marta turn the sun is peeking through. Cresting the final ridge, there is the little town below us, bathed in glorious sunshine, roads steaming as they dry, the pyramid-shaped mountain with the sugar-cube cottages clinging to it's sides, the church towers, the castle and the turrets of the ruined city walls, all sparkling after their soaking. Andy is spellbound. 'Hey, look at that! You were right, matey. It's nothing like bloody Manchester!'

'That's my house over there' I observe, pointing to the higgledy-piggledy jumble of houses below the castle, 'the white one with the terracotta roof.'

'And there's mine, look' Jake pipes up, indicating area below the church tower, clinging to the hillside, 'the white one with the terracotta roof.'

Silence from the back seat for a few seconds while Andy digests these nuggets. He had an early start this morning, poor chap, getting to the airport. 'You pair of pillocks!' he cries, as the penny finally drops. 'They're all white, with terracotta roofs!'

Jake is clearly excited, seeing the old town again. 'Anyway, we'll be up there in about ten minutes, sipping cold ones on my patio! Can't wait!'

'Don't forget it's Sunday, mind' I caution. 'None of the supermarkets will be open, if you need to get any food and drink.'

My friend chuckles. 'Ah, listen here! I stocked the fridge with beer, my last visit, and Maria, the old lady next door who has our key, was coming in last night to turn on the electric. The beers will be chilling nicely, as we speak. And we don't need any food, of course. I am on holiday, not here to do any cooking.'

This time, the shouting from the back seat is instantaneous. 'DON'T NEED ANY FOOD? WHAT ARE YOU TALKING ABOUT? Me belly thinks me throat been cut! All I had was a biscuit, at stupid o'clock this morning. And we couldn't get anything to eat at the airport, BECAUSE YOU WERE LATE, and you were too mean to spring for a sandwich on Paddy-Air, and my money was in my suitcase, AND I AM BLOODY STARVING!'

Jake is calmness personified under this assault to his eardrums. 'Ah ye of little faith! There is a chicken shop just down the road from the house. That is where we will be getting our lunch, fear not!'

His buddy brightens considerably. 'Fantastic! I love KFC!'

Now it is Jake's turn to holler. 'NO! NOT K-EFFING-C'. *Funny that, I always thought the 'F' in KFC stood for 'fried'*. 'It's a little local shop, on the hill down into town, spit-roasted chicken, coated in garlic oil, they serve it with chips and about a yard of crusty bread. The Spanish go crazy for it at the weekends, so that is what we will do. Then tonight, when we sample the delights of the local bars, you get a free tapas with every drink. They are not huge, but a little plate of food with each beer you will be surprised how it fills you up. FOR NOTHING! So you won't need to get your wallet out your suitcase, WILL YOU? Then in the morning, the bars are all open for breakfast, great long lengths of crusty bread, toasted, cut in half, smothered in chopped tomato with olive oil, cup of eye-wateringly strong coffee, just over a euro, all in. So no, I ain't buying any bloody food and I ain't doing any bloody cooking!'

We are all laughing now. 'Don't forget the *sol-y-sombra* for breakfast' I remind him.

'Sally who?' Andy giggles. 'Is this some local senorita you've been keeping quiet about?'

This time it is my turn to be on the receiving-end of Jake's bellowing. 'SHUT UP! I TOLD YOU NOT TO SAY ANYTHING ABOUT SALLY! ROS WILL KILL ME!'

Andy is in his element. 'You dirty old dog, Mitchell! No wonder you keep popping over here all the time. Now I know your secret, you dark horse, so I won't have to get my wallet out at all, this holiday, WILL I?'

Grinning widely, Jake turns to face his accuser. 'It's a drink, OK? *Sol-y-sombra*. Sun and shade. Brandy and anise, which they brew over here. Blows your head off. And there are no optics in the bars, they just slosh it in the glass, straight from the bottle. You end up with about half a pint, for a couple of euros.

Andy is not having it, however, and folds his arms defensively. 'Don't believe you. A drink, my eye. It's a woman. I know you Mitchell, you randy old goat. And I'm gonna spill the beans, when we get home, unless you refund my airfare, AND pay for the K-EFFING-C, AND all the beer, AND the breakfasts. My wallet is not getting unpacked, this trip!'

I can hardly see where I am going for tears running down my face, and Jake is doubled up. 'Who was that plasterer fellow from South Africa, used to have a *sol-y-sombra* for breakfast every day? What was his name? Is he still alive?'

'A Plaster-ER?' Andy cackles, 'don't you mean a plaster-ED!'

'Who, Pieter, you mean?' I croak. 'The fellow who reckoned he was in the South African SAS, thirty years ago? Said he shot his wife's lover, after catching them in bed? Abseiled down from the chimney and burst through the window on them? Came round to our house last winter, said he could get me a job as a tractor driver picking olives, drank almost a whole bottle of my Laphroaig, and collapsed in the street? Yes, he's still around. A couple of months ago he met this Belgian fellow who'd bought a house in his street, the chap said he was a painter and decorator, so Pieter gave him carte-blanche to paint his front room. The Belgian thought Pieter was English, apparently, and might appreciate a Union Jack theme, so painted the room red and blue, with white walls. Anyway, Pieter came home late that night, him and Del had been out for a session, and found his house looking like the British Airways check-in desk at Heathrow airport, and promptly booted him up the arse. People are still whistling 'I'm Mandy, Fly Me!' at Pieter to this day!'

Jake is roaring with laughter. 'Yeah, those new BA flights I read about, from Heathrow to Santa Marta! You speak with forked tongue, Mr Richards!'

I am struggling to steer. 'I swear this is true!'

Jake is getting nostalgic. 'And what about the Cockney, Phil, and that dim wife of his? Bought a load of Spanish cockerels, expected them to lay eggs? What was her name?

'The lovely Jackie? She is history, they had a massive row, ooh, a few months ago, I think. What happened was that Jackie was back in London visiting her daughter, and while she was away Phil found out somehow that she was having an affair with the son of the bloke who supplied the chickens! They'd been having it away in the barn, so the story goes. Anyway, Jackie came back and went absolutely ape, the chickens were all gone and the beautiful hen-house, which I'd built, in ruins. Then Phil kicked her out! She's back in London, as far as I know!'

My passengers are in fits. 'Is everyone in this town completely potty?' Andy ponders.

Jake and I glance at each other, and in unison, 'YES!'

I drop the blokes outside Jake's cottage, then head home to get on with the rest of my day, which hopefully will consist of nothing more strenuous than a few dips, and a snooze in the garden. Wrong! I have only been home half an hour or so when I receive a text, from Jake. 'Wonder if you have a spare sack of yesso handy? If so please could you drop it up, soon as possible? Ta!'

Chrissie, understandably, is less than impressed. 'I thought you said they were planning on sitting in the sunshine for three days, drinking beer?' she complains, in the kind of voice women often adopt when referring to men who are planning on sitting in the sunshine for three days, drinking beer.

That's what they told me' I concur, 'maybe he found a bit of plaster off somewhere, decided to fix it now, before the serious boozing starts. Can't be much anyway, can it, only one sack? I'll take it up now, before I get too settled.' So strapping the mortar to my old shopping-trolley frame, which now performs sterling service as a yesso-transporter, I struggle, perspiring freely in the afternoon sunshine, up the cobbled streets to Jake's place, to greeted at his front door by a rubble-encrusted figure, unrecognisable as the jolly tourist I dropped there not an hour since. Plaster, brick-dust, mud and fragments of bamboo are clinging to his hair, face and clothing, a truly grotesque apparition on a Sunday afternoon, when there is a fridge-full of lager just waiting to be consumed. 'Oh my God, Jake, what on earth has happened?'

The look on his face tells me all I need to know. A disaster, of some sort. 'Follow me' he splutters, rubbing detritus from his eyes. I follow him into the hallway and into the sitting room, where Andy is slumped on the sofa, head in his hands, then up the stairs, past the main bedroom, across the landing and into the guest room, where I am confronted by a scene of utter devastation. Where once was a plaster ceiling is now a gaping hole maybe eight feet across, above which are the tree-trunk timbers and shafts of bright sunlight filtering through what might at one time have been described as a 'roof', but which now resembles a collection of random fissures. Piles of debris and shattered terracotta-tiles are strewn across the floor, the bed and side-tables have been pushed to one corner of the room, and he has clearly made an effort to begin clearing the mess, but it is a hopeless task.

For a few seconds I am rendered speechless. What can I possibly say which will not sound wildly inadequate? 'Oh Jake, your poor house. At least no-one was hurt, imagine if Andy had been lying in that bed? And it can all be fixed, of course.'

He rubs his plastery hands through his hair. 'Quite honestly I don't know whether to laugh, or cry. But you are right, someone could have been seriously injured. Anyway, come on back downstairs, there is nothing more we can do up here.' And he closes the door on the carnage. As if that were possible.

He gestures me to sit, and plonks himself on a footstool. 'And it just gets worse. Our electric has blown, so the beers didn't chill, the electric is off everywhere at the top of town, so all the bars, the corner store, the chicken shop, everything is closed. Nothing to eat, nothing to drink, and no roof. We are, as you might say, utterly buggered.' Andy meanwhile has slumped even further into his chair. An air of total despondency permeates the air. 'Anyway' he continues, 'maybe you and Del can come round tomorrow, give me a quote, let me know what I am looking at, to get it fixed?'

*Shall I, or shan't I? Laugh or cry, he said.* I blow out my cheeks, the way builders often do. I suck in my teeth, as garage mechanics are known to behave.

'What? What is it?'

I perform my routine again, puffing, and sucking, with a slow shake of the head thrown in for dramatic effect. 'Well, I don't know quite how to tell you this, my friend.'

'WHAT? TELL ME! TELL ME!'

I screw up my eyes, to prolong the agony a few more seconds. 'The thing is' I whisper, nodding towards the sack of mortar standing forlornly in the hallway, 'I'm not sure one sack of yesso will be enough…'

'YOU ABSOLUTE SWINE! YOU TOTAL ROTTEN SOD! You really had me going there. You wait, Richards, I'll get you back for this!'

Andy meanwhile is crying with laughter. 'He got you there, Jakey! You should have seen your face!'

*Shall I continue down this path? Hell, why not?* 'How many bedrooms do you have here, Jake?' *Knowing the answer already, of course.*

'Two' he confirms, sighing loudly. 'Well, actually only one, at the moment, for the foreseeable future, as the guest room is completely destroyed.'

'So how many beds do you have in your room?'

'Only the one, mine and Ros's double, why?'

*Here we go…*'Oh no reason really, I was just wondering which one of you is having that bed, that is all.'

'I AM!' they both holler, in union.

'No no no', Andy splutters, 'I am the guest here, I get the bed.'

'Well, it's my bloody bed', Jake affirms.

'Yes, it might technically be your bed, 'Andy persists, 'but any book on etiquette will tell you that in these circumstances, the host has to give way to the guest, and sleep on the sofa. Just good manners, really, isn't it?'

Jake almost chokes. 'THE SOFA? THE SOFA? You're sitting on it! And what do you know about etiquette, and good manners, you savage?'

His buddy is now frantically scrabbling to examine his seating arrangements. A small, two-seater sofa. A tiny woman might just about curl up on it, but a six-foot bloke? Forget it. He seems less than impressed. 'Well that is just fan-flaming-tastic. First you promise me wall-to-wall sunshine, and we get a Biblical deluge. Roast chicken, tapas, a fridge full of beer, toasty breakfasts? Nope, there ain't any electric. AND NOW YOU WANT TO BLOODY SLEEP WITH ME!

Now I have tears rolling down my cheeks. 'What if he bought you dinner and a bunch of red roses? Would you think about it then?'

'Not even if he got down on one knee and produced a diamond engagement ring!'

There is silence for a few moments as both men consider the appalling prospect of sharing a bed together for the next three nights.

'Jake?'

'Yes mate?'

'Do you wear pyjamas in bed, usually?'

'No mate, totally in the buff. What about you?'

'Same here. Bollock naked. Mind you, I am keeping my pants on, tonight!'

'Well I am keeping my bloody JEANS on, tonight, don't you worry!'

*Priceless. Absolutely priceless. And I still have one more up my sleeve.* 'Did anyone see that film 'Planes, Trains and Automobiles? Steve Martin and John Candy, where they have to share a bed, and wake up in the morning with their hands round each other's butt-cheeks, which they thought were pillows?'

Clearly they have, as both men spring to their feet, start beating their chests, and flapping their arms. 'AAAAAAAAAAGGHHHHH!'

'Did you see that bears game last week?' cries Jake, in a theatrically deep voice.

'Hell of a game! Hell of a game!' growls his friend, 'Bears got a good team this year.'

Andy is still flexing his muscles but Jake is keen to get on. 'Right, better get cleaned up, and head down into town, hope the bars are open down there. Lucky the hot water in this house runs off the gas bottle!'

'Yes, I think you will be better off down there' I confirm, 'in the circumstances.'

'Well yes, with the electric cut off up here in the top of town, you mean?'

*Still got a last one in reserve.* 'No, it was the other circumstances I was thinking of, actually.'

A frown appears on his dusty countenance. 'What other circumstances? What are you talking about?'

'Well, it's a bit more traditional up here in the old part, isn't it?' *I'm enjoying this.* 'They are more easy-going down there, about that sort of thing.'

His scowl deepens. 'What sort of thing? You are talking in riddles, Richards.'

'Well, you know, men sleeping together, that kind of malarkey.'

Andy is rocking around on the sofa but Jake raises himself to his full grimy height, and points dramatically to the door. 'Be gone, thou vile miscreant! Ne'er darken these doors again!' Always fancied himself as a Shakespearean actor, did our friend.

I raise my palms, placatingly. 'Hey, it's the twenty-first century, live like you wanna live, baby. Just one word of advice, before I take my leave.' And I open the front door, to make good my escape. 'Just don't hold hands, when you are walking past the church, OK?'

And I skip off down the street, leaving the yesso where it is. *Only a quid a sack. Worth every penny.*

Luckily, Jake's reply is carried away on the breeze…..

A week or so later I am digging the foundations for a new wall in the lower part of our garden, when my phone rings. Chrissie, who is up at Ros and Jake's place, having been tasked with putting the bedding and towels on to wash. 'Help! I cannot get the water to come on. Something is wrong with it.'

Resisting the urge to curse, I mentally run through the options. 'Have you made sure the stopcock under the sink unit is turned on?'

A healthy dose of sarcasm comes my way, down the phone-line. 'Duh! Oh why didn't I think of turning on the stopcock?'

*So that is a yes, then.* 'Well what about the water-meter door out in the street? Perhaps it is turned off there.'

I can feel another caustic remark heading in my direction. 'Well I need that special key, don't I, to open that door?'

'Well there must be a key hanging up there somewhere, surely?'

My wife takes a deep breath. 'Do you really think I would be wasting my time, and phone credit, talking to you if I had that key?'

*So that is a no, then.* 'Well, you can open the water door with a pair of long-nosed pliers. Do you have anything like that up there?'

'Oh, just let me check in my bag. Purse, tissues, hairbrush, house keys, but for some strange reason, I forgot to bring the long-nosed pliers. What an empty-headed woman I am.'

*Another no. But two can play at that game.* 'What, you forgot your Swiss Army knife with the thing for getting stones out of horse...'

'FOR PITY'S SAKE! Just get up here with the pliers, will you!'

Ten minutes later, mentally cursing Jake for turning off his water when he had specifically asked Chrissie to do his washing, I arrive at his front door, brandishing my trusty pliers, to find my wife leaning on the wall, drumming her fingers. 'Look! This is what you need in your bag, instead of all that crap you carry around with you!'

She narrows her eyes. 'Oh, you mean that crap like YOUR wallet, YOUR car keys, sweets for the journey to fill YOUR fat guts, you mean?' *She got me again.*

Snapping the pliers dramatically, I proceed to unlock the door, and pull it back with a grand gesture. 'Open *sesame*!'

Strangely however, instead of grateful thanks, I get a burst of uncontrolled laughter. Bending my head to peer inside, I am stunned to find nothing there. Where there should be a water-meter with attached stopcock, is simply a void, with two unconnected pipes on either side. Some criminal has nicked his meter! Unbelievable. Why would anyone do that? Surely they have no value? Or maybe they do. Perhaps Jake's reading was low, on account of him not being here that often, and some scallywag has decided to nick Jake's, and install it in his own house? Whatever has happened, it is clearly the work of Lad-Ronnies. Or is it Lad-Rios? Forget now. I step back in utter amazement. 'The thieving swines!'

Chrissie however has other ideas, and shoves her head into the void cavity. 'No, look at this. The pipe on the left has a seal across the end. The meter hasn't been stolen, they've been cut-off!' Sure enough, an official seal bearing the legend *Aqualia*, the water company, has been permanently affixed to the pipe leading up from the mains, thereby preventing anyone from re-attaching a meter, or indeed simply connecting the two pipes and stealing the water. So is that what has happened? Haven't they been paying their bills? And when were they cut off? Must have been in the last few days, as Jake and Andy actually went home last Thursday, and it is only Wednesday now. Can the water company do that? I thought that water was a human right, and didn't I read somewhere that in the UK at least, they weren't allowed to cut someone off? Clearly it is different here, but didn't *Aqualia* send a reminder? Surely they don't just take the meter away without sending at least a warning letter? And besides, I imagine Ros and Jake pay their bills here by direct debit from a Spanish bank? So don't they have sufficient funds? Not our business of course, but so many questions. I need to speak to the man himself.

He answers after three rings, and I decide to dispense with the formalities, and start right in. 'Who's been a naughty boy, then?!'

'Oh good morning John, yes I'm fine thank you, good to hear from you too, hope you are both well, yes we had a good flight home thank you, I had a window seat and Andy ……'

'Never mind all that! Your water has been cut off!'

'WHAT? WHEN? WHY?

*That got his attention.* 'Well we were hoping you might have some of the answers, actually. Chrissie is here attempting to do your dirty laundry, and *Aqualia* have removed your meter and sealed the pipe. So I repeat, who's been a naughty boy, then?!'

I have my phone on speaker, so we can both hear the spluttering from a thousand miles away. 'When you asked me to do your washing, Jake' Chrissie chuckles, 'I assumed you would provide the water!'

'THE BLOODY BASTARDS! They took the meter, you say? We pay through the bank, so I just don't understand. I mean, Ros takes care of all of that, so I am guessing this is her fault, but...'

'DON'T YOU DARE BLAME YOUR POOR WIFE!' cries an outraged Chrissie.

'No no no, I am only joking of course! Anyway, it doesn't matter right now, does it. Sorry about this Chrissie, sorry to waste your time, but just leave the laundry for now, we are coming over again next Easter, so we will sort it all out then, OK?'

NEXT EASTER? That's four months away. *Clearly he has forgotten something.* 'Er Jake, you remember Del and I are fixing your roof?'

Laughter down the line. 'Blimey, how could I ever forget that cursed roof! Next Monday you said, didn't you? Starting next Monday, take you about a week, you said?'

'Well actually there's been a bit of a delay. We can't start Monday now.'

Panic down the line. 'What? Why not? When can you start, then?'

*I am going to enjoy this.* 'Ooh, we probably can't start until next Easter, now.'

'WHAT! NEXT EASTER? THAT'S FOUR MONTHS. CHRIST, IT CANNOT WAIT THAT LONG! I mean, I know you put a tarpaulin up there, but that was only temporary, right? The roof needs fixing before the winter storms, you said. You ordered the bloody materials, you said. I PAID you for the bloody materials. So why in God's name can't you start until bloody Easter?'

*Loving it, I am.* 'Well sadly there is one material we don't have. I mean, I thought we had it, but now we don't. There's a shortage around here, apparently.'

'What materials? I gave you a hundred bloody quid. You said you had everything in hand, in fact you made a big play about how organised you were. Those yard-long bricks, for spanning the beams, the mortar to bed them in, the thick PVC sheet to make everything watertight, the reproduction roof tiles to replace the ones that were damaged. I am not happy about this, I have to tell you, in fact if you can't start until Easter then we will have to have a re-think, get someone else to do it.'

*Oh yeah and best of luck with that, matey.* 'Sorry Jake, we forgot about the camel.'

'WHAT BLOODY CAMEL? What the hell are you talking about? You are crazy, Richards, you know that?'

'Well we will need a camel, sorry. Get him to drink about a hundred gallons, then lead him up to your patio, stick one of those plastic beer-taps into his hump, so we can draw off some WATER. You know, the wet stuff which comes out of taps? Only it doesn't do that here, any more, because you are too stupid to pay a WATER bill. You remember? WATER? That stuff we will need to mix the CEMENT to fix your BLOODY ROOF?'

The noise coming down the line is incredible, not sure if it is crying, laughing, choking or a mixture of all three. 'Sorry, sorry, sorry! Yes I forgot, all right? It was the shock, all right? I am in work, middle of a big job, not thinking straight, all right? This is all Ros's fault, I will giver her hell when...'

My wife, who was leaning on the wall crying with laughter, is up like a shot. 'THIS IS NOT ROS'S FAULT! DO NOT blame her. YOU were here last week. YOU were obviously too drunk to check your post. YOU were too busy sleeping with your boyfriend!'

*Ouch. Bit below the belt, that one.* Jake sees the funny side however. 'Yeah, well, you know what they say, you cannot beat the real thing!'

Time for a woman to take charge, clearly. 'Where do you keep your mail, Jake?'

He has to think, for a moment. 'Try on the kitchen unit, on the right, as you enter.'

She nips off, returning a few seconds later with a hand-full of envelopes, mainly water and electricity bills by the look of it. 'Ooh look, a RED envelope, from *Aqualia*. And what is this? A recorded delivery note from the postman, they tried to deliver a registered letter, so you have to go to the post office to retrieve it. And all these communications were shoved on the kitchen unit, so unless the postman limbo-danced under your front door, and placed them there, then YOU clearly saw them, YOU were too drunk to care, which means that WE have to go to the *Aqualia* office and WE have to get your water reconnected so that MY husband can start work on YOUR CRAPPY ROOF! So don't you DARE blame poor Ros!'

We can feel the shame wafting down the phone-line. 'Blimey, a bit fierce, your missus, John! But she is completely correct, I have stuffed up. Can you open the red envelope and see what it says, please? I just can't understand it, there is plenty of money in our Spanish bank to pay the bills, Ros usually checks the account online, to make sure…'

'This red letter is dated fifteenth September, Jake' my wife interrupts. 'It is all in Spanish of course but it does say in bold capitals they will be cutting the supply in two months. So it was here, all the time you and lover-boy were rolling around amid the empty beer-bottles. So what do you want us to do?'

He is clearly hugely embarrassed. 'I am so sorry to put you through all this, of course we need the water back on, and of course John and Del need it for next week. Can I ask you to try to sort it out, with Aqualia?'

I take over the conversation. 'I have a new student, Lydia, she is studying for her 'C-level' English exams, and was thinking about starting a translation service in her spare time, helping dumb Brits who have had their water cut off! Maybe you can be her first customer? She was only planning on charging a nominal five euros an hour. We have a class in the morning so I can explain it to her and hopefully she can get to the bottom of what has happened?'

The relief is palpable. 'That would be fantastic, whatever it costs, no problem, thank you so much, just add it to the bill for the roof.'

Chrissie is having the last word, however. 'Don't you need to check all that with Ros first, Jake?'

*Ouch again!*


The following morning Lydia is delighted to have acquired her first dumb Brit client, so immediately after our class we head, *a-back-o*, to the *Aqualia* office. One of the delights of Spanish life for many expats here is that it reminds them of how the UK used to be, fifty years ago, including offices for the water and electricity boards, where customers can actually go, a feature of British life sadly long since consigned to history. Entering the building, my first impression is of a doctors waiting-room. In the middle is a desk, behind which sits a middle-aged female receptionist, listening disinterestedly as an old man recounts what appears to be his life story. The other half-dozen customers however are seated around the edge of the room, in no particular order seemingly, busily nattering away in one giant conversation. As we seek a couple of spare seats, we receive the usual *Buenas Dias* from the entire room, who are no doubt wondering exactly who this Englishman and his daughter actually are, as Lydia bears absolutely no resemblance to any Spaniard I have ever seen, certainly in these parts. Tall, five-eight maybe, mid-twenties, blue eyes, blonde hair, although thankfully for her, nothing like Prince Charles, Bobby Ewing or Jim Bergerac, she could easily pass as offspring number three. Until she speaks, that is. Within about thirty seconds she has gleaned the complete history of every single client, something no glowering Brit would ever be bothered to do, even if they could speak the language fluently. And I have to say, it certainly passes the time in a delightful manner. The old man next to us, for instance, should be getting his tractor ready for the olive harvest, which starts next month, but his wife has gone to visit her sister in Granada, so he has to come here and pay these *Bastardos*. His olive trees are on the left as you leave town in the direction of Malaga, in case you were wondering.

Meanwhile the old woman in the green coat is meeting her daughter here, but she phoned to say she was running late, on account of the dog vomiting all over the kitchen floor. A Labrador, apparently. Not sure if it is black, chocolate or golden, however. The dog I mean, not the vomit.

And the chap with the gammy leg should be at the social security office really, but he received the red reminder from these *Lad-Ronnies* yesterday so didn't want the *Bastardos* stealing his meter, which THEY DO, you know.

Were you aware the best crusty *pan* in Santa Marta can be had from that little baker next to the post office? The woman with the stiff, 1950's-style perm goes there every day, apart from Sunday of course as they are closed, and just bear in mind you have to get there before ten, when it is still warm from the oven. Good job Chrissie isn't here, she is still madly in love with Jose *sexy-eyes* pan-man, who fulfills her daily order of a hot stick, but not on Sundays of course. *As far as I know...*

The young woman with the baby is not happy, however, as young *Felicia* is not sleeping nights, and she is completely worn out. 'Try some whisky in a little warm milk' olive-man advises, although whether to administer to the mother, baby, or both, he does not specify. Not sure about that, personally. Surely brandy would be better? Or just forget the milk?

In the far corner is a stick-thin woman in running kit, who is constantly tapping her feet in an agitated manner, whilst checking her Fit-Bit. Does sitting in the water board office count towards her ten-thousand daily steps? I suppose we shall never know. Although Lydia could probably arrange for us to meet up again, in case we were curious. Let me know, OK?

Then of course it is time to explain who we are, and why we are here. 'You bought the house of Jose Ocana Pastor' smiles fifties-perm, which comes as rather a shock as I have never clapped eyes on the woman, until five minutes ago. 'Lovely swimming pool you have there, and you have a nice colour from sunbathing in your garden.' Has Loli been handing out photographs? We have a large parasol obscuring the view of our new Carrefour free-standing, tubular-framed, heavy duty rubber pool, from Loli's observation deck, and the fig tree is still in leaf, so short of encasing our entire garden in a concrete bunker there is little more we can do, is there? Still, slightly spooky when complete strangers comment on your suntan, isn't it? Hopefully she's just referring to my face? At least I am not in Speedo's, AM I, Fernando? Imagine snaps of that doing the rounds.

Lydia meanwhile is in full flow. 'We are here about the house below the city wall' she cheerfully confirms. 'The owner and his boyfriend were here last week, he found a big hole in his roof, and now the water has been cut-off.'

*Did she actually just say that? Boyfriend?* 'Er, Lydia, Jake was not here with his boyfriend, he is married, to a woman, his wife stayed in England and Jake came for a few days with his friend. A mate, as we say.'

She looks somewhat confused. 'Oh my God, sorry, I thought you said they were sleeping in the same bed!'

*Well Jake did keep his jeans on, allegedly.* 'No no, sorry Lydia, I have confused you, they had to sleep in the same bed as there was a big hole in the roof of the other bedroom, and the spare bed was soaking wet. They are not, you know, boyfriends!'

Too late, however. Olive-man is wagging his finger. 'Ommo-sexuals! Tut tut tut...' *Oh, I cannot wait to recount this tale to Jake....Worth paying Lydia out of my own money.*

After what seems like about three-hundred years, it is finally our turn, I produce the red reminder and Lydia recounts the sorry tale, of which disinterested-woman is clearly less than impressed. Heard it all before, no doubt. Although, to be fair, neither of us has questioned her parentage, or her honesty, yet, which must earn us a few Brownie points, surely? Apparently not. A rapid exchange of Spanish ensues, and I can tell from the tone of water-board woman it is not going well. 'She is a plug!' giggles our translator, under her breath.

Why do they employ all these plugs here? These miserable receptionists with faces like slapped arses? Can't tell Lydia that though, can I? And I doubt the term will crop up in her English exams. Maybe I can explain it later. 'Shoe-in. It's not what you know, it's *who* you know.'

Meanwhile Plug is still rattling on. Lydia is really earning her fiver-an-hour. 'She says, the bills have not been paid, by the bank, for three months, and the amount Jake must pay is one-hundred and fifty-nine euros.'

HOW MUCH? FOR THREE MONTHS? Ours works out at less than a tenner a month, including filling two swimming pools, and we live here. Jake and Ros only came twice last year, once this, so far, and I don't imagine Andy drank much water... 'How can it possibly be that much? Sorry Lydia, but can you ask her again please? Has she made a mistake?'

Apparently not. In a surprising demonstration of technology, Plug taps away at a keyboard, followed by the sound of a printer springing into life. She roots around under the desk and emerges with a sheet of A4, detailing the breakdown of the extortion, which our friend translates. 'Water nine euros, re-connection fee twenty-five, new meter twenty five, and new contract one hundred.'

'New meter? They still have the old one, somewhere. And a new contract? Why the hell do we need a new contract, and why do we have to pay?'

Lydia is probably regretting not charging double, for these dumb Brits. 'She say that the old meter is gone, and in Espain you always need to have a contract for water and electricity, and you must to pay.'

New meter my eye. Probably they have the old one in the back of the van, just give it a wipe over and refit. Plug's paper should read 're-connection of old meter fifty euros, but we did wipe it off for you.' And a contract? For a hundred? Just a sheet of paper? And it's not even a change of name, is it? Same address, same bank presumably, Jake did say there was plenty of money in it, so none of this seems to be his fault. *The Lad-Ronnies.*

Suddenly, Plug turns her gaze in my direction. '*Ha-cobo?*'

'Si.'

*Now why did I just do that? Why did I say 'yes'?* Every single Spaniard here has cautioned us against agreeing with something we don't understand. The thing is, though, I do actually know what *Ha-cobo* is. A fritter. Indeed, a ham and cheese fritter, covered in breadcrumbs, and deep-fried. Phil and I were given one each as a tapas, in the bar, a few weeks ago. Deep-fried breadcrumbs would not be my first choice, but gift horses and all that. Went down a treat, too, with a glass of *San Miguel*. Just as I was about to make a polite enquiry, *como se yamma in Espanol*?, the artist beat me to it. 'What the bladdy 'ell is this, Antonio?' The diminutive Spaniard regarded my friend without warmth. '*Ha-cobo*.' So there you have it. A fritter. Unless Antonio was really saying something like 'get stuffed you ignorant English peasant.' Doubt it, knowing Antonio. *He was probably thinking it, mind you.*

So do they give away tapas in the electricity board? Surely not. Actually there is a big dish of sweets on the counter, of which the locals have been freely partaking, but I cannot smell anything cooking. Still, if she is just popping into the back to bring out a tray of *Ha-cobo*, I am having one. *But I still don't know why I said yes.* Greed, probably. To cover my embarrassment, I fish out my wallet, with which I have been entrusted today, under pain of death, and proffer my credit-card, tapping the bill.

Plug wags her finger severely. *Maybe we are not getting a savoury snack after all.* 'No. *Effect-eebo* only.' Damn. I have no cash on me. Well, twenty maybe, but not a hundred and fifty-nine. So they are not all that advanced, at the water board, are they? The expats here are correct. Spain is like Britain was fifty years ago. Perhaps they will start accepting cheques, in the next decade?

I give Lydia the nod, and smile graciously at Plug, in a *save me a Ha-cobo if you're getting them out* kind of way. '*Vamos al banco*', and the pair of us stumble gratefully into the sunshine. My student seems concerned about something, however. 'John, why did you say that? Is very serious, to impers, to impers. How you say, to pretend to be a person?'

'Impersonate?'

'Yes. Of course, impersonate. Why you impersonate plees?'

'Sorry Lydia, I don't understand, who have I impersonated?'

'*Ha-cobo.*'

What? Impersonating a fritter? Or have I got it wrong all along? Does *Ha-cobo* actually mean 'you ignorant English peasant'? 'Sorry, I thought *Ha-cobo* was something you eat? Cheese and ham?'

My pupil has to lean on the wall, while she wipes away the tears. Of laughter, hopefully. 'Your friend, Jake! In Espaniss his name is *Ha-cobo*. She was asking you if you are he. J.A.C.O.B. *Ha-cobo*. And you say yes! The ham and cheese food is *San Ha-cobo*. Saint Jacob. In bar we say only *Ha-cobo, give me Ha-cobo*, but is the name Jacob.' And she delves into her bag for a pack of tissues.

So Jake's name is Jacob. Who knew? I mean, we were introduced to them as Ros and Jake, and I'd had a few to drink at the time, so Ros and Jake they have remained. Never gave it a minute's thought. She must be Rosalind, or something like that, I suppose? *So Jake has been sleeping with his boyfriend, and is named after a Spanish fritter? I'm gonna love this conversation with him later. Worth paying his hundred and fifty-nine euros, plus Lydia's time. Oh my GAAD, as Amador would say!*

Returning to *Aqualia*, wallet bulging, we have of course lost our place in the queue, and there is no aroma of deep-fried anything, of course. There is however a golden Labrador tied up outside the door, looking decidedly green around the gills, although whether from this morning's bout of bilious, or whether he's just polished off a plate of Ha-cobo's, is unclear. Anyway, I plan on keeping shtum, if Plug thinks I am Jake, and providing they don't want to see my knee, and why would they as she already has those details, maybe I can get away with it, if I am lucky. And if not, I can always claim I didn't understand, and thought she was offering me refreshments. *Reckon I can wing this*. Wrong! Another dispute has arisen, it seems. 'This bank, it no longer exists' Lydia explains. 'Three months ago, more or less, in the *creesis* we have here in Espain, this bank of Jake went, how you say, boof?'

Bankrupt? Blimey. We did of course read, in our British online newspaper, about all these banks here going boof, Caja-this, Caja-that, Caja-something else, the equivalent of Building-Societies in the UK, I suppose. Ours is Uni-Caja and that certainly didn't go boof, as I have just been there, unless of course it happened in the last two minutes. So is Jake aware his Spanish bank went boof? Has he lost his money? No idea. Did a new bank take over? Surely he was notified? And if I am supposed to be *Ha-cobo*, why don't I know the answers? See what happens when someone offers you free food? I smile sheepishly. 'Please tell Plug my wife deals with banking matters, so I will have to ask her, and we can return here tomorrow with the new direct-debit details, but can I please pay the arrears now, and arrange to reconnect as soon as possible, as I have a big hole in my roof, and need some water to mix the cement to fix it?' Not sure exactly how many lies I have just told, but only little white ones, surely? And I did meet St Peter last Easter in the surgery of Dr Have-a-Hard, didn't I? He knows I'm a decent sort of chap. I hope.

Right, pay Plug, sign the contract, remembering to put 'J Mitchell' and not 'J A Richards', which is fraud for a start, but only a little white one, nobody will care in the slightest, hopefully, and no-one can read my squiggle, anyway, pay Lydia, over the odds to buy her silence, home, recount the sorry tale to Chrissie, lunch under the fig tree, asleep in less than a few seconds.

Waking from my slumbers, and dreams about being refused admittance to Heaven, It is time to call Jake. 'Hello, me old fritter!'

He is laughing already. 'I've been called some things in my time, 'me old mate', 'me old mucker', 'me old china'. But never 'me old fritter!'

'Well that is what you are, a Spanish fritter. A deep-fried, breadcrumb-encrusted, cheese and ham fritter! It's what your name means in Spanish. Jacob. *Ha-cobo*. A fritter!'

'Ooh, I like them' he giggles, 'is that what they are called? Me and Andy had them in the bar the other week. I am a really tasty geezer, you know! Anyway, enough of all that, did you manage to get my water put back on?'

'Well I have good news, bad news, very bad news, and really, really bad news. Which do you want first?'

'Oh here we go' he is still chuckling, 'come on, lets have the good news first?'

'Well, the good news is that your water will be re-connected in the next few days, hopefully in time for Del and I to begin work on Monday.'

He is so relieved. 'Great, well done. So what's the bad news?'

'Well, the ordinary bad news is that you owe me a hundred and seventy-nine euros. A hundred for a new contract, fifty for a new meter and re-connection, and twenty for Lydia.'

'WHAT? HOW MUCH? The thieving, robbing swines. Hang on a minute, that is only a hundred and seventy. Where did the other nine go?'

'That was the actual water used!'

He is huffing and puffing, moaning and groaning. 'So the very bad news? Come on, give it to me straight.'

'Well, the very bad news is that your Spanish bank has gone bust. Which is why the direct debit didn't get paid.'

Silence on the line for a few seconds. 'Hang on a minute, I think we knew that, we were written to, they said the account would transfer to a different bank, but the money was safe, and debits would continue. This is Ros's fault, she obviously didn't check……'

The phone is on speaker and Chrissie, who has been lying comatose on her sunbed, suddenly leaps into action. 'DON'T YOU DARE TRY TO BLAME ROS AGAIN! YOU were here two weeks ago, YOU didn't check your post. Remember, we have already agreed this? So if I hear any more from you about blaming poor Ros, I will personally go up your house and pour any remaining beer down the sink.'

He thinks he has had the last laugh. His bank funds are safe, and as for the water bill, well it's only money, right? 'Best of luck with that, Mrs Richards. Me and Andy drank the bloody lot! So there!'

There is still one final piece of bad news to come, however. The last laugh is with the Richards family, for sure. 'Right, the really, really bad news. Are you ready for this? Do you remember I warned you and Andy not to hold hands when walking past the church? Well you obviously didn't take my advice, did you. Lydia told the entire Aqualia office that you were sleeping together, so now the entire town thinks you are a pair of woofters!'

'Away, thou beastly reprobate, I scorn you, scurvy companion. Methink'st thou art…….

Thankfully I don't get to hear the remainder of his Elizabethan tirade, as shaking with laughter, I have dropped the phone.

Half an hour later, still chuckling to myself, I can feel my eyes prickling. Been a long day, all in all. 'That was so funny, what Lydia said, in the Aqualia office! Jake was so offended!'

Chrissie seems un-amused, however. 'On the contrary, I think you are both completely childish.'

'Ahh, just a bit of banter, wasn't it. You know I always like to have the last laugh!'

'But you haven't, though, have you?'

I regard her through half-closed eyelids. Something is coming, just that I cannot figure out what. 'I think you will find I did, when he started on his Shakespe….'

'Think about it, you buffoon. That Plug-woman thought you were Jake, right?'

'Correct.'

'Then she thinks YOU are the woofter!'


## CHAPTER 9. WHO LET THE PIG OUT?

It was just an ordinary day in Cordoba. We had already enjoyed a delicious lunch in one of our favourite restaurants there, *albondigas* for me, meatballs in a rich tomato sauce, and *salmorejo* for Chrissie, basically a chilled, thick, spicy tomato soup, and were meandering through the narrow, winding alleyways with their white-washed cottages, some affording tantalising glimpses of their inner, flower-bedecked courtyards, ruminating over how best to spend the rest of our afternoon in this World Heritage city. Truly we were spoilt for choice. We had already strolled across the Roman Bridge spanning the *Guadalquivir* river, admiring the ancient water-wheels and mills, then through the *Juderia*, the former Jewish quarter. Maybe a visit to the *Alcazar*, the Palace of the Catholic Kings, with the imposing ramparts and towers bordered by sweeping gardens and fountains, and the old Roman city wall? Perhaps the ruined Roman temple itself? The Andalucian Riding School, home of the Royal Stables and their magnificent pure-bred horses? Or the jewel in the crown, the *Mezquita* Cathedral, breathtaking in its construction, the most significant example of Moorish religious architecture in Spain, and possibly the Western world?

Or as we are doing right now, gazing in the window of *Bimba y Lola?* Nope, me neither. A ladies dress and shoe shop, apparently. With a few handbags thrown in for good measure. Fascinating. I could spend all afternoon doing just this. Who cares about two-thousand years of history when there are handbags to look at? Tearing myself away, my attention is drawn to a passing taxi, which just goes to show how interested I am in the delights and wares of *Bimba y Lola.* A white taxi, actually, a Peugeot, or possibly a Renault, maybe a SEAT, amazing how these modern cars all look the same, isn't it? *She is still looking at the ruddy handbags*. There is a passenger in the taxi, which is slowing to a halt, a bloke, definitely, although I cannot see more due to the tint on the windows, not a dark tint but enough to obscure his features. *Has she finished yet?* No. Ooh look, the back door of the taxi is slowly opening, but strangely the passenger seems to be on the opposite side. So who has opened the door? A child, maybe. Cannot actually see anyone on this side of the back seat. Suddenly, the door springs back on its hinges and out jumps a pig. A real, live, grunting, pig. Nothing in my life so far has prepared me for this moment, but there it is. In the flesh.

'Look, a pig has just jumped out of that taxi' I whisper, as I don't want to make a noise, and scare it away.

'Oh you are so predictable, and childish quite frankly. Is that the best you can come up with, a pig in a taxi? I'm only looking in the window, surely you can manage to let me do that for a few minutes without being so utter……there's a pig standing behind you.'

Indeed there is. Not your average British porker, pink with stubby nose, and curly tail. Not your Gloucester Old Spot, or your Saddle-back. No, a Spanish boar, thick, black, wiry coat, with conical snout, nose-ring, and a spangly, diamante, pink collar. Must be a hell of a size collar too, a belt, probably, judging by the neck on the beast, which starts grubbing around in the gutter in a fruitless search for acorns, or whatever it is pigs eat.

The opposite passenger door crashes open and out jumps a middle-aged bloke in a black leather suit, a ring in his nose, and a punk-rocker, fanned-Mohawk hairstyle, like someone on their way to a Johnny Rotten reunion, although thankfully without the diamante collar. Do people take pigs to Sex Pistols gigs these days? Who knows. And seriously, I haven't seen a haircut like this since about 1976. Is this the height of fashion in this neck of the woods? Is it actually true what they say about Spain being fifty years behind? When were the Pistols actually out? Forty years ago, for sure. Not my era, really, being more of a peaceful long-hair, although I do remember dancing to 'Pretty Vacant' at the Locarno ballroom once, and getting the shirt ripped off my back for my trouble. Mohawk-man whips a heavy-duty steel dog-chain out of his pocket and starts waving it in a large circle, like a skinhead on Brighton seafront on a Bank Holiday Monday, then crouches down crying out 'Lola!, Lola!' And up trots piggy, like a little puppy-dog, allowing Mohawk to attach the lead. *Lola? Isn't that the same name as the shop? Is this a publicity stunt? And is a Bimba about to appear, whatever a Bimba might actually be? Is Sid Viscous about to rock-up, with, say, a goat on a lead? Is all of this actually happening, or were those black flecks in the meatballs, which I assumed were pepper-grounds, something more* wacky?

Mohawk stands up, leans into the back of the taxi, emerging with a dog bowl and a litre bottle of water, which he proceeds to splash into the vessel, allowing Lola to gulp gratefully. He then slams both doors, taps on the roof, and the taxi glides gracefully away. Now don't get me wrong, I'm all for people taking their farm animals out for a stroll on a Saturday afternoon, but isn't this taking 'free range' a bit far? And might the inside of the taxi be a bit, well, piggy? You know, off to a wedding, and end up with hog-shit on your best pinstripes? Imagine the other guests, at the reception. Had a shower in the last month, have you, Jonno?

Lola laps up the entire contents, Mohawk tucks said bottle and bowl under his arm, and the pair of them, in best Barbara Woodhouse fashion, step daintily across the pavement, and into the shop. So this *was* a publicity stunt. Must be. The two girl assistants are making a huge fuss of the creature, stroking her back, tickling behind the ear, meanwhile two thoughts are racing through my tortured brain. Firstly, thank God. There is no way Chrissie is buying a handbag now, infused with essence of sow. Secondly, however, I step back apprehensively, in case this *Bimba* thing turns out not to be a goat, but a creature of fiercer temperament. A carnivore, not a ruminant. Don't laugh, all right? It's OK for you, sat in your comfy armchair, but I'm out here, in the wilds, and right now a pair of jaws might be about to come snapping round the corner.

Mohawk slips out of the shop, minus his porcine companion, pulls a battered silver cigarette case out of his pocket, flicks it open and gestures me to take one. A sheltered upbringing I have had, clearly. Never before have I been offered a fag by a bloke with a pig. You just never know what to do in these situations, do you? And nothing I have learned at the library conversation group is going to be much use, is it? Should I start singing a few Sex Pistols lines? *'Cause I, wanna be, anarchy? We're so pretty, oh so pretty, vacant?'* Probably not a great idea. Maybe he's not actually a punk rocker at all. Perhaps his hairstyle is a statement of post-modernist irony, or is he just, I dunno, a bit of a nut-job? Up close, the hair, which should strictly be a thick mane, is actually thinning badly, with gaps, like a secondhand garden rake. Still, who am I to criticise, devoid of any thatch on top whatsoever. 'So is Lola a companion animal?' I enquire, using the Spanish phrase for 'a pet.' I love that expression, you often see notices in parks or gardens. *'No companion animals.'* Wouldn't work in English though, would it? Can you imagine being a teacher's companion animal, for instance?

He lights his ciggy and inhales deeply. 'Yes, she is a companion animal, and a friend.' *Definitely a nut-job.* I am dying to ask him where the creature sleeps, but don't know the word for 'sty', and am scared stiff he might reply 'in my bed', which would be a step too far for me, having just polished off a dish of meat-balls. Best leave it there. The senior of the two shop assistants, no doubt concerned about her career, having just remembered the CCTV, leads Lola back out into the street, handing the lead to Mohawk, who bends and caresses her snout affectionately. The pig I mean, not the shop-girl, although personally, given the choice…..

Chrissie meanwhile crouches down, extends the back of her hand like you would to a dog, allowing porky to sniff, and then starts tickling her head. And I swear the pig grins, parting her lips pleasurably. My wife smiles, 'here, you have a go, look, she loves it! Hello Lola!' *Hello?* Shouldn't that be *Hola?* Is the creature bi-lingual, as well as domesticated? Besides, it's all very well for Chrissie, she is vegetarian, whereas I, a lifelong consumer of pork-pies and sausages, am putting my fingers nowhere near a pig. They know, don't they, our four-legged cousins? A sixth sense or something? And surely Lola could detect the fragrance of meat-ball about my person? I actually watched all those episodes of 'All Creatures Great and Small', back in the day, wizened old Yorkshire farmers getting trampled half to death by rampant, yellow-toothed swine. Anyway, Chrissie is good with animals. Probably explains why we have been married for almost forty years. She can do the stroking, I am keeping well away.

I have to say however that my wife is doing a great job, Lola is arching her back in apparent ecstasy, when suddenly, without warning, a foaming, frothing jet of urine comes sloshing across the pavement, a veritable puddle of pig piddle, flooding her shoes and causing splash-back on her jeans. I am rocking with laughter and have to turn away with my knuckles stuffed into my mouth, as my splattered spouse jumps back, almost knocking Mohawk clean off his feet. The assistants have witnessed the flood, and one comes dashing out of the shop with the obligatory bucket of soapy water, which all Spanish businesses seem to have to hand, although not specifically for hosing down swine-slash, while the leather-clad punk gathers the lead and with an embarrassed 'sorry!', he guides his disgraced companion animal off down the street. Chrissie then narrowly avoids another anointing as a cascade of soapsuds splashes across the pavement, and both assistants emerge with brushes to sweep the stinking tide into the gutter. The show is over.

I am still giggling as I start to head off in the direction of the historic part of town. 'Oh, that was so funny, you should have seen your face! Johnny Rotten looked a bit shocked, too, didn't he? Don't worry about your shoes, they will dry soon in the sunshine, but I'd prefer it if you took them off, in the car, for the journey home! And best keep the passenger window open, give your jeans chance to dry out! Anyway, where do you fancy going now? The riding school? You'll feel at home there, what with the pong of the horses!'

My wife narrows her eyes, and fixes me with a venomous glare. 'So you thought it was funny, did you? Found it amusing? Appealed to your schoolboy sense of humour to see your poor wife drenched in pig-piss? Want to take me to the stables, do you? Well let me tell you this. YOU can go to the stables if you like, I really don't care where YOU are going. But I know where I am going.'

*She is going to burst out laughing any second now. Tears will be streaming down her face, she will grab my arm and we will head off, laughing together, towards our next destination.* 'So where are you going, my dearest?' I grin.

*I was wrong, again. She has not burst out laughing.* 'Bimba y Lola of course! I have to buy some new shoes, and some new jeans, and I see they have some of both which are reassuringly expensive. And don't forget I have YOUR wallet in my bag, containing YOUR credit card. And I know YOUR pin-number. So off you go, down the stinky stables. I am going in here, and I am going to have fun. AT YOUR EXPENSE!'


**CHAPTER 10. THE OLIVE-PICKER'S HOLE**


'Thees day we show you hole of olive-picker!' Doesn't sound very nice, does it, olive-picker's hole, but Rafi at the library group sounds quite excited at the prospect, so I am guessing she is not referring to, well, you know, *that* sort of hole? No idea, really. Gun-shot wounds, possibly? Wouldn't surprise me, actually, as the town is chock-a-bloc with olive-pickers of all shapes and sizes, cannot move for them, on the roads, in battered Land-Rovers and wheezing, smoking tractors crammed with shadowy figures, trailers groaning under the weight of the crop, queuing at dusk, blocking the streets outside the olive co-operative factory, or in the supermarkets, where they appear to subsist solely on crusty-bread and this hideous-looking sausagey-baloney thing, as thick as your arm, and consisting, I imagine, of beaks and trotters, with a sprinkling of mare. Not an easy life, that's for sure, being an olive-picker. And where do they all come from? One day the town was entirely normal, the next it was as if an invasion had taken place overnight, hundreds of men, and a few women too, shabbily dressed, some dragging battered suitcases, others making do with black plastic sacks, all their worldly goods, I imagine, congregating around the bus station, where a number appear to be bedding-down for the night. The more fortunate ones share houses, apparently, and legends abound regarding fortunes to be made letting rooms, basements, outbuildings even, for the season, which runs from early December to February, or until every last olive has been plucked. And there are plenty awaiting plucking, I can tell you. And where they go after that remains a mystery, Seville or Valencia, some say, picking oranges, where their peripatetic lifestyle begins all over again.

Surprising how many families in these parts have a few olive trees, too. Many of our students are gainfully employed at weekends, helping with the harvest, and we are regaled during the lessons of how they are exhausted by this back-breaking work, the poor souls. The popular image of an olive-picker, as characterised on paintings, engravings and small silver figures on sale in jewellery shops, is of a wizened countryman whacking the tree with a long wooden pole, and they still use that method today, although in this more mechanised age, accompanied by a petrol-driven shaker which presumably does exactly what it says on the tin. The gentle whirring of the motor, followed by the sound of thwacking, typifies the olive harvest, for me. The sound of winter in Andalucia.

Last night, heading out for our evening *paseo*, we were confronted by a dust-covered figure, a man of ninety seemingly, in battered, ripped overalls, struggling painfully up the cobbled street. In his hair, all over his face and neck, his lips and teeth, the only part of his body not covered by thick layer of grime were his eyeballs. The poor fellow looked as if he'd been buried in the desert for about a hundred years, then trampled by elephants. 'Hello, neighbour', he croaked.

*Blimey, it's Fernando! Completely unrecognisable*. 'Been picking olives, Fernando?' I smiled. Stating the bleeding obvious, wasn't I, but hell, if they can do it, so can I. Turning Spanish, I am, gradually.

'Fifty euros a day, neighbour!' he spluttered, coughing horribly. 'You come with me, tomorrow.'

'No thank you!'

'*Por-que*? Why not? Good money! Black money, too, in your pocket! No need to tell those BASTARDOS and LAD-RONNIES in the Government!' And he tapped the side of his nose, dislodging about a pound of soil.

'Because I am too old for this work!' I answered, truthfully, pointing at his grotesque appearance. 'And it is much easier, lying on my sunbed!'

He roared with laughter. 'Yes, we know how much you English like lying on your sunbeds, neighbour!' And off he limped. *Probably made it home by about midnight, if he was lucky.*

'Actually, I don't know why you don't go with him tomorrow' Chrissie queried. 'Fifty euros a day? We could do with that!'

*Wondered when that was coming.* 'Did you see the state of the bloke?' I exclaimed. 'Death warmed up! And it's only about the second or third day. Imagine what he will be like by February?'

'Yes but fifty a day, that is three-fifty a week. One-thousand four-hundred a month. Almost three grand for two months work. That would pay for that Caribbean cruise you've been promising me!'

'Oh, wonderful.' I protested. 'You'd have me olive picking seven days a week, for two months? How much are funerals, around here? About three grand, I imagine. SO FORGET IT!'

But she had the last laugh, as always. 'No, I'd get Fernando to bury you out in the olives, so zero for the funeral, three grand for me! Probably get two cruises for that, find myself a rich old man, get him olive-picking next year….'

*She was joking, I hope….*

The crack of dawn at this time of the year is around half-seven, I imagine, as I've never actually seen it, eight o-clock being a more civilised hour to start thinking about getting up, but our early mornings are enlivened by the sound of the pickers clearing their windpipes, making their way drowsily down the street, to the centre of town, where they are collected and taken to the olive groves, then in the evenings around dusk it is a favourite pastime of mine to sit on our patio, with a cold beer, watching the sunset, keeping an eye out for the flashing orange lights on the tractors, coming back into town from the fields, with the day's haul. I feel a glowing sense of collective satisfaction, somehow, of a job well done, even though I haven't actually been involved in anything physical, heaven forbid. Or maybe it's the beer, who knows? But one thing is for certain; the entire livelihood of the province depends on the humble olive.

And typically of Spain, there is even a fiesta to celebrate the occasion. A long weekend of it, to be precise. An exhibition at the library, a silver band concert, a medieval market, flamenco, a kiddies fun-fair, and general lazing about under parasols. All this for something you cannot actually eat, the fruit here being used solely for the oil. The kids are off school, too, so I am guessing there is yet another public holiday in this country of endless public holidays. One every month since the summer, plus the inevitable 'Days of Bridges', which the *Gobby-Enry* in Madrid were meant to be outlawing, but presumably haven't got around to yet, as no doubt they are all sat around under parasols instead of actually governing, means that the pace of life here remains sedate at best. The locals can scarcely believe it when I tell them there are zero Bank Holidays in Britain between late August and Christmas Day. 'No wonder you moved to Espain, neighbour!' Indeed.

So, this hole of olive-picker. Rafi is quite religious, so no way is she being rude, but ideally we would like to know what we are being shown, before we are shown it, in case of, well, not sure really, just in case I suppose. 'Yees, thees day we go to fack. See hole of he.'

*Getting worse, isn't it?* Luckily Juan comes to the rescue. 'Fabrica. How you say fabrica in Eengliss plees?'

Fabric? Chrissie is wearing a canvas nautical-style top, even though we are sixty miles from the sea, which she smooths lovingly. 'Fabric?'

Heads shake around the table, and Marie is thumbing through her dictionary. 'Factory. Ees factory. Thees day we go factory of *assy-etty*. How you say hole of olive-picker in Eengliss plees?'

Well that is English, actually, isn't it? The problem is that there are absolutely no olive-pickers in the UK, last time I checked, so it doesn't actually translate into anything we can understand. Unless they are being rude. Anyway, all will no doubt be revealed at the oil factory, which I assume is olive oil and not Castrol GTX, although you never know in this country. I have been wrong before...

Into the room comes Anna, chief librarian and town historian, smiling, bidding a warm welcome to the British guests, and inviting us to accompany the group to the *fabrica de assy-etty*, to see the *oyyo assy-tun-ero*, a tantalising prospect if ever I heard one. There then follows the usual melee, coats, scarves and gloves are donned by the Spaniards, muffled up as if we are visiting the north pole, whereas Chrissie and I have light jackets, undone, just to show willing, and the group files excitedly into the street. After about fifty yards we reach a large stone archway, and it appears we have arrived at our destination. We have seen this place before of course, but in the complete absence of signs or any visible activity, had no idea what it was. A factory of *assy-etty* was the last thing we imagined. Through the arch and into a cobbled courtyard, we are greeted by an old man with a walking stick, the boss of the *fabrica* presumably, who introduces himself as Alonzo, 'but sorry I speak no English!' *Now how did he know we were English?* Must be our complete lack of polar accoutrements, no doubt, unless Historian-Anna phoned through to warn him that foreigners were coming.

Glancing around, my attention is drawn to three trestle tables set up under a covered area, on which a dozen or so round crusty loaves, about a foot in diameter, have been placed. So is this actually an olive oil factory, or a baker's? Suddenly, from a doorway comes a woman bearing a tray of what looks like small pieces of white fish, cod maybe, judging by the flakes, followed by another carrying three glass pitchers of Castrol GTX. No, hang on a minute, not Castrol, what was that other engine oil they had back in the seventies, which was dark green in colour? Duckhams! That was it. Never used it myself, always put Castrol in my Ford Anglia, but I knew people who swore by the green stuff. So what is happening here? Loaves and fishes? A re-enactment of the feeding of the five thousand? And what does the Duckhams have to do with it? No sign of an olive-picker either, with or without a hole. The Spanish are becoming highly animated, they obviously know what is happening next, whereas we, on this voyage of discovery, have not the foggiest.

Alonzo is still babbling away to no-one in particular, when suddenly he stumps off, beckoning us to follow, to a different part of the courtyard, where we are confronted by a huge piece of apparatus, cast iron, maybe fifteen feet high and ten across, clearly a press of some sort. I saw something similar on the Somerset Levels in about 1971, on a school rugby trip, where having administered a hefty beating upon the local yokels, our rugby master Jack Allen, who legend had it once played for Bristol, directed the coach down a bumpy lane to a cider farm, where he proceeded to get us royally bladdered. To this day I can picture Jack with a pint glass wedged between his gums and his lips, gargling the first verse of 'God Save the Queen'. Not going to happen today I imagine. *The wussy Spanish don't drink pints, right?*

The structure is basically a giant vertical screw set in a massive frame, with various wheels, cogs, circular raffia mats and a huge wooden bucket at the bottom. Olives have already been shoveled into the contraption, between the mats, and it doesn't take a genius to work out what is happening next; someone, or something, needs to turn the screw. A donkey on a treadmill, perhaps? Wrong. Two ruddy-cheeked countrymen emerge dragging a huge wooden beam, which they thread through a corresponding hole on the apparatus, pausing for effect, milking the encouragement from the crowd, before taking up position either side, and applying their meagre weight, the gears grind and the beam creaks painfully in a clockwise direction.

Nothing happens for a few seconds, when suddenly comes the sound of liquid dripping into the container. Olive oil, I assume, although at this rate it will take until next year's harvest to get it finished. This is all so quaintly low-tech, and surely they have some form of mechanisation, bearing in mind there must be a million olive trees in the province? No idea. The old fellows are really cranking up the pace now, however, they might even overtake a few snails, before sundown, at this rate, the Spaniards are clapping, cheering, shouting encouragement, we are applauding politely, amid splashing and gurgling, and strangled oaths. *Still no sign of the hole, though.*

The men pause for a breath, worn out as they are, the poor chaps, and Alonzo steps forward clutching a glass canister, which he holds beneath a tap in the wooden bucket, and after a few solemn words he turns the peg to release the first taster of this season's crop of...Duckhams! It is green! Surely this isn't olive oil? The stuff we buy, admittedly from the supermarket, is oil-coloured, clear, translucent, golden-brown. This substance is reminiscent of a cross between cat vomit, and nuclear waste. I have it figured out, however. This is just like when they change a barrel of beer, when about a gallon of froth and murky detritus has to be drawn off, before it can be enjoyed. They need to get rid of this cloudy, green rubbish, but do what with it? Oil some hinges? Paint it on some rusty gates? Feed it to the pigs? Pouring it down the drains is clearly not an option, unless they want to stain the Mediterranean the same colour as Shrek's underpants. Jose digs me in the ribs. 'First press.' *Well fine, but when's it gonna start running clear*?

Alonzo holds up the glass to the heavens, and recites a monologue. What is this, a prayer? Is he offering thanks to the Almighty for the harvest, or cussing about the impurity. Are there harvest festivals in these parts? Are we off to church, next? I hope so, actually. Harvest was always one of my favourite times of the school year, taking a basket of fruit and veg for distribution to the old folks. 'Thank the Lord for all His mercies, and these the first fruits of His hand.' *But what about the hole*? Alonzo then directs us towards the trestle tables. 'Now we see hole of olive-picker' smiles Rafi, eyes aglow. 'Plees, take you breath.'

What is this? Does she mean hold my *breath*? Is there a vile stench about to be released? Will there be noxious fumes from the olive press? Wouldn't surprise me, judging by the state of what has just trickled out. Or are the slices of cod humming? Looks like they might be, actually. Certainly not the freshest bits of fish I have ever seen. I glance at Chrissie who looks totally bewildered, and shrug. Her sense of smell is acute, especially when I am around, whereas personally my olfactory powers are not that great, due no doubt to having been whacked on the hooter once too often, in the scrum. Rafi clutches her loaf. 'Plees, take you breath, we making hole of olive-picker!'

'Bread, Rafi.' Chrissie grins. 'Bread, with a 'd'.'

Our dear friend is struggling however. 'Breath'. Like many locals, she simply cannot enunciate a terminal 'd'. Which explains why their capital city is often pronounced *Madreeth*. Like the famous football team, *Ray-al Madreeth*. Who knew? Giggling, she tries again. 'OK, plees to take you breath-d, and make *oyyo*, like thees.' And she starts plucking away at the centre of the loaf until a circular hollow has been excavated, maybe two inches in diameter. The locals have already performed this task, and the table is starting to resemble a battlefield in a bakery, with crumbs and lumps of dough strewn everywhere. *So is this the infamous olive-pickers hole?* Has everyone taken a day off work just for this charade? And what does the manky cod have to do with it? Quite honestly I could have stayed home and prodded my finger through one of Jose the Pan's offerings. *More satisfying, certainly, pretending to poke a hole in the twinkly-eyed lothario.* I dig my fingers through the crust, which is easier said than done, actually, could do with my thing for getting stones out of horses hooves, but eventually I have a passable imitation of hole of olive-picker. Now what? This is rather like being back in primary school quite honestly. 'Have you all made your holes, children?' Or an episode of *Blue Peter*. 'Here's one I made earlier.'

Jose certainly has. 'Now, plees to take you *assy-etty* and fill you *oyyo*, like thees,' and he proceeds to slop a generous measure of Duckhams onto his creation, completely filling the orifice, allowing it to soak in. *This must be some form of satanic ritual.* And what is the point of ruining a perfectly good loaf by slathering it with this slime? Why not slice it in half, butter both sides, whack in some ham, or cheese, or both, and bring out the Branston? And what is he doing with it now? Oh. My. God. He is eating it. Or drinking. Getting it all down his coat, more like. Alonzo produces a pile of paper napkins, and the others follow suit. 'Plees' he splutters, spraying soggy crumbs over the table, 'eat you olive-pickers hole!'

No way, Jose. There is more chance of me lying underneath the car, undoing the sump nut and drinking the contents of the engine. And that's not happening any time soon. Glancing across the table, however, everyone else is at it, tearing savagely at their loaves like a pack of wild hyenas, oil dripping everywhere, over the tablecloth, the floor, and, almost inevitably, their clothes. OK, so the first rule of travel is 'do what the locals are doing', nobody has died yet, so hell, why not. Chrissie is looking decidedly apprehensive, so I have to score one for the geezers, right? So just the merest dribble, to start with. I can always claim an urgent hospital appointment, if this stuff tastes as bad as it looks. I fact I might need a hospital appointment come to that. Anyway, I've always had the constitution of a *booey*, so here goes.

'Jonneee! No! Not a drap, come on! Like thees!' and Jose snatches the container and swills about a pint of the viscous fluid onto my bread. Sadly my hole is not deep enough so the whole lot overflows, across the table, and I have to jump smartly to avoid the splashback. There you go, another tip about living in Spain. Make sure your olive-picker's hole is nice and deep. Ordinary supermarket olive oil is a beggar to get out of your clothes, and I imagine this Duckhams stuff will take the colour out. And the skin off the back of your hand. No way am I picking this unholy mess up, so I decide to go the delicate route, break off a small piece, and holding a napkin below my chin, pop it into my mouth. And swoon. My taste-buds think they have died and gone to heaven. Rich, fruity, peppery, with not the slightest hint of engine. How can this be so utterly different from the stuff we buy? Ripping off a larger piece of loaf, mopping up the *draps* from the table, to hell with getting it down my chin, in it goes, caressing my tongue like a heavenly host of angels, and I roll my eyes in rapt appreciation. Chrissie is following suit, slurping and dribbling, and the Spaniards are clapping and whooping like madmen.

'Jonneee, you enjoy you hole of olive-picker, no? Cristina, what you think?' And Rafi is roaring with laughter. Problem is we are unable to speak, so have to make do with enthusiastic nodding, although truly, I am concentrating on the intense flavours and have lost the powers of speech. 'Now, plees' she continues, 'you must to eat you *back-allow*! How you say *back-allow* in Eenglees?'

Ah yes, the *back-allow*. I wondered when we were coming to that. I know this one of course, from my lessons with Vic the Fish. Cod. Although the fillets we get from him are fresh, whereas I deeply suspect that the slices laid out on the table here are the salted variety. Salted cod. Never tried it. A leftover from wartime rationing I always thought, my grandparents ate it, talked about it, but mother didn't buy it and I thought it had long since disappeared from sale in the UK. Here, however, it is everywhere, and not just fishmongers. Grocers sell it, huge great lengths of stiff, unappetising-looking cricket-bats, wouldn't give it to the cats, quite honestly, but it must be popular here or they wouldn't sell it, would they? And it's not as if refrigerated transport hasn't been invented yet in Spain, so why do they need a foodstuff which originated in the Middle-Ages? Bizarre. Actually, there are several recipes for it in my Rick Stein cookbook, it needs to be soaked in water for about a hundred years or something, but the locals must like it, presumably. Personally, I think it looks unspeakably vile, but it seems as if I am about to try some, doesn't it? 'Cod.'

Once again however, Rafi's pronunciation is letting her down. 'Coth. Codth. Cothd.' Poor woman just cannot get it. Mind you, I struggle with *Madreeth*, personally, so it works both ways. And you should hear me talking about *Hee-HHON*. The Spaniards around the table are all practicing their new English word, and suddenly we have a chorus of *coth, codth and cothd*, intermingled with breadcrumbs, tears are being wiped away and the whole scene resembles a tea-party in a playgroup.

I'm not getting away with it, though. 'Plees, to be eating you coth now' Juan instructs. 'Like thees.' And he breaks the offending seafood into its component flakes, mixes it with pieces of loaf, drowns it in Duckhams and swallows the whole thing. OK, so the fifth rule of travel used to be 'eat what the locals are eating', but this had to be amended following a dish of *Pho* in Vietnam, which as far as I can remember was the only time in my life I had to give up on a meal, containing as it did slices of a pink substance which might or might not have been rodent, from an earlier century. So the fifth amendment now goes something like 'eat what the locals are eating unless you suspect there might be lumps of rat in it', which I think is fair enough. Anyway, cod is not vermin, is it? On the other hand, in its cricket-bat state, this stuff looks as if it might have spent its entire life swimming up a drainpipe, but again, what the hell, I can only die once can't I? Following our friend's example, I take a generous pinch of *back-allow*, a goodly lump of crust, a healthy dose of Duckhams, open my mouth, then snap my jaws theatrically onto the weird combination. And my taste-buds resurrect themselves, die once again, and travel, via heaven, on an inter-galactic voyage into uncharted universes. Utterly. Sensational. The cod is salty, but offset somehow by the intense flavour of the oil, and already I am looking forward to olive-picker's hole day, next year. Oh my GAAD, as Amador might have said, were he here.

Right. I have some questions. 'So why is this oil so different from what we usually buy in the Donna, sorry, *Mercadonna*?' I enquire of no-one in particular. *Blimey, I was about to use the English word for our local supermarket, then.*

Juan snorts with derision. 'How much pay you, for thees?'

I glance at Chrissie for support. 'Not sure, about three euros a litre?'

He waves his hand dismissively. 'Ees fine for cookee, but for eatee you must to buy first-press, sabor, sorree, flavooo much intenso, ees good for you. Yees. I understand, you no have olive-trees in Eengland, you not know thees, but here in Espain ees much tradition of *assy-etty*.'

Yep, I get that. We've been buying the industrial oil, mass-produced, bottom of the barrel stuff, probably not even Spanish, some impostor blend, French possibly. A bit like that 'Old Farmyard' wine-flavoured beverage they had on the boat. Certainly not Spanish Duckhams, that's for damn sure. 'So where do we buy this first-press flavooo much intenso, then?'

Alonzo is grinning wildly, waving his stick. He's got us, hook, line and sinker. '*Ben*. Follow me. Thees way, plees!' And off he stumps, across the courtyard, the group following animatedly behind. Mind you, the locals are animated in everything they do. Even when they are asleep, I imagine. He leads us to an emporium, reminiscent of the dispensary in Doctor Finlay's Casebook, complete with dark, wooden shelving and ornate glass bottles of varying vintages and styles, some with stoppers, others with corks, each containing the same deep, dark, intense oil. We have been transported back in time to the premises of a Victorian apothecary. All we need now is for Doctor Cameron to pop up....AND THERE HE IS! Behind the counter sits a whiskery old gentleman, and, I swear, if he speaks with a Scottish accent, I will surely faint. We are back in Tannochbrae, for sure. I wink at Chrissie. 'Och aye, Doctor Snoddy!' She whacks me on the arm, and turns away, shoulders shaking.

Jose meanwhile is grinning. 'Why you laugh, plees?'

What can I say? He wasn't even born when Doctor Finlay was on TV, and my translation skills are not that great. 'Oh, we were amazed at this museum. What a wonderful place!' *There, that should cover it.*

It seems not, however. 'No thees not museo, thees shop. Here you can to buy you *assy-etty*. You want buy *assy-etty* thees day?'

I am certain we do, but we are pensioners on a budget, after all, and this is a premium product. Got to watch the pennies, right? What if it is wildly expensive? Be a bit embarrassing, wouldn't it? 'Do you know how much it is, please Jose?'

Alonzo senses a sale, however, and slips his arm companionably around my shoulder. He points towards Doctor Cameron, who has craftily assembled three different-sized bottles on the counter, while we were looking the other way. 'Small, three euro. Medium, five-fifty, and large, eight.' Hell, that is cheap, we pay three for the olive-oil flavoured beverage from the supermarket, and the large bottle Doctor Cameron is caressing lovingly is easily twice the size. And it's surprising how much we get through, for cookee, obviously, but also for eatee, drizzling it on salads, crusty bread with ham and cheese for lunch, sliced tomatoes on toast for breakfast, the list goes on. Who knows, I might even need to get some salted *back-allow*, poke it in my olive-picker's hole, after this eye-opener of a morning. I smile at Chrissie in a 'please get my money out' kind of way.

She raises her eyebrows innocently. 'Did you want something?'

Always drags it out, does my wife, this carrying my money business. Can't blame her, really, but the alternative is surely to be stranded in a foreign country with no bank cards. And how much does a wallet weigh, anyway? I bought her the blooming handbag, with a little Scottie dog hanging from it. Surely that earns me certain transportation points? I grin pleasantly. 'Would you mind giving the man eight euros, please?'

'No.'

'Eight euros of *my* money, please?'

'No.'

'And why not, pray?'

She narrows her eyes. 'Because YOUR money is in YOUR wallet which YOU left home this morning.'

*Like pulling teeth*. 'So could you possibly see your way to lending me eight euros of YOUR money, please?'

'No.'

The Spaniards are all chuckling at this British soap-opera, and I glance at Jose and shake my head in a 'women, eh' fashion. 'Just for half an hour, until we get home?'

She exhales dramatically. 'I didn't bring any money, YOU didn't bring any money, because YOU didn't say we needed any, did YOU?'

I turn to Alonzo. 'I am sorry, my wife forgot my money, we will return tomorrow and buy the *assy-etty,* then', and step smartly backwards to avoid the left-hook, but instead walk into a right-jab, which earns my wife a loud cheer from the crowd. And me a painful rib. *Always the butt of the jokes round these parts, aren't I?* Still, learning a language has to be fun, hasn't it? And acting the goat has been my life's mission, from my early schooldays, and I'm still at it. The epitaph on my gravestone should be *he liked a laugh*.

Anyway, it seems as if the group is breaking up. Been a long old morning, all in all. Learned some great new Spanish phrases, too, and I cannot wait to inform Loli I have been eating hole of olive-picker. Imagine the kudos she will reap telling the other neighbours that, in the street tonight. Juan has other plans, however. 'Plees now we go to see olive tree *mee-lon-arry-o*. You will be exciting see he!'

*Mee-lon-arry-o*? Is that a millionaire? A millionaire olive tree? Surely not. I've heard of Million Dollar Baby, courtesy of Mr Eastwood of course, but a tree? Is this a local legend of some sort? Did the tree up-root itself, stroll down the newsagents, buy a lottery ticket, and hit the jackpot? Or did some unfortunate olive-picker, in days of yore, hide his stash under the trunk, meet an untimely end, the loot being discovered many years later? I am assuming we are talking pesetas here, not euros, and as we all know, a million pesetas is worth six grand. According to Fernando, working seven days a week for the entire harvest would only earn you half that, at today's prices. And it's not as if the picker could work overtime, bearing in mind it is absolutely pitch dark in the olive groves at night, so he couldn't see what he was picking, could he? Or is the tree a valuable tourist site, worth a million? Did, I don't know, some Spanish king, in ancient times, shelter there from his pursuers, rather like our Charles the Second? Fairly useless, actually, olive trees, for harbouring royalty, or anyone else for that matter, given that the branches are only a few feet off the ground. 'I see you, come here plees, you Majesty, I chop off you head, thees day!' Are there hundreds of pubs dotted around Spain called the *Royal Olive Tree*? Not seen any, to be honest. I smile warmly at our friend. 'Millionaire?

Which produces uproar. Chrissie is looking puzzled, either struggling, like me, with the concept of a wealthy fruit-bearing plant, or at my stupidity because she knows from her Spanish O-Levels that *mee-lon-arry-o* means something entirely different, but everyone else is doubled up. 'Jonneee no!' cries Juan, wiping tears from his cheeks, 'no millionaire, thees tree have one towsand jeer!'

Rafi is not having it, however, wagging her finger severely at her compatriot. 'Juan, you no correct. Cristina and Jonneee tell we that in Eengliss you no *have* jeer, you *are* jeer.' And she glances in our direction, seeking confirmation. *Don't look at me missus.* My wife cottons on, thankfully. 'That is correct, Rafi, in English we say 'I am twenty, you are twenty, she is twenty.' In Spanish you say 'I have twenty.''

Alonzo meanwhile is flapping his arms, calling for silence. He takes a deep breath. 'Thees. Tree. Of. Olive. Ees. One. Towsand. Jeer. Oldth.' And he exhales, grinning widely. *Incredible! And he told us he didn't speak any English.* I'd buy some olive oil from the bloke, if only my wife had remembered my money.

Anyway, so where is this venerable plant? I mean, it's knocking on towards lunch-time, not that I need anything to eat having polished off a square foot of breadth, and all that *back-allow*, but it's the principle, isn't it? We knock-off at one. The Spanish however, being officially in the wrong time-zone, which the

*Gobby-Enry* are supposed to be doing something about, in the next fifty years, possibly, sit down around half-two, so there is plenty of time. We follow a dusty track out into the olive groves, the Spaniards all chatting away excitedly, whereas we are looking out for a signpost indicating the location of this *mee-lon-arry-o*, a ridiculous notion actually, in this country where directions are the exception, rather than the rule. Still, the others must know where they are going, but best of luck finding the thing, in this endless ocean of olives, which to my untrained eye all look the same. Obviously, there are minute differences in each tree, but they say that about snowflakes, don't they? Low, squat, no more than fifteen feet high, (the olive trees I mean, not the snowflakes) they say olive wood is extremely slow-growing, which is not that surprising, quite honestly, in this country.

Historian-Anna is leading the expedition, and suddenly she arrives at the stump of a broken fence-post, indicating we need to turn off the main track. 'Thees was sign for *olly-bow mee-lon-arry-o*, when I was cheeld,' Jose confirms, 'but *Gobby-Enry* no fixy yet.' Well what's the rush? Probably sat under a parasol somewhere, aren't they. Get round to it in the next fifty years, no doubt. Do the time-zone, and the signpost, all in one go.

We head up a short rise, then the ground drops away, and there it is! Unmistakable, towering over its neighbours, dominating the landscape. And I am transfixed. We stroll reverently up to it, and I notice that even the Spanish have fallen silent. A thousand years, imagine that. I reach out my hand and caress the gnarly bark of the oldest living thing I have ever encountered. The trunk has divided into what appears to be five separate trees, all emanating from one massive root, spreading more than ten feet across the ground in every direction. The canopy is easily thirty feet, maybe more. Humbling, the history this tree has witnessed. It was a mere sapling at the end of the Dark Ages. The Norman Conquest, the Renaissance, the Reformation, the Dissolution, the Spanish Armada, the Civil War, the Restoration, the Industrial Revolution and more recently, the world wars of the last century. All have come, and gone, and still this beast stands. My head is spinning. What a remarkable morning this has been.

Strolling homewards, Chrissie squeezes my arm. 'I was really proud of you, this morning' she smiles.

I feel a warm glow spreading through my person. 'What, my Spanish, you mean?' I whisper, modestly. 'I am getting better, aren't I? And we are so lucky, having such wonderful friends to teach us, and to share it with.'

She guffaws unkindly, breaking the spell. 'Your Spanish? Do me a favour! You sounded like some Westcountry yokel! No, it was the olive-pickers hole, I mean. All that olive oil, and you didn't manage to get a drop down your shirt, and trousers!'

*Always the butt of the jokes round these parts, aren't I?*

## CHAPTER 11. WHERE DID ME FLOOR GO?

'Wow, what a difference! I can't believe it's the same room! You have been busy!' Sunday evening, and I am admiring Del-Boy's freshly scraped, filled and painted walls in his sitting room. The exposed beams have been stained, the floor tiles re-grouted, and his 'coffee-table', which previously consisted of three sacks of white mortar piled on top of each other, has been replaced by the real thing. Harvested from the street, no doubt, as it bears the scars of wear and tear, but a complete transformation from his previous living arrangements, which were, and he would be the first to agree, medieval. He has even stocked the fridge with a pleasing selection of beers, one of which is nestling comfortably in the pit of my stomach, a second cradled in the palm of my hand. Tomorrow morning we will begin the replacement of the damaged section of Ros and Jake's roof, Dirty Diego the Dumper Driver is scheduled to appear at the stroke of the crack of dawn, or about half-nine, the weather forecast is good, and we hope to have the whole place at least water-tight by Friday.

And seriously, I am so pleased that Del is finally getting himself together, from his previous existence of chaotic, abject poverty. Rocking-up in Santa Marta around seven years ago, in a battered Ford Transit with twenty-five grand in used tenners stitched into the passenger seat, according to local folklore, a fugitive from a messy divorce in London, he proceeded to sink the whole of his funds into two dilapidated cottages near the top of the mountain, *'one to live in, one to do up an' sell, nah wot I mean?'*, subsisting meanwhile on a Navy pension which would barely keep a mouse alive in the UK, but which here should have provided the basic necessities of life, were it not for his unruly pack of canines, who consume huge sacks of dog food, and his meagre budget, at a rapid rate of knots. Speaking of which, I cannot detect the cacophony of barking which usually provides the soundtrack to my visits here. 'Where are the dogs, Del? I didn't hear their usual greeting!'

He rubs his hands across his face. 'Dead, mate. Well three of 'em is, Harley, Suzy an' Piddle. Happened when you was in England, they musta caught summat, in three days they was goners. I only got the three puppies of Suzy, now.'

*Me and my big mouth.* And he dearly loved his pets, despite them almost wrecking his house, stealing his food, raiding his fridge, attacking the local wildfowl, escaping at regular intervals and being confounded nuisances generally. But hang on a minute. Three dead, three puppies left, but didn't he have seven bow-wows, previously? Mental arithmetic has never been my strong point, despite spending my entire career in the accountancy profession, but surely one is missing? 'So what happened to Squirt, Harley's son?'

He roars with laughter. 'Oh my Gawd, that was so funny! Phil the chicken got him. You know when he booted that dim Jackie out for having it off with the neighbour? Well I think he regretted it after, he used to turn up here, pissed, going on about how lonely he was, so I suggested he got a dog, only joking really, but you ain't gonna believe this, Squirt musta read me mind as he came bursting out of the kitchen an' leaped on Phil, I fought he was gonna get him round the froat, but he started licking his 'ead, Phil was laughing like 'ell, an' they just bonded. Two bloody lunatics togevver, if you ask me! An' you ain't heard the best bit yet! You know Phil reckons he's an artist? Got all them pictures wot he says he painted? Well Squirt et 'em! Some of the paintings is up on easels, like, but there was about half a dozen on the ground, all laid out like it was that bloody Louver-place in Paris, so Phil comes home one day an' there's bits of wood, canvas, you know he painted all them topless women? Well they all had teef-marks over their 'eads, bits of chewed-up women all over the floor, he went bloody spare, I think he was gonna kick Squirt out an' all, but he musta learned his lesson about Jackie. Anyway, Squirt is prettier than her!'

'More intelligent, certainly!' I confirm, and the pair of us are rocking with laughter.

'Fing is though' he continues, 'ee musta got a few bob from somewhere, as he said he wanted to buy me Transit!'

I am astounded. 'Surely it isn't running? I thought you said it was clapped-out, falling apart, rusting away on that waste-ground on the edge of town?

It is, it was! It never had a MOT when I drove it 'ere! But it still starts, just about, I used to go there once a month and turn it over, completely illegal of course, and utterly useless here, don't go down the narrow streets, too wide, and his street is even narrower than this 'un. But he reckoned he could get it changed to Spanish plates, get the ITV done on the cheap, so he gave me two-fifty for it, the silly sod! An' it gets better, he said he was gonna start a chainsaw business, cutting up olive-wood he thought he would find, at the side of the road, an' selling it to dopey Brits for their wood-burners. So 'ee goes down that DIY place in Granada and buys a petrol chain-saw, an' first time 'ee goes out in the van, 'ee gets caught red-handed by the old-Bill nicking wood, well you know how lazy the coppers are here, so they says provided the van disappears, completely, they will turn a blind-eye, say no more about it! So he had to pay these Moroccans to come with acetylene torches an' chop the van up! Oh my Gawd, they done it on the waste land in the middle of the night, all you can see now are scorch-marks on the ground, an' a few bits of rubber trim! Phil was going crazy, comes round 'ere demanding 'is money back, says it all my fault, my bloody dog eating his pictures, my bloody van getting 'im in bovver with the law, my bloody fault Jackie left!'

I have tears streaming down my face. 'How could Jackie leaving possibly be your fault? That is completely ridiculous.'

''Cause I introduced her to the chicken man!'

Tears are streaming down my tears, and it is several seconds before I recover the power of speech. 'Well at least you got the van off your hands, and two-fifty will get you a couple of beers!'

My friend is consumed by a paroxysm of coughing. 'Not two-pound-fifty, ya numpty!' he splutters, 'two 'UNDRED an' fifty!'

'TWO HUNDRED?' I choke. 'Are you serious? He must have lost his mind! Anyway, I know where the money came from. You heard the story about how Chrissie found those paintings in the street? How Phil took them home, then sold the one of the giant retriever to the Irishman, Ronan, for two hundred and fifty? I cannot wait to tell Janie and Nigel, when they come over next month. That is total serendipity!'

A puzzled look crosses Del's face. 'Sarah Dippy? Do I know her? Is she Jackie's sister? Jackie Dippy, and Sarah Dippy!' He rises unsteadily to his feet. 'Anyway mate, let me get you another one, then we gotta sort out what we're doin' termorra.'

At that precise second there is an ominous cracking sound from the ceiling. Several eddies of white dust drift nonchalantly past my head, and we both instinctively glance upwards. Suddenly there is an enormous, hideous crashing sound, I jump to my feet but am hit squarely on the bridge of my nose by a huge chunk of cement maybe two feet square, which stuns and knocks me clean off my feet, and I tumble in an ungainly heap into oblivion. I must have only been out cold a few seconds, if that, as I am aware of lumps of masonry raining down all around me, choking dust in my eyes and throat, red and green lights swirling around in my head and a shattering, searing pain behind my eyes. Writhing and groping amid the devastation, a disembodied voice is calling 'quick, get up, the effing house is falling down' and I feel a hand dragging the belt of my jeans, a vain attempt by the diminutive Cockney to haul fifteen stones of Westcountry muscle, OK, blubber, to safely. Somehow I manage to scrabble onto all-fours, and my first coherent thought is of Chrissie, who last year begged and pleaded with me not to get involved with this dilapidated structure, and who was proved right, yet again. And ironically, after all the work we have done making the place watertight, poor Del is back to square one.

Groping for the doorway, I somehow manage to haul myself upright, and the pair of us stumble gratefully into the sweet evening air, and crash down onto the cobbles. I pull up my tee-shirt to wipe the blood from my shattered forehead and nose, which seem to have ballooned in size, although miraculously, nothing seems to be broken. 'What the hell has happened, Del?' I croak, coughing up lung-fulls of dust.

My business partner has his head in his hands, presumably either mentally checking his third-party insurance cover, or crying. 'Well, while you were rolling round on the floor like a bladdy girl' he sniffs, 'it looked like part of the back wall had fallen away, and two of the bedroom floor beams above had dropped, a couple of foot. So what we gotta do, mate, is get me scaffold tower out of the other 'ouse, right now, an' prop up those beams, somehow, stop the whole bladdy lot falling in.'

*So not checking his third-party insurance policy, then*. 'Oh, and how are you feeling, John?' I cry, as sarcastically as possible, given my circumstances. 'How is your head? Is there anything I can get you? Do you need to go to the emergency department to get checked-over? Sorry you were almost killed in my shitty hovel. Sorry to ruin your clothes, and your Sunday evening, and sorry I am asking you to give up even more of your precious time saving me from being completely HOMELESS!' He leans across and places his hand on my knee, which I hastily knock away. 'And you can pack that in, you pervert, taking advantage of me, at death's door. I read about people like you, on the internet!'

He buries his head in his hands. 'Mate, mate, I am so, so sorry. You must be heartily sick of me. You must rue the day we ever met. I am nothing but a total nightmare, for you.'

I nod in agreement. 'All of that is true, of course. But it gets worse, actually.'

He replaces his hand, and once again I brush him off. 'Worse? How could I possibly be any worse, for you?'

I pause for dramatic effect. 'Because Chrissie is gonna kill me, when I get home!' He roars with laughter. 'But it gets even worse than that, actually.'

'Even worse than that? How could it possibly get any worse than being killed by your missus?'

I place my hand on his knee, and give it a playful squeeze. 'Because, my little Cockney buddy, my bottle of beer is buried under all your bloody rubble! So give me a hand up, then go and get me another, RIGHT NOW!'

One curiosity of Del's 'main' residence is that it was originally two cottages, now knocked into one, so effectively he obtained three dwellings for his twenty-five grand in used tenners. Sounds a bargain, doesn't it? But then you haven't seen these structures, have you? Trust me on this one. You don't really want to. I would strongly advise anyone thinking of retiring to Spain not to go down this route. Buy one which has already been restored, unless you are a builder. Or an optimist. Anyway, Del is as certain as he can be that the collapsed section, effectively the middle cottage of the three, is structurally sound, and that all we, and note he implies 'we', have to do is crank the fallen beams back into place, support them temporarily with something called an *Acro*, rebuild the back wall, remove the *Acro* and hey presto, all will be 'cushtie', as they say in the building trade, apparently. But then, he is an optimist, after all. Me? I am keeping 'schtum', as they also say in the building trade.

Del has his thinking-cap on. 'Wot we better do mate, is go out into the garden and check the back wall of the 'ouse, it should be all right as it's about a yard thick, I fink it's just the inside bit of the wall wot has collapsed, where the rain was getting in last year, but we better check, right? So come on, don't just stand there like a bleedin' dummy!' *Oh a bleedin' dummy am I*? And there was me, minding my own business, when half his house fell on my head, which now feels as if I have been clubbed senseless by about fifty cavemen. And *garden*? Describing the area to the rear of Del's house as a *garden*, is a laughable statement of wild optimism, quite honestly. No self-respecting Moroccan would be seen dead sawing up a Ford Transit out there, that's for damn sure. A fly-infested, faeces-encrusted, Third-World hell-hole would be talking it up, frankly, and that would be a gross insult to the Third-World. And hell-holes everywhere. *Keeping schtum though, aren't I?*

Head thumping, I groggily follow the annoying Londoner through the undamaged section of his property, out into the medieval plague-pit, sorry, garden, site of the dead goat and the flapping turkey incidents last year, and immediately, despite my fragile condition, I notice something has changed since my last visit. Takes me a few seconds to figure out what is different, but yes, the concrete floor has been dug up in several places, and replaced by tamped-down hardcore. 'Trouble with the drains, or something, out here, Del?'

He regards me without warmth. 'Yeah, thanks for reminding me, mate. You're standing on Harley's grave. There's Suzy, look, and Piddle is in the corner.'

I stifle the urge to burst out laughing, but only just. I'd forgotten he had no actual earth in this so-called garden. Concrete, and piles of rubble only. He spots the corners of my mouth turning up. 'Yeah, you can laugh' he grins, 'you know how big Harley and Suzy were, like bloody mountain lions. Took me a solid day to dig three holes. Nearly killed me.'

'So how far did you go down?'

'About a foot!' he chuckles. 'Nah, about a yard, actually. Dynamite wouldn't get me down any further, would it?' And he gestures at the granite mountain, towering above us.

My befuddled brain meanwhile has one major concern. Don't want Del and his three puppies turning up at our house tonight, begging accommodation, do we? I'm in enough trouble as it is. 'So where will you sleep tonight, mate?'

'Oh, no problem, I can use the other part of the 'ouse. The spare room, got a bed in there, ain't I? That's the good fing about 'avin' two 'ouses knocked into one, innit?'

He is not serious? 'You mean that room with the pile of wardrobe doors, the dog-food sacks, and the bed strewn with rubble, and weeds growing out of it. The bed with the shat-in sheets?'

'Yeah, why not? The wardrobe doors and dog-food sacks is gone now, used 'em on the roof, didn't we? An' I cleared away all the rubble, an' the weeds all died back, so it's like a bloody palace in there now. I was thinkin' of doin'

Airbnb, before all this happened.' He pauses for a few seconds. 'Ain't changed the sheets yet, but who cares? I'll give 'em a bit of a sweep, be fine. Slept in worse, anyway, over the years.' *Slept in worse? Bedding down in a scrap-yard would be preferable, if you ask me. Still, at least we're not having house-guests, tonight.* 'Anyway, the back wall of the 'ouse is fine, so that's a hell of a relief. But obviously, we ain't gonna be able to start Jake's job tomorra, are we?' *I was wondering when this was coming.* 'Can't leave them beams just dangling, can I? Gotta get 'em back in place, and the new support wall built at least, ain't we?' *That Royal 'we' again.* 'Anyway, Jake's roof ain't leaking, is it? We got the tarpaulin up, ain't we? So a week or so ain't gonna matter, is it? *Questions, questions. I'm keeping schtum, however.* 'So you can meet Dirty Diego termorra, can't you? Get all the materials stowed away? Then maybe you can ask him to deliver me a coupla *Acro's*?'

My schtum quota has just run out. 'How do you say *Acro* in Spanish?'

'Gawd knows, *Acro* I imagine, it's a trade name, innit? And p'raps you better call Jake, later, tell 'im there been a slight delay, but we'll get round to it as soon as.'

I am now in negative schtum. 'Right, let me see. I have to go home tonight, permanently disfigured possibly, explain to my wife how I almost died, why I look like I've gone ten rounds with Mike Tyson. And bearing in mind she never wanted me to work on this shitty hovel in the first place, she is gonna KILL ME. Then I have to phone Jake and explain why we won't be starting on his roof tomorrow, and he will quite possibly want to KILL ME. Then tomorrow I have to meet with that disgusting Dirty Diego, listen to him gobbing and flobbing, watch him scratching his balls, after which I will no doubt want to KILL MYSELF. And then, to cap it all, you want me to come back here on Tuesday, and help you restore this desolate bog-hole for about the tenth time, but you won't be able to pay me will you, *oh sorry mate, bit skint at the moment, have to pay you after Kingdom Come*, so then I will have to KILL YOU. And then I will have to explain to Chrissie how I've been working all week with sod-all to show for it, and she will KILL ME ALL OVER AGAIN! So yes, I AM heartily sick of you. I DO rue the day we ever met. You ARE nothing but a total nightmare, for me. Probably save us all a load of grief if I beat you over the head with that shovel, right now, and bury next to your confounded DOGS!'

My little East-Ender is laughing so much he has to hold on to the wall.'Save me a load of grief an' all, mate! Whack me on the 'ead right now, bury me next to me pets, 'an I'll be a 'appy man! Don't know how much more o' this I can stand, actually. Seven bloody years I been fixin' up this 'ouse, and look at the state of it. Come on, 'urry-up, get it over wiv!'

I pick a bit more grit out of my ear. 'I can't, at the moment. Sorry.'

'Why not? Quick whack acrost me 'ead, boof, in the 'ole, sorted.'

I wipe the smile off my face, as best I can. 'Because I need you to tell me where you've hidden that two-hundred and fifty you got from the artist, so that I can spend it on your wake. The whole town will want to get totally rat-arsed!'

He shoots me a hunted look. 'Too late, mate. Spent it, ain't I?'

Which explains why Del is still alive. For now….

## CHAPTER 12. THOSE *LAD-RONNIES* FROM THE WATER BOARD, AGAIN!

The second week of December we receive a letter from our dear friends at *Aqualia*, the water company. *Addressed to Jose Ocana Pastor*. Chrissie is outraged. 'What is the matter with those idiots? The bills are all in your name, so why are they writing to Joe Shepherd? The left hand doesn't know what the right is doing, clearly. What is it in Spanish? *Mano izquierda* and *mano direcha*? I've a good mind to go down there right now, and tell them that! The TONTOS!'

Quite impressive, isn't it, getting cross in a foreign language? And I bet she never learned that for her O-Levels, all those years ago. 'But have you actually read the letter? What do they want? They might be offering us a refund, or who knows, a contribution to Del's wake! Read the rest of it, before you start having a go!'

Yes, sadly, or fortunately, depending on your point of view, and I am keeping schtum on the subject, the Crafty Cockney is still with us. We have repaired his back wall, built a complete new one with concrete blocks, reduced the size of the sitting-room by six inches or so but at least he won't have to worry about the floor above collapsing, when he is having a quiet beer of an evening. And no, the Spanish for *Acro* is not *Acro*, for all you budding builders who intend to completely ignore my advice, and buy one of these ruins. *Poonto*-something, I forget now, although I do vividly remember causing mayhem in the builder's yard that morning, asking for 'two iron tubes with a screw in the middle for holding up a beam in an emergency', which I thought was a pretty good attempt, all in all, seeing as how I didn't study Spanish for O-Level. Cue blank faces in the office, however, which meant a search of the entire yard accompanied by Dirty Diego, gobbing and flobbing, and scratching his balls, until we came upon a pile of the cursed things. What a morning that was.

And no, we haven't managed to fix Jake's roof yet, either. Or 'El Fritter', as he is now called, to his extreme annoyance. Del's emergency repairs took rather longer than expected, and then we had about ten days of unsettled weather, but the sunshine is back now thankfully, so we absolutely, one-hundred percent have promised the fritter we will get it done before Christmas. Starting the day after tomorrow. Got to, as Chrissie and I are off to the UK for the holidays, flying Granada to Manchester on Christmas Eve, a brand-new service from that orange airline, but don't mention that to Phil the artist if you see him, visiting our elder daughter who has just started a new job in north Wales, then heading 'down west' to our younger daughter, and Chrissie's mother, travelling back Bristol to Malaga. Cheap flights, too, as we are going in the opposite direction to the mass exodus of Brits seeking winter sunshine. *See what good advice I am giving out? Travel against the flow, and don't buy the first old wreck you encounter. Saving you thousands, in the long run, and so much grief!*

Anyway, this letter. Chrissie is frowning with concentration. '*El contador*, we have to change *el contador*. The water meter. It has to be moved, ours is inside the house, apparently, *good job they told us, we've been looking for it, these past fifteen months, haven't we?,* and it has to go outside, according to some law passed in 2010, and another law from 2011, and then......the *BASTARDOS!* If we don't do it within thirty days of this letter, they will cut our supply. *Suministro.* That's supply, right? .....AND THE LETTER IS DATED 30TH

NOVEMBER. Where the hell has it been, this last ten days, coming from…..SEVILLE! I could have crawled from Seville in ten days. So that means we have effectively until Christmas to do this, or we will get cut off. What a way to treat a paying customer. That is completely outrageous.'

I have to agree. It's not as if we have ever been late paying, although the letter is actually addressed to old Joey Shepherd, maybe he always waited for the final demand before getting his cash out? 'Are you sure that is what it says, cut us off? Sounds a bit extreme, to be honest.'

She narrows her eyes, and flings the letter across the table. 'Well you have a read, Mister Russian O-Level, and a fat lot of good that did you, living in Spain! Unless you intend moving to Vladivostok.' *Anywhere to get out the way of you, my dearest…*

I finger the missive disinterestedly. 'Ah well, we knew this was coming, didn't we? A few of the neighbours have had to change theirs, Del and I can knock this off in………HANG ON A MINUTE! The bloody swines! We are gonna be tied up with Jake's roof until Christmas. Oh my God! We're gonna have to pay a plumber!'

Chrissie is chuckling. 'Not so tranquil now, are we! And no, WE are not going to pay a plumber, YOU are going to have to pay one!'

I have calmed down a bit, however. 'Don't worry, Lydia is coming here for a lesson tonight, I will ask her if she can come to the Aqualia office tomorrow, explain to them that we are busy this next two weeks, then going to the UK for Christmas, but will move the meter in the New Year. That is common sense, right? And the letter was in the post for ten days, not our fault was it? Surely they will grant us a short extension?'

'Oh that plug-woman in the *Aqualia* office?' she giggles. 'The one who thinks you are *Ha-cobo*? Who is convinced you are a woofter? Well best of luck with that, sunshine!'


The following morning Lydia and I make our way, a-back-o, to the office of the cursed water people. When I suggested to my student that she start a new career as a translator to dumb Brits, I never envisaged I might be one of her clients. Bit embarrassing, really, but what the heck, good practice for her, translating into English, and for me too, hopefully picking up a few choice phrases along the way. And renewing my acquaintance with those cheery souls of *Aqualia*, who today appear to have acquired a new member of staff. Plug-woman is still seated behind her desk, maintaining her slapped-arse demeanour, dealing with an old man, otherwise the place is deserted. But a new lady is seated at the back of the office, behind a completely clear desk, performing a passable impression of absolutely nothing. Mid-twenties maybe, tight sweater, even tighter jeans, and stilettos, a great improvement on her colleague I have to say, but still with that *couldn't give a toss about you losers* look on her pursed lips. Not the full slapped-arse style yet, she is new, obviously, still in training no doubt, but a cat's-arse, most certainly.

I turn to Lydia. 'Is she a plug, also?' I giggle.

'Oh yes, of course' my student replies. 'She is doing nothing!'

Just then the telephone rings, and I expect to see young-Plug spring into action. No doubt this is her moment, she has been lying in wait, like a coiled spring, a lion in the Serengeti, ready to pounce on an unsuspecting gazelle. Not that there is a telephone on her desk, mind you. Perhaps she has one of those modern ear-pieces buried under all that hair, explaining why she is constantly flicking it? Wrong. She remains completely immobile, and impassive, while old-plug answers the call. The old man turns to us with a *'don't you just hate it when that happens, I walked all the way down here, with my bad leg, early, and now some lazy swine, who is no doubt still tucked up in bed, or sprawled on the sofa, has called up and interrupted'* kind of look. 'I'm paying my water, *chica*!' he informs us, proudly, in case we happened to be wondering exactly what he was doing in the water board office, clutching what looks suspiciously like a red demand. *Well he certainly isn't here for the Christmas cheer, that's for damn sure.* Glancing round the office, you would never know it was the season of goodwill. Maybe that is what young-plug is up to. Perhaps she will start digging out the decorations, a tree with fairy lights, tinsel, balloons, paper-chains, a string of Christmas cards sent by appreciative customers, a box of crackers, and a tin of Cadbury's Roses for the counter. And here she goes, look! Now we're going to see something! She rises to her feet, slips her coat off the back of her chair, struggles into it with a heft of her chest, picks up her bag, and with a cry of 'I'm off to breakfast' to no-one in particular, totters across the room and out through the door.

*Breakfast? At eleven o'clock*? Didn't she have it, I dunno, but here's a suggestion, before she came to work? And why does she need sustenance, anyway? Not done a stroke, since we've been here, certainly. And how many calories has she expended, preening her hair? About three? Unbelievable.

Maybe I misunderstood. 'Did she say she was going to breakfast, Lydia?'

She seems unperturbed, however. 'Yes, it is usual, with these public employees. They allowed breakfast, during the morning.'

I am staggered. 'And how long are they allowed? And didn't she have her breakfast when she got up, this morning?'

'Oh, about an hour, I think' she smiles. 'In Espain it usual to have a break, middle morning, tostada, coffee, thees kind of thing.'

AN HOUR? They only work mornings, for pity's sake. This place will be locked and shuttered by half-one. At least the shops will open again at five, after the siesta. But this lot, like the electric board, and the council offices, only put in a paltry morning. And what is young-Plug actually doing? Is she training? Why doesn't she answer the phone, leave old-Plug to get on with serving the customers? Would make sense, surely. Questions questions. I can just imagine the uproar in Britain, social media, the local newspaper, about people doing absolutely naff-all, then going for a breakfast. I know, I know, Spain is different, but honestly, there are times….. Then again, I imagine young-Plug is now seated contentedly under a parasol, outside a pavement cafe, sipping a *cafe solo*, gossiping with her friends possibly, flicking through her messages, stress-level zero, cholesterol entirely normal, blood-pressure and heart-rate no cause for concern.

The old man meanwhile has turned and is regarding the departing figure with undisguised lust. 'Nice arse!' he comments, with a grin. *Don't look at me, mate. I am keeping schtum, in front of my student.*

Eventually, it is our turn. Now, I have already rehearsed the possible scenarios, for this very moment, given that just a few weeks ago I was here, with Lydia, inadvertently posing as someone else. My pupil has the offensive cutting-off letter, addressed to old Joey Shepherd, plus one of our previous bills, addressed to me, so we have agreed she will do the talking, and I will remain seated, until called upon to do something, no idea what, as this cannot be that difficult, can it? Letter was in the post for ten days, let your left hand know what the right is doing, please, we are off to the UK for Christmas, but we promise to get the meter shifted after the New Year. Simples, as they say. *Wrong*. Plug studies both communications intensely, gazes across at me, opens her mouth as if to speak, closes it again, glances at Lydia, studies the paperwork again, taps her keyboard, and pauses while the gears turn in her head. Something is about to happen, but what? Surely, she will smile, sheepishly, say something like *'oh those accounts people, what are they like? Yes, no problem, sort it out after Christmas, have a good holiday in England, take a warm coat, mind!'*

*Nope*. She looks me square in the eye. *If she accuses me of impersonating Hacobo, and implies I am a woofter, I will jump up, beat my chest, and start talking about the Bears match last weekend, in a deep voice, hell of a game, hell of a game. But if she asks if I am Jose Ocana Pastor, I will blow my top. There are not two people in this town who are that stupid, surely*? But no, once again I am caught completely flat-footed. 'Tee-too-lar?'

*Not a clue*. I stare helplessly at my translator. 'She is asking about your title.'

*Well, that is an easy one*. Chrissie has been known to refer to me as *Your Royal Highness*, or *His Lordship*, on occasions, for some strange reason, but bearing no connections to the aristocracy, I am of course plain old *Mister*. I stifle the urge to giggle. 'Mister.'

Now it is Lydia's turn to look puzzled. 'No sorry, your title. *Tee-too-lar*. How you say thees in Eengliss?'

Well sounds like *title* to me, to be honest. 'Well, title, your designation, Mister, Mrs, Miss, that kind of thing.'

She takes a deep breath. *Not easy, this translation stuff, is it.* 'No, your title, on the bill. It has not been changed.' And she taps the account, which clearly reads *Austin John Richards*, followed by our address.

Can't see the problem, quite honestly. I smile serenely. 'Well those are my names, in the wrong order actually, but that is me!'

'No no, the title, it was not changed, look!' and she points to some minuscule printing, barely visible to the naked eye, about a third the way down the page, bearing the legend *Titular. Jose Ocana Pastor.*

Well so what? Big deal. Someone forgot to change the *Titular*. Woopy-doo. My name is on the bill, so who cares? Get it changed, and let's get on with our lives.

*Wrong*. 'No, sorree, you need a new contract. Thees contract still in name of Jose Ocana Pastor.'

My turn to take a deep breath. 'Sorry Lydia, but I didn't type the bill, did I? My name must be on the contract, as there it is! Our lawyer did all this, when we bought the house, and the bills arrive each quarter with my name on. I don't see what the problem is.' And so confident am I of being entirely in the right, I wave the bill at Plug, tapping the name and address box. 'Mi nombre!'' *So get your typewriter out and get it changed.*

Plug narrows her eyes. *If she calls me a fritter that is it, I am off*. She turns to Lydia, and an exchange of Spanish, containing the words *titular*, and *contracto*, takes place. My star pupil exhales deeply, puffing out her cheeks. 'I know it sounds ridiculous, but the bill is still in the name of Jose Ocana Pastor. Your name is the address, only. You understand? They put your name, above the address, but the contract was never changed. You need new contract, now.'

Ridiculous? No, this is way, way beyond ridiculous. How can one single sheet of paper show two different names? Official paper, too, as arranged by Pedro, our Spanish lawyer. Anyway, I need a new contract. 'So where do I sign?'

Cue more discussions. 'She say, you must to pay fifty euros, and seventy-five centimos, for new contract. Plus, she need to see your knee.'

*HOW MUCH? FOR A BIT OF PAPER? And what is the extra fifteen-bob for? A Mars Bar, for young-Plug's breakfast?* Inwardly seething, but trying not to show it, in case someone calls me a fritter, or Jose Ocana Pastor, I turn to my student, who is clearly enjoying this, unless she too is inwardly seething. At me. 'Look Lydia, I have to get this sorted today, as we are starting on Jake's roof tomorrow. I will call Chrissie, ask her to come here with the knees, so I need to go to the bank right now, get the money out. Are you coming?'

Of course she is, no point staying in the office talking to Plug, especially when there is free, intelligent English conversation to be had, is there? Well something like that, anyway. The cash-point is only a few hundred yards up the street, and the news is bad. It only has fifty-euro notes. *On the other hand...*'Do you know what the English expression *'getting your own back'* means, Lydia? Well, the contract costs a ridiculous seventy-five cents extra, and I only have two fifty-euro notes, so Plug is going to have to give me forty-nine euros and twenty-five cents change!'

'My student has the decency to sound concerned. 'Oh no, no, don't worry, I have seventy-five cents I can give you!'

I smile widely. 'No. Thank you, but no. I will make her give me the change, as punishment for having such a stupid price. That is *getting my own back*!'

Chrissie is waiting outside Aqualia with the knees, but cannot stop as she is meeting Marie from the library for coffee. 'If you bump into young-Plug down there, say hello from me!' She has not the faintest idea what I am talking about of course. That will be a conversation for later.

Right, back into the office, and I hand over two crisp fifties, smiling sweetly. Plug looks as if she's swallowed a lemon. 'Do you have seventy-five centimos?' We both shake our heads, stifling huge grins, so huffing mightily, she flings open her cash drawer and pointedly slaps down my change. My own back has been got. *Wrong*. Time for Lydia to request a short extension, on the cut-off deadline. And you can guess what the reply is, can't you? Not Plug's fault about the post, was it? And the cut-off has been ordered on the computer system, a laughable notion given that they don't even have cashless payments, in this throw-back to 1963. *Didn't get my own back, did I?* Plus, I am now going to have to pay a plumber, and I don't know one, in this town. Well I do actually, but his name is Del, and we are going to be fifty feet off the ground, tomorrow. Curses, as Dick Dastardly might have said.

'Does Plug know the name of a plumber, please?' I enquire. She does, it appears, pushing a business-card across the desk. 'Electra-Man' he is called, apparently, which doesn't inspire confidence that he might know anything about moving water meters, does it, although the small-print at the bottom of the card assures us he does.

Now, already I am having heart palpitations about letting a stranger loose on my house, and we haven't even spoken to the bloke yet. But the fact remains that many local tradesmen and DIY-ers can be complete bodgers. Some of the lash-ups you encounter in this town defy belief, quite frankly, and a large proportion of those horrors involve new water meters. Basically, a rectangular aluminium trap-door, maybe fifteen inches by ten, has to be fitted into the outside front wall of the house, maybe six inches or so above street level, and the meter, and associated pipework, go inside the door. Del and I have performed a number of these tasks, and we usually charge around thirty euros, plus materials. Mark the outline of the door, cut a neat, straight rectangle in the wall using an angle-grinder/disc-cutter, then punch a hole through to the inside of the house for the new pipe, using an electric chisel. The door then fits neatly, secured by a flop of mortar the same colour as the wall, and there you have it, a lovely neat job. Inexplicably, however, the locals just bang a huge hole in the wall using the chisel, whack in the door, and flop a load of mortar, usually the wrong colour, into the jagged, irregular hole, then go and sit under a parasol somewhere. Incomprehensible. I cannot think of a single reason why someone would not cut a neat rectangle, even if they had only the bare minimum amount of pride in their work. But that is the reality.

But not on our house, however, of this I am adamant. We have a beautiful grey and cream granite finish on our facade, and no way am I permitting electric chisels anywhere near it. Lydia calls Electra-Man, who by a stroke of good fortune can do the work this week, and impresses on him the need for a neat and tidy job. A hundred and thirty euros, all-in, including a brand new meter supplied by Aqualia, who are good friends of his, apparently. *Yeah, I bet they are.* Clearly Del and I are under-pricing….

Two evenings later and Electra-Man arrives, armed with pipes, fittings, the aluminium trap-door, a new meter from his 'friends' at Aqualia, *but no disc-cutter*. Grrrr. 'No corto-disco?' I enquire, politely but firmly. 'Remember, I want the wall cut straight, like this one?' And I indicate Loli's water-door, fitted neatly, perfectly, into her facade, which is the same finish as ours, just a different shade. He babbles something along the lines of 'don't worry' and 'it'll be fine', but I'm not having it. 'It'll be fine' doesn't cut the mustard, so I pop downstairs and dig out my disc-cutter, plus extension-lead, then mime cutting a nice straight rectangular hole, just so that no-one is under any doubt. He nods in agreement, but is no doubt thinking *'fussy English idiot, what's wrong with just banging a huge hole, then filling it with plop? I got a parasol I need to sit under, after all.'*

Leaving the front door ajar, in case Electra-Man needs to borrow any more of my tools, I head back inside and flop on the sofa. I am utterly beat, I can tell you. Completely whacked. Been a hell of a few days, on Jake's roof, long days too, up and down steps and ladders, lifting, carrying, and the damage was worse than we feared, too. Should be watertight by Christmas Eve, though, it *has* to be watertight by Christmas Eve, but boy oh boy, I am feeling my age. And my evening's work is not complete yet, either, I still have an English class on Skype with Rosa, my student who moved to the north of Spain, but who was reluctant to give up her lessons. Great to be popular, and in demand, but who knew early-retirement was going to be like this?

The unmistakable sound of a disc-cutter, hopefully travelling in a straight line, invades my tranquility, but that is a good thing, all in all. Get the job done, get Aqualia off my back, one less thing to worry about. And I am being completely un-Spanish about this work, too. One of my least-favourite aspects of life here is the extremely annoying, to me, habit of the locals to just stand around and stare at any form of construction. Just last week there was an electrician in the road fiddling with the street lights, and there must have been half a dozen neighbours gathered round the foot of his ladder, shouting advice, like a pack of hounds baying at a cat up a tree. So no way am I watching a bloke cutting a rectangle in a wall. He is a professional. He knows what he is doing. There is nothing I can add to the narrative, no value to my presence. Besides, I need to get my laptop out, ready for my pupil.

The next hour passes quickly, as it always does with Rosa on Skype, albeit punctuated by the noise of construction, and the shouting of Spaniards, emanating from the street. Just as well Electra-Man quoted for the entire job, rather than by the hour, as I wouldn't want the neighbours holding him up, and inadvertently increasing my bill, would I? I close down the computer, and am suddenly aware of the silence. Has he finished? Has he got fed up with being bellowed at, and cleared off? Surely he must be used to that, being entirely normal, for him? Why wouldn't people gather round, and holler? Opening the front door, and stepping into the street, I am confronted by the grotesque spectacle of my alleged plumber with his hands in a bucket of white mortar, sloshing it into the two-inch gap around the water door. *He cut the rectangle out perfectly. But he cut it too big.* He glances up, spots the look of sheer horror on my face, and smiles. 'Almost finished! You can paint the mortar grey, when it dries.'

I am sick to the pit of my stomach. Our beautiful facade, ruined by this complete, utter cowboy. Paint it? I'll give him paint it. I want to grab the bucket, stuff the remaining mortar into his mouth, hold him by the ears until it dries, and paint it a different shade of fleshy-pink. See how he likes it. Patching this mess now would be like fixing a hole in a tiger with a slice of zebra. Beyond belief, surely anyone with a grain of intelligence would have cut the oblong the same size as the door, just a few millimetres over all round, and fixed it discretely in place with grey cement? Instead of this play-fight in an infants school, this rampage by toddlers. Too late to complain now, of course, the damage is done, for all time. In sheer, utter rage I snatch up my cutter, furiously wind up the cable, place them in the hallway, grab the money, stamp back outside, slap it in his hand, and dive back inside, slamming the door, and collapse on the sofa in sheer abject desperation. Inconsolable.

Thus Chrissie discovers me, half an hour later, when she returns from her student. 'What in the name of all things holy is that God-awful mess outside?' she wants to know. 'Have we been visited by lunatics? Is this how so-called professionals behave? I could have made a better job than that with one hand tied behind my back, and my head in a paper bag. And do we actually have any water? Is the new meter in place?'

'No idea' I groan. 'I was so angry, I forgot to look' and I slouch into the kitchen, turn on the tap, and after a few feeble splutters, a goodly flow of water appears. So there must be a meter in the street, but I haven't the heart to go out and check.

'So what about the metal key, for the water door? Or do you have to get your pliers out again, as we did for Jake's?'

'Dunno.'

'So what about the meter, and the stop-cock? Has he done it correctly? Please don't tell me you have paid him, without checking?'

I take a deep breath, and place my head in my hands. 'I was so furious when I saw what he'd done, ruining the front of the house, I just wanted him off the premises as soon as possible. So I didn't get a receipt, or anything, didn't check, didn't look. And I haven't moved off the sofa since.'

She flops down next to me and slips her arm round my shoulder. 'So can you do anything to make it look better?' she enquires, softly.

I raise my face to the ceiling, exhaling softly. 'Yeah, I've got it all worked out, actually.' A smile crosses my face for the first time in about an hour. 'My huge man-brain has it all figured! At the builders they sell these edging-tiles, in grey, over a foot long, two or three inches wide. What I am going to do is make something like a picture frame, an edging round the trap-door, mitre the corners, you know, on an angle, just like a frame, so that will cover the horrible white plaster. The tiles will be a different shade of grey, a contrast, not fifty shades, just two, but it will look great, will finish it off beautifully.'

She brightens considerably. 'Fantastic! Can you really do that?'

'Of course, of a certainty, one hundred per-cent.'

'Great! So why are you so upset? I mean, Electra-Toss has made a huge mess, but you can rectify it, put it right, so what's the matter?'

'Well the problem is I cannot do it until the New Year, can I? I am completely tied up until Christmas, then we are off to Manchester, then the builders will be closed, probably, so it will be New Year until I can start.'

She is doing her best to sound sympathetic. 'So, you're busy. That isn't your fault, is it? You will get round to it in good time, won't you? What is the problem?'

I am rubbing my face with my hands. 'The problem is, that horrible, crappy job will be on full display, to people walking up and down the street, for the next three weeks or so, and I just cannot stand the thought that people will think that I did it, that people will say 'blimey, look at the lash-up that Englishman made of his water-door. It's my pride, isn't it? Actually I'm thinking about putting up a sign, *this wasn't me, it was Electra-Toss!*'

She is really laughing now. 'Do you really think that anyone Spanish will worry about that? Have you seen some of the monumental disasters in this town? And what British people will see it? Seen the state of some of the houses in this street, lately? More cracks than Cheddar Gorge! Just stop worrying, and forget all about it.

At that moment there is a loud rat-a-tat-tat on the front door. Just what I don't need right now, some nosey Spaniard telling me what a balls-up the front of the house looks. I struggle to my feet, and open the door a crack. *Deep joy. Fernando.*

'*Jabby del passo*, neighbour!' he cries, at deafening volume. *That reminds me, Chrissie was asking what I wanted for Christmas. I need to put ear-defenders on my list for Santa. Essential equipment, living in Spain.* I do my best to look confused. '*Jabby del passo!*' he repeats, gesticulating wildly at something in the street. *He's not going away, is he? Better see what this jabby thing is. No peace until I do.* I follow him into the street, and sure enough he is indicating the water-door. *Yeah yeah, I know, I know, no need to rub it in, is there? How do I say it wasn't me, it was Electra-Toss, in Spanish?* It seems however that Chrissie might have been correct. 'Beautiful job, neighbour, but you need to pick up your *jabby*.' And he points at the little metal key, protruding from the new door.

'Thank you, Fernando' I smile, bashfully.

But he isn't finished with me yet. 'What you must do, is get some grey paint, and cover the white plaster, when it dries. Then it will be perfect. No rush, after Christmas will do!' *Well blow me down. Why didn't I think of that?*

I slump back on the sofa and start to laugh. Such a huge release of tension after a traumatic couple of hours. *A beautiful job, neighbour.* Who'd have thought it? Never ceases to amaze me, Spain. Just one small fly in the ointment, however.

*Really got her own back, old-Plug, didn't she?*


## CHAPTER 13. AND WE THOUGHT LAST CHRISTMAS WAS CRAZY…..

Two days before Christmas Eve, and I am utterly, totally and completely exhausted. Shattered, battered. Beaten up, beaten down, covered in wounds and abrasions, aching in places I would not have believed possible. If I never see another ladder, another bucket of mortar, another yard-long brick, another length of rubber sheeting, another roof tile, and another whingeing, whining Cockney wide-boy before Kingdom Come, that will be fine by me. But we did it. Jake's roof. All done. A day early, too, praise be. And this was no *Electra-Man* job, either. Put our very souls into it, I can tell you, and there are pieces of my soul scattered all over that roof, went the extra mile, we did, proud of ourselves, we are. Climbed down the cursed ladder for the final time, and hugged. Let go again pretty swiftly, mind you, as we were both absolutely reeking, but still, it's the thought that counts, right?

And now, all I want to do is sleep, hibernate until Spring, like Yogi Bear and Boo-boo. Wake me up in April. Can't do that, of course, as we are off to north Wales the day after tomorrow, which, now that the thrice-damned roof of *El Fritter* is out of the way, I can start really looking forward to. Chrissie has it all organised, as always, given that I have been living and breathing nothing else but mortar these past few weeks. The passports and boarding cards, which she always does anyway, bearing in mind that if I cannot be trusted not to lose my wallet, being stuck abroad without a passport would be a monumental disaster. And the parking at Granada airport, wherever that is, given that, despite being frequent visitors to that magnificent city, we have never seen a single aeroplane flying about. Malaga yes, Michael O'Leary's finest are often to be seen circling, plus the orange ones too, and whisper this, but not to Pieter, please, the occasional red, white and blue of BA, and there is even a giant DIY warehouse at the end of the runway where you can plane-spot, if you are that way inclined, whilst trying desperately not to drop that box of expensive tiles you are attempting to stuff into the car boot. But Granada airport? Not a clue. Still, there will surely be a sign, won't there? Although hang on, this is Spain, so maybe there will be a complete absence. Perhaps I need to ask Mr Google.

So anyway, here are my plans for the next two days, providing I can heave my broken corpse out of this bed. Breakfast, a plate of ham and eggs on toast, washed down by a pot of coffee. Morning paper on the Kindle, with my feet up. Maybe check that Chrissie has packed all my holiday gear, which actually will fill less than half of a Ryanair-size carry-on, although I distinctly recall that camping trip to Jersey in 1982 when she forgot to pack my shoes. Still haven't completely forgiven her for that one, especially as she waited until I'd got my trainers soaking wet on the beach, before breaking the bad news. Can you imagine the embarrassment for me, a Jim Bergerac-lookalike, trying to blag my way into the *Royal George*, in a pair of sodden Reebok's? *So gotta keep her on her toes with my luggage.* Then, late morning, stroll up and see if anyone fancies a swift Christmas half, following which, as that looks distinctly like blazing sunshine forcing its way through the shutters, lunch in the garden, might even uncover the pool, water will be icy but I can bake in the sun for a while then plunge into the depths, get the old corpuscles pumping. People pay a lot of money to have that done to them in fancy spas, so I've heard. Then, at sunset, up on the terrace with a cold one to watch the olives coming in, a Rick Stein special for dinner washed down with a couple of glasses of red. Is that a plan, or is that a plan? And the following day, repeat.

My wife, however, has other ideas. Although she does at least grant me a temporary stay of execution, until after the eggs, and half the coffee, have been consumed, before informing me of how the next two days will actually pan out. 'Right, listen to this very carefully.' *Words almost guaranteed to make my eyes glaze over, actually, but it will surely turn out worse for me, in the long run, if I fail to pay attention.* 'Tonight' she smiles, 'we have been invited to a kiddies' Nativity play, at St Francisco school. Paloma's little sister will be appearing, and she has asked us if we would like to go, it's usually only family who are invited so we are really lucky. You didn't say you had any plans, did you, so I said we would love to go, seven o-clock this evening.'

*I'm struggling to keep up, quite honestly, and yes, my eyes have glazed over, although hopefully only I know that.* To be honest, I'm not that keen, although give the Spanish their due, they do organise these childrens' events well, and we really enjoyed the nippers Easter procession, plus the choral concert last year, and besides, I was a kid once, believe it or not. A king too, in our school Nativity when I was about ten, and of course, the sheer joy of watching our own daughters' school plays and activities, in years past. *So snap out of it Richards, you old grump.* Christmas comes but once a year. *But Paloma? Do I know her? I'm struggling here, quite honestly.* Hang on, though, wasn't she the girl who came to the original conversation classes at the library a few times, before Chrissie took her on as a private student? About eighteen, wasn't she, studying to be a teacher, or something? But her little sister? Did I know she had one? Have I been told about her? Blowed if I can remember. *Not going well, so far, is it*? What could the sister's name be? Anna, probably, I mean, it's not my fault I get confused, with hundreds of different women called Anna, in this town, Chrissie is constantly regaling me with takes of Anna this, Anna that, and as we all know, I'm a bear of very little brain.

She narrows her eyes, having twigged, no doubt. 'You really don't have the foggiest idea what I am talking about, do you?'

I haul myself, painfully, to my full height in the chair, and adopt my best indignant-face, with an added Paddington Bear stare. *Right, time to wing it.* 'I will have you know, my dearest, that I am fully conversant. San Francisco school is next to the church of the same name. Paloma is the trainee teacher, your student. And her little sister is Anna, I remember you telling me all about her.' And I poke out my tongue, then rapidly withdraw it, in case traces of fried egg are still in evidence. 'So there!'

She doesn't believe me, I can tell, but in the absence of proof to the contrary, by some miracle I have passed the first test. *Oh yes!* With her eyes locked firmly on mine, in an *I know you are bluffing, really* way, she reaches behind her and produces a travel agent's flyer bearing the legend *'Viaje a Belen'*. Trip to Bethlehem. 'There. I bought you that as a Christmas present!'

Oh. My. Giddy. Aunt! as my mother used to say. I have always wanted to visit the Holy Land. Blimey, this must have cost her a packet, what a wonderful present! I mean, her pension is kept for use as a 'travel fund', but I had no idea she had squirreled that much away. Ignoring my shattered spine, I leap up and plant an eggy kiss on her cheek, which she wipes away, theatrically. I am grinning from ear to ear. 'Yes' she continues, 'it means an early start tomorrow morning, unfortunately, but I thought it looked good fun, what do you think?'

Hold on, tomorrow morning? We're off to Wales the following day, so how can we possibly be…….. maintaining my smile, I return my gaze to the notice, and continue reading. '*De chocolate. En Rute. Autobus ida y vuelta. Precio 7 euros.*' So we're not off to Israel, then. *Cursed Spanish.* The word *Belen* does indeed mean 'Bethlehem', but also 'Nativity Scene', a fact I was well aware of, given that our own, all six feet by four of it, is standing proudly in the lounge, erected heroically by Chrissie last week, with man-shepherds, house where live donkey and shitting gypsy, while I was fixing that cursed roof with that cursed Cockney. We are off to see a chocolate Nativity, in some place called Rute, a return coach trip, apparently, and scanning the rest of the pamphlet, which I should have done first, of course, it appears the trip also includes visits to museums of sugar, anise, Spanish ham and chorizo. *That'll teach me to wing it*. Sounds great, actually, but just one potential fly in the ointment. 'An early start in the morning? How early?' And Del and I were originally supposed to be working tomorrow, so how did you know we would be finished, when you bought the tickets?'

She beams with pride. 'I called Del a few days ago, swore him to secrecy, and he said you would probably finish yesterday. And the travel agent said we need to be at the bus station at seven thirty, bit early I know, but it looks a fun day out, don't you think?' I do indeed, and to prove it she gets another eggy cheek. The other one this time, a matching pair. *Probably best if I keep quiet about the Holy Land, however, so don't say anything, please, if you bump into her in town…..*

The rest of my day goes pretty much as planned, apart from the olive-pickers and the beer on the terrace, and just before seven we arrive outside the school, as we're British and therefore always punctual. To find a massive hullabaloo going on inside. Has it started early? Surely not. Chrissie giggles. 'Listen to that! No doubt we are in the right place, is there? This is why there is no need for signs, in this country. Just listen out for the noise!' Into the entrance hall and we are confronted by about a million pushchairs, all left in a haphazard fashion to seemingly cause the maximum chaos. 'And they park their buggies like they park their cars! Have you ever seen anything like this?' We start picking our way through the melee, when a thought crosses my mind. Pushchairs? For ten year-olds? Obviously, there will be younger siblings, and the Spanish do tend to have large families, but realistically, how many people can be inside? Say twenty-five kids in the class, plus the parents, but not all of those will be able to make it, so forty adults possibly, call it seventy people in total, tops?

I open the door for Chrissie, to be assaulted by a barrage of noise, and a scene reminiscent of opening-time at John Lewis on a Boxing Day morning. Blimey, is this supposed to be a Nativity play, or a small war? A seething scrum of humanity, bellowing, hollering, like last orders on a New Year's Eve in a pub full of thirsty dockers. I have a good six inches on most of the crowd, but all I can see are heads. Mums, dads, grandparents, aunties, cousins, plus, it wouldn't surprise me, Old Uncle Tom Cobley and all. Together with his old grey mare, for all I know. Who the hell are all these people? Suddenly, a female voice calls out, 'Jonneee, I here!'. Well that's as maybe, whoever you are, but I'm wedged in, some joker is standing on my foot and I sincerely hope that is not a hand, jabbing me in the groin. Chrissie meanwhile has completely disappeared, trampled underfoot possibly, but who can tell in this stampede?

Suddenly, without warning, there is a brief lull in hostilities, and I am able to inch my way around the back wall, extracting my privates from someone's sweaty grasp, and find myself in a blessed six inches of space, and a better view of what is happening on the far side of the hall. What the…. there is nobody there! We are all hemmed in on this side, like sardines on our way to a canning factory, yet maybe two-thirds of the room seems empty. I cannot actually see the floor, but is there a fence of some sort, preventing free movement? I glimpse Chrissie chatting away happily to Paloma, so at least she has made it unscathed, being far nimbler, and closer to the ground, no doubt, whereas I, conscious of my size, am wary of treading on some diminutive Spaniard. Or inadvertently grasping anyone's groin, of course. One thing is for certain, there is no way the play is starting at seven, not that we seriously expected it to, knowing, as we do, that start times in this country are mere suggestions, bearing no relationship to actual reality.

Gradually I am able to squeeze my way towards the girls, and for the first time snatch a glimpse at the floor, and the precise cause of this ridiculous chaos. *Toddlers*! A Nativity for two-year-olds. Oh my word, how utterly charming, there must be thirty of them, at least, arranged in a living village scene, tiny nursery-school tables and chairs forming authentic-looking market stalls, with bakers, fishmongers, fruit and veg, a butchers, a haberdashery, a cake shop, with each little 'stall-holder' dressed in Biblical costume. Standing behind the village is a cardboard-box Roman fort complete with centurions in togas and tiny sandals, waving plastic swords, then the Three Kings, one of whom is in authentic black-face, regally clutching their precious gifts, a couple of angels with huge fluffy wings, and finally the stable, Mary, Joseph, and in a tiny straw-filled manger, a plastic doll wrapped in swaddling bands. In the middle of this enchanting scene is the *piece de resistance*, a baby, eight or nine months old maybe, a little girl, sitting up, on a patch of plastic grass, surrounded by a white picket fence, dressed in a sheep's costume, a fluffy ball of white, so unbelievably cute. And guarding her, outside the fence, four little shepherds, with tea-towels around their heads, dressed in hessian sacks.

Overcome by emotion, choking back the tears, I approach the girls, and we hug. Paloma first, then Chrissie. No idea why I am gripping my wife, actually, as I last saw her not five minutes ago, but it just seems the right thing to do, incapable as I am of speech, without blubbering. Truly, in my lifetime, I have never witnessed anything like this, and all my Christmases have come at once. 'What do you think of my little sister?' Chrissie's student smiles.

Blimey, in all the kerfuffle I had forgotten about the sister. Not a clue. What was her name again? Anna? Is she here? *Time to wing it again.* 'Yes!' I lie, although hopefully only I know that. 'So pretty!' There, that should do it, hopefully, although my wife is staring in a *you are so full of bull* kind of way. She knows me, is well aware that my man-brains, although more than capable of figuring out how to cover Electra-Man's hideous cock-up with a tiled frame around the water-meter door, simply do not have the capacity for remembering people, or names, especially all these blinking Annas. *Got away with it for now, however. Maybe.*

Meanwhile the toddlers, being toddlers, are misbehaving mightily. The centurions are staging a massive sword-fight, the baker is whacking the butcher with a plastic loaf, who in turn is jabbing the fishmonger with a rubber steak. One of the angels is behaving in an extremely un-angelic manner in the cake shop, and the shepherds are poking the baby sheep with their crooks, trying to make her baa. Chaos descends upon the Nativity village. Mothers are attempting to separate the warring stall-holders, dads with smart-phones are taking photos, grannies are waving madly and Paloma dives into the melee like a modern-day Bo-Peep, to rescue the little lamb from a severe prodding. And this being Spain, everyone is bawling and shouting at the same time. Chrissie and I, meanwhile, are leaning against the wall, shaking with laughter, shedding a few emotional tears, no doubt. I know I am. Unbelievable. Simply unbelievable.

Suddenly, if it were possible, the noise intensifies, as through the door crash three blokes dressed as kings, Gold, Frankincense and Myrrh, each bearing a large sack of festive gifts. The kiddies, forgetting their Nativity-Wars, hurtle across the room, en-masse, pushing and shoving, struggling between the legs of the frazzled parents, in one huge unholy bunfight. Three chairs are rapidly produced for the royal visitors, just in time too as within seconds they are engulfed by rampant nippers. Several school-helpers dressed as fairies attempt to restore order, and to steer the exultant ankle-biters into an orderly queue, but there is no chance. Within seconds, each King has at least three little terrors clinging to his robes, others scrambling for the best positions, and the fairies appear to have abandoned all hope of quelling this kindergarten riot. One fortunate centurion has wrenched a football from one of the kings and is attempting to dribble his way past the baker, who is laying into all and sundry with his loaf, when suddenly the little girl from the cake shop dives on the ball like an All-Black, a rubber steak flies through the air catching the fishmonger on the side of his head, he bursts into tears, then snatches a shepherd's crook and shoves it unceremoniously between the legs of Frankincense. Who looks less than impressed to have had his Christmas ruined, quite possibly. As does one of the fairies, who I imagine might well be Mrs Frankincense, in real life. That's Christmas night gone for a Burton, in their house.

Time for us to bail out of this lunacy, before I have a sheep-tending implement shoved where the sun don't shine. Hugging Paloma, who has somehow shed her fluffy burden, we stumble gratefully, breathlessly, into the silent street, reflecting on what was undoubtedly the craziest Nativity scene of our entire lives. 'Did you see the look on that king's face?' Chrissie splutters, 'I bet he will be speaking with a high voice, for a few days!'

'And walking with a limp, I imagine!' I giggle, 'and his wife didn't look too chuffed, either. She won't need to get her Christmas underwear out, this year!'

'Well that's one blessing, I suppose!' comes the not-unexpected reply.

We walk along in silence for a few minutes, before my wife takes my arm. 'Right, now, be honest, you didn't have a clue what was happening tonight, did you? I could see that far-away look in your eyes! Come on, time to confess!'

*Told you, didn't I? Rumbled.* I puff myself up in mock indignation, all the while crossing my fingers. 'Not at all. I recognised Paloma, of course. I must admit, I did think it was going to be a proper Nativity story, a play, and I didn't realise the kids would be toddlers, but I think you will find I was completely up to scratch with everything.'

'So what did you think about her little sister Anna?'

*Not letting go, is she?* 'Well, you will admit it was fairly chaotic in there, to say the least, wasn't it? So in the general melee, I have to admit I didn't actually spot the sister. I was bluffing, to Paloma. Now please leave me alone! I am having enough trouble hauling my earthly remains up this damned great hill, having toiled NON-STOP for the last few weeks! I need a beer, after all that HARD WORK!'

*Nope. Not happening.* 'So you didn't see the little lamb, then, in the middle of the Nativity village?'

*And I run my neck right into the noose.* 'Of course I did, that was the cutest thing I have ever seen, having a baby dressed as a sheep!'

*Checkmate.* 'Oh, so you do admit to seeing Paloma's little sister, then?'

It takes a minute for this latest nugget to permeate my grey-matter. *Not my fault, is it? Been a hard couple of weeks, right?* 'A baby? Blimey, Paloma is, what, eighteen? Bit of a gap, isn't it!'

I suddenly realise I am alone, as Chrissie has stopped dead. 'That is it, I am taking you to the doctor, when we get back after Christmas. You know all this. Second marriage, isn't it. Rosa, Paloma's mother, was married before. We went to see the new baby, last Spring, didn't we? Louise made a little patchwork quilt, for the cot, didn't she?'

I am scratching my head, in desperation. 'Well I forgot, all right? Last Spring? I can barely remember my name, these days. A quilt? What does that have to do with me? And who is Louise, anyway?'

She is open-mouthed, rooted to the spot. 'You steaming, blathering nincompoop. Louise? Our elder daughter? Remember her, do you? Where we are going, the day after tomorrow? Her latest hobby is quilting? She made that beautiful patchwork one, don't you remember?'

I screw up my eyes, in a vain attempt to get my feeble brain into gear. I just need to sit down, with a glass of red. Or four. Rick Stein can go to hell, we're having sandwiches. Puffing, we reach the top of the hill, and our front door. 'Anyway, never mind all that nonsense' I pant, indicating the water-meter door, 'what I reckon is four of those long edging tiles, mitre the corner joints, some of that grey fix-n-grout, will look lovely, don't you think?'

Which earns me another bruise, to go with my collection...


The following morning, at the unearthly hour of seven-fifteen, we exit our front door, to be swept away in a torrent of olive-pickers and a rhapsody of windpipes, heading down *aback-o* towards the bus station. Never seen so many people on the move at the same time, in this town. So this is what it's like, before the dawn cracks. Who knew? Although quite why we are assembling in the middle of the night Heaven only knows, as a quick check on Mr Google revealed this *Rute* place to be lying in the hinterland, on the borders of Jaen, Granada and Cordoba provinces, not a million miles from where we live. Half an hour, max, in the car, I am guessing, although there might be huge great mountains in the way, requiring a thirty-mile detour, and I cannot imagine a coach negotiating some of these crazy hairpin bends. Impossible to tell, from an online map. Mr Google might be all-powerful, but he ain't no *Ordnance Survey*, is he? All will no doubt be revealed, in the fullness of time. Another Spanish voyage of discovery. Or it will be, when I eventually come-to, in about three hours time.

'NEIGHBOUR! Where are you going?' Oh for pity's sake. It is pitch dark, I am barely awake, my body still thinks it is yesterday. Who is shouting, at this hour? Isn't there a law about that kind of behaviour? Ahead, illuminated grotesquely in the streetlight, stomach bursting out of his ratty overalls, it can only be one person. Fernando. Going olive-picking, no doubt. *Right, I'll teach you, matey, disturbing my sleep like this.* Has to love sweets, doesn't he, with a gut like that? Can't all be beer, can it? 'We are going to the Belen of CHOCOLATE, Fernando! In Rute. On a coach.' *There. Give him something to salivate about, whilst he is harvesting.* Although we have previously wondered what his function might be, in the team. Cannot possibly be bending over, gathering up the fallers. I bet he hasn't seen his feet in years. And whacking the tree with a damn great stick? Hardly seems likely. Shouting, we reckon. Bellowing advice. That must be his task, for which he is eminently qualified, if you ask me.

'Well bring some home for me, neighbour!' he brays, waking-up the rest of the town. *Oh we will, neighbour. The empty wrappers...*

Outside the bus station is the usual total Spanish mayhem. Tractors and trailers, wheezing and belching out fumes, and olive-pickers, well, just wheezing, completely blocking the street. The air is thick with the enticing aromas of diesel, and phlegm. 'I hope the coach is here already!' Chrissie giggles, 'imagine trying to drive through this lot?'

'Well watch where you're stepping' I warn. 'you know the old saying, *as slippery as snot*!'

She screws up her face in disgust. 'Oh, you horrible old man! You're putting me off my breakfast.'

'Just telling you, darling' I snigger, 'don't want you getting anything on those extremely expensive shoes, and jeans, you bought in that *Bimba* place in Cordoba, do we? Just remember what happened to you, the last time we had a day-out, when you trod in that pig-piddle?'

'SHUT UP, RIGHT!'

*Oh yeah! One-nil to the boys, and it ain't even daylight yet!* But hang on a minute. Breakfast? Two rounds of toast and a mug of instant, due to this ungodly departure time? Call that a breakfast, on a Christmas? Or as near to Christmas as makes no difference? Actually, we have no idea what is happening about meals, on this little jaunt, given that the bumph we got from the travel-agent was vague to the point of being worse than useless, regarding a return time. *Tardey* was all it said, afternoon, and bearing in mind there is no Spanish term for 'evening', that could mean any time from mid-day until getting on for midnight. Still, the seventh rule of travel is *something will turn up*, and in this country of a million cafes where *menu del dia*, three courses plus wine, can be had for as little as seven euros, we are unlikely to go hungry. *And we're off to a chocolate factory....*

Stepping gingerly around the harvesters, keeping a wary lookout for slippery, unsavoury deposits, we squeeze our way into the bus station, where a single coach is drawn up in one of the bays. Cannot be ours, however, as about a hundred shouty Spaniards are crowding around, many of whom are bearing Ryanair-approved hand luggage. The sides of the bus are raised, and the harassed-looking driver is shoveling suitcases on board for all he is worth, like the fireman on the Flying Scotsman. Baggage safely stowed, the passengers attempt speedy-boarding, all at the same time, a physical impossibility given the girth of some of the back-sides in evidence. 'So where is our coach, then?' I groan, 'late, as usual, I imagine.' I just need to flop down in my seat, any seat, and catch up on my beauty-sleep. Wake me up when we arrive in chocolate-city.

'That is it, look', Chrissie confirms, 'the sticker on the window. *Zeus Tours, Belen de Chocolate, Rute.* That is us, quick, get on board, before they leave without us!'

*'Leave without us?* Are you insane? Ever heard the expression threading a needle with a sausage? Gonna take about a year to squeeze this lot on. And besides, what's with the luggage? You didn't say anything about stopping overnight, we're flying tomorrow, so that is it, we can't go, I am off home.'

My wife regards me without affection, tearing savagely at the contents of her handbag, emerging with the tickets. 'Right, look, seven euros. You don't get overnight accommodation for seven bloody euros, do you? The travel-agent said we would be home in the *tardey*. So just get on the damned bus!'

*I am quite enjoying this. Gonna be two-nil to the geezers, any minute now.* 'But which *tardey* did she mean? Boxing Day *tardey*? And I repeat, we don't have any luggage, we will look a right pair of losers, with no bags! I will need clean pants, at the very least, by Boxing Day! Possibly.'

She calms down slightly, maybe at the thought of me in my pants, or then again, no. 'Well I don't know about the suitcases, all right, but this is definitely a day-trip, because I checked. You know what the Spanish are like, maybe they've brought extra coats, scarves, gloves, thermal underwear, who knows?'

'Extra coats? They are bundled up like Sherpa Tenzing as it is! Where do they think we are going, Mount Everest?!'

She smiles sweetly. 'Well, the melee has thinned out. Let us have a look on board, maybe ask the driver, shall we?'

I follow her up the steps, to be greeted by what appears to be a small general store. Spread out across the dashboard are a bottle of wine, a fruit cake, a box of biscuits, various shower products in a cellophane bag, a tin of chocolates and a cuddly toy. All right, I made one of those up, but what is this, a bus, or a duty-free? Are we crossing frontiers? Have I looked up the wrong *Rute*? Is there another one, in, I dunno, Portugal? Could we get from here to Portugal in a day? Easy. In fact, I romanticise about being able to see it from our terrace, even though I know it is not possible. But are we headed in that direction, hence the luggage?

The middle-aged, balding, paunchy driver is grinning widely, although whether he has expectations of us buying something from his shop, or wind, is impossible to tell. 'Tee-kay?' he grins. Now we are sufficiently au-fait with the language to know he is not referring to that jumble-sale shop you find on many British high streets, where I was unfortunate enough to be dragged once, and once only, unless of course he is opening a small branch here. *T.K. Coach*, anyone? No, he means 'ticket', which Chrissie produces with a flourish. Wrong. He is in fact pointing to his wares. 'Tee-kay Sort-ayo?' Blimey, we *are* expected to buy something. Got my eye on the fruit cake, actually. Were I to be marooned on a desert island, provided there was a plentiful supply of pork pies and fruit cake, just forget all about having me rescued, OK?

I tap my chosen delicacy on its wrapper. 'Quanto?'

'Two euros only' he smiles.

Blimey, give the man the money! Unless it has gone way past the sell-by date, that is the bargain of all time. And fruit cake keeps for years anyway, doesn't it? Not that one has ever lasted more that a few days, in our house, mind you. Chrissie is delving for some coins in her purse, and I reach over the dashboard and grab my purchase. Wrong again. A massive hullabaloo kicks off, the driver and passengers are laughing and shouting, which is the default setting for Spaniards, even before the crack of dawn, apparently, but it appears I have committed a faux-pas. What? Am I expected to leave it there, on display, sun blazing away through the windscreen, when it eventually rises? Do I pick it up later, at the end of the day? Will it be delivered to my seat by the cabin-crew? Or does he think that because I am British, he will drive round a few mountain passes, open the door, let it roll out and watch me chase it down the hill? I don't care what he read in his English text book, when he was a kid, I don't go in for that malarkey, and anyway, as we all know, that was cheese, not cake.

Suddenly there is an almighty kerfuffle from the back seats, and a young woman comes trip-trapping down the aisle. 'Jonneee! Cristina! Ha ha ha ha!'

NOOOOOOOOOOO! PLEEEEEEEEEASE! Elena. Crazy Elena. Totally. Barking. Mad. Elena. Batty, scatty. Potty, dotty. Completely round the bend, and back again Elena. My latest student, of two months, although, believe me, it feels like two hundred years. In a country of nut-cases, Elena is a surely the original

Fruit-and-Nut-case………. It all started on that fateful morning, at the library conversation group, fifteen bonkers minutes engraved on my very soul, for all time. There we all were, the usual crowd, Teri, Rafi, Marie, and the fellows Jose, Juan and Amador, plus Chrissie of course, totally minding our own business, with me attempting to explain Halloween and the Guy Fawkes Gunpowder Plot, under the general heading 'Autumn Fiestas in Your Country', when suddenly there was a scuffle in the corridor, and into the room burst this rather scary-looking lady, mid-twenties maybe, dressed entirely in black, tight jumper, short skirt, thick woolly tights and high heels. With her long chestnut hair, she reminded me of the Cadbury's Milk Tray woman, if there is such a person, and if not, why not, in the twenty-first century? *Anyway, don't look at me, love, all because I prefer Quality Street.* She fired a rapid broadside at the locals, who, totally passing the buck, nodded sheepishly in my direction, the *bastardos*, whereby Milk Tray glanced at me, seemingly for the first time, broke into a manic cackle, bumped into the desk, thudded clumsily into the chair next to me, grabbed my arm and uttered those immortal words, which will surely follow me to my grave. 'Ello, my name Elena. What you name plees? Ha ha ha ha!'

*Why do they always attach themselves to me, these lunatics*? Alicia was the same, until she got expelled from the group, for being a complete nut-job. Do I cut a professorial air? Hardly. Drunk too much beer, eaten too many pork pies, plus the odd fruit cake, to ever project a scholarly image. I promise you this, there are no leather elbow-patches on my Harris tweed jacket. I did have an inkling, of course, of what she was after, and no, it was not my body, strange as that may seem, what with me being a dead ringer for Jim Bergerac and all. English lessons, of course. *Well bad luck, Mrs, I am fully booked, well into the next century.*

She flapped her arms vigorously, either calling for complete silence, or attempting a vertical take-off. 'Plees. I study Eengliss at official school, ha ha ha ha.' *Well congratulations, you don't need me then, clearly, as I am so not official. In fact, I am so unofficial as to scarcely exist.* She glanced suspiciously round the room, either struggling to concentrate, or admiring the institutional decor. 'Sorree, I nervous!' *You're nervous? I am bricking it*. 'Ha ha ha ha!

Plees, in official school, no speaky moocho Eengliss. I prepare my examins, Deathy-embray, ha ha ha ha, es good for me speaky Eengliss with joo.'

Across the table, Amador, who had clearly been itching to interject, glanced at me and, under his breath, muttered 'Fox me!' Del-speak for *well I never did!*

Chrissie seemed to be enjoying the charade, however. 'Which particular day were you hoping for English classes, Elena, before your exam in Deathy, I mean December?'

Once again Elena looked shocked at the presence of other people, staring vacantly at my wife. It's like she is here physically, but mentally on another planet entirely. 'Ha ha ha! You Eengliss also? You woman of he? Plees you speaky Eengliss with me, ha ha ha!'

Not great tactics, I felt, referring to Chrissie as *my woman*, but she refused to feel offended. 'Sorry, I have no spaces left at the moment, but Johnny does, don't you dearest? So which day do you want?'

*Being stitched right up, wasn't I*? Elena was bouncing on her chair, like a manic toddler on Santa's knee. 'Ha ha ha ha, I to go official school on Wed-nest-day, plees I speaky joo antes thees?'

'Before this?' *Now why did I say that?* Me and my big mouth. Should have just kept schtum, denied everything. Now I've gone and implied I'm available. Done myself up like a kipper, as Del-Boy might have said.

Elena sprang out of her seat and enveloped me in a bear hug. 'Ha ha ha ha, ees perfecto, nine-and-half on Wed-nest-day. You come my house plees, ha ha ha ha?' As the spider said to the fly, I seem to recall. And she does bear more than a passing resemblance to a Black Widow.... The opposite side of the table seemed highly amused at this turn of events, which earned them a mild Paddington Bear stare, I recall, but my new student seemed highly delighted, to put it mildly. Hopping from foot to foot with excitement, although perhaps she needed a bathroom break, who knows, she jotted down her address, crashed into the table, and with a final frenzied cry, departed the room, leaving us in a state of complete bewilderment, like we had been struck by a whirlwind.

Jose was the first to speak. 'Good lucky with she!' And the group dissolved into uncontrolled laughter.

Fixing Chrissie with a severe Paddington, I continued where I left off, half a lifetime ago. 'Anyway, in the Houses of Parliament, on the fifth of November………'

My first English class with Elena was unlike any educational experience since education was first invented, I imagine. Usually, I ask a question, and let the pupil speak, correcting as required, but with someone studying for an exam, a little more structure is necessary, following the syllabus. Arriving apprehensively at her door, I was dragged across the threshold, dumped on the far end of the sofa, against the wall, penned in by a coffee table, unable to escape. And it was one of those sofas where, if you lean back, you end up with your knees round your ears, almost. 'Ha ha ha ha! Jonneee! Good see joo! Happy morning! I show you my syllaboooo! Ha ha ha ha!'

Barely able to speak, what with my windpipe resembling a concertina, I hauled myself to the edge of the settee. '*Good* morning, Elena, please show me your syllaBUS!'

'Ha ha ha ha! No, first I show you my cock! Plees, come, see my cock, thees way plees!' And she grabbed me by the hand. *Oh my good God. Please let this be a chicken.* Although where she might be storing a fowl in an apartment heaven only knows. Across the sitting room, onto a small outside terrace, and there, deepest joy, sweet blessed relief, was a cockatoo, in a cage.

Wiping cold sweat from my brow, I found myself croaking. 'Cockatoo. You have a cockatoo. *Cock* means something different. Are you talking about your pet in the exam? What is his name, and what colour is he?' *Flaming hell. Just wait until I see my spouse, later this morning.*

'Ha ha ha ha! Yees, I speaky my cock, in examins. But now I show joo my keetcheen. Thees way plees.'

This woman has the attention-span of a goldfish, but time to assert some authority. 'No, Elena, please, we only have an hour, and we need to talk about things which you must practice for the exam. Now, sit next to me, and tell me about your pet cockatoo.' *God I felt old.*

She grabbed me round the shoulder, batted her eyelids, and directed me back to the sofa. 'Wrrrrrrrrr! Jonneee, you so machisto! Ha ha ha ha! I love mans machisto.' She flapped her arms. 'OK. My too-cock, he name Pedro. Ha ha ha ha. I show you keetcheen, plees, now?' *Not gonna pass this exam, is she? Might as well go and look at her bloody kitchen, for all the good I am doing here.*

Suddenly, there was the sound of a key turning in the front door, and into the room stepped a young man, who I have to say looked entirely unconcerned at the sight of his girlfriend virtually horizontal on the sofa with a grey-haired old bloke. 'Ha ha ha ha! Thees my friend-boy Won-ma! Say 'ello my teacher of Eengliss, Jonneee!' I struggled to my feet and gripped his hand, smiling, all the while keeping a wary eye out for a swift knee in the groin. *Well you just never know do you? These hot-blooded Latin types.* I needn't have worried, however. 'Won-ma he make brax-fass. Joo want see keetcheen, plees?' This time a stern wagging of my finger was sufficient to bring my errant student to order. 'Wrrrrrrrrr! Jonneee, you so machisto! Ha ha ha ha!' And she leaned across, and breathed into my ear. 'Won-ma, he no moocho machisto, like joo!'

The rest of the lesson passed in a similar vein, and couldn't end soon enough, for me, as somewhat punch-drunk, light-headed, and stunned, I made my way unsteadily up the hill homewards. If ever I deserved a cold one on the patio…. Oh and by the way. If you were interested, that is. Pedro, the too-cock? He was white, with a few yellow, punk-rocker, fanned-Mohawk feathers on the back of his head, rather like a Johnny Rotten lookalike taking his pig to a Sex-Pistols concert…


And so today, this general store with a small bus attached, down the aisle comes the vision of craziness, who launches herself at the pair of us, almost knocking me into the bag of shower products. 'Ha ha ha ha! Jonneee! I so 'appy! I win tee-too-low! I passy my examins! Thanks to joo!' *Bloody hell! She passed?* Unbelievable. Good to get the credit of course, but honestly? Did I do a scrap of good? The woman was unteachable, as far as I was concerned, up and down like a Weston donkey, unable to focus for more than a few minutes at a time. We had six lessons all-told, her kitchen wasn't even that great, to be honest, and I was utterly sick of talking about that cocka-flaming-too, come the end.

Suddenly, a thought crosses my mind, and I dig my wife playfully in the ribs. 'One hundred-percent, eh? What about that, then!'

'More by luck than judgement! comes the frosty reply. *Oh yes!*

Elena is still bouncing around, making an awful song and dance of herself, as my mother would have said, but which the Spaniards in the first few rows seem to regard as entirely natural, although they must surely be wondering why this lunatic is cavorting with two Britons, in the front of the bus, at half-seven in the morning. Crazy-woman puts them out of their misery. 'My name is Elena, and I passed my English exams last week!' she hollers, 'and this is my English teacher, Jonneee! Ha ha ha ha!' And the whole coach, including the puzzled-looking driver, burst into spontaneous applause, cheering and stamping their feet. Hell, you don't get this on the National Express, do you? We travelled from Exeter to Gatwick airport once and didn't speak to a single soul, the driver merely grunted when I handed him the cases, and there were no fruit cakes on sale, that's a fact.

My former pupil quietens down slightly, but only slightly. 'Plees, you have no bags?' Why you have no bags?'

I decide to let Chrissie answer that one, as she bought the tickets, and I'm still unconvinced we are not headed overseas. She smiles confidently, although I suspect she was bluffing, really. 'Why do we need a bag? We are only going for the day. Aren't we?' *See what I mean, that little uncertainty at the end?*

'Yees, one day only, ha ha ha ha, but you need bag for you *em-boo-tea-toes*.' *Nope, me neither.*

My wife feels vindicated however. 'See? Thermal socks, for cold toes? Told you we were only going for the day, didn't I?' *Didn't mention the 'em' or the 'boo' or the 'tea', though, did she?*

'So what are these tea-toes things please Elena?' I query.

She breathes deeply, flapping her hands. 'I not know how you say *em-boo-tea-toes* in Eengliss, ha ha ha ha! Theengs to eat. You see, thees day, at fack-toey.' *So not thermal socks then.* Not sure I fancy eating body parts, however, thees day, or any day. And the fifth rule of travel might need to be amended again to *eat what the locals are eating unless you suspect there might be lumps of rat in it. Or toes.* We shall see, if ever this damned trip actually gets going. Not yet however, as Elena is still hopping. 'Plees, you buy tee-kay? Sort-ayo? Ha ha ha, how you say sort-ayo in Eengliss?' *Oh for pity's sake, not the flipping tee-kay again?*

At that moment, her eyes come to rest on the driver, seemingly for the first time, as if she was maybe expecting the coach to steer itself. Who knows? 'Hello, ha ha ha ha, my name is Elena, what is your name please? And do you know how to say *sort-ayo* in English?'

He thinks he has pulled, no doubt about it. Sucking in his gut, puffing out his chest, and failing miserably, at both, he leans nonchalantly against his seat back. 'My name is Pepe, but sorry, I don't speak a word of English, but don't worry, I will ask the passengers.' And he cups his hands to his mouth, and hollers down the bus. 'Anyone know the English for *sort-ayo?*'

Pandemonium ensues. Everyone is shouting at once, some wag bellows 'I thought you just passed an English exam, Elena, don't you know?' but sadly it appears no-one does. And none of the old duffers has a smart-phone, either. *Well so what? Not life and death, is it?* Or do we have to remain here, until we get to the bottom of the mystery?

Mercifully, Pepe comes to the rescue by rummaging around behind his seat, and bringing forth a book of raffle-tickets. A RAFFLE! So that is what all this is all about, although why we need to have it now, in the middle of the night, and not on the journey homewards, I guess we will never know. Chrissie still has her two euros to hand, which she exchanges for a strip of tickets, on the pink, and grabbing me by the arm, Elena leads us down the aisle. 'I have seat in back, plees you seat with me thees day, ha ha ha ha!'

*Oh deepest joy*. And there was me, hoping to catch up on my sleep. A ridiculous notion, I know, in this crazy country, but we live in hope. Elena crashes down next to the window, I shepherd a reluctant Chrissie next to her, and I take the middle, from where I can see the driver, tidying away his raffle prizes. *Take care of that fruit cake sunshine, it's got my name on it*. He fires up the engine, steers round about a hundred milling olive-pickers, and, half an hour late, just as what I assume might be the dawn is breaking spectacularly over the mountains to the east, we are on our way.

I close my eyes, ease back my head, and try to catch forty winks. Been a hell of a morning already, and I need to conserve my strength for the trials ahead, later this morning, of which there will undoubtedly be many. At least I know the Spanish for *raffle*, which can only be a good thing, right? Hopefully Chrissie can natter away quietly with Elena, get to know each other better, just don't mention the cocka-pigging-too, darling, and you'll be fine. And I can just drift away……

Wrong! Annoying-woman catapults to her feet, narrowly missing impaling her head on the parcel-shelf, 'PEPE! PUT SOME MUSIC ON! HA HA HA HA!'

*Oh please, for the sake of all things holy*. Can't a man get get a bit of peace, around here? Hopefully the wag will tell her to get stuffed, and the other passengers threaten to mutiny. Not a bit of it. There are shouts of agreement, someone calls for Christmas songs, and suddenly Pepe is driving one-handed as he rummages through a cubby-hole, bringing forth a CD case, which he opens with his teeth, and steering erratically around a Land Rover full of startled-looking pickers, shoves the disc into the player. And over the speakers comes the sound of Wham! *Last Christmas, I gave you my heart, but the very next day, you gave it away…..* Oh. Can. This. Day. Get. Any. Worse? An image of George Michael and Andrew Ridgley, cavorting in the snow outside a ski chalet, mullets waving majestically in the frosty air, comes into my mind, and stays there. Chrissie and I have our heads in our hands, but the rest of the bus appear to have been electrocuted, with cattle prods. They are singing, clapping, waving their arms, *thees yeer, to-say-me-fro-teers, I gib-it-to-someone-especial.* They don't understand the lyrics I suppose, but who cares? This is the same as us Brits, joining in with foreign language classics, like *Nessun Dorma*, by Pavarotti, for example, which was all about a London cabbie called Vin Cherry, apparently. I look at Chrissie, she looks at me, and we both start laughing hysterically, at the utter lunacy of the situation, then start singing. Well, the twenty-fifth rule of travel states that *if you are the only Brits on a coach in Spain in the middle of the night and the passengers start singing Wham! songs, you must join in, to avoid looking miserable, even if in your minds-eye you can picture George Michael with tinsel round his neck.*

Next up is a mangled version of the Bing Crosby classic *I dreamy-of-a-why-cree-maa*, then that other huge Christmas number one, *Sweet Caroline*, by Neil Diamond. Who knew that was a Yuletide classic in this neck of the woods? Problem is they've changed the lyrics, so instead of *Sweet Caroline*, we get *Es Navidad*. And no *da, da, da* afterwards. Whatever next? It might well be Christmas, but you gotta have the *da da da*, right? Well we do on this bus, I can tell you. Chrissie and I are singing along, English lyrics of course, *I've been inclined,* **da da da***, to believe they never would*. Elena, who is waving her arms above her head like a star-struck teeny-bopper on *Top of the Pops*, turns to us. 'You singy the wrong words! What the fox, ha ha ha ha!' Her English is coming on in leaps and bounds, don't you think? *Clearly she has met Amador again. Or Del*.

Suddenly the bus is pulling into a huge car park, next to a large, modern building. Is this the chocolate Nativity? The Spaniards are all donning hats, gloves and, it wouldn't surprise me, snow shoes, and a mad dash for the exit ensues. Funny that, I didn't notice a sign saying *You are now crossing the Arctic Circle*, or even the *Circulo Arctico*, as it might be called here, possibly, and meanwhile Pepe is bellowing 'one hour please' at the top of his voice. Elena has trussed herself up like a festive turkey, and ushers us down the steps into what must be fifteen balmy degrees at least, even at this early hour. She stumbles on the stair and I have to grab her unceremoniously to avoid a pile-up on the tarmac, 'Wrrrrrrrrr! Jonneee, you so machisto! Ha ha ha ha!' *No not really, I just cannot stand the sight of blood, when I'm supposed to be looking at a display of confectionery.* Wrong. 'Brax-fass. We take brax-fass now, plees.' So not the chocolate Nativity, then. Breakfast? An hour stop for breakfast? Hell, back in the day we used to consume a right gut-buster full-monty, including chips and steak, at my favourite greasy spoon, the *Frying Pan* on the A303, on our way to Twickenham, in about twenty minutes flat. Including a steaming-hot mug of Ty-Phoo. Still, when in Rome, and all that…

Inside the restaurant is the usual Spanish anarchy. People are milling around absentmindedly, removing ski-wear, scraping back chairs, hollering at their friends, while behind the counter a bemused cashier is doing her level best to add to the confusion. Now I know why Pepe said an hour, it will surely take that long to even place an order. Elena rugby-tackles a passing waitress. 'Hello! My name is Elena, what is your name? Three *cafe solo*, and *three tostada*, please. Ha ha ha!' Do we actually want heart-stopping black coffee, plus about a foot of toasted crusty bread, smothered in chopped tomato and olive-oil? Daft question, and if Chrissie cannot finish hers, it won't go to waste, trust me on that. And in less than a minute, Anna the server returns balancing three laden plates on her tray. How does Elena do that? I would still be queuing, that's for sure. Or not even bothering, more like, given my extreme dislike of waiting in line for half a minute, let alone half an hour. *Great this, though, isn't it*? And I might even need to propose a new rule of travel. *If you get accosted by bonkers-woman on a coach, just go with the flow.*

Back on the bus, Pepe puts flamenco on the sound system. *And there was me hoping to catch forty-winks*. Sorry Mr Diamond, but *Sweet Caroline* doesn't get the locals going like a spot of manic strumming. The cattle-prods have clearly been replaced by bare wires, connected to the mains. *Berserk* barely covers it. And Elena's dance-moves are something to behold, even though she is sitting down. Imagine someone picking an apple from a tree, taking a bite, then throwing it behind her, all the while stamping like a wild mustang, and you are not even close. Chrissie has to shuffle along the seat to avoid losing an eye, and glancing down the aisle is like being in the middle of a mass brawl in an orchard. *And this lot haven't even been drinking*. Unless they've been on the *sol y sombra*, of course. And they've had an hour, plenty of time to get absolutely blotto on the old solly-whatsit.

Another forty-five minutes of this lunacy passes pleasurably, before we once again pull into a car-park, outside what is undoubtedly a factory, with a huge banner draped across the entrance bearing the legend *Cristiano Ronaldo Here Today*. For those fortunate enough to have never heard of this person, he is an oily, preening, prancing, show-pony of a footballer, for Real Madrid, or Ray-al Madreeth, as they say in these parts, and I am not a fan, not sure if you could tell that or not. My wife, however, who should surely know better, at her age, is salivating at the prospect. 'Ooh ooh ooh! Cristiano! Oh my God! Get your camera out.' Not sure I want to get grease splattered all over my best Nikon, actually, as I surely would, getting it anywhere near that slimy specimen, and besides, I have just spotted, from my higher elevation, some especially good news, which causes me to burst into uncontrolled laughter. Ronaldo is indeed here, *but made from chocolate*. Oh yes! Elena and Chrissie have their faces pressed against the window, when suddenly my dearest spots the error of her ways. 'Oh bugger!'

My former pupil looks suitably confused. 'What mean this *oh bugger*, plees?'

Disappointed-one takes a deep breath. 'It means, Elena, that we will not get to see the real Cristiano today, only a chocolate version!' Then she brightens visibly. 'Still, every cloud, and all that. Do you think he will be milk, or plain? Will I be able to sink my teeth into his pecs? Give his abs a crafty lick?' And she closes her eyes and mimics performing such unspeakable mummy-porn, rather like the woman in the Cadbury's Flake advert, all those years ago.

Elena is wiping away the tears. 'Oh Cristina, you are, you are, how you say in Eengliss?'

'Dirty cow!' I bellow, grinning widely, 'go on, tell her, you are a dirty cow!'

Elena takes a second to compose herself, flapping her hands, a look of fierce concentration on her face, and the Spaniards, who seconds ago were jostling for position, scrabbling with their polar-region sub-zero daywear, turn as one, and fall silent. 'Cristina, ha ha ha ha! You are dirrrteee cooo!' Uproar ensues. They don't understand a word, I imagine, although a swift staccato burst of Spanish from Elena, including the words *Cristiano* and *Ronaldo*, followed by a protruding tongue, rather like a tomcat cleaning his privates, soon puts them right.

Several of the women are nodding vigorously in agreement, but I have had enough. Time to clarify where my allegiances lie, and put an end to this smut. 'Forza Barcelona!' I chuckle, raising my arms, which elicits a chorus of good-natured booing, and one or two cheers. Oh my word, this has to be the best seven euros I didn't actually spend, and we haven't even got there yet. I can just imagine the chatter in the streets of Santa Marta this night. *An English teacher turned up on our bus, he tried to steal the fruit cake and it turned out he was a Barcelona supporter, the bastardo lad-ronny.*

We heave our way down the steps of the bus, cross the car park in a giant scrum, and attempt to force our way through the door of the factory. All apart from us, of course, who do it the British way, with decorum, and besides, Elena has been swept away in the throng, allowing us a brief respite. At the doorway we are met by a woman selling tickets, one euro for admittance, which causes me to pause. 'You go on in' I tell my wife, 'I am not paying to see that smirking narcissist, even if he is made from Dairy Milk. I will wait here, in the sunshine.'

Which doesn't go down too well, I have to say. 'Get. In. There. Now.' I am commanded, 'you have the camera! I have already paid. And I want my photo taken with the greatest footballer on the planet.'

I do my best to look indignant. 'Well just remember, if I get drips of baby-oil from that glistening buffoon on my lens, you are paying for it to be cleaned!'

Nursing a painful arm, we head up a flight of stairs and out onto a suspended walkway, overlooking the factory floor, into what appears to be a time-warp. Difficult to judge the size of the place from up here, half a football field maybe, but there is almost a complete lack of any mechanisation. Did the Industrial Revolution ever come to Spain? Virtually everything is being done by hand. A woman in a white coat is sorting sweets into boxes, another is placing cellophane over the top, a third is carrying each individual box to a device resembling a one-armed-bandit, where she pulls a lever to stretch and fix the packaging, and a fourth lady conveys the finished article to a large cardboard box and stows it carefully inside. Are we back in the nineteenth century? In another area, trays of what look like biscuits are being deposited inside an oven, on the other side of which a bloke is meticulously placing each individual one into display boxes, and once again the cellophane procedure begins afresh. Incredible. And despite the walkway being packed with excited, chattering locals, not one of the workers gives us a second glance. This must be horrible, surely, being gawped on from above, by all and sundry, your entire working day, like a human zoo? I know I would hate it, and feel overwhelmingly sorry for these poor people having to be a part of, what seems to me, a grotesque sideshow.

'I can't stand this, I am off' I tell Chrissie, and squeeze my way past the spectators and away from the platform, to be confronted by a chocolate figure, maybe three feet tall, a miniature Ronaldo, possibly, although it could actually be a gnome bearing a Real Madrid crest. Oh how the mighty are fallen! I am giggling so much I have to hold on to the wall. Why is he only a yard tall? Did they run out of chocolate? Surely not, in a chocolate factory. Did he melt, under the lights? Was he nibbled by excited women? Or what about this? Did half a dozen Barcelona supporters creep in, under cover of the night, and decapitate him, with samurai swords? *Wouldn't that be fun?*

At that moment, Elena comes bouncing into the room, dragging Chrissie, already licking her lips in anticipation, in her wake. 'Oh my gaad! Ha ha ha ha! What is thees leetle boy?'

My wife's face meanwhile is an absolute picture of crushing disappointment. 'What a load of rubbish, he's only three feet!'

Bonkers-woman squeals with delight, leering suggestively. 'Cristina, ha ha ha ha! You are dirrrteee cooo! He no have three feet, only two, he middle foot, how you say, he pen-yes, ees like thees!' And she starts waving her pinkie finger suggestively, just as the remainder of the passengers come barreling through the door.

From crushing disappointment to red-faced embarrassment in five seconds flat. 'No no no, I don't mean his middle wicket, I mean he is three feet tall. About a metre.' And she shoots me a hunted look.

*Oh I am absolutely loving this*. 'Well, I have only one thing to say to you. Well two things, actually. This is your fault, for being a dirty coo. And, FORZA BARCELONA!' *Gonna need to rub some liniment into my arm, though, aren't I, before the flight tomorrow?*

The diminutive figure of Ronaldo is greeted with outright derision by the Spanish, many of whom must have witnessed Elena's gesture, and are crowding round, taking photos, little fingers prominently on display. The noise is incredible in this enclosed space, so heading for the exit, we find ourselves in a gift shop, to be greeted by a woman bearing a tray of goodies, which she proffers, mumbling 'Disgusting!'

Not sure if I fancy a lump of disgusting, actually, bearing in mind the recently-amended fifth rule of travel, but what the heck. This stuff looks like it might have passed through the digestive system of a rabid dog, several years ago, and been left out to bake in the sun, but here goes. The girls also grab a piece each, and for a few blessed seconds, silence prevails. Blimey, this stuff is like eating dust, with the merest hint of chocolate, but mostly dust. I pull a face, 'she wasn't wrong there, was she? It is actually disgusting!'

Chrissie splutters. 'You idiot, she wasn't saying *disgusting*, she was saying *digustation*. A tasting.' She swallows, grimacing. 'Then again, you were right first time!'

My ex-pupil meanwhile is at it again. 'Hello, my name is Elena, ha ha ha, what is your name?'

Mumbling tray-woman appears somewhat taken aback. *I bet she is called Anna. Guaranteed.* Wrong. 'Hello, I am Marie, how can I help you?'

'Ha ha ha ha, one kilo of *polbo* please!'

A KILO? Hell, that is over two pounds, in weight. Couldn't she have made do with a quarter? And *polbo*? We know this word, on account of the clouds of dust which waft up our street, every time Isabel gets her brush out. So this excrement stuff is actually called 'dust'? What a peculiar country this is. 'Why are you buying a kilo of dust, Elena? We get it for free, in our street, when the neighbours start sweeping!'

She flings her arms around my neck, like a drunken sailor. 'Oh Jonneee, you so funny! Ha ha ha! Ess Cree-mas! My family love thees sweets for Cree-mas! And now we taste manty-cado! Plees, you try manty-cado. Marie! Digustation manty-cado plees!'

Marie disappears round the back of the counter, and returns with a tray of what looks suspiciously like chocolate-chip cookies, only without the chocolate-chips. 'Manty-cado' she mutters, 'take, please.' In for a penny, and all that, and I need something to take away the taste of dust. I take a tentative bite, and the thing just crumbles away, some down my chin and the rest on the floor. More ruddy dust! With a trace of lemon, possibly, but there is just nothing holding it together. I've fallen asleep on the beach before now, woken up with a mouthful of sand, and it tasted better than this.

Elena is rolling her eyes in ecstasy, whereas Chrissie and I are frantically casting around for somewhere we can spit the stuff out. 'Marie!' cries the nutty-one, 'one kilo of manty-cado plees! Ha ha ha.'

'There's a toilet in the corner!' my wife whispers, brushing crumbs off her blouse, 'got any Polo's?'

'I thinth I goth a packeth in my pocketh!' I splutter, heading for the bathroom. But truly, what a let-down this visit has been, so far. A chocolate pixie and the sweepings of the factory floor.

Having thoroughly rinsed my teeth and throat, I return to the fray to find Chrissie perusing a different display. 'What is this you are looking at, don't tell me, Paignton beach, infused with wee?'

'Actually, it is marzipan' comes the reply. 'You know my mother loves marzipan. I think I will get her a box.' *Did I know that? Search me.*

'Well, you'd better ask Marie for a disgusting digustation, hadn't you? I smile. 'Check it for dust-content. And piddl….'

'JUST SHUT UP, RIGHT? Elena, are we allowed a taste of this?'

Our friend looks as if she has been poleaxed, for a few seconds. 'Oh my gaad! Massy-pan! Massy-pan! I love massy-pan. Marie! Ha ha, digustation massy-pan, plees!'

Well the woman can hardly refuse, can she, having just sold two kilos of particulate matter? A plate appears, bearing half-a-dozen generous slices. 'Ten-to-one it tastes of dust!' I mutter, not quite under my breath. But, lo and behold, massy-pan it indeed is. The real thing. Could do with a layer of icing above, and a Christmas cake below, mind you, but beggars, and all that.

Chrissie is scrabbling for her purse. 'One please', she smiles.

Elena is stunned. 'One? One? Only one? Why you buy only one? I am buying six! Ha ha ha.'

Suddenly a massive hubbub heralds the arrival of the other passengers, who descend on the freebies like a pack of wolves. Two other members of staff have been drafted in to assist with this orgy of pushing, shoving, hollering and grabbing, and we have to step back to avoid being swept away. *This is a factory, for heaven's sake, they are not going to run out*. Or are they? Shelves are being stripped, carrier bags filled, fist-fulls of euros changing hands, and glancing out of the window, I spot Pepe with the sides of the bus open and people already grappling to fill their suitcases. So is this the famous *em-boo-tea-toes* thing Elena was warning us about? Come to think of it, I did actually spot a box of what I'd assumed might be fudge pieces, before the looting started, which could have been ten little piggies all in a row. Too late to tell now, however, as this place resembles Old Mother Hubbard's cupboard. Bare.

The Wag comes struggling towards the door, laden down with four bulging sacks of plunder. 'Did you English buy anything?' he grins, perspiring mightily.

'Yes we did!' Chrissie smiles, opening her bag to reveal the single box of marzipan.

'IS THAT IT?' he roars. 'ARE YOU VERY POOR?' Then performs a double-take. 'OH MY GOD, Massy-pan! DOLORES? DID YOU BUY ANY MASSY-PAN?'

He needn't have worried. A rotund little woman, Mrs Dolores Wag I suppose, performing a passable impersonation of a beast of burden, barges her way breathlessly through the crowd, dragging a bag-for-life, nodding vigorously, seemingly incapable of speech.

'Fancy a cigarette?' her husband chortles. 'Come on, get this lot on the bus!' And the pair of them, wheezing and coughing like a pair of copulating elephant-seals, wend their way across the car park.

God I need some air, before my head explodes, and nodding at the girls, I stumble, stretching and yawning, into the warm sunshine. Strange place, this Rute, I had assumed it was a village or small town, but we are in the middle of nowhere, on a country lane, completely isolated. Glancing up the hill, I notice another factory, almost identical to the one we have just visited, maybe two-hundred yards away, with a huge banner strung across the entrance which appears to proclaim *Belen de Chocolate*, but I am struggling with my vision at this distance, even with my glasses. *Been a hard morning, and my senses are reeling, all right?* A stream of cackling behind me indicates that Elena, at least, has followed me out, and I turn to see the pair of them, arm in arm, heads together, and I catch the words *Ronaldo* and *pen-yes*. Good to see them bonding, isn't it? *And it will get bonkers-woman off my back for half an hour, hopefully.*

'Is that the chocolate Nativity up there, in that factory, Elena, do you know?' I enquire.

She screws up her eyes, but appears to be having trouble concentrating. 'Ha ha ha! Yees. We go there now. Get on bus, plees!'

'Well actually' I smile, 'we are going to walk, stretch the legs, as we say in English.' *Plus the fact it will take about a hundred years to get this lot installed on the coach.*

She reacts with horror. 'Walk? Walk? I cannot to walk! Ha ha ha! In these boots! Oh my gaad!'

I have not really been paying any attention to her attire, due to my sleepy state, and glance down for the first time to find that she is clad in a pair of skin-tight jodhpurs, shiny at the front, matte at the back, and ankle boots with spike heels. *Oh my gaad indeed.* Is she on a coach trip, or taking part in a gymkhana in a sex shop? Bizarre. I indicate her compatriots, who are crowded around the bus, chaotically stuffing confectionery into their suitcases amid a barrage of bellowing. How can such an innocuous task require any vocals whatsoever, let alone disorganised yelling? *Put it this way! No no the other way! Give me the case! Put the massy-pan on the top!* Not for the first time, or the twentieth, I am amazed at the ability of the Spanish to turn a simple task, via a drama, into a crisis. *Then again, we could be stuck in Gordano Services on the M5, in the drizzle, not speaking to a soul.* 'I just thought it might take some time to get everyone on the bus, so we could maybe walk, that is all.'

She lurches into me, grabbing my arm. The painful one. 'Ha ha ha! Jonneee! I luff my classes of Eengliss with you! You teach me, see things with you eyes. We crazy Espanee peoples! We makey much noise! We shouty always! Look these persons!'

Chrissie grabs her other arm, and plants a kiss on her cheek. Time for a group hug. Well this is Spain, after all, not Gordano Services. And not a hint of drizzle in sight. 'Yes, but we love you for it!' Enough said.

*So we are not walking, then.* Back on the coach, and the vocals begin again. *We bought two kilos of polbo! We got polbo and manty-cado! I have massy-pan, polbo and manty-cado! Did you see that rubbish Ronaldo?* After about thirty seconds, we stop, and the whole disembarkation debacle begins again. *Could have walked it by now.* Another one-euro ticket, more stairs, another walkway overlooking a Dickensian factory, we squeeze past and are in the front of the group again. *And, breathe.* Ahead are more confectionery figures, life-size this time, four dark chocolate, and one Milky Bar. Not the little kid in a cowboy outfit and round glasses, but a bloke, white chocolate, with his arm outstretched. 'PAPA!' cries Elena. *Oh please, no.* Are her family here? She once explained that her mother was just like her, only crazier, which in Elena-speak must mean off-the-scale bonkers. Can my frail constitution stand any more of these loons? Strange though, I cannot see anyone else in the room, or more to the point, hear anyone. 'PAPA!' she cries again. 'Plees take photo with me, and papa! Ha ha ha ha! I take photo of you, with he!

Hang on a minute, surely I recognise this figure? As we approach, and my eyes begin to focus, I spot a sign on the floor. *Papa Francisco*. Of course! Pope Francis. And who are these other people? Letizia, Felipe, Sofia and Juan Carlos. Not a clue. Chrissie senses my confusion. 'The Spanish royal family. Come on, get your camera out! Me and Elena with the Pope, and the King!' So why couldn't the other place have made Ronaldo this size, instead of that jokey little midget? Ridiculous. These figures are incredible, however, such detail, from the faces, to the clothing, all in chocolate, and we are grinning like schoolkids, posing and snapping away merrily. What a contrast.

Into the next room and here we are, what we have come to see, the chocolate Nativity scene. And I step back breathlessly, in sheer amazement. For it is not simply a *Belen village*, but a recreation of the Seven Wonders of the Ancient World. Even Elena is stunned, momentarily, into silence. Set on a huge plinth, maybe thirty feet square, ten feet or more high, surrounded by perspex to keep little fingers at bay. At the highest point are the Hanging Gardens of Babylon, the columns and terraces in dark chocolate, but the trees, shrubs and flowers in exquisite detail and colours.

Stone steps, in plain and milk, lead down to a huge statue of Zeus, with ivory-coloured skin, and gold encrusted robes, seated regally on a throne, winged figure positioned on his right palm, and moving to the left, the Great Pyramids, instantly recognisable of course. Further round is the lighthouse of Alexandria, minutely carved, and on the far side of the display, the Colossus of Rhodes, crown of sunburst on his head, right arm extended, the Statue of Liberty of the pre-Christian era.

Next up is a figure of a lion, which a small sign announces is from the Mausoleum at Halicarnassus, and finally, bringing us back to where we came in, the ruined columns of the Temple of Artemis. Astounding. Elena is gripping Chrissie's arm, as we wander around again, trying to take in as much as possible, before we are engulfed. In my lifetime I have never seen anything remotely like this, the bricks, the stones on the footpaths and in the walls, the vegetation, the people, almost beyond belief that this was hand-carved, from chocolate.

Elena links her arm in mine, and whispers, softly 'Jonneee, do you like to live thees times?'

I have a lump in my throat. 'Good question, well done! Let me ask you. *Would* you like to *have lived* in these times?'

She giggles, pulling my wife closer. 'Only if Cristina and me were Queens!'

So that is two circuits of the exhibition, and so intently have we been concentrating, we have almost forgotten about the actual Nativity village, intertwined around the Seven Wonders. Narrow cobbled streets, shops and stalls selling bread, fish, meat, carpets, bales of cloth, fruit and veg, pitchers of wine, sacks of corn, bales of hay. A forge, a well, a stream with fishermen, horses, cattle, pigs, chickens, dogs and cats, and of course the villagers, stallholders, all in authentic Biblical clothing. A Roman fort, centurions, then a group of shepherds tending their flock around a camp fire, three kings on camels, and finally, a stable all forlorn, containing the Holy Family.

Suddenly, from the other room, comes urgent shouting. 'ELENA! YOU ENGLISH! COME HERE!' Blimey, what could possibly have happened? Has one of the group had an accident? Is the place on fire, and we have to evacuate? Our friend trip-traps her way back, and we follow, to find a jostling mob crowding around the Pope. 'PHOTO! PLEASE, GROUP PHOTO, WITH PAPA! And there was me imagining a matter of life and death had just occurred. *'You big English, stand at the back! Elena, at the side. Woman English, in the front. No this way! Here! Not like that! Get off my foot! Move over, I can't see the Pope!* For pity's sake, it's only a photo. Drama, crisis, and all that. But we cannot help laughing, as this is Spain, after all.

Disentangling myself from someone else's footwear, holding my camera aloft, I gesture to the unruly crowd that I will take a picture myself. *With a decent camera, not a manky Instamatic.* Lining up the shot, I suddenly crane my neck around the lens, and shout *'Kay-so!'* Do they say 'cheese' in this country? No idea, but it produces the hoped-for laughter.

I fire off about four shots, then the Wag steps forward. 'Fay Boo?'

*No idea who she is, quite honestly*. 'Que?'

'Fay Boo, Fay Boo!'

*Not a clue, mate*. Elena reads my mind. 'Fay Boo. You no weeth Fay Boo?'

*Sorry, I thought I had already made that clear*. Several others join in, Fay Boo, Fay Boo. *Look, I don't know Fay-bloody-Boo, all right*. 'No comprendo!'

Our friend cackles, and flaps her hands. 'Ha ha ha ha! Fay Boo. Social media!'

Social what... Facebook! 'Are you saying *Facebook*?'

'Yees!' comes the chorus.

*Blooming Spanish!* They will keep eating their words. 'Look, Elena, these are two English words. Face. Sssss.' I slap my cheeks. 'Book. With a Kkkk.' And I mimic opening one. 'Face Book!' And suddenly, just about everyone is slapping their heads, and opening imaginary publications. Face sssss Book kkkkkkk. *Priceless*. This is supposed to be my day off, of course, I have finished until the New Year. But I can just imagine the chatter tonight. *An English teacher turned up on our bus, he tried to steal the fruit cake and it turned out he was a Barcelona supporter, the bastardo lad-ronny. But he did teach us how to say Fay Boo.*

I smile widely. 'Sorry, I am not on Facebook, but Cristina is! She can post the pictures. Probably!' Which earns me a glare, but what the heck. It's Christmas.

Moving on, we find ourselves in another sweet shop, with another tray-woman, this time bearing *Too-Ron*. 'You take plees.' Now, we know this one. Chocolate, with crispy bits inside, rather like the 'Dairy Crunch' stuff they used to sell in Britain, and might well still do, for all I know, but about five times better. Chocolate heaven, it comes in milk, plain and Milky Bar versions, about eight inches long, over half an inch thick, and costs not much more than a euro, a ridiculously low figure when you consider they were asking fifteen-bob for a reduced-size Mars Bar, in the UK last August.

My former pupil meanwhile is in a state of delirium, 'Too-Ron, too-Ron!' whereas Chrissie and I have to turn away, shaking with laughter. *Too too Ron Ron Ron, too too Ron Ron!* 'Hello, ha ha ha ha! My Name is Elena, what is your name plees?' I forget what tray-woman said, actually, as I have *I met him on a Monday and my heart stood still* going round in my head, but whatever it was, Elena seems to be ordering five bars.

Chrissie however is concerned for her welfare, not to mention the state of her bank balance, and teeth. 'How much is this *Too-Ron* here, Elena?'

'Ha ha ha ha! Cristina! Three euros! You buy?'

*Not a chance.* 'But Elena' she whispers, just in case tray-woman speaks English, 'it is only a euro-twenty in *Mercadonna*.'

'No no! Ha ha! Thees chocolaty, artisan product. Ees much better than supermarket!'

Well it isn't, actually, as I've just had a square, and it wouldn't surprise me to learn that the factory bought the entire *Mercadonna* stock, removed the wrappers, and substituted their own labels. By hand, of course. And trust me, I know cheap chocolate when I taste it, having polished off a whole packet of doggie drops belonging to Peter Allen's dachshund, when I was about seven. And to this day I cannot look a sausage-dog in the face without feeling decidedly green about the gills. 'Elena, I think it tastes exactly the same, and this chocolate is more than twice the price!'

She turns to tray-woman. 'My English teacher says your chocolate is the same as Mercadonna, and double the price! Ha ha ha ha!'

*Well I didn't expect you to tell her that, did I?* The bearer of *Too-Ron* looks suitably offended. 'No, all our chocolate is hand-made!'

*Yeah, but only 'cos your boss is too mean to spring for a machine.* And who cares if it was treaded by barefoot, topless maidens? All about the ingredients, right? But what the hell, never gonna see her again, are we, until next year at the very earliest? I smile warmly nevertheless. 'Sorry, but to me it tastes the same.'

At that moment a tumult of Spaniards comes stampeding into the shop, with cries of *Too-Ron, Too-Ron*!, and we have to step lively for the second time this morning to avoid becoming accident statistics. Death by chocolate, anyone? 'English!' cries Mr Wag, 'bought any Too-Ron?'

I open my mouth to reply, but before I can draw breath Elena wades in, with both feet. 'NO HE HASN'T! Ha ha ha ha! He says it is the same as Mercadonna, and twice the price!'

*Oh. You. Great. Blabbermouth*. Will the ground please open up, right now. This has to be my most embarrassing chocolate moment, since I was caught by Mrs Allen with a mouthful of doggie drops. Tray woman looks furious, with good reason. 'Gone and done it now, haven't you' Chrissie whispers, under her breath.

'Me?' I cry, indignantly. 'I seem to recall it was you who started this, actually, telling Elena the price. Don't try to blame me.'

The Wag reaches across, and grabs a square of Mercadonna's finest, sorry, artisan Too-Ron, from the tray, sucks in his gut, and pops it onto his tongue, rolling his eyes, like a sommelier with a goblet of finest *Cotes du Rhone*. For a few seconds, silence prevails. The suspense is unbearable. Could go either way, this, although I surreptitiously check the direction of the exit, in case it turns ugly. 'It's the same!' comes the verdict, and suddenly, everyone is talking at once, as the group heads chaotically towards the exit. *It's cheaper in Dia! No it isn't, Mercadonna is better! Dia have three-for-two offers! The Englishman was correct! Dia does one with orange bits in! Get off my feet! Did you get a photo of the Pope?*

I just want to curl up somewhere, and glancing back, I spot tray-woman, all alone, open mouthed, in the middle of the shop. I feel so wretchedly sad for the poor girl, she was only a youngster, barely into her twenties, now mentally scarred, possibly, by the day an English teacher came to call. None of the Spanish appear to be wrestling with their consciences, however, as squeezing onto the bus, Pepe fires up the engine, and we head off to our next destination on this bizarre voyage of discovery. *Did you buy any Too-Ron? Not at those prices! I will go to Mercadonna tomorrow! Don't forget it is Noche Buena! They close early! No, plenty of time! Are you going to his mother's? Yes, miserable old cow! I cannot stand her sister! You should have seen what she wore, last year! Not surprised, with that arse!* Christmas. A time for peace and goodwill.

We are now coming into a village, Rute according to the signs, and Pepe pulls over outside a rank of shops. 'Right, museums of *Azucar, Anise and Em-boo-tea-toes.* Hour and a half, then we go for lunch. Back here at two PM.' Now, I understood every word of that, and it was actually in a foreign language. No need for any discussion whatsoever, in my opinion, we have ninety minutes to visit three places, so that is, let me think, half an hour in each? Wrong. Pandemonium breaks out. *What about the suitcases? Are you staying with the bus, Pepe? I want to buy three bottles of Anise! Where are you going first? I want to see Marilyn Monroe! I haven't got my Christmas chorizo yet!*

We stumble onto the pavement, giggling at the absurdity of not having your chorizo yet. Christmas is the same day every year, so why aren't they organised? Serve them right if it was all gone. And what does Marilyn Monroe have to do with it? This is more than my brain can cope with, quite honestly, but Elena is still in full-on mode. 'Ha ha ha ha! We go museo of *em-boo-tea-toes* now! We alone! Others they go drinky *anise*! We visit biggest *booty-farra* in world! How you say *booty-farra* in Eenglees, plees?' And she grabs us by the hands, and guides us towards what appears to be a butcher's shop.

No idea about any of this, of course, although I suspect it might have something to do with meat. A meat museum? Is that a thing? Entering the premises, it seems I have to amend my first impressions, slightly. Not a butchers, exactly, but a delicatessen. A sausage shop, to be precise. A glass counter, twenty feet long, possibly, containing every shape and size of banger imaginable, thick, thin, long, short, every possible shade of brown, pink, white and black. One particular gruesome, knobbly specimen wouldn't look out of place at a certain kind of *Gentleman's Club*, so I've been told, you understand,

and another resembles a copper's truncheon and would certainly administer a mighty whack to a fleeing miscreant, I can tell you. Chorizo I recognise of course, plus black and white pudding, and it gives me particular pleasure to spot what looks remarkably like Cornish hog's pudding, but the rest of them? Not a clue.

It appears, however, I am to remain in ignorance no longer, as a friendly, smiling woman behind the counter is slicing frantically, laying out free samples onto around twenty plates. Thank my lucky stars, I have died and gone to heaven, and were this a desert island....well you know the rest. The only decision is which ones to try. Now, let us be clear on this, I could easily polish off the lot, especially if I had a beer on the go. But that would be greedy, wouldn't it? Not British in fact. I have to save some for the other customers, especially after they have been on the *anise*. So, with that in mind, as I already know the puddings, black, white and hog's, plus the chorizo, naturally, and as the thirty-sixth rule of travel states *if you are in a sausage museum and get offered something which appears to have spent its formative years in a gentleman's club, go for it, my son,* that has to be my choice, right? Plus a slice of copper's truncheon. Tough job, and all that.

Before I can get my sticky mitts on my selection, however, there is a cry from the far side of the room, whom I had momentarily forgotten, amid this largesse. 'JONNEEE! Ben akee! Come here, plees! *Booty-farra*! Ha ha ha ha!' Having removed my glasses, all the better to view the delicacies on offer, I am unable to make out anything other than a large shape on the ground, but as I approach it appears something has been dragged out of the sea. Hell's bells, it's a creature from the deep, possibly, a humungous, brown-grey tube, thick as a tree trunk, in a perfect 'U' shape, which if it were stretched out straight, would be thirty feet long, easily, and tied up at each end by a thick, white length of cord, to what, prevent it escaping? Hardly, it's been dead for thirty years, surely? A Spanish Loch Ness Monster? Didn't see any lakes on the way in, on account of being half-asleep, but I make a mental note not to go paddling, any time soon. Then the image of Vic the Fish trying to haul this beast onto his counter flashes through my mind, and I start to laugh. Chrissie has gone pale for some reason, but Elena reacts with suitable outrage. 'Jonneee, why you laugh, plees, ees biggest *booty-farra* in world, you no like to eat? *Sall-chee-chon*?'

Eat? I'd rather chop off...hang on a minute, did she say *Sall-chee-chon*? The Spanish word for sausage? I screw up my eyes and rub my hands across my face. Sounds reasonable, doesn't it, in a sausage museum, but I told you, I'm finished for Christmas, my brain has been switched off, I am running on autopilot, the lights are on, but no-one's home. Bonkers-lady is not giving up, however. 'Jonneee, ha ha ha, how you say *booty-farra* in Eengliss, plees?'

Well, we don't really have these weapons of mass destruction in the UK, do we? Bangers, yes, dozens of different varieties in butchers' shops up and down the land, but here they are cured, I imagine, left out to dry for years. 'Giant sausage' I smile.

She turns to my wife. 'Cristina, you like giant shosh-shage, plees?'

My dearest narrows her eyes. 'Chance would be a fine thing!'

Elena explodes into laughter. 'Cristina! You dirrrteee coo! Ha ha ha ha!' I also have tears running down my face, not from this slight to my manhood, which will be a conversation for another day, trust me on that, but the image of the talking dog on *That's Life!*, forty-odd years ago. *Shosh-shages*! Priceless.

At that moment, there is pandemonium behind us, as around twenty passengers from the coach come barreling in, fighting their way to the counter, and proceed to strip the plates bare in around twenty second flat. The savages! The lad-ronny bastardos! There was me, teaching these peasants to say Fay Boo, and what do I get for my troubles? A few miserable pieces of rind. Chrissie, a life-long vegetarian, is giggling mightily, but my ex-pupil is scandalised. 'Ahh, thees Espanee people are goats!' No, I wouldn't say that, actually. I love goats, inoffensive creatures as they are. Plus, I am a Capricorn. Pigs yes, but goats no. Elena has the bit between her teeth, clearly, and totters to the counter, elbowing her way through her cloven-hooved compatriots, and addresses slicing-woman. 'Hello, my name is Elena, ha ha ha! What is your name please? My English friends have not had any *em-boo-tea-toes* yet!'

The beleaguered assistant grins and rolls her eyes, as if to say *well what did you expect from this bunch of Santa Marta goats*, although it might possibly have been *I will get the sack in a minute if I give away any more*, but she responds with a smile. 'I am Lola, what would you like?' I indicate the gentleman's club and the truncheon, and slicing-Lola gets to work, producing a clean plate and two perfectly carved specimens. Suddenly, the Wag waddles into view, stretches out his arm and tries to grab my delicacies. *My em-boo-tea-toes I mean, not any other delicacies, in case you were wondering*. Luckily for him I whip the plate away from his sweaty grasp, because this is mine, matey, and I will fight for it, to the death. Join the queue, you goat. Sorry, pig.

Gentleman's club reveals itself to be a rich, ruby-red colour, truncheon much darker, both bursting with full, meaty flavour, and I close my eyes, and drift away to a land of…. 'For Pete's sake, what a disgusting stench!' my wife cries, 'I am getting on the internet this evening, see if I can change your seat on the plane, tomorrow. And it's the spare room for you, tonight. Come on Elena, let's go to the sugar museum!' And the pair of them, arm in arm, head for the door.

'Hang on!' I call, 'where's my wallet, I want to get a kilo…' Too late, they have disappeared. I hand my plate back to slicing-Lola, with a sheepish grin. 'Vegetariana' I shrug, and follow in their wake.

Catching breathlessly up with the girls, wiping bits of truncheon from my lips, the *museo de Azucar* is basically a sweet shop, from the front at least, although there is a one-euro entrance charge, so presumably there is something to look at, although what it could possibly be, out of sugar, heaven only knows. Hang on a moment, though, didn't someone make a model of the Tamar bridge, from sugar cubes, a few years ago? Or was it matchsticks? Forget now, slept since then.

The first exhibit is a recreation of a late nineteenth-century sweet factory, using real implements, and tailor's dummies, or mannequins, dressed in period costume. *Or are they mannequins*? Surely they couldn't mould sugar as accurately as this? Standing behind a worktable is an old man, dressed in a cloth cap, a grandad collarless shirt and white apron, arms out like he is about to start mixing a huge bowl of flour, but his skin is perfectly formed, rosy cheeks, a red drinker's nose, eyes staring guiltily across the room, as if the boss has just walked in and almost caught him doing something illicit. Does he have a hip-flask hidden in the flour, perhaps? Would account for the colour of his hooter, certainly. Opposite him is a grey-haired old woman in a hooded frock and knitted shawl, head down arranging a tray of biscuits, but with a knowing smile on her lips, as if she too is in on the secret. Her cheeks are flushed, clearly she enjoys a tipple, and I can imagine the pair of them, as soon as we have passed by, relaxing with a wee dram. Delightful, and whoever the artist was has certainly created a tableau of huge skill, and humour. 'Look Elena' I giggle, 'that old man has a bottle of whisky, hidden in the bowl of flour!'

She roars with laughter. 'Jonneee, no! Ha ha ha ha! Not wicky! Thees Espain, he drinking Anise! Ees factory opposite!' *Ooh yes, I'd forgotten the Anise factory……*

'I tell you what' Chrissie grins, 'this sweet factory is more modern than the *manty-cado* place we visited earlier! The staff look happier, here, for sure!' *Well yes, the manty-cado staff didn't have chance for a swift tot, did they, being constantly gawped at…..*

Into the next room, and Elena is jumping for joy. 'Doo Kessa! Doo Kessa! Ha ha ha ha!' *Well that clears it up nicely.* All I can see is a life-size figure of a spectacularly ugly old woman, pouting trout-lips like a mans-sall-mon on Vic the Fish's counter, a turned-up nose and a bleached-blonde curly perm that no self-respecting poodle would be seen dead in. Arm raised regally, she is wearing a long, spangly red dress with white frilly edging, and a white ruff round her neck such as you might find on a circus dog. The sculptor has done her no favours, clearly, as she has a tummy to resemble Fernando. Who on earth is this? A sign affixed to the perspex screen reads *Duquesa de Alba y Lola Flores*. Nope, me nether. A Duchess, presumably, hence the long Spanish name, but famous here for what, precisely? Simply being a Duchess, I assume, a bit like Fergie? *Although that is not a road we wish to go down right now. I have some Anise to drink, very shortly.*

'So who is this Doo-Kessa Alba Lola Flores, Elena?' I enquire, not unreasonably, I feel.

Wrong. Bonkers-woman almost topples off one of her spikes. 'Ha ha ha ha ha! Jonneee! You so funny! You make me laughing! Thees Doo-Kessa de Alba!' indicating old fish-face, 'and THEES Lola Flores!' pointing to another figure a few yards away, a woman in a red and white flamenco dress, arm raised as if she is picking an apple from a tree, grinning like the Cheshire Cat.

Chrissie regards me without warmth. 'You steaming nincompoop! Anyone could see that was two different names!'

Out of order, isn't it, kicking a man when he's down? 'Look, I've told you. It is Christmas. I am switched off, until January. It's not my fault this place is too mean to provide two separate signs, for two different people. And besides, I personally guarantee you have never heard of either of these women, have you, eh? Come on, admit it.'

Elena is still giggling hysterically, enjoying the good-natured interplay between a man and his wife, even though she is understandably struggling to follow the dialogue. My spouse remains indignant, however. 'I will have you know, Sonny Jim, that I do actually know all about the Duchess of Alba. Her family used to make record players, I think you will find. And Lola Flores? Well obviously, her dad used to make buttery spread, back in the seventies, the one that Terry Wogan used to advertise. *The margarine for men.* So there!' And she pokes her tongue out, for good measure.

Moving on, the three of us rocking with laughter, we come face to face with Michael Jackson. At last, someone we've actually heard of, as, between you and me, I don't believe the story about the hi-fi and the Flora. A passable impersonation of the King of Pop too, arms raised, milking the applause from an imaginary audience, trilby hat, dark shades and red sparkly jacket. Incredible detail, the clothes on these figures, made from piped icing sugar, I imagine, a skill beyond my wildest imagination, bearing in mind my one and only attempt at icing a cake, when the kids were young, resembled a massacre at the North Pole. Elena, still totally wired, stands next to Wacko Jacko, raises her arms, and starts to sing. 'Billie Jee, es-no-my-lubber, she-jus-the-gir, say-that-I-am-the-won, the-chi-es-no-my-son!' Incredible, her vocals are more legible than the man himself! Now then, I can Moon-Walk. Yes seriously. Usually after six pints of McEwen's at the rugby club, admittedly, but I cannot hear a Michael Jackson tune without an overwhelming urge to get up and boogie. *And we only pass this way once, right*? Elena changes the record, 'Eddy-are-you-okay, are-you okay-Eddie' and I begin my routine. All right, I cannot actually Moon-Walk, bearing in mind I resemble Farmer Bill's Cow-Man, rather than old twinkle-toes, but what the heck. Another group from the bus come hurtling into the room and suddenly there about a dozen of us, arms raised, stomping round the room. It's what I love about the Spanish, their complete lack of reticence. All right, so this lot have clearly been partaking of the Anise, but they throw off their inhibitions at the drop of a hat.

Next up is Marilyn Monroe, which explains the comment on the coach, earlier. Dressed in her famous little white number, hem wafting provocatively in the up-draught from a New York subway ventilator, red garter placed tantalisingly on her thigh, this time it is Chrissie's turn to perform. She is wearing jeans, so unable to heft up her skirt, and I have no idea about the garter, quite honestly, but she grabs an imaginary microphone and in a breathy American accent, begins to sing. 'Happy Birthday Mister President, Happy Birthday to you!'

'Oh my gaad, Cristina, you much sexy!' Elena grabs her in a massive bear-hug, and the pair of them are rolling round the room.'Appy Birthday to yooooo!' And why not?

My wife has a mischievous gleam in her eye. 'Is it time to visit the museo of anneee, now, Elena? My throat is a little dry!' *Oh my gaad, again.* I had forgotten her liking for this particular Spanish spirit, got tipsy on it last year, on a pre-christmas night out with the library girls, I seem to recall, then directed a stream of abuse at my choice of shepherdesses for our Nativity scene. Accused one of them of sleeping with the Roman centurions, of all things. *Gonna need to keep an eye on her, aren't I?*

'Ha ha ha ha! Thees way, plees!' *So that's a yes, then?* Stumbling into the bright sunshine, across the road, and into the next port of call, the Anise museum appears at first glance to be a bar, a long wooden counter, shelves on the wall, crammed with bottles, and a slim little man standing proudly behind.

'Welcome to the *museo de anise!*' he beams, 'the most famous drink in all the world! My name is Rico. Four euros please, includes *digustation*.' Four euros? Bit steep, isn't it? Unless *digustation* in here is code for getting absolutely slaughtered. You just never know, in Spain, do you? And what's all this about the most famous in all the world? I'm sure the Scotch whisky industry would have something to say about that. Never heard of the stuff, before we moved here, and I thought it was a woman's name, first off. *Anneee*. Drank *Pernod* once or twice in my youth, of course, but I'm not sure it's the same stuff. Was my beverage of choice in nightclubs, for a while, mixed with blackcurrant, and sloshed into a half of cider. You should have seen me dancing to *Tiger Feet* after a few of those. Lethal, I was. Literally.

Chrissie hands over the money and our new friend reaches for two bottles, which causes Elena to start cackling. 'Hello Rico, my name is Elena! Ha ha ha ha!'

He eyes me warily. 'And what is your woman called?'

'Cristina!' cries my wife, who intensely dislikes being addressed in that way. Strangely, Rico doesn't ask what I am called….

He delves under the counter for three small plastic tasting glasses, and with millimetric precision pours three identical measures. 'Dulce.'

'Sweet' translates Elena.

We knew that already, but good practice for her of course. So now, what is the form here? Swig it back, sip it gently, or bung it into half a cider? Can't see any bottles of *Taunton Natural Dry* to hand, so I decide on the genteel route, take in the aromatic bouquet, and imbibe, gently. Huuuuuuuuurrrr. Oh my gawd, as Del-Boy might have said, my throat is on fire, my eyes have crossed, and it wouldn't surprise me if steam was issuing from my ears. I remember this stuff from last year, in the house of a sweet old couple who had organised an open house, to view their Belen. The girls, meanwhile, have necked theirs, and are holding up their glasses for more.

Rico chuckles and goes through the same ritual. 'Seca.'

'Dry. Ha ha ha ha!'

'Hang on a minute!' I protest, gulping down my remains, 'I haven't finished this one yet!' Hell, it is strong, quite viscose too, or should that be vicious? Both of those, actually, and I need to be careful, having eaten only sand, a square of Too-ron and two slices of shosh-shage since before dawn. *Don't want to get shoshed, do I?*

Our host then steers himself round the bar, and heads through some double doors. 'This way please, we will begin the tour now. Come please, Elena and Cristina!' I assume I am included in this, unless Rico thinks I am a complete waste of space, bearing in mind I haven't started upon my *seca* yet. *Well I'm taking it with me, OK, enjoy it on the way round, unlike these two gannets.* He switches on a bank of lights, revealing four rows of antique glass cabinets, each crammed with bottles, jugs and containers of every shape and size. He steps back and holds out his hands, proudly. 'Estupendo, no?' It is, actually, a really impressive collection, there must be over a hundred different brands on display, in this row alone. 'As I was saying' he continues, 'Anise is the most important alcoholic drink in the world, much bigger than Scotch whisky, for example. It is drunk in the Spanish-speaking world, south America, in Africa, Asia, Europe, and England also!' *Well it certainly was in Chaser's Disco, that's for sure.* 'Phenomino, no?' That is quite phenomenal, actually, I had no idea it was that popular. I remain sceptical about the Scotch claims, but clearly have no way of knowing.

He continues along the same vein. 'Look at the artwork on the bottles, phenomino, no? Compare with Scotch whisky, how you say, Tea-chairs?' Is he saying *Teacher's?* He's correct though, isn't he, the label on that fine spirit bearing little more than the name, and a small crest, whereas the brandings on this stuff are like small portraits, many of which feature smoldering, dark-eyed senoritas clicking castanets, strumming guitars, or picking apples. Others depict bullfighters in ridiculously tight trousers flapping capes at two tons of charging, horned flesh, Roman goddesses crowned with laurel leaves, and Don Quixote-like figures astride laden mules. 'Estupendo, no?'

*Blimey, are there no other words in the Spanish language?* And is it really necessary to keep banging on about it? Yes the drink is phenomino, the artwork is estupendo, the antique bottles, the posters, the thing with pipes sticking out of it for boiling up the brew, or whatever, it is all estu-flipping-pendo. We agreed with you the first time, so just shut up and let us enjoy the exhibition in peace. AND STOP TAPPING ME ON THE BLOODY SHOULDER. Nothing I hate more than being prodded, when I'm trying to enjoy a glass of seca. The problem is, our responses are hindered by our lack of vocabulary. *Que bonito* is one, beautiful or pretty I imagine, *pressy-osa* another which we have picked up, which appears to be on similar lines, and we have employed both on several occasions already in the last few minutes. I did actually hear *Que Mono* used as a term of surprise and delight recently, which is something to do with a monkey, literally, but Marie at the library suggested it was an expression used by teenage girls, so possibly not a phrase to utilise in front of Rico, who clearly thinks I am a bit of a wuss for not sloshing back my drink. And sometimes, these words do not exactly translate. *Stupendous* is not a term we use a lot in English, is it, but here they do. Juan 'The Dustman' is particularly fond of it, which causes additional problems due to his absence of front teeth. It is bad enough trying to learn a foreign language on the hoof, let me tell you, without having to keep a wary eye out for incoming projectile spittle.

Suddenly, I become aware of a change of atmosphere, somehow. Is it something wrong with my hearing, a strange ringing in my ears? I glance across at Elena, who appears to be in a world of her own, away with the fairies, in a trance-like state. Has gulping down the rot-gut left her tonsils in turmoil? Is she spaced-out on the anise fumes? Or is she just biding her time, waiting to grab an empty bottle, and bury it in the back of Rico's head? Now, let me tell you. I'm typing this by hand, on my laptop, two fingers maximum. So it takes a long time, right? Been at it for months, already. Then I have to correct my frequent mistakes, review what I have written, then re-read each chapter. And I'm only two-thirds the way through, with plenty more to tell you about. Then I have to take a photograph of a sunset, convert the whole text to some Amazon thingy so they can review it for inappropriate content, then wait while they transfer it to e-book format, and the paperback, when that comes out. So none of this happened the Christmas just gone, OK? But trust me on this, I have it down in my diary, in black-and-white, 23rd December, half-one in the afternoon. ELENA SHUT-UP FOR TEN MINUTES!!!! *Estupendo, no?*

Meanwhile Rico is still in full flow. 'There were more than forty anise factories in Rute, in the last century, and five hundred in Cordoba province. Phenomino, no? The spirit was made in every region of Spain, the Canaries, and the Balearics, estupendo, no? Cristina, look, anise from Barcelona, this one dates from 1885.' And to emphasise the point, he sketches an imaginary date about a foot from her face. 'Phenomino, no?'

'Si, que bonito.'

'These bottles are from Madreeth, friend. Look at the designs, 1889 this one is. Estupendo, no?'

'Si, pressy-osa.'

'And look here, Hee-HHON, Santander, San Sebastian, all in the north. Phenomino, no?'

'*Si, que mono.*' He will just have to think I'm a big girl. I've run out of things to say. *And the will to live, quite honestly.*

Suddenly, from behind me comes a sound like a male elephant-seal in a state of arousal, I spin around and catch Elena mid-yawn, mouth wide open. *Yeah, I saw you eating your breakfast, Mrs. I don't need to see it again.* 'Oh my gaad, I am so boring. Bottles, bottles. Give me some more anneee, Rico!'

I cannot help chuckling. They all get this one wrong. 'We say *I am so bored*, Elena. I am bored, she is bored. The *feeling* is bored. But the *situation* is boring. This is so boring, that is so boring. Do you understand?'

'Ha ha ha ha! Yees, you are bored, Cristina is bored, I am bored, we all bored! Come on Rico!'

I was speaking generally, of course, but she is correct, I am bored rigid. As my mother-in-law might have said, *seen one bottle of anneee, seen 'em all*. Still, the first few minutes of the tour were quite informative, and Rico is clearly passionate about his subject. *Just as well he doesn't speak English, though...*

Back in the bar, our guide produces more bottles, one of which he claims to be forty-eight per-cent proof. 'Ha ha ha ha! This one please!' giggles Elena. Narrowing her eyes, she squints at the rest of the line-up. 'Then I will have the coffee, and the blueberry. Ha ha ha ha!' Blimey, it seems you can infuse this stuff with just about anything, although, sadly, there doesn't seem to be a *Taunton Natural Dry* version, which is probably just as well in the circumstances, given that my knees are a bit stiff these days. I could probably manage to do the *Juke-Box Jive*, but would need half an hour's notice, to get limbered up.

Time passes pleasantly, hazily, before raucous shouting from the street alerts us to the fact that the bus is about to depart, but not quite yet, apparently, as Elena has her purse out. 'Rico, give me one *dulce*, one coffee, and the forty-eight! Ha ha ha ha!'

He beams, widely. 'That will be nine, twelve and fifteen euros, a total of thirty-six.' *Is it just me, or is everything in this town over-priced*? Chrissie bought a bottle of the ordinary stuff last Christmas, from Mercadonna, and I swear it was only six-something. And it had a sultry maiden on the label. Keeping schtum this time, though, aren't I? *Look what happened before.*

We stumble into the blinding sunshine. 'Pepe! Where is my suitcase! Ha ha ha ha! I need to put my anneee away!'

'Did you buy an anneee, English?' bellows the Wag.

I indicate my former pupil, frantically stowing her purchases. 'No. Elena bought the whole shop!'

We crowd, laughing noisily, onto the bus, and Pepe sets off again. *Did you buy any em-boo-tea-toes? Yes I got some booty-farra! What about the anneee? Yes two bottles! Coffee and seca! I got a kilo of sweets in the sugar museum! That Doo-Kessa is ugly! Did you see her lips? Putting on weight too! I want a garter like Marilyn Monroe! Give Alfonso a Christmas treat!*

After a few minutes we arrive at what appears to be the centre of the village, consisting of a huge square containing around a dozen market stalls, and the usual Spanish mayhem. An extremely ancient Old-Bill is frantically waving his arms, at no-one in particular, and Paco skillfully ignores him and steers his coach around the melee into a parking space, and switches off the engine. 'It is just after two now, back here at six, please. Enjoy your lunch!'

FOUR HOURS FOR LUNCH? OH MY GAAD! We only wanted a sandwich. What the devil are we going to do for four hours, for pity's sake? Be easier to walk home, quite frankly. Elena however seems delighted at the prospect. 'Yees, we have it above the table! Ha ha ha ha!'

*I beg your pardon*? Did she actually say that? Have what, pray? I narrow my eyes, and do my best to look confused. 'Can you repeat that, please?'

'Ha ha ha ha! Yees, we have saying in Espain, *sobre la mesa*. It mean 'above the table'. You no have above the table in Eengland?'

*Not in polite company, certainly.* I steal a furtive glance at my wife. 'Have what above the table, Elena?'

'Ha ha ha ha! Lunch, of course! We find table, we have lunch, *sobre la mesa*. Come on, follow me plees!'

Oh well, what can we do? We will just have to spin out the time as best we can, I suppose. But seriously, four hours? Have you ever heard anything like it? Still, the thirty-second rule of travel states that *if a Spaniard invites you above a table for four hours, just go with it,* so why not?

Still cackling, bonkers-woman leads us to a building marked *Taberna*, which clearly means 'tavern', into which around five hundred people have crammed and all started shouting at the same time, and the prospect of spending four minutes, let alone four hours, in this bedlam is laughable. Not to mention the fact that there is barely a square inch free, let alone a table, so we won't be *sobre la mesa* any time soon, that's for sure. However, as has happened before in this ridiculous country, I am proved wrong. 'Elena, I am here! You come, plees!' All I can see are bodies, but we squeeze in the general direction of the voice, then my heart sinks into my boots. *Oh. Please. No.* It is tray-girl, from the Too-Ron factory. Writhing with embarrassment, wishing a large hole would open up, a sickly grin on my face, we approach her table, which is less than a yard square. *Oh what a shame, no space.*

'Anna!' cries the mad one. 'How are you! Ha ha ha ha! Do you have room for us?' It appears she does. Sliding a stool for Elena from beneath the table, she directs Chrissie and I to what might optimistically be described as a 'window-seat', but which actually would be better characterised as a 'plank', and we shoe-horn ourselves in.

Right. I am British. I have to get this cleared up. 'Look, Anna, I am sorry about the Too-Ron, and Mercadonna.' And I adopt my best contrite-face.

It seems I was concerned about nothing, however. 'Ah do not worry!' smiles tray-Anna. 'I am student of Eengliss at University of Granada, thees is holiday job only, for the Crees-mas. I hate thees, the customers are goats, and you are correct, the too-ron is cheaper in the supermarket!' *Phew*! She then grabs a passing waiter by the bum. Not, mark you, a playful pinch, but a full-on handful of butt-cheek. The startled young man spins on his heels, ashen-faced, almost dropping his tray, then bursts into a wild fit of giggling. 'Thees my boyfriend, Alberto! Say hello to Elena, and my new Eengliss friends...'

'Cristina and John' I smile, keeping my hands in full view.

''Ello' he splutters. 'Anna, she ver bad! What you like, plees?'

Unbelievable. We've done it again. And there was me thinking it would take about a hundred years to get served in here, and now we have our own personal server. Plus, it appears, a choice of tapas. Now *that*, Rico, is estupendo, no? Three beers appear as if by magic, together with a plate of king prawns, and bearing in mind the thirty-first rule of travel states *if someone offers you free shellfish whilst seated on a plank, just wolf it down*, we do.

Suddenly, my eyes are drawn to a TV screen in the corner showing what appears to be a funeral, of someone quite famous, I imagine. There are shots of the cortege, then old footage of a woman with a poodle haircut, trout lips, a turned up nose and a bit of a belly…hang on a minute, isn't that the Duchess of record-players? 'Look at that' I command of no-one in particular, 'is that the Doo-Kessa de Decca? Is she dead? We only saw her half-an-hour ago, just down the street!'

Chrissie almost chokes on a sliver of shell. 'Not Decca, you blithering idiot, Alba!'

'Well who cares if she is called Decca, Bush, Ferguson, PYE, HMV or Dansette, quite honestly? We were just looking at her!'

The Spanish girls are roaring with laughter, although it is doubtful they get the references to ancient British radiograms. 'Yes, she is dead!' giggles tray-Anna.

Right, this is Spain, so if the funeral is today, that must mean she died, what, yesterday? What a hell of a coincidence. 'Did she die this week?'

Elena is still chuckling, although I'm still uncertain it's about the Hi-fi joke. Surely she is too young to have had a collection of forty-fives? 'Ha ha ha ha! She die three, maybe four jeers, I forgetting now!'

Chrissie is looking puzzled. 'So why are they showing the funeral on TV today?'

Tray-Anna is concentrating. 'Yes, I think maybe four years ago, but it was thees time of year, Cheesmas time. ALBERTO!' Her boyfriend is passing with a loaded tray, but thankfully for those standing within range of a possible spillage, notably me, he escapes another groping. 'When did *La Alba* die?'

He turns aggressively towards the TV, and despite his burden, still manages an obscene one-handed gesture. 'Ah who cares, the old *puta*!' *So not a fan, then.*

And so the time passes companionably, but strangely the lunchtime rush shows no sign of dying down. I would have expected the place to start thinning out a bit, but if anything it is more crowded than when we came in. People are squeezed into impossibly small spaces, standing-room only, tapas balanced in one hand, drink in the other. Is this what they mean by *over the table*? Is this the only bar in town? Who is that with their elbow in my neck? Will my hearing ever recover from this cacophony? Will Elena ever stop cackling? Who knows?

The TV is now showing a clip of the Doo-Kessa standing next to Camilla Parker Bowles, an image which will surely disturb my sleep this night, so easing my tortured posterior off of the plank, but well away from tray-Anna's reach, I indicate to Alberto, who appears to be taking a short break, that he might like to take my place on the board for a few minutes, take the weight off possibly.

And get me facing away from the telly. 'I am estudent of engineer at University Granada' he begins, 'and is necessary for me have exam in Eengliss. Phew!' And he shakes his head, sadly. 'Anna much better, but for me is ver diffy-cool.' Just as we are about to sympathise just how diffy-cool learning a foreign language is, he catapults off the seat. 'Me gas! Me gas!' *Oh. Please. No.* Surely he is not about to break wind? In front of strangers? In this already stifling atmosphere? Completely hemmed in, he is twisting his body, painfully, like Uncle Tom Cobley's old grey mare, with a nasty dose of colic. Whatever is coming, is gonna be a biggie. I recognise the symptoms.

Elena, meanwhile, is jerked to her feet, as if attached by wires. 'Me gas! Ha ha ha ha! You want me-gas, plees?' What is this, a farting contest? Has the appearance of the Doo-Kessa, or dare I say it, Camilla, sparked an outbreak of competitive flatulence? Alberto is squeezing his way through the crowd, although he should presumably be heading for the door, or the gents, surely. The noise is unbelievable, people are pushing and shoving, whereas Chrissie and I are still perched precariously, open-mouthed at this lunacy, on our window seat.

Tray-Anna seems to be the only sane person left on the planet. 'You ever had me-gas?' My wife is shaking with laughter but what can I say? We were only formally introduced to the girl half an hour ago, and this is not the rugby club. Quite honestly I can think of at least half a dozen ribald replies, each one less suitable than the last, and having already blotted my copybook earlier this morning, I am tongue-tied.

Before either of us can frame a suitable response, Alberto comes weaving through the throng clutching a large plate of what appears to be something you might find splattered across the pavement outside a Wimpy Bar, on a Sunday morning, together with a hand-full of forks. 'I have the last plate!' he cries, triumphantly, 'you take, plees!'

*Not a chance mate.* Peter Allen's sausage-dog would surely not have given this concoction a sniff, and neither will I. 'Er, what actually is it?' enquires Chrissie, peering dubiously at the greeny-brown, lumpy, congealed concoction.

'Fried breath!' Elena confirms, cheerfully. 'Hoder! Ha ha ha ha! Eengliss ver difficult. Breadth. Breathd.'

'Fried bread!' Anna corrects, better able to get her tongue around the pronunciation.

*They have to be joking*. I am a lifelong consumer of fried bread, usually with an egg on top, admittedly, and never before have I seen anything even remotely resembling this. What on earth have they done to it? Has to be just about the easiest thing in the world to cook, surely? Oil in the pan, in with the slice, turn a couple of times and leave to go the required shade of brown. Add fried egg, job done. This stuff looks like it has been pulverised by sumo wrestlers, left outside to rot, and blended with giblets. And that might be talking it up, to be honest. Still, other people's countries and all that, and besides, Alberto went to war to get it for us, didn't he, so we don't want to appear ungrateful. I smile warmly, inwardly cringing, although hopefully only I know that. 'It looks very different from the fried bread we have in England!'

'Ha ha ha ha! Eengliss brax-fass! Oh my gaad!' Elena giggles. 'I see thees in my school book!' *Al right, all right, just don't mention the cheese-rolling, OK*?

Tray-Anna comes to the rescue. 'Crumbs. Crumbs of bread. And you have different bread in Eengland, no? Here in Espain we have the pan, Espanee pan, so we use the crumbs from yesterday, mix with garlic, olive-oil. Espain was ver poor, years ago, people have no food, me-gas was cheap, fill the stomach. You can mix me-gas with chorizo, shoshage, beans, anything. You take, plees.' Yes, wondering when this was coming. Not too keen to be honest, although the ingredients sound innocuous enough, don't they? I just don't understand, that being the case, why it's the colour of bile. Still, you know what they say, *Pete's dachshund was a right wussy little creature. Get a forkful down you, Jonno*. So I do, and I have to tell you, it tastes fine. Nothing to set the taste buds alight, and I doubt I'd order it by choice, although bung a few lumps of shoshage in and I might think about it. The Spaniards show no such reticence, however, digging in with relish, although that is it for me thank you very much, not being a fan of sticking my fork where other people have just had theirs. Not terribly hygienic, is it, especially among strangers? Is there a shortage of crockery in this town? Or washer-uppers? Search me.

The Doo-Kessa is now strolling regally, arm-in-arm with some ageing lothario, although Camilla appears to have disappeared, a *Black Sabbath* number is belting out from a speaker, and all around the bar the locals are wolfing down their crumbs of breathd like there is no tomorrow. *Never like this at the Rose and Crown on a lunchtime, was it*? Which is the whole point about living in another country, obviously. Suddenly, for no apparent reason, I feel decidedly mellow. Whether it is the manty-cado, the polbo, the too-ron, Ronaldo's tiny todger, the gentleman's club, the truncheon, the Pope, six tots of anneee, Marilyn Monroe's garter, Old Trout Lips, or, unlikely as it may seem, Camilla, or maybe a combination of all of the above, I am overcome by peace and goodwill. *Well, it is Christmas, right*? Chrissie, sensing my mood, squeezes my hand. I smile lovingly. 'You don't happen to have a pair of ear-defenders in your bag, by any chance, do you!'

Thus passes the afternoon, and before we know it, incredibly, the spell is broken by irritable honking from the street, and Pepe's coach appears outside the window. The stragglers are being rounded up. Us. Have we really been four hours above the table? Incredibly, it appears we have. Climbing the steps to ironic applause, the Wag is still in full flow. 'Get lost, English, did you?!'

I smile warmly, and crinkle my eyes. 'No. *Sobre la mesa*!'

We slump into our seats, and suddenly I am overwhelmed by weariness. Back with my head, I am asleep in seco……Wrong! 'Got any DVD's, Pepe?' hollers Elena. *And there was me thinking she would be worn out, enabling me to catch forty winks*. Our nutty driver performs the usual swerving manoeuvre as he rummages for the tape, and suddenly the two tellies on the ceiling crackle into life and the opening credits of a Mister Bean film are rolling. *Surely not*? Will the Spanish find this funny? Isn't he a bit, well, *British*? OK so there is no dialogue to worry about, but are the bumbling antics of a tweed-jacketed Englishman humourous, to the locals? It would appear so. A buzz of anticipation grips the passengers, and within seconds virtually the whole bus is shaking with laughter, tears streaming down cheeks, tissues being produced, proving beyond doubt that comedy is universal. Incredible. 'Would you like the middle seat, Elena, so you can see better?' I enquire, always the gentleman, although only I know that I really mean *so that I can wedge myself into the corner and nod-off*. Which I do, although I would have been better awake, quite honestly, as I drift off into a tortured nightmare where I am being pursued by a thirty-foot sausage, with hundreds of legs, which suddenly morphs into the Loch Ness Monster, with dragon's wings and a huge scaly head, breathing fire. In sheer terror I dive through a doorway into a Gentleman's Club, where Michael Jackson, wearing only a frilly red garter, is selling tickets to a stage show featuring the Doo-Kessa, dressed in a pink catsuit, who proceeds to whip me painfully with electricity cable whilst screaming 'I AM ALBA! NOT DECCA!' *Whack*. 'I AM NOT FERGUSON!' *Whack*. 'THAT IS A DIFFERENT DOO-KESSA!' *Whack*. 'I AM ALBA! ALBA! ALBA!' Elena then appears, dressed in gold spangly jodhpurs, impales me through the groin with a six-inch stiletto and wallops me with a copper's truncheon, bellowing 'CLASSES OF EENGLISS! HAHAHAHAHA! CLASSES OF EENGLISS! I WANT CLASSES OF EENGLISS, EVERY DAY! EVERY NIGHT! PLEES, I SHOW YOU MY COCK! CLASSES OF EENGLISS!'

I wake, bathed in sweat, shirt stuck to my back, to find the girls giggling mightily. 'Mary-night, Mary-night! Ha ha ha ha! You have Mary-Night!'

'A nightmare' Chrissie chuckles, 'he was having a nightmare.' *If only they knew…*. 'Come on, Sonny Jim. We are home. Santa Marta. Look, we are in the bus station!'

*Thank heavens*. Surreptitiously checking my nether regions for puncture wounds, we stumble off the bus, and bid fond farewells to our fellow passengers. 'Goodbye English!' grins the Wag. 'You didn't spend much money, but we enjoyed your company!'

'I didn't spend *any* money', I reply, truthfully, adopting my best serious-face. 'My woman has spent it all!' Which earns me a whack, but also the expected roar of approval. *So that was all right, then, but God I need my bed*.

Elena has not quite finished yet, however. She envelops us in a massive bear-hug, then starts flapping her hands. 'Plees. Ha ha ha ha! I enjoy my day weeth you, moocho, I decided to continue weeth my examins of Eengliss. The next, how you say, level? So plees, Jonneee, we continue after the Cree-mass, weeth classes of Eengliss? Plees you say me yes! Ha ha ha ha!'

*Well there's a Christmas present I will never forget. Oh deepest joy*. My wife, however, seems delighted. 'I am sure John will be happy to continue the classes, after the New Year, Elena!' she smiles. 'I will contact you on Fay-Boo, sorry, Face-Book, to arrange it, in January!'

Staggering wearily up the cobbled street, she squeezes my arm. 'Wasn't that an absolutely fantastic day? What wonderful memories, to treasure, don't you think?'

I huff. 'Oh yeah, wonderful for you. Absolutely incredible memories for you. But two things completely ruined it for me, I will have you know.'

She gives me a playful nudge. 'Oh go on, you know you love her really! Ha ha ha ha! Give you something to look forward to, won't it, classes of Eengliss! Anyway, what was the other thing? Come on, let's hear it.'

I am still huffing. 'Well, what completely ruined my day was that we didn't win the raffle for that bloody fruit cake, did we?'

## CHAPTER 14. WHAT LAD-RONNY NICKED ME TYRES?

As a motorist, there is one major drawback in living on a narrow, cobbled hairpin-bend, halfway up a mountain; there is nowhere to park. It might be possible, if you are extremely lucky, to bag one of the few spots where the streets widen, but as that involves a stress-inducing drive around the switchback, dog-legged zig-zags, on the off-chance of finding somewhere, we simply don't bother. Some of the neighbours do, even though they pay for spaces on a municipal site, which we have christened *El Scrapyard*, on account of the motley collection of broken-down, abandoned, dirt-encrusted vehicles with flat tyres, sunken into the weeds, which are to be found there. Plus a length of plastic trim from Phil the chicken's sawn-up Transit van. No. A pleasant ten-minute stroll from our house, where the old part of town gives way to the new, are full-width streets, with pavements, and a two-hundred yard length of garden wall, where we can leave the car without blocking anyone's view, or causing any obstructions, and where a space is virtually guaranteed. Plus, we avoid the usual Spanish shunting, which is what passes for parking in this neck of the woods, thereby reducing considerably the risk of battle-damage on our pristine white paintwork.

I said one major drawback, but there are a number of minor ones, too. Cleaning? *Forget it. No water.* Vacuuming? *Not possible. No electricity.* Checking oil levels? *On a mountain? Are you having a laugh? Nowhere flat, this side of Madreeth.* Other little maintenance jobs? *Too hot.* See what I mean? Not easy, is it, this retirement business? Having said all that, there are wash & vax places dotted about, and I am sure you could find a relatively flat spot on a petrol-station forecourt for checking the levels. They say you should let the engine oil settle a bit before getting the dipstick out, don't they, so while you are waiting, follow the Spanish example and go for a coffee. Virtually every *gasolinera* here has an excellent coffee shop attached, and no, not branded national chains selling weak, overpriced slops, but full-strength, heart-stopping espresso for just over a euro. Throw in about a foot of toasted, crusty bread smothered with chopped tomato for the same price, and you won't need to eat again any time soon. And your oil will have returned to normal in the interval, too.

Seriously though, we didn't think about all this when we bought the house, although you pay peanuts and all that, and as we only use the car at weekends, I guess we can live with it, but for anyone considering going down this cheap town-house route, my advise would be to scope out the local area for likely car-parking spots, before you sign on the dotted line. There you go, might just have saved you a load of aggro!

Mind you, in theory we have no such problems, because outside our caravan on the Camping Rural site, there is an abundance of electric, water, level ground, shade, and most importantly in this country of constant questions such as 'what you doing neighbour?', privacy. I say in theory, but so far it hasn't worked out that way, however. Look, a day toiling away, or should I say boiling away, on the beach, wears you out, right? A cold shower to wash away the sand and the salt, an even colder beer, and a long sit down in a camping chair with a book, after what has been a strenuous week, is just what the doctor ordered. So hands up, I confess, it is all my fault, no excuses, should have known better. We bought the little white SEAT in the autumn, and here we are in mid-February, and I haven't done a stroke, in terms of basic maintenance. Nothing. I am ashamed of myself, quite honestly.

Until this evening. Bonnet up, oil and water fine, screenwash needs a drop, though. Headlights on, all good, round the back to check the tail………OH MY GOD! Look at the rear tyres! I have been seriously negligent here. We knew, when we bought the car, that the tyres would need replacing in a few months, but all this sitting around in the sunshine must have addled my brain, what little there is left of it. OK, there is no canvas showing through, but there is little tread visible, either. They used to say, didn't they, you could use a two-bob piece to check the depth of your tread? Well, I don't have any English coins on me right now but there would be little point, anyway. Smooth as a baby's bottom. Right, thinking-cap on. There is a tyre garage just off the motorway near Malaga airport, and we have to go to the DIY place on the industrial estate there tomorrow on the way home for a few bits and pieces, so kill two birds with one stone, call in for two back tyres. There is a shopping centre down there too, near that giant blue and yellow Swedish warehouse, I cannot mention the name as I would get heart palpitations and need to lie down in a darkened room for a couple of hours, and I have all this writing to do, but you know the one I mean. They sell meatballs, I believe.

So sounds like a plan, but I have a small dilemma. What do I tell Chrissie? Don't want her lying awake all night, worrying about the tyres going pop, do I? Which I know she will do. It's how I was brought up, OK? My father was old school, and I can hear him now. 'Don't say anything to your mother, son, but…' All right, it's the twenty-first century now and those attitudes should rightly be consigned to history, but I was born in the fifties. It's what us chaps do. Suddenly, the caravan window opens wider and my wife's head pops out. 'Have a look at those back tyres while you're there, will you? We need to get some new ones, the tread is almost non-existent, and I don't know if your life-insurance policy is up-to-date. Those tyres are like you, completely bald. There's that *Maris* place near the airport, so first thing in the morning, you can drop me at the shopping centre, and you can sort out the tyres, like you should have done, TWO MONTHS AGO!'

*Well that little quandary sorted itself out quite well, didn't it?*

So the following morning we arrive outside *Maris*, having successfully avoided the giant blue and yellow Swedish meatball emporium, and are greeted in the customer area by a cheery, middle-aged man going by the name of Ramon, according to the name-badge pinned proudly to his spotless overalls. 'Buscando dos neumaticos para trasera de mi coche' I announce. There, what do you think of that then? I hope it means *I'm looking for two back tyres for my car*, but then again, possibly not.

'No. Ruedas.' Ramon smiles.

Now I know this word, *ruedas*, for some reason. It means 'wheels'. But I don't need any wheels, obviously. 'No, neumaticos!' I confirm, for the avoidance of doubt.

His grin tightens, slightly, and I get the finger wagging, too. Only one finger, for now, but clearly I have transgressed in some way. 'No. Ruedas.'

For pity's sake. I have the wheels already. Those circular, metal things, bolted onto the axles. I need the circular, rubber things, otherwise known as 'tyres'. *Neumaticos* in Spanish. Luckily, there is a poster on the office wall, featuring said components, so in a not-quite-a-Paddington-Bear-but-almost kind of a way, I gesture at the black rubbery things. 'No, I have the *ruedas*, I need the *neumaticos*.'

He throws back his head and roars with laughter, although Chrissie and I fail to see the funny side. 'Sorry, here in Spain we say ruedas, I need to change my ruedas!' Oh yes, absolutely hilarious that was, wasn't it? I don't think. So let us be clear on this. There are separate Spanish words for both wheel and tyre, but if you need a new tyre, you ask for a new wheel. Who knew that? Right now, there are people stuck in rainy old England thinking we are living the life of Riley over here in the sunshine. Let me tell you, it's just not like that, OK? And why is there never a branch of *Halfords*, when you need one?

Summoning up the last of my dwindling supply of smiling, I turn on my heels, head back towards the door, then swiftly about-turn. 'Buenas dias. Buscando dos RUEDAS para trasera de mi coche!' *And if that doesn't do it, I am off. Probably get another fifty miles until we are down to the canvas.*

It seems however this was simply good-natured banter all along. Ramon never imagined he would be encountering a dafty Englishman who couldn't tell a wheel from a tyre this day, did he? 'Your Spanish is very good!' he grins. 'What car do you have?' I gesture out the window at the little white SEAT standing forlornly in the car park. He performs a double take, as if he was mistaking me for Lewis Hamilton and expected there to be a Formula-One racing-car outside. 'We have this range of *Maris*-branded wheels which are perfect for you, good quality, made by *Hankook*.' And he rummages under the desk and emerges with a price catalogue. OK, I have heard of this brand, sounds fair enough to me. Little does Ramon realise but he is looking at a bloke who made do with remoulds, in my earlier motoring career, at least until the kids came along. Wouldn't do that now, of course, having achieved a slightly less poverty-stricken level, but quite honestly I don't care if they are made by Hankook, or Han Solo. 'Seen one neumatico, you've seen them all' as mother-in-law might have said.

He runs a grubby finger down the page. 'Twenty-four euros, each' he confirms. Blimey, that seems like a bargain. No idea what I was expecting really, all I can do is compare it with what the price might have been in the UK, and just over twenty quid a throw sounds cheap. Bearing in mind the population of Spain is only two-thirds of Britain's, with twice the land area, I would have thought that distribution costs here would be higher. I am no economist of course, and other factors such as lower wages and warehousing here come into play, but yeah, I am well 'appy, to paraphrase Del. *Or not.* 'Do you want them mont-akky?' Ramon enquires.

Mont-akky? Mont? Mount? Mounted? *What, like a stag's head, on the wall*? Or is he asking if I want them fitted? Well actually mate I was planning on taking them home, putting them on the patio, filling them with earth and planting them up. Or hang on, what is this in my pocket? Ooh look, a pair of tyre levers for me pushbike. Nah, don't worry, I'll mont-akky them myself. What else can I say? That thing for getting stones out of horses' hooves is going to be no earthly use at mounting tyres, is it? 'Si.'

Chrissie has turned away, so I cannot see if she is giggling, or cursing. Ramon meanwhile taps away at a calculator. 'Equilibrio?'

Has to be balancing, I am guessing. Equilibrium. *Not gonna be twenty-four bucks a piece, are they, these wheels*? Does my wife have one of those laser pens, and a handful of lead weights in her bag? No? Therefore it has to be 'Si.'

More tapping. 'Balbo?'

Unless he is referring to one of those African trees, which grow upside down, he must mean 'valve'. Damn it, forgot the Wrigley's. Could have chewed some up, and stuck it over the air hole. What is this anyway, twenty questions? Surely all of these 'extras' should be included in the price as standard? Come on, who would possibly want to fit their own tyres? Go on then, chuck in a balbo. 'Si.' Right, that is the lot, surely? Nothing else he can stiff me for. *Wrong*.

'Eye-ree especial?' Nope, you got me there, Ray. Eye-ree? I narrow my eyes in a *not-the-foggiest* way. 'Si, eye-ree. Oxy-hen.' And he purses his lips, exhaling dramatically.

My wife meanwhile is still fixated on something she can discern through the window into the workshop behind. 'Air. He is asking if you want special air. Oxygen. You know, puff puff!'

AIR? They are charging for air in this place? That free stuff that just floats around in the sky? Does he think I just beamed down from a galaxy far far away, with Han Solo? *Arriba mi cuerpo*, as they say in Santa Marta. Special air, too, which immediately reminds me of Chrissie's mother, who always refers to a stiff G&T as her *special water*. Ramon senses conflict in the room over this latest turn of events, and produces a glossy leaflet extolling the virtues, in Spanish of course, of the special air, which gives a more responsive ride, apparently. *Yeah right. Ding dong.* 'No, gracias.'

Some final adding-up, and wheel-seller has a total for us. The final, final total, hopefully. 'Seventy-six euros. Baly?' Actually, that is still pretty good, I think. A remould for the Ford Anglia was about a fiver, back in the day, but seventy quid for two tyres? A result, Jonno!

'Come back in one hour' Ramon suggests, 'you can visit *Thee-en Montaditos*, in the shopping centre.' I nod in agreement although clearly only he knows what he is talking about. *Thee-en* is a hundred, I believe, and a word ending in *itos* usually signifies a small, or little, something. So a hundred little monty's, whatever they are, possibly? Wonderful, this journey of discovery, isn't it? Little did we know, when we left the caravan this morning, we would be learning all about special air, and a hundred little somethings, this day.

Chrissie, strangely, seems reluctant to leave the office, gazing wistfully into the workshop. Usually she would be champing at the bit at the mere mention of a shopping centre. What could possibly be so fascinating about a pile of tyres? Sorry, wheels? 'So, are you, er, coming, then?'

'Actually' she purrs, 'I think I will stay here. Check out the totty! I think he is completely commando, under those overalls. What do you reckon?'

WHAT? I stare angrily through the glass but all can see is a swarthy, snake-hipped Spaniard wiggling his arse in a manner which would surely earn him a stiff kicking, in certain pubs I could mention. 'YOU DIRTEE COO! Pack that in, right now. A woman of your age! If I was caught leering like that, there would be hell up!' And adopting my best aggrieved-face, I turn to Ramon. 'Miras. El coolo! Women, eh?'

He guffaws, loudly, then turns, shaking his own posterior. 'Look, I have a beautiful bum, too!' *Why didn't I just run the cursed tyres down to the canvas? Not like this at* Halfords, *is it?*

Dragging my reluctant wife behind me, we enter the shopping *plaza*, and just about the first building we spot is proudly proclaiming the legend *100 Montaditos*, although whoever painted the sign was clearly drunk, as the number '1' resembles a snake which has just been run over by a steamroller. Curious. Still, every cloud, as the place is clearly a cafe-bar, and as the sixteenth rule of travel states *never pass a strange restaurant with a splattered serpent in the title*, and bearing in mind it's been a hard morning already, we flop down at an outside table. Placed in the middle are a couple of laminated, pictorial menus, a notepad and a ball-point pen, and it appears these *montadito* things are miniature baguettes, four inches long or thereabouts, and yes, there are a hundred of them. Now, it is my usual custom to ignore restaurants displaying photos of the food, on the grounds that I am fully aware of what egg and chips look like, but this is different, as I cannot even begin to imagine a hundred different sandwich fillings. Not that there are a hundred separate pictures, you understand, which means we are going to struggle identifying many of the offerings. What could a *christorra* possibly be, would you suppose?

The first sixty or so *montaditos* are one euro, another fifteen are one-twenty, and what are described as *Super Monty's* are one-fifty. There are also items *para picar*, at two yo-yo, including bowls of chips, onion rings and something described as *palomitas*, which I thought was the word for pigeon, but then again…. It is not yet official Spanish lunchtime, so the place is not particularly busy, and the noise levels should therefore be tolerable, but I cop a sneaky peek at a group of five teenage girls three tables away who are writing down their selections, swiping their smart-phones and gabbling at maximum volume, all at the same time. Remarkable. How do they do that? I am struggling to remember what day it is. I mime theatrically to Chrissie to make a note of her choices, and she cottons on to the joke and cups her hand to her ear. 'WHAT?'

'I SAID, WRITE DOWN YOUR CHOICES!' I giggle, loudly

'WHAT?'

'I'M HAVING A NUMBER SIX, A FIFTY-FOUR, ONION RINGS AND THE PIGEON!'

'DON'T THEY HAVE ANY ME-GAS? OR WOLF?'

Strangely, not a single eyelid is batted, on the other table. That was normal volume, for them. Anyway, we have made our decisions, so what happens next? There is not a single waiter in sight, does this mean we order inside? In a country where going up to the bar is uncommon, to say the least, it appears we do. Well, that is what the girls are doing, so who am I to disagree. I am about to follow when suddenly my wife snatches the list. 'You stay there, old man, we don't want you drooling in there, do we? I will place the order, you just sit here and LOOK THE OTHER WAY!'

I am rightly aggrieved. 'Oh heaven forbid I should as much as glance at those young ladies. Unlike you, who was blatantly perving at commando-boy in the garage, not half an hour since.' She giggles, pokes out her tongue, and hurries off to place the order, leaving me to ponder the injustices of life.

Around five minutes later, sipping our lemonades, just as we were beginning to wonder what was happening, I almost jump out of my skin, as someone has surely crept up behind me and started bellowing into a megaphone. 'CRISTINA, POR FAVOR!' I slump, ashen-faced onto the table, while my heart rhythm reduces to something like normal. Dear Go.... 'PILAR POR FAVOR! MARIA POR FAVOR! ALICIA POR FAVOR! LOLIS POR FAVOR! PATRI POR FAVOR!' Hell's teeth, this is like sitting inside Big Ben. I have spilled about half my drink down my shirt, and turn, head spinning, to see that we are positioned in front of a speaker, and that up at the counter, some half-wit is hollering into a microphone.

Chrissie finds this immensely funny, of course. 'Al right, all right, I will go. They said they would call me, but they weren't supposed to blow your bloody head off!'

*Never like this in Gregg's, is it*? And we are going to have to move tables, as any more shocks to the system I will surely peg it. Or was that her plan all along.... Now clearly I cannot move nearer the girls, lest I am accused of further lewd behaviour, and the only other spare places are on the other side of the terrace, and she will not know where I have gone.....quickly I gather up the glasses, tiptoe away, then chuckle to myself as she emerges, balancing three large, heaped plates, staring in disbelief at the empty seats. *That will get her back for salivating at some spotty youth*. Hang on a minute. *Three* plates? I dash across to give her a hand. 'How much have you ordered, you have enough to feed an army here! I am sure there will be other occasions, we don't have to try the whole hundred on the menu today!'

'ALBERTO POR FAVOR! MANOLO POR FAVOR!'

She flinches at the aural assault. 'This isn't all of it, there are three more plates to come!'

'So why did you buy so much? I only ordered two montaditos! You have about eight here!'

'JOSE POR FAVOR!'

She returns with the three extra platters, each one piled high. 'Look, I got confused, right? He was babbling on about his brother, or something, I don't know, I was saying no no, four only, he was shouting si si, you take, and the brother business. Anyway, nip up to the bar and get the chips, onion rings, and two lots of pigeons!'

'PACO POR FAVOR! MANUEL POR FAVOR!'

Our feast barely fits on the table. 'Bloody hell, Ramon said to come back in an hour, we will be here until next week, eating this lot. How much did you spend, for heaven's sake? We have the tyres to pay for, don't forget!'

'ANGELA POR FAVOR!'

'It came to twelve euros-something. Not a lot, really!'

I perform some quick mental arithmetic. 'You have almost twenty-quids worth here, are you sure this isn't someone else's order? And why do you have two lot's of pigeon?'

'FATIMA POR FAVOR!'

'OH SHUT UP! Palomitas aren't pigeon, you plonker. This one is deep-fried brie, with cranberry. Yours are chicken bites, with barbecue sauce. My *montadito*s are goat's cheese, smoked salmon with cream cheese, tuna with tomato, and the rest are for you! Now stop moaning, and get it down you!'

'LOLA POR FAVOR!'

I stare in disbelief at the mound of food in front of me. We won't be needing a Rick Stein special when we finally get home tonight, that's for certain. Before I start tucking in however I have one further question. 'So which one of these is the *christorra*?'

'RAFI POR FAVOR!'

After what seems like about fifty years, we waddle painfully back to *Maris* to find the little white SEAT standing proudly outside the workshop door, new rear tyres gleaming in the afternoon sunshine. 'There you go, look!' I exclaim, proudly, bending over to examine my new *neumaticos*, sorry *ruedas*, 'see how the new tread pattern has been designed to......' Where has she gone? Vanished! Glancing angrily around, I spot my errant spouse peering expectantly through the workshop window. THE DIRTEE COO! I stomp into the office to find Ramon in full flow. 'Yes my brother is the manager of *Thee-en Montaditos*, so I called him to give you a small discount! I hope you enjoyed it there! Now, you must return here next month to change the front wheels, OK?' Chrissie is nodding expectantly, like a breathless schoolgirl, all the while keeping an eye peeled for commando-spotty-youth, who to my huge delight seems to have disappeared. Amazingly, she then delves into her bag, fishes out her credit-card and, simpering, hands it across. *Well well, looky here*! Has she been hypnotised? I am keeping schtum.

Spilling out into the warm sunshine, I fire up the engine, and, shifting my seat back a notch to accommodate my extended belly, gingerly edge out of the car park and along my secret short-cut, under the motorway and past the golf course, to the far end of Torremolinos beach. I need a long lie-down, and a snooze, before the journey home. Settling into her beach-chair, my wife still appears to be in somewhat of a trance. 'Ahhhh, well that was a lovely morning, wasn't it? And we have to come back again next month, too! Oh, by the way, did you discover what that *christorra* thing was?'

I raise my head off the towel and look her firmly in the eye. 'I have only one word for you after today's performance. Shoshage!'

A few weeks later we are in the city of Jaen, or HH-ayen, as it is pronounced, throatily, in these parts. Capital of the province of the same name, Jaen forms the northern point of our inland triangle, featuring Granada in the east, and Cordoba to the west, and one of its most attractive features is a hilltop castle, part of which has been converted to a *Parador*, an upmarket hotel. A track leads along the summit to a huge, white concrete cross, thirty feet high maybe, from where commanding views over the twisted, tortured mountains to the south can be obtained. The *piece de resistance* of the city however is the Renaissance-style cathedral, home to the Holy Veil, which according to legend, was used to wash the face of Christ. The twin towers of its Baroque facade guard the surrounding labyrinth of narrow streets and arches, and it was there that we dined Royally, at a pavement cafe, on *blan-kettas marineros*, which might or might not translate as 'sailor's blankets', large chunks of crusty bread the size of a boxer's hand, topped with smoked salmon, tuna and sliced tomatoes, smothered with toasted cheese. Angels sang, let me tell you, especially when they learned the price; less than three euros each. *Estupendo, no*? We certainly thought so.

Returning to the car, late afternoon, we discover a glossy publicity notice shoved under the windscreen wipers, announcing the opening of a local tyre garage, *Neumaticos MK*. A wide range of new and secondhand wheels, at competitive prices, with friendly service, it confidently predicts. Hmmmm. I wonder….. 'This looks good,' I smile, 'there is a map on the back, and it is only a few streets from here. We could swing by there on the way home, and see about those front tyres we need to get. What do you think?'

My wife's face is a picture of crushing disappointment. *Now, why do you think that could be*? 'But I thought you said we would go to *Maris* again? We had good service there, didn't we? Old Ramon was good fun, and he got us that discount at Hundred Montaditos, didn't he? We could go there again, for lunch, couldn't we?'

*I am struggling to keep a straight face*. 'Yes, but we both agreed our weekend breaks are sacrosanct, didn't we? You complained before about me going to that DIY warehouse, and you having to mingle with a load of sweaty blokes, when you could be basking in the sunshine. Correct? That time at Maris was an emergency, wasn't it? And besides, my guts still haven't shrunk back to their former size, after eating all those *Montaditos*. So I suggest we have a look in this *MK* place, while we are here, and if it's no good, fine.'

She splutters. 'Your guts haven't shrunk to their former size since you were about eighteen, I think you will find! But I really liked it in Maris, there was a good atmosphere, I thought, they were good people, and you know I have a sixth sense about these things.'

'Sixth sense be beggared! Just be honest, I know why you want to go back to that place, which I thought was totally unhygienic by the way, people going to work with no underwear. Eughhh! Anyway, for all you know, this *MK* might be stuffed with oiled-up 'totty'. So get in the car, get hold of this map, 'cos you are navigating!

It takes us around twenty minutes to arrive at *Neumaticos MK*, situated on a nondescript trading estate, after what I suspect were several deliberate misdirections on the part of the 'navigator', due in part to the screwed-up nature of the map where it had been snatched from my hand, but we eventually pull up on the forecourt and step inside, to be greeted by Kevin Keegan from about 1976, complete with curly mullet and sideburns. 'There you go, look!' I mutter, 'I said there'd be totty, didn't I?' The place is huge, with no 'customer' area, glossy magazines or complimentary coffee, but an impressive display of tyres, floor to ceiling, lining the right-hand wall. Sadly however, I am unable to spot any remoulds, but otherwise we could have been beamed back to a previous century. My kind of place. And, blessed relief, the handful of old men standing around are properly clothed, in the underwear department, I would imagine.

'Buscando dos ruedas *delantay*, para mi coche' I smile, ignoring my wife who appears to have returned to the car, for some unknown reason. Now then. Please pay particular attention to my word *delantay*. It means 'front', and there will be questions on it, later.

Kevin glances outside. 'For the SEAT?' And he leads me across to the far wall, indicating a small selection of different brands, in my size, which I have carefully memorised. My attention is drawn to a pair of Michelins, and I reach out my hand and lovingly caress their rubbery flanks. I always aspired to a Michelin, back in my remould days, but simply never possessed the wherewithal. Great tyres, right? Kev senses my interest. 'Seventy euros, the pair, all included. Good price, no?'

It is indeed, but I just have to check. 'Including *mont-akky*, *equilibrio*, and *balbo*?' I query. Not worth mentioning the *special air*, was it, bearing in mind the last forty years haven't happened yet, in this particular emporium?

He nods emphatically. 'Everything.'

Well that's it settled, as far as I'm concerned, but 'I need to speak to my wife a moment' I inform him. Heading back outside, she is seated in the car, glowering. 'They have a pair of Michelins for seventy, all in.'

'Good for you.'

I am really trying here. 'Well that's a good price, don't you think? Top brand, Michelin. I reckon we should go for it.'

'*We*? Who said anything about *we*? If *you* want to do business with that slimy old grease-ball, that is *your* decision, and *your* money.'

I try a different tack. 'You don't fancy Kevin Keegan, do you?'

'FANCY HIM?' she hisses. 'I was a Leeds United supporter. 'Course I don't bloody fancy him! The Michelin-Man is better-looking than him! Just get on with it, and get me out of this ratty old dump.'

Kev is rubbing his hands at the prospect of a sale. 'Come back in half an hour?' he suggests, so we trudge off down the dismal street in search of a diversion, in silence for a few minutes. I am in the dog-house, and she's not keen to let me out, any time soon.

Suddenly, around the corner, we spot a cafe, bearing the legend *Cafe Pingu*, together with the image of a cartoon penguin. 'Ohh, look, a cafe!' I bluster. 'A penguin cafe, too. You like penguins, don't you? Come on, let me buy you a coffee, while we are waiting.'

She regards me without warmth. 'Oh, let me think. The last time we bought tyres, in Malaga, I took you for a right gut-busting lunch. In fact, it was so big, your belly hasn't returned to normal, even now. Followed by an afternoon on the beach. But you bring me to this imitation of a Soviet gulag, and try to buy me off with an invitation to a greasy-spoon.'

I cannot help chuckling. 'So is that a yes, then?'

After an excellent coffee, admittedly without the drama of the Montaditos experience, or any sand, we head back to Senor Keegan's and are somewhat surprised to see the car jacked up at both ends, and all four wheels lying on the floor. Kev freezes for a second, a guilty look etched on his face, as though he's been caught red-handed doing something he shouldn't, although I cannot work out what. '*Equilibrio*?' I smile.

'*Si, Si*' he nods, frantically, teeth exposed in a sickly grin. 'Another fifteen minutes.'

We head off, puzzled, in the opposite direction. 'I know I am only a mere woman', Chrissie ponders, menacingly, 'but I thought that *Maris* had balanced those tyres on the back already. What do you imagine old slimy was doing, just then? He is up to something, you mark my words!'

'Well, I cannot imagine what, quite honestly. Perhaps he feels the rear tyres need re-balancing, I don't know, but he is the expert after all.' *If only we knew then, what we know now.*

We walk for another aimless ten minutes, then back to Kevin's, to find the car standing proudly on the forecourt. *Right, don't have to think about tyres for another year, do I, apart from checking the pressures, occasionally?* I pay the man, cash only of course, and we head homeward.

Dusk is falling as we arrive back to Santa Marta, the western sky shot with crimson, and, avoiding scuffing my new purchases on the kerb, I step regally out of the car. 'Right, come and see this. Ta da ta da! Presenting, new Michelins to the front, and….'

'SECONDHAND TYRES TO THE REAR!' bellows my furious spouse.

'Yeah, yeah, very funny!' I giggle. 'OK, so you didn't get to see commando-boy this time, but I promise that when we need to have a service, we will go to Maris, OK? But you must admit that was a great price on the Michelins, wasn't it?'

'Yes, such a great price, that he had to STEAL THE MARIS TYRES TO MAKE UP FOR IT!' she fumes, gesticulating angrily at the rear wheels. 'Look, come and see what Mr Greaseball has done.'

What the hell is she is talking about? Stealing my *neumaticos*, what a ridiculous…….WHERE THE BLOODY HELL HAVE MY TYRES GONE? The nearly-new Maris ones have been replaced by a pair of scruffy old things. I simply cannot believe this. 'Hang on, hang on, let me get the penlight out of the glove-box a minute, let me check properly. I flop down onto the road, face about six inches from the wall of the tyre, shining the torch, and read out the brand name. '*Cheng-something.* Chinese remoulds? THE DIRTY THEIVING SCUMBAG! THE ABSOLUTE BASTARD.' I am stunned. Completely and utterly poleaxed. Beyond my wildest comprehension. How can something like this have happened, at a tyre-dealer? Boiling with rage, I stagger to my feet, and administer a swift kick to one of the offending *ruedas*. Hurts like hell, of course, bearing in mind I am wearing espadrilles, but it deflects my anger for a second or two. From hopping mad, to hopping painfully, in two seconds flat.

Chrissie is indignant. 'Oi, stop kicking Juan like that' she fumes, using her pet name for the little white SEAT. 'It's Keegan who needs a swift boot up the arse. Speaking of which, what are you going to do about this unholy mess you've got us into? I told you that low-life was up to no good, but you wouldn't listen.'

I have my head in my hands. Had I any hair to speak of, I would have torn it out by now. 'All right, all right, it's me who needs a damn good seeing-to, with a size ten. Come on, let's get the hell out of here, maybe the walk home will give me time to think. I need a few minutes to clear my head.' My mind is a jumble of rage, fury, and yes hurt, that this has happened to us, but by the time we reach home I have it mostly worked out in my head. 'Right, it's too late to go back there today, so I will go tomorrow. I know exactly what to say, and how to say it, to get him to put the Maris tyres back. The problem will be if he starts arguing, or denies all knowledge. I will need to go to the police, and I have no idea where the police station is in Jaen, or whether it would be the local Old-Bill or the Guardia Civil. So we need to ask one of our Spanish friends to come with me, and it's a big ask, isn't it, several hours out of someone's day?'

'What about Juan?'

I screw up my eyes. 'Yes, he would be perfect, but I don't want to keep asking him things, bothering him with our problems all the time.'

Chrissie is one step ahead of me, as always. 'Don't you remember he said he was on a course at Jaen university, for the next few weeks? Travelling there and back three or four days a week? Maybe he could meet you first thing in the morning, or when he finishes in the afternoon? Give him a call, I'm sure he won't mind.'

*Now why didn't I think of that?* Our dear friend is suitably outraged. 'Thees man is lad-ron! He is teef! He picker of olives! He *cholo!* We go he shop of wheels, tomorrow, we frighty sheety of he! Yees! Don't to worry, Jonneee! I must to start at university at eleven hours o-clock, so I meet you at ten-and-half, I know thees place, I see you there!'

I spend a restless tortured night, my mind a jumble of angry thoughts. At one stage I am dreaming I have stuffed Keegan inside a tractor tyre, encased in concrete, leaving only his sideburns and mullet flapping in the breeze, following which I take him to the top of the nearest mountain, and push him off, like a grotesque wheel of cheese. He rapidly picks up speed, then hits a huge bump, catapulting into the air, where he soars like Eddie the Eagle, coming back to earth directly on top of Neumaticos MK, completely obliterating the building, leaving nothing but a huge, steaming crater. Suddenly, from out of the pit, like a creature from the deep, crawls a curly mullet, which is grabbing and shaking me by the arm…. I wake to find Chrissie gently caressing my shoulder. 'Come on, the alarm has just gone off, you need to get going if you are meeting Juan at ten-thirty. You just have time for a quick coffee, and a slice of toast.' *Yeah, not only has that slime-ball nicked my tyres, he's denied me a decent breakfast. Don't know which is the worst crime, quite honestly.*

I am just finishing off my mug of instant when Chrissie squeezes in next to me on the sofa, and places her hand on my knee. 'Now look, I don't want you getting angry today, OK, and doing something stupid. We are totally in the right, just remember that, please. I will be worrying about you up there, so give me a call when you get it sorted.'

I smile sweetly. 'Don't worry, I will give him a Paddington Bear stare, and he will swap the tyres back in a jiffy!'

She giggles. 'Paddington Bear? More like Yogi Bear, you mean!'

I laugh for what seems the first time in ages. Such a huge release of tension. I adopt my best Yogi voice. 'But I'm smarter than the aver-age bear, Boo-boo!'

On the drive north I am endlessly rehearsing my speech. Do I act calm, or fly into a rage? I need to stand firm, clearly, but do I charge in, or wait for Juan? My pride is at stake here, so do I let him do all the talking, or attempt to sort it myself? It is only ten-fifteen as I round the corner past the Pingu Cafe, no sign of our friend yet, so decision made, I am going in, and to hell with the consequences. And strangely, the red mist clears. I am calmness personified. The garage doors are open so I steer across the forecourt, into the workshop, and I step out of the car and lock the door. Going nowhere, until this is sorted. Keegan is on the far side, talking to what appears to be a customer, patently ignoring me, so arm extended, finger pointing, never mind Yogi Bear, I adopt my best ten-foot grizzly, with a raging toothache. I frighty sheety of me, let alone he. 'YOU! HERE! NOW!' And I point my arm towards the car.

Grease-ball makes a big play of apparently spotting me for the first time, although he does look startled. He mutters something to his customer then scuttles across, sickly grin on his face. He knows he's been rumbled. 'Buenas dias!'

Buenas dias my arse. I fix him with a fiery glare. 'Yesterday, I bought a pair of Michelins here, for the front of my car.' And I make a sweeping gesture in their direction.

'Yes, yes, I remember' he whimpers.

Slowly, I pull the Maris receipt from my pocket, and make a big play of unfolding it under his nose. 'Last month, I bought a pair of wheels for the back, at Maris in Malaga, and here is the bill.' *And he is actually reading it...* Theatrically, I indicate the back tyres. 'Look, here they are.... oh, where have they gone?' And I raise myself to my full height. **'YOU ARE AN EFFING THIEF! CHANGE MY WHEELS BACK, NOW!'**

The effect is spectacular. Like a whipped puppy, hopping from foot to foot, he almost disappears up his own backside. 'You want me to put the Maris wheels back?'

That is indeed what I said. And he knows it. 'YES. AND MY LAWYER WILL BE HERE IN TWO MINUTES.' And at that precise moment Juan comes striding into the workshop, thunderous look on his face. Consider yourself frighty sheety, Senor Keegan, who is dancing around, desperately trying to open the car door. I hand him the key. 'Equilibrio, and new balbo, also', I hiss.

I embrace my friend warmly, as always. Wouldn't do that to my alleged lawyer in the UK of course, but here is different. And you can certainly say that again. 'I think you frighty sheety of he already!' he giggles, 'what say you to he? Thees *cholo* move much rapido!' He has indeed. One rear wheel is already off and grease-ball is frantically searching for the tyres he stole from me yesterday. 'I think I speaky weeth he now!' And he winks, conspiratorially.

'I have told him you are my lawyer, don't forget!'

'Perfecto!' And he strides across the workshop and engages Kevin in serious conversation, amid much arm-waving, while I lean on the wall and enjoy the squirming. The other customer, meanwhile, has departed. Juan comes strolling back, while *cholo* resumes his hectic tyre-changing. 'He say me, he no understand you Espanees, he think you want back wheels changed also. But I say he, we maybe go to polices-mans. He very frighty!'

I narrow my eyes. 'He is lying, Juan, why would I want nearly-new wheels changed? That is completely ridiculous. And I know the difference between back and front, *trasera* and *delantay*. And I didn't mention the word *trasera*. He stole my tyres, and he knows he did, end of story.'

Soon, the changing of the neumaticos is complete, and Kevin backs the car out of the workshop, avoiding eye contact. But I have one last comment for him. 'I live in Santa Marta. I need money for the petrol.' And I click my fingers, and hold out my palm, in best grizzly-bear fashion. Like a bulldog swallowing a wasp, he delves into his greasy overalls, producing a small wad of ten-euro notes. *Oh, if you insist, Kevin. A fiver would have done.* I flick my fingers again, and like a bulldog who's swallowed the wasp and started sucking a lemon, he peels one off and hands it over. I hold it up in front of him, and proceed to tear it up into tiny fragments, easily done with this Euro paper Monopoly-money, and fling it across the workshop, where it flutters down to earth like expensive confetti outside a church. With fire in my eyes, I raise my finger at the pathetic, cowering figure, invading his space. 'Fay-boo. Tonight.' And turning, Juan and I stride out of the workshop, heads held high.

Out on the forecourt we embrace. Getting to be a worrying habit, this cuddling of men, isn't it? 'OOH, JONNEEE!' You magnifico! Destroy he money! I laughing so much! You no need me!'

I grip my friend warmly by the hand. 'No, you were a big help, Juan. You gave me the confidence to do what I did! I could not have done any of that on my own. Thank you for being such a good friend to us.'

Driving home, I have time to reflect on what has undoubtedly been the most unpleasant episode of our lives in this country. OK, so nobody died, and one bad apple and all that, but this has left a nasty taste, I can tell you. And I am beginning to realise why the locals always scrutinise their tradesmen closely. In many cases they simply cannot be trusted. Had we remained in the workshop, and not gone for the coffee, there is no way this could have happened. Same with Electra-Man and the water-meter door, had I drawn up a chair and sat watching him in the street, as Loli or Fernando would undoubtedly have done, I could have prevented him cutting an over-sized hole in our wall. Are we too trusting, us Brits? I think so. Certainly something to bear in mind in future.

And, I have already alluded to the fact I am a slow typist, so you appreciate none of this happened in the Spring just gone. Therefore I have recited this tale to many people hereabouts in the interim period, and tellingly, none of the locals seemed that surprised. Despite his claim to the contrary, there is no doubt in my mind that grease-ball saw an opportunity to relieve a tourist from his property, thinking we would be back home before we discovered the deception, although clearly he didn't possess the intelligence of a goat, as why would a holidaymaker be driving a vintage, Spanish-registered, car? A shiny new rental, yes, but a little white SEAT? His comeuppance was well deserved.

All in all a valuable lesson learned.

## CHAPTER 15. VOTING, SPANISH-STYLE.

Back last summer, we each received official letters from the government of Spain. Always a bit nerve-wracking getting contacted by the Government, isn't it, especially this one, the Gobby-Enry, *Bastardos,* as Alicia calls them. We needn't have worried, however. All they wanted to know was, did we want to register to vote, as was our right as European citizens? So clear and easy to understand were the letters we didn't even need to refer them to our Spanish friends at the library group. Yes or no, sign the form, and post it back. 'Should be good fun, at least, to see what a Spanish election is like!' Chrissie giggled, ticking the 'yes' box on her form.

'I cannot begin to imagine!' I replied, doing likewise. 'The only thing for certain is that it will involve a lot of shouting!'

Into the post, then we promptly forgot all about matters of democracy.

And now here it is. A local election. The mayor, and town council, it appears. Which is actually of great interest to us, benefiting as we do from council tax of eighty euros per year, with free everything, fireworks, the fiestas, processions, band concerts, cultural visits, flamenco shows, daily rubbish collections, legions of council workers sweeping the streets, pruning the trees and shrubs in the public areas dotted around the town, and numerous other events. And personally, as I studied Local Government finance and administration as part of my higher education, I am fascinated how the Town Hall can afford all this stuff, on the amount we pay them. Just doesn't seem possible, particularly when compared to Britain, and what we used to pay, with services stripped to the bare bones. Now clearly, local services are funded differently here, but none of our educated Spanish friends are able to explain whether the money comes from the central government, or the Andalucian administration, which must itself be funded by Madrid. A complete mystery. All they will ever say is that all politicians are *Lad-Ronnies*, quite a few are *Bastardos*, they all live in big houses and have deep pockets. Corruption is rife, apparently, with more than a whiff of European money sloshing around. Have we seen the plethora of traffic signs on the country lanes, for example, with road surfaces like billiard tables? We have indeed.

This was brought home to us recently, with the resurfacing of a little lane from the middle of nowhere, to the back end of beyond. Little more than an olive track, used by grizzled old farmers in Jeeps and tractors. Up went a huge sign at the side of the road, announcing a complete re-construction, at a total cost of seven-hundred and ninety-five thousand, three-hundred and sixty-six euros, and seventy-five centimos. *Seventy-five centimos?* That is less than fifteen-bob. Who on earth could have costed out re-tarring a road down to the price of a Mars Bar? And who would possibly care? 'I wonder what the seventy-five cents will be spent on?' Chrissie laughingly observed. 'The bolts holding up the sign?' Mind you, they were stainless-steel. And the surface on the finished result could have hosted the World Snooker Championships, if only there had been pockets at the side of the road, and little white spots at strategic points. Better look out, Crucible Theatre, Sheffield. Next year's event could be coming to Andalucia.

So this stuff matters, right? Plus the fact that we are on more than good speaking terms with the current mayoral incumbents, Francesca and Paco. Quite why there are two mayors is uncertain, something about the previous contest being more or less a draw, so the pair of them decided to divide the role between them. Now one rather special, if somewhat embarrassing, aspect of being a Brit in this town is that we seem to be singled out at the various events. Francesca in particular always makes a point of coming up to us and saying how pleased they are that we are interested in the local customs, and introducing her 'English friends, who live in Castle Street, near Loli, Isabel and Fernando, and who always come to the festivals', to the locals, who quite possibly are muttering 'bloody foreigners' under their breath, but I have to say, always respond with grace.

'Dignified' is I think how we would describe Francesca and Paco. Both in their early sixties, always smartly dressed, not showy, smiling at the townsfolk and behaving in precisely the way Lord and Lady Mayors should, sometimes in their official regalia, but more usually in their own clothes, a discreet dress and sensible heels for Francesca, collar, tie and lounge suit for Paco. We like them, a lot, and sincerely hope they are returned for another period of office, however long that might be.

The election is set for Sunday, and we have received our voting cards, with directions to the polling station, a local neighbourhood association hall. Precise instructions, too, commanding us to present ourselves to table number six, as we enter. Blimey, a bit daunting, to be honest. Makes you wonder what would happen if we rocked up at table two, doesn't it? And we are required to produce identification. *Not those confounded knees again? Think we'll take our passports.* In Britain, I would simply stroll down the scout hut with Nelson, my retriever, who would nose around the assembled electorate, looking for biscuits, while I placed my cross in the box. Easy. This here sounds a lot more, well, regimented. No doubt all will be revealed, on the day.

On the Thursday before, I receive a phone call from Jose, of library group fame. 'Plees to come thees night, a-junty-mento demonstration of loo. Streets of old city, will be new loo. Carlo will coming so opportunity speak with he. We meet at eight and half, *a-junty-mento*, plees.' *Not the foggiest.* Very difficult, to be fair, speaking a foreign language on the phone, so probably best just to go along, and see what happens. A new loo? Are we having a pissoir installed somewhere? Will there be a ladies, in the interests of equality? And how on earth will they squeeze a public bog into these tiny, narrow streets? Carlo? Do I want to speak with he? Not that I was aware.

Chrissie is out with a student, so when she arrives home I recount the tale, and as it's almost eight and quarter, we need to get a move on. 'Oh yes, I saw this in an e-mail from the library. I was telling you about it, remember?'

*Time to bluff.* 'Yes, of course' I lie, 'I had forgotten it was tonight, what am I like!'

She narrows her eyes. 'I keep telling you to see the doctor. You don't have a clue what I am talking about, do you? I knew you weren't listening, when I told you.' *Sussed again*. But am I getting a de-briefing? It appears not.

At eight-and-half we present ourselves outside *a-junty-mento*, the town hall, to be confronted with a group of around twenty townsfolk, including Francesca and Paco, who are talking to a much younger, scruffily-dressed, skinny little man, who immediately reminds me of Mister Potato-Head, from my youth. Mid-thirties maybe, white shirt unbuttoned at the neck, a suit jacket, and jeans. Oh *please*. Does he imagine he is a Hollywood star? Were he a snake-hipped, dapper, dasher, in a stylish pair of Levi's, then possibly. But workman's jeans from the market, combined with a kiddies jacket which doesn't even do up in the front? Francesca and Paco smile at us and wave enthusiastically, whereas potato-head simply stares. *Don't like the guy, whoever he is.*

Just then Historian-Anna from the library steps forward, grabs a microphone, and announces the candidates for the upcoming election, who are asked to take a bow in turn. Francesca, Paco, and, *oh no I don't believe it*, Carlo. Mister Potato-Head. *He is running for Mayor? This refugee from a clothing bank?* Now don't get me wrong, he might be eminently qualified to be chief-executive of a small town, and we all know you shouldn't judge a book by the cover. Francesca and Paco might look the part, but actually be completely inept at managing a budget of what must be millions of euros, although they certainly seem to have made a pretty good fist of it, as far as we are concerned. But come on, first impressions, and all that? We need to speak to a few locals, get their opinions, form our own judgement based on facts. And here is one now, puffing his way up the street, Jose, late as usual. 'Sorree I late! Ahh, ees Carlo, *Lad-Ronnie*. Ees pig, he father mechanico in garage. Ees picker of olives. He sheet.' *Right, not a fan, then.*

Smiling, Historian-Anna then invites us all to follow the three nominees around the old streets, to inspect the new loo recently installed, although the milling, gossiping collection of Spaniards seem in no hurry to move off, so the three of us jump in ahead, all the better to see what is actually happening, and the new sanitary arrangements, hopefully. We have only gone a few yards however when the whole procession grinds to a halt. We appear to be admiring a street-light. *Fascinating*. Actually, the illuminations in the old town are rather quaint, resembling vintage gas-lamps, fixed to the walls of the cottages, rather than on lamp-posts, a ridiculous notion considering how some of the locals drive. I cannot even begin to imagine the carnage, not to mention the hole in the council budget, which would surely be caused by inattentive motorists, were there lamp-posts to avoid. Jose grabs my arm. 'A-junty-mento change all bom-beelos in old city, friendly environment, bom-beelos no illuminate sky, shine street only. Blanco, white. Soddy-oom no. How you say bom-beelos een Eengliss, plees? Soddy-oom?'

*Never mind the sodding soddy-oom, what about the pissoir? I could offer to christen it for them, actually.* Luckily, Chrissie benefits from a much higher tolerance level than me. 'Light-bulbs? And sodium? Yes, I see! The lights have a different shade, there is no more of that horrible orange glow. What a wonderful idea!' She is correct, actually. The light is more diffused, softer somehow, much less of a glare, casting a Dickensian radiance over the up and down, in and out, higgledy-piggledy streets and houses. *Gonna need that pee soon, however.*

As is usual around dusk, elderly residents of the street have emerged to gossip, after the heat of the day has subsided, a number leaning against walls, and many perched precariously on ancient wooden chairs, with raffia seats, for me one of the emblems of Andalucia. Nattering Spaniards on rickety furniture. As the politicians approach, smiling and waving, the atmosphere turns, if not actively hostile, then certainly antagonistic. 'Oh look, here they come!' mutters one old woman. 'Must be an election coming. Where have you been, Paco? Not seen you for four years!'

Her companion is equally unimpressed. 'What are you doing for me, Francesca? Nothing, as usual?'

Consummate politician as she is, the Lady Mayor brushes off the criticism. 'Well, today we are unveiling the new street lights, see? This will cut down on light pollution, and make it easier for you all to see at night, walking around.' And she puffs out her chest, as she and Paco gesture proudly at the recently-installed illuminations.

Suddenly matters deteriorate. A squat old man, forty-six waist, twenty-two inside leg, maybe, squeezes out of his front door, but only just. 'Why do we need new street lights, you stupid people? Where is all the money gone? You are a bunch of LAD-RONNIES.'

Writhing with embarrassment, I turn away. The Spanish are nothing if not direct, but surely he could have chosen his words more politely? Once again, however, I am reminded that British sensibilities do not apply here. The mayoral incumbents seem to regard this level of abuse as entirely normal. Everyone is shouting at once, and whereas in the UK a scuffle would surely have broken out, here it appears that a healthy dose of bellowing allows honour to be maintained all round, and peace breaks out again. Paco shoots me a sly wink and a grin, as if to say *'Spaniards, eh?'* and we continue on our way.

Up the hill come the stragglers, at the usual snails-pace, and eventually, after what my bladder considers to be about a century, we reach a look-out, where we can gaze down at the maze of buildings and alleyways below. And the effect truly is magical. Gone is the light pollution, above us are Orion and the Plough, the only constellations I am able to recognise, and here comes Paco, beaming widely. *'Estupendo, no?'* Indeed it is my friend, and may you reign for another four years. *But where is this bloody toilet?*

Strangely, the party seems to be breaking up, and Jose gestures us back down the slope. *I am hopping from foot to foot.* 'So what about this loo, Jose?' I whimper.

'Ees wonderful, no? So much better than before! I hated that orange *loo*. Was orriblay. Francesca and Paco do *phenomino*. I vota for they. I no vota for pig Carlo!'

My innards are completely destroyed. I am so utterly stupid, that I feel like banging my head against a wall, if that would knock any sense into my thick skull. Which it wouldn't. *Luz.* Pronounced in official Spanish *Looth*. 'Light', but also 'electricity'. However the local populace cannot speak official Spanish, can they, so the word comes out as *loo*. And if I don't find one in the next thirty seconds, there is going to be an accident of *phenomino* proportions. By the grace of God, we are outside a bar. 'Fancy a quick beer, Jose?' I command, shepherding him inside, and handing him a fiver. 'You order, I just need to nip to the TOIL....'

Election day dawns bright and sunny, and in view of the fact that we just know that the voting process will be anything but straightforward, we decide upon a fairly *Lazy Sunday*, a stroll around the olive groves in the morning, sunbeds in the afternoon, *close my eyes and drift away*, then the polling station around six, on our way to the cliff-top church, for half-an-hour of quiet contemplation. *Yeah, right.* At the allotted hour, armed with voting letters, passports, and with 'table number six' etched firmly on our minds, we approach the parish hall to find ancient Old-Bill leaning nonchalantly on the wall. Nothing unusual about that, quite honestly, they have so many venerable coppers in this town they could monitor every voting site from here to Madrid. Struggling through the usual melee outside, the first thing we notice is that there are only four tables, labeled one to four, unsurprisingly, but of number six there is no sign. 'Are you sure we have the right place?' Chrissie whispers, keen not to draw attention to ourselves, but already it is too late.

'NEIGHBOUR!' Every eyeball in the place focuses on us, distressingly. Fernando, sitting resolutely behind table number four, although mercifully he has foregone his florescent Spandex, and squeezed his gut inside what appears to be someone else's shirt. This bloke turns up just about everywhere, usually when we could do without him, although today he could actually be a blessing in disguise, which is not something you will hear me say that often.

'We are looking for table six, Fernando', I giggle, spreading my arms in a 'what the hell is all this gesture.'

'I AM TABLE SIX, NEIGHBOUR!' he hollers, just in case anyone in the next village was looking for it. 'GIVE ME YOUR CARD!'

No point being reticent about it, is there, in a foreign country where we don't have the first clue what is happening? I didn't come to Spain to be reticent. The melee outside have crowded in to get a ringside seat, and ancient Old Bill is peering through the throng, although bellowing is nothing to get excited about, in this town. 'No! You are table number four. We want table six' and I gesture exaggeratedly at my note, folding my arms and pursing my lips.

Now Fernando has a slight stutter, which usually only manifests itself when he gets excited, or agitated, which is just about always. 'NEIGHBOUR, I AM TABLE F-F-F-FOUR, TABLE F-F-F FIVE, AND TABLE S-S-S-SIX! GIVE ME YOUR CARD!'

Chrissie has to turn away, knuckles stuffed in her mouth, but around us there is uproar. An old woman barges her way through the pack. Mercedes, rocking from side to side on her gammy hips, like a drunken sailor on shore leave. 'Neighbour, are you here to vote?'

Stating the bleeding obvious again. *No, we are here to piss Fernando off, but we might do a spot of voting, later, if there is time.* 'We would like to vote, yes, but it says table six, look, but there is no table six!' And I shove my card under her nose.

She studies it carefully, then fixes our corpulent neighbour with a glare. 'Fernando, what is this? The English come here to vote, and there is no table six. *Hombre*, you are a *TONTO!*'

Priceless. I am willing to bet there is nothing on Spanish TV this evening to match this. We could all be YouTube superstars, if any of these old duffers had a smart-phone. Poor old chap, he only volunteered for this job to get away from his sisters for the day. 'MERCEDES, IT IS NOT MY F-F-F-FAULT!' And he leans forward, shirt buttons squealing under the pressure, and tries to snatch my card, but in a split-second I whip it away.

'Say por-favor!' I grin. But enough teasing. I hand him my letter, and he smiles in gratitude, although it could actually be in frustration. Or wind. He gestures Chrissie to do the same, places our communications neatly in a box, and hands us a plain, white envelope each. I look at my wife, she looks at me, and we both look at Fernando. So what happens next? Now clearly, they have their systems here, and Fernando, and no doubt everyone else here present, assumes we know what to do. Presumably the envelopes are for putting our voting slips in, once we have actually cast our crosses, but how? And glancing round the room, I realise for the first time there are no actual voting booths, with table-tops and pencils on strings. And quite honestly I am beginning to feel a bit of a lemon, standing here grinning. Nothing unusual in that, of course, spent a goodly part of my life standing around like a lemon, grinning, but not generally surrounded by about twenty Spaniards.

Mercedes to the rescue. 'Get a voting paper, neighbour. Look, over there!.' And sure enough, near the door are three separate piles of A4-sized sheets, lying on an un-numbered table-top. I stroll nonchalantly across, as if this were an everyday event and I actually know what I am doing, really, to be confronted by a list of around ten or a dozen names. Now we thought there were only three candidates, and had already decided I would vote for Paco, and Chrissie for Francesca, and nothing for the Pig, of course. We don't actually know the surnames of our preferred candidates, but how hard can it be to pick them out from a list of three? But who are all these other people? And to be honest, the printing is quite small. Do we simply tick the name we want to vote for? Do we cross the others out? And in any event, there are no actual boxes to tick, or cross, or whatever it is you do in this crazy country.

I take two sheets of paper from the first pile, hand one to Chrissie, and slink back to Fernando's table. 'Do you have a pencil, please?'

He stares as If I have completely lost my mind, which is a fair approximation of the truth, quite honestly. 'WHAT DO YOU WANT A P-P-PENCIL FOR? JUST PUT THE F-F-FORM IN THE ENVELOPE, NEIGHBOUR!'

'In our country, we put a pencil cross on the form' I confirm, but fearing another barrage I do as commanded, as does Chrissie. Fernando sticks out his tongue in a gesture I take to mean *just lick the envelope, neighbour*, although he is no doubt thinking *now get out of my polling station you pair of lemons*, then he nods towards a tin box with a slot in the top, standing in the corner. I can feel my wife shaking with subterranean mirth as she grabs my envelope, stuffs it in the box, and we both crash through the door, squinting in the bright sunshine, and flop against some railings, laughing uncontrollably. Ancient Old-Bill is still there, smiling, clearly he senses something funny has just happened, but cannot figure out what could possibly be humourous about the Spanish electoral system. We, on the other hand, have tears running down our cheeks. What the hell just happened? We came down here, failed to find table six, stuffed a list of people into an envelope, *but didn't actually vote for anyone*. Utterly and completely bizarre. This place is beyond bonkers. Passers-by are staring so we need to get ourselves together before we get run out of town. Chrissie produces a couple of tissues from her bag, we dry our eyes, and head up to the cliff-top church, away from this madness, a half-hour of relative tranquility. And the sunset over the olives, of course.

Our route homewards takes us past the polling station again, where the general milling-around of earlier has been replaced by complete anarchy, it appears. 'NEIGHBOUR!' Oh blimey. Loli. This woman could cause a riot in an empty room. 'Are you voting?'

I smile serenely. 'Already have, Loli!' Beat you to it. And no doubt Fernando will give you a blow-by-blow account, later.

'Did you vote for the Labrador, neighbour?'

Now I am sufficiently au-fait with the lingo to know she is not referring to a retriever, but a worker, although for all the good it did we might as well have voted for a poodle, or a tom-cat. Still, not going to make much difference, is it, our two votes? From what we have seen of the opposition, Francesca and Paco are going to win by a landslide. Whatever, I am looking forward to recounting the tale, tomorrow at the library group, of the time we didn't actually manage to vote for anyone, animal, vegetable or mineral. Right, home, glass of beer, and a prawn paella from my Rick Stein cookbook.


The following morning the library is a-buzz with the election result. Or rather, the non-result, due to there having to be a re-count, the first tally being too close to call. 'So do you voted for Francesca and Paco?' Jose enquires. No point being coy about it, is there? I mean, it is a standing joke among the Spaniards at the group that we get singled out for special attention by the mayors, so clearly we are going to vote for them. The problem is, as we try to explain, we don't think we actually managed to vote at all.

'I no understand!' giggles Rafi.

'Why you not know who you vote for?' Teri queries.

'Plees say me you no vote for pig?' Jose wants to know.

*This is worse than paying the rates.* Quickly, I sketch out a UK voting slip in my notebook, with three names on a list, and three squares next to the names. I then dramatically rip the page from the book, place a cross in one of the boxes, and mime putting it in a tin container. 'There! That is how we vote in Britain, with the cross against the person you are voting for. We didn't do that yesterday, the list had maybe ten names, and we just stuck it in the envelope!' *Phew!*

Total bemusement on the opposite side of the table. 'But you did voted!' cries Rafi. 'You no put cross in box in Espain.'

This could go on until the next election, quite honestly. They know what they mean, we know what we mean, but ne'er the twain shall meet before one of us dies. *'Ee-keep-o'* Teri explains. How you say *ee-keep-o* in Eengliss? In Espain, you vote for *e-keep-o*.' *Oh, so not the Labrador, then?*

'Team!' giggles dictionary-woman Marie. 'In Espain we vote for team.'

Does she mean a political party? I didn't think the town council elections were like that here. I didn't see any political affiliations being banded about during the campaign, there might have been of course, but I got the impression this was about who had done what, on a purely local level. Maybe I am wrong, but honestly, I am losing the will to live. Let Chrissie see if she can get to the bottom of all this.

'So how many people are in these teams, usually?' she enquires.

'Ten, or maybe twelve persons, depend on the team.' Marie confirms.

'But there were only ten or twelve names on our list, something like that, the one we put in the envelope. There were three candidates, so that is almost thirty names in total. There were definitely not thirty names on that list!'

Teri is laughing, and I am starting to develop a sinking feeling about all this. *Someone has cocked-up again.* Not sure how, yet, but I am willing to have a small wager it might possibly have been yours-truly. 'Cristina, are three lists separate! One for Francesca and she team, one for Paco, one for Pig. Which list you put in you envelope, plees?'

*She has it figured out, of course. Told you someone had cocked-up, didn't I?* 'I don't know which list, Teri' she whispers, menacingly. 'You will have to ask HIM.'

Suddenly, all eyes are on me. *Not really my fault, though, is it? I didn't know there were three separate lists, did I? Anyway, all these damned Spanish names are the same, aren't they? Jose-this, Antonio-that, Maria-the other, and don't get me started on all those bloody Anna's.* 'The first pile, by the door. I just picked up the first one I found. Could have been any team. I was confused, OK. I was expecting just three names, and three boxes to tick. I was voting for Paco, and Cristina for Francesca.'

'BUT YOU VOTY FOR CARLO!' Jose explodes. 'Thee first pile, by the door, was pile of he. I also voty een thees place, I know thees.'

At that moment the door bursts open and in crashes Amador. 'Sorree I late, I RUNNY. Who vote for CARLO?' Four Spanish fingers, and one English, are pointing in my direction. 'Oh fox ME! Why you vote for thees ANNY-MALLY? Thees picker of OLIVE? Thees oink-oink, how you say, PEEK? Jonneee, you say me you voty for PACO! Why you voty for thees BOOEY? I will tell Paco, and Francesca next time I see THEY! Oh my GAAD!'

I am waving my arms like a crazy-man. 'No, no, please don't say anything to Paco and Francesca. It was an honest mistake, I swear. Please don't tell them! PLEASE!'

Amador grins widely. 'OK, I no tell they, on one CONDITION!'

'I agree! What is your condition? Anything!'

The locals are all smiling. They know Amador, and they know what is coming next.

'We go pub, after CLASS! You buy me CUBO! WE GET PISSY!'


The following morning Chrissie is checking her emails and Facebook, after breakfast. 'Oh look, a post from the council. The election result. And guess who won? By a mano-something. And what is a *mano*? Do you know this word? Of course you do! It is a hand, isn't it? A handful of votes. Car-bloody-lo has won the election. And it's all your fault, isn't it? Well you better pray he doesn't impose an austerity budget, hadn't you? Treble our council tax. Put a stop to the fireworks, the processions, the fiestas, the flamenco, the cultural visits with free lunches. This wonderful life we have here, could all be coming to a grinding halt, because you were too stupid to read a slip of paper.'

*That's a bit rich, isn't it?* 'Well don't forget, you also voted for Carlo. Your envelope also contained his slip. You will be just as much to blame as me.' *She is joking, I know she is.*

'Not at all! YOU gave me the slip. All I did was lick the envelope. And best of luck finding my DNA, among hundreds of others. Anyway, we have that procession this coming weekend, and now you won't be able to go, will you?'

'What are you talking about? Of course I can go. I remember that one from last year, they gave away free paella afterwards. Of course we are going!' *Surely she is joking?*

'No no. I am going, of course. My conscience is clear. But you cannot go. What if you bumped into Francesca and Paco? You wouldn't be able to look them in the eye, would you, responsible for them losing their jobs? You couldn't possibly face the pair of them, could you, knowing this was ALL YOUR FAULT!'

*She wasn't joking. I think.....*


## CHAPTER 16. RAMBLIN' ON MY MIND

One Saturday evening, a few weeks later, approaching midnight, just as we are getting ready for bed, a text message comes through on our Spanish mobile. Wouldn't happen in the UK, would it, phone messages, at this time of night? Here, however, the locals show no such reticence. We have even received texts at two in the morning, which explains why we now switch it off during the night. Chrissie grabs the phone, and raises her hand. 'Shut up, all right? I've got it! Stay there!' I do my best to look aggrieved. *Haven't said a word, have I?* 'It's from Juan' she confirms. *'Plees to meet tomorrow at eight and half in morning outside library for sendero. See you!'* She pauses for effect. 'So, do we know what a sendero is?'

'Why are you asking me?' I chuckle, having benefited from several large glasses of wine during the evening. 'I'm going to bed. My brains are switched off! Just text him back and say we'll be there.'

She eyes me accusingly. 'I wasn't actually aware you had switched them on this morning. Off, on, it's all the same to me. Anyway, I think a sendero is a car. A Romanian car, a *Dacia Sendero,* you know, Jose at the library has one, in white, and there are a few others dotted around here, all of them white. They must be quite popular.'

I am struggling to get my grey-matter into gear one last time, today. 'So why would Juan be taking us to see a car, at half-eight in the morning, pray?'

'Who knows, perhaps there is a dealer open-day? Or maybe he has bought one himself, and wants to take us out for a spin? And were you listening to what I said about half-eight in the morning? You know what you are like about getting up early, moaning about missing your breakfast. I don't want to hear your stomach rumbling from the back seat, when we are supposed to be enjoying a leisurely Sunday drive!'

I still have my aggrieved-face on. Seems to be the default, these days. 'Well there is one easy remedy for that, then, isn't there? Just put your alarm on, and make my scrambled eggs a bit earlier than usual. Plenty of seasoning, don't forget!' And despite my sleepy state, I dodge what would have been a painful blow.

The following morning we present ourselves outside the library at eight and half, keeping a lookout for a gleaming new white Dacia coming from the direction of Juan's flat. Five minutes pass with no sign, when suddenly from the opposite direction comes an urgent honking, and there is our dear friend driving some scruffy, beat-up wreck of indeterminate make, and vintage. *Maybe today is the big trade-in, and we are invited to the key handing-over ceremony. Who knows? I've had my scrambled eggs on toast with two mugs of coffee, my brains are switched on again, only half-power mind you, as it's a Sunday, so all Is well in my world. Another day of discovery in this bonkers country.* He rolls down the window. 'Plees. I sorree, I ver late, hop on, like London bus! Hop on, hop off! Mind the gap! We must to go quickly!' *Blimey, whatever next? Is this supposed to be Spain, or have we been beamed back to*

*London? Late? Quickly? I cannot ever remember hearing those words over here, and certainly not from a Spaniard.*

We barely have time to fold ourselves into the back seat before he roars off down the street, we reach the edge of town in about thirty seconds and hurtle down a country lane, out into the olive groves. He is throwing the ancient jalopy around the bends like some demented rally driver, and I am in imminent danger of a close encounter with an olive tree, or a plate of scrambled egg, or maybe both, when mercifully, he screeches to a halt, almost mowing down a dozen or so people who are milling around in the main street of what appears to be a one-horse town, only smaller, with no horses. Describing this place as a hamlet would be a wild exaggeration, and there is no sign of a Dacia dealer either, so what is happening, heaven knows. Nigel Mansell turns to face us. 'Sorree, my drivey ver bad. Hop off, plees!' Apparently we have reached our destination, although what these other people are doing, I have no idea.

Trembling, we extract ourselves from the venerable conveyance, and breathe deeply while our heart-rates return to double figures. Surprisingly, bearing in mind a number of them were almost hospitalised, there is a great deal of good-natured banter between Juan and the group, who clearly bear him no ill-will. Just then, one of the number detaches himself from the throng, and approaches us, hand outstretched. 'Welcome! My name Ar-hona. You Eengliss free-end of Juan. He say me of you. Plees, sign here!' And from behind his back he produces a clip-board to which is attached a list of names, addresses, signatures, and, oh no, NIE numbers. Not the dreaded knee, on a Sunday morning? Thought I had done with knees, when we bought the car. And why exactly do we need to give our names and addresses, anyway? Don't want to look a complete dork of course so I fill in my details, put a dash through the knee bit, sign the thing and pass it to Chrissie. That will have to do, no way am I going home from here to get a bit of paper, or heaven forbid, the deeds of the house.

Formalities dispensed with, we appear to be ready. For what, search me, but ready we are. 'Follow me plees! Sendero!' grins our friend, and the whole group trudge off into the olives. There is no path as such, no fences, no signposts or way-marks of any sort, just olive trees, by the million, as far as the eye can see, although clearly someone knows where they are going, Ar-hona presumably, as he appears to be in the lead, with us bringing up the rear. 'Plees, I show you Trinny.' Juan grins. 'She naturista.' *Please let most of that be lost in translation.* He calls out to a blonde, slim, serious-looking, middle-aged lady dressed in hiking gear, with copious pockets, who has a small bunch of grasses and plants in her hand. 'I know in Eengliss thees word have different meaning' he whispers, 'but here in Espain she ees Padre, Hijo and Espiritu Santo. No laughy, plees!' Father, Son and Holy Ghost? Trinity? *This is a very strange country. Especially at this time of the morning.*

'Ello' she beams. 'My name ees Trinny. Plees to see you! Look! Different flowers yellow. Are you interest naturista, plees?'

Before I can blunder in with both feet, Chrissie takes over. 'Good morning, we are Cristina and John. Yes, we are interested in nature, but in English we use the word 'naturalist'. A 'naturist' is something different.'

Ahead, the whole group has stopped to listen. 'So what mean naturist, plees?' Juan enquires.

My wife smiles politely. 'A naturist is someone who likes to go without clothes occasionally, in public, often with others of the same interest.'

'NUDISTA!' cries the horrified naturalist. 'OH MY GAAD! I NO NUDISTA!' And she is hopping from foot to foot, while the rest of the group are roaring with laughter.

'Trinny, get your clothes off!' cries a male voice. 'Look, I will take mine off also! We can be nudistas together!'

Juan is looking aghast, but eventually the group settles down, and we move off again, us bringing up the rear. 'There are no Russian cars around here', I complain, through gritted teeth, after a few more minutes. 'This is more like a bloody route march. What the hell is going….' I turn to see my dearest propped against an olive tree, tittering helplessly. It takes a few more seconds for the penny to drop. 'You swine! You absolute rotten….'

'What thees swine, plees?' our friend enquires.

'Her, look!' I splutter, indicating the woman who is still clinging to a leafy branch. 'She told me a sendero was a car! A Dacia Sendero! I thought we were going to look at a car this morning. Juan, what am I going to do with her?!'

The rest of the gang, meanwhile, have paused to ridicule the Brit who thought a hiking trip was an Eastern European vehicle. Total uproar. 'Hey English, my feet are aching!' 'Can I get a ride please?' 'Take me home, I am tired!' 'Careful not to hit any olive trees!' 'Can we go to the beach? Malaga?'

I spread my arms out wide, in a 'I feel like a right lemon, but who cares' kind of way. 'No hablo mucho Espanol' I grin, which is my standard 'get out of jail' card in these circumstances. *No speaky Spanish.* Which usually does the trick, as it does on this occasion. Breaks the ice, too. Off we march, again, heading heaven knows where, but at least I am no longer keeping a weather-eye out for traffic. Chrissie still is wiping her eyes. 'So, just as well I didn't wear my flip-flops, this morning, wasn't it? Would have looked an even bigger idiot, wouldn't I, thank you very much.'

She is still finding the whole thing hugely funny. 'That is why I strategically placed your trainers in the hall, wasn't it, so that you would put them on automatically, what with it still being the middle of the night, in your world!'

I glance down at my trainer-shod feet. *Been done up like a kipper, haven't I, as Del-Boy might have said.* 'So how long have you known about this hiking trip then?'

'Since last week' she cheerfully confirms. 'Juan asked if we wanted to go, but he wasn't sure he could make it. No idea where you were at the time, away with the fairies probably, but he promised to message us last night. Anyway, I thought it would be a nice surprise for you, so here we are.'

Suddenly, from up in front, comes the sound of muted shushing, and Trinny appears, holding up her hands in a plea for silence. 'Weeld dohhs, in the trees, up ahead! Look!'

*In* the trees? I must have mis-translated? Dogs in the trees? Who do they think they are, these dogs? Leopards? Craning our heads for a better view we can see a small group of maybe half a dozen canines, fawn-grey in colour, flecked with black, like small Alsatians, fifty yards ahead, *and the hair on the back of my neck stands up.* They are jumping, from a standing start, up the trunk, into the branches. In my life, I have never seen anything like this. *And are they actually dogs?* To me, they look just like... no, surely not? Here, in Andalucia? I saw a wolf once in the zoo and these creatures look suspiciously similar, pointed noses, sticky-up ears, the same general size and colouration...

We are edging gradually closer, Chrissie keeping herself tucked in behind me, although the creatures seem entirely unconcerned by our presence, glancing in our direction occasionally but continuing their frolicking. What can they be after, in an olive tree? Certainly not the famous Mediterranean diet as all the fruit was picked several months ago, by Fernando, maybe, and all that remains are tiny white flowers, the beginnings of next years crop. Grubs, possibly? Small insects? Juan squeezes my arm. 'Incredible, no? Weeld dohhs. Thees ver especial. I never see they, so closely, like thees.'

'But are they really dogs?' I whisper. 'They look like a different species, to me.'

He blows out his cheeks. 'I know, you think maybe *lobo,* how you say, wooooolf? There ees wooooolfs een *Sierra Morena,* north of Cordoba , maybe forty kilometres from here, border weeth *Castilla,* but honesty we not know. Exist no fence in *Sierra Morena,* so ees possible they travel here, are no towns to prevent they.' And he beckons to Trinny.

*'Canis lupus?'* she murmurs softly, smiling. 'We must to take care, people frighty of they, so we say dohhs weeld, maybe they living here, we are study at university of Granada, now.....'

Suddenly from the crowd comes the frantic sound of multiple sneezing, and as one, the dohhs weeld prick up their ears, and go galloping off across the countryside, disappearing into the distance. A bloke in the group is blowing his nose, eyes streaming. 'Sorry, I have allergy!' Trinny is dumbfounded, staring, open-mouthed, in disbelief, in a *height of the hay-fever season, olive trees and spring flowers in full bloom, and he comes out on a nature walk, scaring away the wildlife* kind of way. Not happy, is our nudista.

The show over, we resume our sendero, with us still bringing up the rear. Just then I become aware of an engine, a vehicle approaching from behind. A rattly diesel, getting louder, and I turn to see what looks like an old farmer in a beaten-up four-wheel-drive, about twenty feet behind us, making no attempt to overtake. For pity's sake, we are in the middle of the back of beyond, and here is this annoying motorist, acres of space in which to pass. And I really dislike people behind me, whether I am walking, or driving. I stop, smiling politely, and wave him through, but no, he resolutely refuses, pointing at something ahead. What, he cannot pass twelve people? With all these millions of acres? First someone frightening the wooooolfs, and now Reginald Molehusband. Grrrr. Just then, Ar-hona comes striding back. Excellent, he can shoo this motorist away, and leave us in peace. Wrong! 'Brax-fass!' he grins. 'Who is ready for brax-fass?' Well me obviously, even though I have already had one already this morning, but all this walking makes you peckish, right? Only one slight problem, however. Where are we partaking of this repast, in this wilderness? Suddenly, old Reggie switches off his engine, wrenches up the handbrake, squeezes his gut from behind the wheel, stumbles out of the vehicle, and adjusts his groin in a manner not fit for publication in respectable circles. Charming. He then lifts the hatchback, and drops the tail-gate, to reveal two huge rubber buckets, filled with ice and stuffed with cans of beer, lemon and orangeade, and Coke. Another fellow opens the side doors and extracts two folding tables, which are hastily erected, a large sack of crusty rolls is dragged from the car, followed by cool-boxes crammed with slices of cheese, chorizo, Spanish ham and various em-boo-tea-toes. A bowl of ripe, beefy tomatoes, a stack of paper plates, knives for slicing and a pile of serviettes completes the ensemble. Brax-fass is served, and I have to say what a bloody nice bloke that Reggie is, driving all the way out here to keep us fed.

The Spaniards need no encouragement, diving on the largesse like a pack of, well, dohhs weeld, really, whereas I do have reservations. Only slight ones, you understand, but reservations nevertheless. I turn to my wife. 'Did you actually remember to bring any money today, amid all the deception? You remember, Dacia dealers, and all that? I mean, had I known about all this I would have brought my camera, got some shots of the lobos, instead of some distant, grainy images on my phone, which could be of half a dozen mice, quite honestly.'

She regards me without affection, opening her mouth to speak, and then closing it again. She rubs her hand across her face. 'Look, Juan didn't say anything about food, all right, so I have a couple of small bottles of water in my bag, and two cereal bars.'

*Ooohhh! Might be one-nil up here, for a change.* 'Yes, but do we have any money, perchance, to pay for the brax-fass? It would be embarrassing, you must admit, if they come round for contributions, and you don't have any. I, of course, have a perfect excuse. So what flavour are your power bars? Not those horrible apple ones which taste like chemicals, I hope!'

'About five euros, all right?' she hisses. 'Now get out of the way and let me get to the cheese, before all these ruddy meat-eaters grab…..'

'Plees, you take beer? Chorizo? Come on, diggy in, as you say!' Our good friend seems concerned lest we become faint, and with good reason, in my case. Anyway, five euros should be more than sufficient for a Spanish breakfast, so without further ado, I diggy in. Not beer, you understand, as my name is not Del, but a ham and tomato roll goes down a treat. And glancing around, it's probably a good job that old sneezy frightened away the wooooolfs, as doing battle with six sets of snarling fangs would not go down too well when we are having our brax-fass, would it?

It appears we have not eaten enough, however. Maybe we still have forty miles to go, before nightfall, as Ar-hona is keen for us to take on further nourishment. 'Benga! Eaty! Bocca-dee-yo! How you say, sand-wee! Coca-cola! Yees!' *Oh go on then, twist my arm.* Saw some Spanish black pudding in the box earlier, and a crusty roll stuffed full of that, washed down with a lemonade, will set me up nicely, for whatever awaits.

Bidding farewell to old Reggie, we are on our way again, and fully fueled, and now fully awake, I am able to discern a definite pathway through the olives, having hitherto felt we were simply following our noses in some vague direction. *All right, so I am lost, OK?* Difficult to spot, amongst all these olive trees, but we are on some kind of a trail. 'So where are we heading, Trinny?' I enquire of our naturist.

She gathers her thoughts, and breathes deeply. 'OK, we follow can-yadda. How you say can-yadda, een Eengliss?' I think my face gives it away. Not the foggiest. 'Juan! Come here plees! How you say can-yadda, een Eengliss?' *Well if I don't know, I doubt he does, but then again...*

He whips out his smart-phone, and types 'Canada' into his translator app. 'Canada!?' I splutter, 'are you serious? We are walking to Canada? Is that the country to the north of the United States, or is there one in Andalucia?' *No wonder Ar-hona wanted us fueled up.....*

Our friend wags his finger. 'No, I not typy Canada, I typy can-yadda. Look!'

Now then. Hands up all those of you who knew there was an additional letter in the Spanish alphabet? Go to the top of the class if you did, cos we sure as hell didn't, when we moved over here. But it is true, there are two letter 'N's. The ordinary one, pronounced 'en-ny' and a second one, with a squiggly line above, like a little snake, pronounced 'en-ya'. I cannot prove it to you, as I'm typing this on a British keyboard, but trust me on this, next time you look at the Spanish version, there it will be. And they use this letter for words like 'Espana', *Espan-ya,* 'senor', *sen-yor,* and most famous of all, 'manana', *man-yanna.* So twenty-seven letters, but confusingly, to fit them all in, there is no '@' key. Who knew? And best of luck typing an email in the local library.

I glance again at his screen to see that he has indeed typed 'canada', but using the en-ya letter. The little blue wheel is spinning, and there seems more likelihood of picking up a signal in the Bay of Biscay if your name is Elton 'Bobby' John, but eventually the Spanish Wi-Fi creaks painfully to life and some wording appears. Our friend frowns. 'Drow-berrs row-ad.' he smiles. 'Can-yadda is drow-berrs row-ad.'

*Of course it is! Oh silly me!* 'Let me see that, please' I grin, peering over his shoulder. 'Drovers road! So this can-yadda is a drovers road?' I cannot help chuckling to myself. *Drow-berrs row-ad* indeed. See what we are up against, over here? It ain't easy, I can tell you. Especially on a Sunday.

Trinny is keen to elaborate. 'Yees, is ancient direcho, how you say, right? From medieval epoch, I think, for person take they anny-mally to different part of countree. Coos, sheeps, like thees.' Which is all well and good of course, but I have one burning question. What anny-mally? There is a complete absence of coos, sheeps or indeed farms, in this area. A few goats of course, scrabbling around on rocky mountainsides, tended by gnarly old goatherds, ably assisted by a couple of mangy curs, but I am unable to conjure pastoral images of wide, sweeping plains, luxurious grasslands stretching majestically to the horizon. And these olive trees didn't just spring up overnight, did they? We have already encountered one allegedly from a previous millennium. Maybe it was different hundreds of years ago, dusty gauchos driving herds of wild steers down to, I don't know, the Costa del Sol for their holidays? A conversation for another time.

The morning passes quickly and Trinny is performing sterling service, bringing the local flora and fauna to life. Insects, lizards, bugs, butterflies and caterpillars are drawn expertly to our attention, and as the gardener of the household, Chrissie is particularly interested in clumps of wild iris, buttercups, ox-eye daisies and some straggly lemon-coloured weeds growing in profusion around the bases of the trees. But of human habitation, nothing. We might as well be on the moon. Suddenly, there comes the sound of excited murmuring from the group, and a building appears on the near horizon. Civilization! Two buildings, a cluster in fact, with a few pine trees, which make a pleasant change after a morning of nothing but olives. 'Cor-tea-HHo!' Juan exclaims. 'We visit cor-tea-HHo now!'

Ah yes, we know this word, having originally intended buying one. Cortijo, with the phlegmy third syllable. A Spanish farmhouse. An extremely well manicured farmhouse in this case, with wrought iron gates, a paved driveway featuring an ornamental fountain, stone and whitewashed buildings forming three sides of a square, a massive arched doorway with a bell-tower above, flowers and shrubs sprouting artfully from ancient stone pots, palm trees providing dappled shade, and bizarrely, a complete absence of old bed-frames and rusty chicken-wire. What is this place, a five-star hotel? It certainly looks that way, and suddenly I feel shockingly under-dressed, in my Primark polo shirt, grubby shorts, and trainers. My appearance could be best described as 'scruffy-casual', and that would be talking it up, quite frankly. None of the others are in black tie of course, but embarrassingly, I have the Waterloo Station tramp look down to a fine art. Still, not my fault, is it? I was told we were calling in on a car-dealer, not visiting the Ritz. *We all know who to blame, don't we Mrs Richards?*

At that moment the massively-timbered doors open, and out steps a lady, in her seventies, clad tastefully in a Chanel two-piece suit, string of pearls and matching earrings, exquisitely coiffured. A Lady of the Manor, at the very least, a Doo-kessa possibly. Not the *Alba* one, as we all know what happened to her, ending up in a sugar museum, but a close relative, surely. I instinctively duck down behind Juan, in case she spots me and summons the police, *get off my land,* although it appears I was worrying about nothing. 'Welcome to *El Cortijo*' she beams. 'Follow me please, and I will show you around.' So were we expected? Is this part of the sendero experience? I glance at Chrissie, surreptitiously fingering the collar of my polo in a *do they let scruffy British oiks in here* kind of way, but she just shrugs, pokes out her tongue, and moves on, following the group.

Her Ladyship leads us through into a parquet-floored entrance hall, with beamed ceiling and minstrels gallery, all the while providing a regal commentary, which I am struggling to hear as I am bringing up the rear, as far to the rear as possible, then through another huge doorway into what was once possibly a massive wine-cellar, with ancient stone arches, and curved brick ceiling, all laid out with tables and chairs. 'Is this a wedding venue, by any chance, Juan?' I whisper.

'Yees' he smiles. 'Baptisms, weddings, parties, reunions, all of thees things.' *So not wakes, then….*

'Now I will show you my private quarters' she smiles regally, pushing open yet another huge wooden double door. Blimey, what is this, the full tour? Will there be a ticket booth, a liveried footman handing out audio-guides, in twenty different languages? Is there an entrance charge, with glossy souvenir booklets? *Well best of luck with that, your Highness, as we only have a fiver, and that has been earmarked for the breakfast.* This room is a massive banqueting hall, with a beamed ceiling, but planed, sanded and varnished, not knobbly tree trunks like Del-Boy has in his kitchen, wood-paneled walls hung with family portraits, and tapestries, and a table in the middle, fully twenty-five yards long, and simply groaning with food. Blimey, are the family coming to lunch? Bone china crockery, silver cutlery, crystal goblets, at least five different plates of cheese, myriad sausage, chorizo and em-boo-tea-toe platters, dishes of pate, bowls of ripe, beefy tomatoes, *empanadas* of various shapes sizes, quails eggs, little toasted montaditos, sliced, crusty bread with little curls of rich, yellow butter, triangles of tortilla, and on a sideboard, the desserts, flans, trifles, sweet biscuits and fruit. On the far wall is the wine table, the whites, chilling away regally in silver ice buckets, and the reds, breathing freely. And not your everyday *Mercadonna* plonk, either. Oh no, this lot is off the top shelf of the *bodega,* I can tell you. How big is this family? There must be enough here to feed a small army. Or is this some sort of a formal function? Will there be dignitaries, ambassadors, Archbishops? Not Royalty, clearly, *as there are no pork pies or scotch eggs,* but this is one hell of a banquet.

But hang on a minute. The food is already out, so the arrival of the distinguished guests must be imminent. I can imagine about a mile of red carpet being laid out, as we speak. So won't their eminences be a bit cross to find their grub being breathed on by a dozen dusty, sweaty ramblers, and an English bum? Curious.

Her Royal Highness smiles sweetly, heading for the door. 'Enjoy your lunch, please, and I will return later to see you all, before you leave.'

Oh. My. Good. God. In panic, I turn to Chrissie, nodding my head towards the exit, and taking our friend by the arm, 'look, Juan, we are going to wait outside, in the courtyard, OK? We will meet you when you leave.'

He looks completely flummoxed. 'What? You no want you lunch? Plees, sit down, we must to take lunch, now!'

I swallow hard. 'It's a bit embarrassing, because we didn't bring much money. We have enough to cover the breakfast, so don't worry about that, but we will just wait outside, now, and see you later.'

He narrow his eyes, frowning. 'I no understand. Why you need money, plees?'

I want a big hole to open up. *Why does he keep going on about it?* 'Juan, please, we only brought five euros with us, we didn't know we were having lunch, and we have no money to pay for it. But don't worry, we can sit outside, in the sunshine. Cristina has some biscuits, in her bag. You enjoy your lunch, and we will see you later.'

He throws back his head and roars with laughter. *For God's sake will you shut up? I am starting to get annoy….* 'Plees. You no need money. Thees food is free! Brax-fass, lunch. Not to paying. All is free. *Todos.* You not worry about thees!'

I am staring at him like he has lost his mind. 'Sorry, how can it be free? A car full of food for breakfast, and now all this. It cannot be free, somebody must be paying. Who is paying for all this?'

He is still finding it extremely amusing. 'The a-junty-mento paying! How you say, hall of town? They will to pay. Now don't worry, take you foods, plees!'

The town hall? Is this serious? The council are treating us to a day out, with enough food to last us a week? My brain, admittedly only on half power, is unable to process this information. We only paid them less than forty quid for a half-year. Two breakfasts, two lunches, glasses of wine, cans of drinks? This is beyond belief, no wonder this country is virtually bankrupt, carrying on like this. Two grand a year in England and they don't even collect the rubbish every week. 'But why do they pay for all this, Juan? You know how much we give them for our ee-bee?

'Because a-junty-mento, they say, ees good for healthy, sendero, like thees. They no want people fatty. And Espanee people say you must to buy lunch for we! Ees normal! Plees! Eaty!'

*Well if you insist, my friend.* The wooooolfs are already diggy in, so without further ado, we join them. Someone hands me a glass of expensive rioja, and I make a beeline for the em-boo-tea-toes. Could murder a scotch egg mind you, but beggars, and all that. I still can't really believe this is on the town hall, maybe that is why we had to sign the form, and perhaps the year after next someone will shove a manky yellow slip into our letterbox. *Should have said I was old Joe Shepherd, shouldn't I?* Anyway, what the hell, we eaty.

A companionable hour and more passes in this fashion, before the doors open and Her Excellency returns, smiling graciously, *thanking us* for coming, and slowly, we are making for the door. No bill, no tin plate for donations. I love Santa Marta council, did you know that, the forty bucks we gave them has to be the best value in the known universe. *And I did, of course, vote for the mayor…..* 'She is a lovely lady, Purity!' smiles our friend, under his breath, as we head off into the olives once again.

Chrissie looks puzzled. 'Is that her name? Purity? I have never heard that one before!'

He frowns. 'No, her correct name Conception, but she called Purity.'

She giggles. 'Well I never heard of Conception as a name, either!'

'Ees older name, not much popular thees days', he frowns. 'I not know why, but Conception ees *Purity.* Also, Jose ees *Pepe,* and Francisco ees *Paco.* But Miguel ees *Miguelito.* I am *Juanito.* I no understand!'

*Well if he doesn't, neither do we…*

The pace after that huge lunch is modest, and the mood relaxed.This morning we were rambling, now we are ambling. By rights, I should be having a little nap under a certain fig tree right now. Suddenly, there is a burst of activity from the group and one of the blokes goes tearing off through the olive trees, returning with what looks like a glass jam-jar. Fair play to him for litter-picking I say, and may the fleas of a thousand camels invade the nether regions of the moron who left it there. I detest people who would do that, leaving glass around, a danger not only to wildlife, but a real risk of forest fires too, in this arid countryside. So lazy. We have barely gone another hundred yards however when it happens again, the original picker, and another chap, hurtling across the parched soil, where, after some good-natured tussling, the second one claims an identical prize. Who the hell is eating all this jam, out here, anyway? Actually, scrub jam, the containers look like the jellies with fruit which were produced in the sixties, by Hartley's, was it, or Chivers? Mother used to buy them for picnics, whereupon a scuffle would ensue, as the whole family attempted to avoid the green one. Dad invariably ended up with that. Anyway, back to the present, fruit jellies are still made, of course, but surely in plastic containers these days? *Although they do say that Spain is fifty years behind the UK…..*

I glance at Trinny, rolling my eyes, expecting her to be suitably outraged, but for some reason she seems amused. Just then, incredibly, a third jar appears, half-buried, and three of them go sprinting off, and Juan is shouting encouragement. He turns to me, smiling. 'En-dessa!' he confides.

En-dessa? The electricity company? The *only* electricity company, at least in these parts. The people who continue to issue bills, admittedly for extremely moderate amounts, at irregular intervals, to Jose Ocana Pastor? Never had any dealings with them, other than that, but they have an office in town, similar to the water company, staffed by plugs, I would imagine. Might have to pay them a visit, next week, providing I can learn the Spanish for *please tell your blokes not to leave their jelly-jars scattered all over the damned countryside.* Someone has to make a stand, right?

One of the fellows then produces a hanky from his pocket, polishes off his recycling, and holds it out for the rest of us to examine. Hang on a minute, it's not from a fruit flavoured dessert at all, it appears to be an electrical insulator of some sort, from a telegraph pole, or the like. I glance skywards, but cannot actually see any cables, *because they've been removed.* Duh. En-dessa have been out here, I can see it now, a row of wooden poles, in amongst the olive trees, and the cables have either been buried, or re-routed. Still doesn't excuse the savages though, does it? Anyone know the Spanish for *please tell your blokes not to leave their glass insulators scattered all over the damned countryside?*

'Collectable' our friend chuckles. 'Would you like one? There might be more, if you are quickly!' Well actually, they are quite interesting..... I glance at my wife, who, like wives everywhere, is able to read my mind, somehow, and has a *don't even think about displaying that crap on the mantelpiece* kind of look on her face. She is correct, of course. 'De-cluttering', we called it, when preparing to move to this country, or 'never again will we accumulate any more of this rubbish', when boxing up our possessions to take to the car-boot sale.

The sun is sinking slowly in the western sky as we arrive back at the no-horse town, from the opposite direction to what I had been expecting, proving that my built-in compass is not always accurate, after what has been a memorable day. Our friend drops us back at the library, but instead of heading home, he jumps out of the car, and asks us to join him on a nearby bench. 'I have some news for you' he smiles. 'I have new job. I want to tell you person, not with the others. All is thanks to you, helpy me so much, I am so happy!'

We are delighted, of course, and to prove it my wife envelops him in a huge hug, followed by a kiss, then from me a man-wrap, with added back-slaps. We are somewhat puzzled, however. 'How did we help with your new job?' Chrissie smiles. 'What did we do, exactly?'

'EENGLISS!' he chuckles. 'You teach me Eengliss! You know I was working research, at university, but in past I was not possible to speak to lecturer or estudent in other countrees, only Espain. Now, I prove to they I can have conversation in Eengliss, so can to speak to persons in United States, Eengland, Germany, Holland, rest of Europe. Ees ver good for me, and thanks to you I so 'appy!'

'But we didn't teach you German, or Dutch!' I protest. 'Anyway, your level of English was very good when we first met you. We did nothing, really.'

He is still on cloud nine. 'Confidence! You give me much confidence! And Eengliss ees international, so university in other country must to speak Eengliss. I learn much vocabulary from you. And weeth new job I continue work at home, same as before, maybe must to go Granada and Jaen university more times but will be ver similar.' And he opens both arms wide, and hugs the pair of us, again.

I have a lump in my throat, and Chrissie is wiping away a tear. Such a lovely young man, a wonderful friend, and we are delighted for him, naturally. 'But you help us too, Juan!' Chrissie snuffles, emotionally. 'We could not manage without you! Pretending to be our lawyer, when we got our tyres stolen, getting our medical cards last year. But we must celebrate your new job, OK?'

He extracts his keys from his pocket, and heads back towards his car. 'YEES! The next week. We go to pub, we take beer, and like Amador say, WE GET PISSY!'

Our memorable day just got even more memorable, and walking up the cobbled streets homewards I feel as if I am floating, emotionally. Be good if I could float literally, up this damn great hill, but you can't have everything, can you? 'Can you believe the past, what, ten hours?' I ponder. 'We thought, sorry,

I thought, we were headed for a car demo. And what did we actually find? A new job for Juan, tree-climbing wild wooooolfs, or whatever they were, free breakfast, that great piling lunch, with wine. It was just…..'

'SHUT UP, RIGHT! Just don't say it, OK? I know you, what you are thinking. Zip the lip!'

*What?* I am flabbergasted. 'What are you talking about? Thinking what?'

She narrows her eyes. 'You are so predictable sometimes. I could see you, those piggy little eyes, scanning that great mound of food, lunchtime.'

I adopt the moral high ground. 'I have absolutely no idea what you are going on about. So come on, spit it out, whatever it is you think I was going to say.'

She pokes out her tongue, and mimics a whiny, kiddies voice. 'It was just a shame there were no pork pies or scotch eggs!'


The following evening, Monday, I am awaiting the arrival of my student, Alberto, when there is a knock on the door. I glance up at the clock. Quarter to six? Cannot possibly be him. Never in the history of the Iberian peninsula has a Spaniard been early for anything, and more often than not he is five or ten minutes late. I open the door to be confronted by a British couple… blimey, Babs, and what was he called, the people who came round on my first morning back in Spain, what, over ten months ago? Andy, that was it, they didn't return for the de-brief that evening, and we haven't seen hide nor hair of them since, so we just assumed they were so shocked by the experience with the Virgin Mary in Antonia's house, and had given up on the whole idea of moving to this crazy corner of Europe. And yet here they are, looking mightily pleased about something, and Andy is holding a huge cardboard box in his arms.

'Come on in' I smile, 'sorry I cannot offer you a drink or anything as I have a pupil coming shortly, but sit down and take the weight off!'

'Actually we can't stop' Babs grins, 'but we brought you a present, for everything you did for us that day! Sorry it's a bit late, but we've bought a house, which used to be a shop years ago, and it's taken all this time for the lawyer to get the change-of-use permission. Or so he said! We got the keys a couple of days ago and have been clearing out, we fly back to the UK in the morning but wanted to see you while we were still here!'

'Oh many congratulations!' I exclaim, 'we thought you had gone off the idea, after your experience down the street! So where is this new place, then?'

Andy rests his burden on the floor. 'It's a four-storey townhouse, with a roof terrace, behind the city wall in the jumble of streets back there. Been empty for donkey's years, it's in pretty good nick considering, just needs a paint up, and we thought we might keep the top two floors as an apartment for the kids, when they fancy popping over, and live in the bottom two ourselves. We're not ready to retire for a few years yet so will just be shooting over for holidays, but it was so cheap that it would have been rude not to!'

'Anyway' Babs chuckles, 'we found this lot in the basement, must have been old stock I am guessing, but seriously, if you don't want it, just chuck it away! And, there are a few leftover food things in the box we couldn't eat, if you can use them. If not, give it to those crazy next-door neighbours of yours!'

'You have me intrigued now!' I chuckle, 'May I?'

I drag the box towards me and open the lid, revealing a pile of dark, rustic, wooden souvenirs of various shapes and sizes, each one bearing the town crest. One is an ashtray, complete with glass centre, then a carved wooden key, maybe a foot wide, with half a dozen or so brass hooks, and a chain for hanging it up. Next comes a guitar-shaped barometer, together with a heart-shaped plank to which is fixed a photograph of one of the town squares, with a thermometer below. 'Wow, I love this stuff!' I giggle. 'And it must be, what, thirty or more years old, look, you can tell by the photos, the clothes people are wearing, and the cars. Is that a Ford Cortina? And it proves what I have been saying for ages, someone must have thought there was scope for tourism in this area, all those years ago, to have commissioned these souvenirs to be made. I mean, Granada and Cordoba get the lion's share, but here, the area in between, there are dozens of little towns and villages, historic old churches, castles, with an abundance of tapas bars! Ripe for tourism, if only people knew about this area. All it needs are a few articles in the weekend travel sections of a couple of newspapers, and this place would be like Benidorm! Anyway, as soon as my student is gone, I will hang them on the walls, apart from the ashtray of course! Thank you so much!' *Chrissie is gonna kill me, mind you, I can just hear her now, I'm not having that crap on display! Better get it hung up before she gets home. Fait accompli!*

Babs turns serious, all of a sudden. 'We just wanted to ask you, what has happened to the British people here, do you know? When we were here last September, for a couple of days, we saw maybe half a dozen Brits, but this time we haven't seen any. Has anything, you know, been going on?'

I glance up at the clock. Five minutes. 'Well, two blokes died, no sorry, three died in the last year. One was divorced, the house is closed up but we have no idea what the family are doing. The second one, his wife sold up quickly and moved back, and the third one has the house on the market but not sold it yet, although she is back in the UK also. Then another couple split up, she went back but he is still here. Another pair had a grandchild so they have moved back, but the house hasn't sold yet, as far as we know. Then two couples were worried about their healthcare after Brexit, they were in really poor health, taking lots of medication, we were away most of August last year and by the time we got back it had all changed. To be honest, we don't socialise like we used to. When we first came here, this house was like party central, a revolving door almost, we were still in holiday mode of course, then after a while we had to step back a bit, it was getting out of hand, all the drinking, and even though booze is cheap here it was still running away with our money! So nowadays we tend to go to the bars in the new part of town, if we fancy an evening out together as a special occasion. There is one place we really like where you can choose your tapas from a menu, as Chrissie is vegetarian, so that is really good.'

Time is up, but predictably, Alberto is late... 'Then you have the Brits with holiday homes, most of them are still around, one couple got too infirm to manage the hills so they sold up, otherwise the rest are still around, so we tend to meet up with them when they are over. That is better, we find, having a good old catch-up a couple of times a year, rather than trolling round the same old bars, week in, week out. Plus of course we have more Spanish friends now, so we meet up with them from time to time.' At that moment, there is a knock on the door, which I get up to open. 'Plus, we are really busy with our

English conversation! Alberto, good evening! Come in and meet our friends, Babs and Andy.'

'Hello, pleased to meet you!' smiles the bewildered Spaniard, glancing at the souvenirs. 'What are thees, please?'

'That is your class tonight!' I grin. 'Two classes in fact, English conversation, and Spanish history! And by the way, I have a present for you. Does anyone in your family smoke?!'


The following morning we are off on another hike, I assume, or maybe not, a visit to the local water supply, wherever that might be, and if our translation is correct, according to the publicity notice hanging in the library. A guided tour, no less, as organised by Historian-Anna, the town archivist. Important stuff, water, right? Can't live without it, and we have often wondered where it comes from in this arid country, given that the locals slosh it around liberally, down the streets in the mornings, to keep the dust at bay, and in their gardens, after sunset. And in a country with three hundred days of sunshine a year, you rarely hear the words *drought* or *hosepipe-ban,* as we used to from South West Water after three dry-ish weeks.

Bizarrely however, many of the neighbours drink bottled water, complaining that the stuff which comes out of the tap *has little stones in it.* Hardly surprising really, given the fact there is a huge great limestone mountain behind the town, and yes, there are occasionally calcium deposits floating round inside the kettle, but I spent my formative years in a similar hard-water area, and it didn't do me any harm, did it……

Dotted around the town, and surrounding villages, are stone horse-troughs, or fountains, with continuously-flowing supplies of spring-water, from ornate brass pipes, even in the height of summer, *agua potable,* safe to drink, where the local populace gather on a Sunday morning, to fill giant plastic containers…. so isn't this stuff the same as what comes out of the tap? And where is the reservoir? Blowed if I know. Never seen one, on our strolls around the vicinity. And we must be walking, as the poster didn't mention anything about a coach trip, although Chrissie has a few euros in her bag, I believe, just in case there is a minibus offering a fruit cake as a raffle prize….

The expedition is scheduled to begin at eleven, so we duly arrive at the main square at five minutes to, punctual Brits as we are, to find a group of around a dozen elderly people already assembled, which causes momentary confusion inside my admittedly tiny brain, as being last to arrive is a difficult concept to deal with, in this country. Can be a bit hit and miss, these cultural visits, quite honestly. The one to the local prison, a few months ago, was hugely interesting, having never been incarcerated, albeit temporarily, before, and I was mightily relieved to discover that Crazy Man was no longer behind bars. Or anyone else who maybe brandished Prestige stainless-steel kitchen implements, in a threatening manner, for that matter. We were also shown the lost property office, consisting solely of a forlorn collection of half a dozen punctured footballs, each one having a parcel label sellotaped to it, showing the date of recovery, and the location. And, I swear I am not making this up, one of the sad specimens was dated 1999. So if that was you who lost their ball, brown leather, a bit scuffed, during a quick kick-about, back in the last century, just call into the nick when you are next in the area. It will still be there.

On the other hand, the hugely anticipated visit to the local ceramics factory was an absolute dead loss. There was Chrissie, slavering at the prospect of adding to her rapidly-growing collection of decorated pottery. Sadly however, or thankfully, depending on whether or not you were paying, it turned out to be a brick factory, the boss of which droned on in a monotone for over twenty minutes about the weather-resistant qualities of his products. Fascinating. We snuck off early from that one. So we just never know what to expect. A voyage of discovery, to the water-works, hopefully.

Historian-Anna steps forward, smiling, bidding a warm welcome to everyone, and lovely to see the British couple, Cristina and Jonneee, which causes a mild scuffle from within the small crowd. 'NEIGHBOUR! What are you doing here?' *Oh, deep joy. Why did she do that? Not as if we are famous, or Royalty.* Who is this? A man's voice…. Pirate Pete emerges from the crowd. Pepe, from our street, neighbour of Auntie Vera and Leopard-skin woman, who, despite shedding his eyepatch many months ago, retains his original nickname, at least in our house. Well into his eighties, limps like an old badger, a few of his own teeth, but only a few, a widower, we often tease Antonia that he would make a good catch for her, which always produces much hilarity, particularly in the case of Manuela. *Not even if he was hanging in diamonds,* was one of Antonia's more printable denials. Sharp as a knife, yet with a permanent look of total bewilderment on his face, Pepe is a treasure, either about to crack a joke, or having just done so. Nothing, or no-one, is safe from his quips, which at his age he can get away with, a fact he plays on, I suspect.

So never mind what we are doing, what is *he* up to, this far from home? 'Are you coming with us this morning, Pepe?' I enquire.

'Certainly, neighbour!' he hollers, indicating a van emblazoned with the *Aqualia* logo, the local water company as beloved of Jake the fritter, which has just that minute drawn up, 'I want to see what those bastardo LAD-RONNIES are doing!' Which elicits a few tuts, and giggles, in equal measure, from the small, jostling crowd. Strange mixture, actually, this lot, a completely different bunch from the sendero expedition a few days ago, much older, and not that agile, most of them, which, given that the only way out of this square involves hills, and uneven cobblestones, is somewhat strange. Maybe we are all going to cram into the back of the van....

The front door of the ageing conveyance springs open and out steps Sean Connery. Not, I hasten to add, from his Thunderball period, but nowadays, minus toupee thankfully, trimmed white hair and beard, strong, handsome features, dark, piercing eyes, causing a certain amount of fluttering amongst the females of the group, including, disappointingly, my wife. 'Ooohhh, looky here!' she purrs. 'His name is Bond. James Bond. And I must say I am shaken, *and* stirred.'

Not right is it, when we're supposed to be visiting a water-works? 'Hang on a minute' I protest, 'didn't *someone near here* once say I resembled James Bond, the current one, with the blue eyes, Daniel-something, emerging from the sea in my swimming trunks?'

'I think you will find I said Basildon Bond actually' she chuckles, eyes still firmly fixed on water-man, who, dressed in a florescent bib as opposed to a tuxedo, bears absolutely no resemblance to ageing film stars, I have decided. 'You looked like a shriveled-up writing-pad, as I recall!'

That is it. I am with Pirate Pete on this. All these *Aqualia* people are nothing but bastardo Lad-Ronnies. Suddenly, Historian-Anna coughs, to gain our attention. 'Rogelio will be our guide, this morning, and he will meet us there. Follow me, please!' Rogelio? Roger? Roger Moore? Priceless. Besides, I preferred him as Bond.....

'Benga arriba!' cries Pete. Arriba? Up where? Up this narrow, cobbled street, it appears, the same one we traversed on that pre-election evening, when one of us was searching in vain for a public convenience. And curiously, old Rog has driven off in the opposite direction…. The group has spread out now, following slowly behind our intrepid historian, and for the first time I am able to take a good look at the make-up of the gang. Pensioners, mostly, so where in the devil's name are we going? Many of them are lucky to have made it this far, quite honestly, and the two old women bringing up the rear, dressed in tweed two-pieces, surgical stockings and patent court-shoes, resemble ladies who lunch as opposed to those who might ramble. Not a trace of Gore-Tex, for sure. The larger of the two reminds me of Hyacinth Bucket, with her strong, manly features, and bosom, while her smaller compatriot wouldn't be out of place on the set of *Monarch of the Glen,* poised regally in front of a roaring fire, stags heads and other hunting trophies fixed proudly to the wall, tartan curtains closed against the chilly winter air.

It is their hairstyles which fascinate me the most, however, lacquered to within an inch of their lives, stiff and unyielding, one honey-blonde, the other chestnut, just like our front door, only more durable, clearly dyed, as my mother would undoubtedly have remarked, unkindly, and I am chuckling to myself, imagining a howling gale sweeping down the street, people shielding their eyes from the debris, bent double, buttoning coats, and yet these coiffures remaining perfectly in place, not a hair disturbed. Pirate Pete, lagging behind, catches me grinning, digs me in the ribs, points openly at the retreating backsides and, laughing, hollers 'Elephante, and Rinoceronte!'

Hyacinth turns, her face twisted into a mask of hatred. 'Who are you calling a Rinoceronte, you disgusting old TONTO! Go away, you stink of orina!' And she swipes at him with the back of her hand, which, displaying remarkable reflexes for an octogenarian, and proving his cataract operation was a complete success, he expertly avoids.

Chrissie is leaning on a cottage wall, doubled over, fingers stuffed into her mouth, trying desperately not to laugh, while Pete grips my arm and whispers, not quite under his breath, 'she was the Elephante, actually!' *And we haven't even gone a hundred yards, yet.* Oh my GAAD, as Amador might have said. But Hyacinth was correct. I am able to detect the faint aroma of old men, emanating from our neighbour....

We are of course entirely familiar with the street we are climbing, leading as it does to the abode of my some-time business partner. 'Maybe you could give Del a quick call, ask him to get the kettle on, organise a refreshment stop, for, ooh, about an hour's time?' Chrissie ponders.

'Well he'd have to serve the tea individually, bearing in mind he only possesses one tin mug!' I observe. 'We would be there all morning. Besides, can you see Monarch of the Glen here wanting to stop at chez-Del? Hardly the Dorchester, is it? *A window seat madam? Certainly, just let me shift this sack of yesso and give it a quick brush down.*'

'I thought he was in the money, now that his state pension has arrived?' she grins. 'You helped him with the online application, and he said it had quadrupled his weekly income, didn't he? Enable him to claw his way out of abject squalor, you said?'

'Yes but I don't think an *Old English Roses* bone china tea-service was going to be his number one priority, somehow. Upgrading from a mop-bucket to a functioning bathroom was slightly higher up his to-do list, I gather!'

The main problem with this particular stretch of uneven cobbles is the uniformity of the gradient. Steep, the entire way, with no little flat sections to take a breather. We are puffing, and the rest of the crew have fifteen years on us, at least. Whether Historian-Anna anticipated a bunch of pensioners turning up for her tour is questionable, but we ain't getting there any time soon, wherever *there* might be. Hyacinth is clinging breathlessly to the wrought iron outside one particular cottage, and Monarch is bent almost double, hands on her meaty knees. Mind you, I have to ask, *tweed?* Were they expecting it to go off a bit chilly, in Spain, in early July? Although, judging by the speed we are going, we might still be here come Christmas.

Pirate Pete meanwhile is doing well, all things considered, and thankfully a light breeze is wafting down the hill, enabling us to keep up-wind, and the severity of the terrain means that his supply of pithy one-liners has dried up, for now at least. Certainly there have been no further sporadic outbreaks of violence, in the last hundred yards. *Give it time.*

Eventually, after what seems like about fifty years, we emerge at the top of the street to be confronted by a wall of rock, hundreds of feet high. Our mountain. Not the Matterhorn, admittedly, but a vicious, grey, rugged, limestone pinnacle towering above us. There is a walking-route to the summit around the other side, but from here you would need serious mountaineering gear to get any higher. Or you could try the hairpin bend, where a ropey old *Aqualia* van is parked, containing a white-haired, bearded, balding old man who to my mind bears absolutely no resemblance to anyone called James, or Bond, slumped in the passenger seat. My wife appears energized, for some reason. 'Ooh, do you think we will be abseiling to the water-works? Will Mister Connery here have to, you know, show me the ropes? Strap me into his harness? Get out of the way, please, I am first in the queue!'

Not nice, is it, when there are people in need of medical assistance, oxygen even? A complete disregard for her fellow travelers, who admittedly will only require strapping into an ambulance, as opposed to a film-star? Hyacinth and Monarch have gone a disturbing shade of puce, and Pete has taken advantage of the break in proceedings to vacate his lungs, the sound and evidence of which is happily being carried away on the wind. Most of it, anyway.

Big problem, however, as far as I can see. Anna claimed that old Rog would meet us there. And, unfortunately, here he is. But where is *there?* Trust me on this one. A few straggly, tumbledown cottages. An Alpine meadow, beneath the cliff-face. And what looks suspiciously like a brick out-house, from when bricks were first invented. But a water-works? Nah. More chance of finding the wet-stuff in the Sahara desert.

Suddenly, over the ridge comes a herd of maybe fifty goats, sniffing, nibbling, rubbing shoulders as they jostle for the best positions and the tastiest morsels, mothers with kids, and a few old rams with curled horns bringing up the rear, followed by two straggly, matted hounds of dubious pedigree, and a wiry old man in a stained, collarless shirt, which might actually have featured a collar in a previous century, whiffy trousers held up with baler-twine which even Pirate Pete would surely have forsaken, and tramp's boots. A bachelor, certainly. Hardly the wholesome image from the *Sound of Music,* but nevertheless I start to croon, softly. 'High on a hill was a lonely goat-herd, lay ee odl, lay ee odl, ley ee oo.'

And my wife joins in. 'One little girl in a pale pink coat heard, lay ee odl, lay ee odl, ooooo!' Julie Andrews eat your heart out.

Slowly, Connery eases his girth from behind the steering wheel and hauls his way unsteadily up the grassy slope. 'Welcome to the system of water' he smiles. 'Follow me, please.' And he trudges off up the field, the Von Trapp menagerie having departed for pastures new. Must have been the florescent bib scared them away. *Or the size of his gut.*

I'm not going up there!' hollers Pete, grinning widely. 'That grass is covered in goat shit. I'm not walking in goat shit, it's slippery, gets all over your shoes. It was bad enough when we had goats running up and down the street, that Jose Ocana Pastor, in your house, neighbour, those animal sheds you knocked down to build your swimming pool. You could have had goats, neighbour! What did you want a swimming pool for?'

Just then, there comes a muffled cry from behind us, and we turn to see Hyacinth sprawled on the grass in an ungainly fashion, legs akimbo, although whether from cardiac arrest, or merely having lost her footing whilst treading on a fugitive lump of ruminant faeces, is impossible to say, as half a dozen of the group are crowding around, fussing. 'Told you, didn't I?' Pete chuckles, unsympathetically. 'Get up, Ann-Hella, you will get goat shit on your coat!'

A number of thoughts cross my mind simultaneously. Shouldn't around five of those people move away, right now, and give the stricken woman room to breathe? Does someone need to call the emergency services? Does anyone have a pack of wet-wipes in their bag, as that does look suspiciously like a brown stain on Hyacinth's knees? Is that her name, *Ann-Hella?* How on earth did Pete know about our pool, given that he lives at the other end of the street? Has Loli been blabbing again? And where on God's green earth is this cursed water-works?

Sometimes, these little problems have a way of working themselves out, don't they? Historian-Anna takes charge. 'Ann-Hella is fine, she is not hurt, she just slipped, but she will rest here a few minutes. Please, the rest of us, can we follow Rogelio? Oh, and does anyone have a wet-wipe?'

Pete snorts derisively. 'A wet wipe? Why the hell would I carry a wet wipe?' *Why indeed? What a ridiculous notion.* Chrissie meanwhile springs to the rescue, delving into her bag whilst picking her way precariously across the grass, brings forth a pack of Poundland's finest and hands it to Monarch, who is remaining behind with her friend, apparently, while the rest of use resume our expedition.

Connery is leaning on the wall of the brick outhouse, fiddling in his pocket for a large bunch of keys, and as we approach I suddenly become aware of a loud rushing noise. A watery rushing noise, emanating from the ……. surely not? A rickety old structure, three yards wide, corrugated roof…. is this what we have come to see?. Our decrepit film-star holds up a hand. 'Please, we have to visit one at a time, as there is not much space inside. So, who is first?'

Suddenly I am shoved rudely aide, as my wife forces her way to the head of the queue. 'Bugger offf!' she giggles. 'Come back in about an hour!' Her whiskery hero unlocks the door, and the pair of them disappear inside.

It appears as if Pete has decided to follow us, after all. 'You want to watch him in there with your woman!' he cries, 'bastardos, those *Aqualia hombres!*' He gestures at the still reclining figure at the bottom of the slope, who is having her stockings sponged off by Monarch. 'I see the Elephante and the Rinoceronte didn't make it! Ridiculoso! Waste of time them coming!'

Before I can frame a suitable reply, the door to the outhouse reopens, and my red-faced, breathless wife emerges, grinning widely, fanning her face with her hand. 'Incredible! she pants. 'What a force of nature! I thought my head would explode! And the water was quite good, too! Your turn.'

'Told you, didn't I?' shouts our annoying neighbour. 'Look at her face. Bastardos, those *Aqualia hombres!*'

Not sure I'm all that keen, now, I have to tell you, but in for a penny and all that. Be a shame to come all this way... I open the door and am almost deafened by a rushing torrent, a cascade of water, in a cleft in the rock, a chasm, almost twenty feet below. A natural spring, clearly, but such a huge shock to the system as I always imagined a dribble, a trickle of water, not a violent deluge like this, which would surely mean certain death to anyone falling in? A set of stone steps leads down to a concrete viewing platform, and Connery is holding out his arm for me to take, which I am extremely reluctant to do as, unlike my wife, holding hands with other men in underground chambers not one of my biggest ambitions, I can tell you. Same as those pleasure-boat rides, on holiday, isn't it, where there is usually some beefy great sailor waiting to take hold of my hand as I step aboard? *No thank you. I can manage.* On this occasion however, gazing into the roaring turbulence of what could easily be a watery grave, especially if I have traces of goat shit on the soles of my espadrilles, I decide that having James Bond on hand, albeit an extremely elderly one, might be a good thing, after all, just in case, and you know what they say, discretion, valor and all that, so I take his arm, firmly, in a *don't I have a firm grip, hell of a game, hell of a game, Bears got a good team this year* deep-voiced kind of way, and allow him to lead me down the steps.

Conversation is impossible, such is the force of the water, but he points out a huge iron pipe, maybe a foot in diameter, with a wheel controlling what I assume is a valve to regulate the flow, leading off to one side of the gorge, in the direction of town. Otherwise, apart from a rusty strip-light flickering away on the ceiling above, everything is refreshingly old-school. No dials, gauges, men in white coats and hard hats, just a crack in the rock which has probably been there about a million years. Welcome to Santa Marta water-works.

Smiling my appreciation and shaking him warmly by the hand, he follows me up the steps, which is good to know, something to cushion my fall, should I lose my footing, and out into the blinding sunshine. Chrissie is sprawled on the grass, so checking for unwanted dung, I join her while we wait for the others to complete their tours, which doesn't take long as Hyacinth and Monarch are sheltering in the lee of a ruined cottage, and Pete is refusing, citing bastardos, Lad-Ronnies and goat shit, not necessarily in that order.

Still smiling, Historian-Anna thanks Rogelio for his informative tour, and us for attending, and we are free to head off. 'Are you coming home with us, Pepe? Chrissie enquires. *Or limping home, more like. Still, it's all downhill.*

He grimaces, wiping something suspicious from the sole of his shoe on a clump of grass. 'No, I will probably have lunch with my sister.'

Lunch with his sister? Have we mis-translated? 'Your sister, Pepe? Who is your sister?'

'Yes, my sister!'

She takes a deep breath, then instantly regrets it, having failed to take into account the direction of the breeze. 'So who is your sister, Pepe?'

He flashes me his best gap-toothed grin, and winks. 'Ann-Hella. El Elephante, of course!'


## CHAPTER 17. THE NATIONAL HEALTH SERVICE, SPANISH STYLE.

Early-retirement agrees with me, and never in my life have I felt so well. The sunshine of course, all that wonderful Vitamin D, (or is it C?) just waking up in the morning and glancing out the window has my spirits soaring. The deep blue sky, the warmth, the wondrous light. Even rainy days don't seem so bad, because we know the sun will return, before long. And keep this to yourself, please, but the odd damp afternoon lets us catch up on all those little jobs we were meaning to do, but just never got around to. By any measure, health-wise, our decision, all right all right, my original idea, to move over here, has been a resounding success.

There are of course a few negative points, just give me a minute while I think of one…. oh yes, the ground is very hard here. No, don't laugh, it is true!

Without a stitch of carpet, apart from the front door mat, these marble tiles in the house don't half play hell with my knees, every time I get down on them, looking for my shoes, which 'someone' has kicked under the sofa, or doing a little job (on rainy afternoons only, of course), so I have had to learn to ease myself to the floor, rather then bump down, but I forget, from time to time, because I am a bear of very little brain, as you all know. So my *Rhodesias,* to give them their local name, are taking their fair share of wear and tear.

Another downside, now I come to think of it, is the terrain, all these damned hills. *Well what did he expect,* I hear you say, *living halfway up a ruddy great mountain?* Well yes, we knew there was this big rocky thing, behind the town, of course, and ours is a mere hillock, compared to some of the humungous ones away to the east. It's just that my favourite forms of exercise, cycling and running, are such blooming hard work. Been a lifelong cyclist, from my tiny pavement trike, when little more than a toddler, graduating to a *Raleigh* all-steel at about five, a shop-bought racer at around eleven, and finally, a self-assembled road bike, a *Mercian* frame from Derby, Reynolds 531 tubing for those in the know, with *Campagnolo* Italian components. And it is here with me now, downstairs in El Woodshed, gathering dust, having benefited from a full factory re-spray the year before we moved, and then 'smuggled' over in the caravan. *Just a shame I never get the time to ride it.*

And running? On these cobblestones? Play havoc with my knees, they do, or that is my excuse, and I am sticking to it. Like the switchback at the funfair, these streets, and a couple of miles of painful jogging, before breakfast, is about all I can manage, these days.

All of which is leading towards a confession, as you might have already guessed. And here it is. What with the relaxed lifestyle, the sunbeds, the complete absence of stress, apart from when the water board rear their ugly heads above the parapet, the rich food and wine, but mainly the wine, I may have put on the odd pound or two, in the last twenty or so months. *What?* OK, OK, a few pounds, a number of them, in fact. *Say again?* ALL RIGHT! Don't keep going on about it. Half a stone! Satisfied? At least my 'House Orderly' skills from my Wolf Cub days fifty years ago didn't go to waste, shifting my trouser buttons slightly to the left. OH STOP! THIS IS THE LAST TIME, OK? Half an inch to the left.

But as a serious point, for anyone contemplating moving over here, just keep an eye on those bathroom scales, OK?

Luckily, Chrissie has no such worries, charging round the town of an evening visiting her pupils. In fact, she even bought a fitness tracker, and regularly puts me to shame, over dinner, announcing her score for that day. No, her main problem has been coping with the dry air over here. Just about the whole of inland Spain is between fifteen-hundred and two-thousand feet above sea level, and that is before you start adding on the mountains, plus the fact that they build towns and villages at the top, rather than in the valleys. Better to spot approaching invaders, I imagine. Our town is the equivalent of living the best part of the way up Snowdonia, for instance, that bit where the little trains pass each other, keen mountaineer as I am. That is where the similarities end, of course, there having been no olive trees growing on the side of Mount Snowdon, the last time we took that stunning train ride, *well you surely didn't think we walked, did you,* together with the reality that any high ground in the UK would be suitably moist, and humid. Over here, the climate is dry and dusty, and she does suffer from a blocked nose, and a dry cough, quite regularly.

But having said all that, we are both well. We feel well, we *look* well, according to our friends in the UK, every time we visit. We are the epitome of wellness. So much so that, having obtained our Spanish medical cards, and registered with the local GP surgery, ably assisted by our good friend Juan, not long after we moved here, we have thankfully had no cause to use them. We did have one brief interaction with the medical profession, a few months ago, when Chrissie lost a filling, one Friday evening, allegedly during the consumption of one of my speciality Rick Stein prawn paellas, an accusation I totally deny, on the grounds that there are no bones in prawns, or rice. *Still got the blame, though...* During the night, she developed a raging toothache, and it was clear by morning she was in considerable distress, the side of her face all swollen. Now, my cure-all remedy for just about anything involves a bottle of whisky, and specifically for toothache, I slosh it round the offending area, rub it over the gum, and hold it inside my mouth, hamster-style. Never fails to bring relief. Tastes good, too. Trouble is, my wife cannot stand the taste of Scotch, having got horribly drunk on it as a teenager, so had to resort to more traditional methods, namely aspirin, which did no good whatsoever.

So there we were, that Saturday morning, dentists all closed, and us not registered with one in any case, with the prospect of a miserable, and for one of us, painful weekend ahead. 'I think Marie at the library has a cousin who's a dentist' she winced. 'I will give her a call, tomorrow evening, see if she can get me an emergency appointment, Monday morning. Meanwhile, could you pop down the pharmacy and get me some stronger painkillers, please?'

Inevitably, leaving the house, I got trapped. 'Neighbour! Where are you going?' *Chrissie might well have toothache, but I have Loli-ache, for which there is no known cure.* I duly explained that La Cristina had *dolor de dientes,* whereupon Her Annoyingness demanded to examine the patient. She gripped my wife around the neck, like a sack of potatoes, and proceeded to prod the affected area vigorously, which I imagine did no good whatsoever, then announced her diagnosis. 'Take her to the *oor-hen-thee-ya,* neighbour!'

*The where?* Is she saying hospital? No, I imagine the Spanish for 'hospital' is *ospital.* The pharmacy? No, that is *farmacia,* we know that one. I am as much use as a chocolate teapot, in these situations. 'The urgency!' Chrissie wailed, from the corner of her mouth. 'You know, that emergency place, just past where we leave the car. Where they park the ambulance. Come on, get me down there, for pity's sake.'

Easier said than done, in this country, running the gauntlet in the street. 'Go to the pharmacy, neighbour!' 'Give her some whisky!' 'Tie some cotton round her tooth, the other end around the door, and slam it shut!' My own teeth were starting to ache, I can tell you, by the time we got clear of the neighbours, that morning.

So what is this *oor-hen-thee-ya* place, given there are absolutely no signs indicating anything whatsoever. A minor injuries hospital? A clinic? A refuge for the poor overworked ambulance drivers, somewhere they might sit all day drinking coffee and eating tapas, given that the sound of sirens in this town is about as rare as hen's teeth? Entering the building, through an unmarked door, was like a visit to the *Marie Celeste* visitor centre on a wet Monday in November. Deserted. Nothing. An empty space. We followed a corridor, eventually reaching a set of steps, at the top of which was a white-coated, middle-aged woman perched behind a desk, moodily filing her nails. Was this reception? Or was she the sweeper-up? 'My wife has very bad toothache' I announced, 'could we see a doctor, please?' *I swear if she tells us to go away I will scream. Could have been down the pharmacy, bought the tablets, gone home, Chrissie could have taken the required dosage and been feeling entirely better, by now.*

She looked up from her cuticles and frowned, as if the appearance of patients was a complete shock to her system. 'Are you English?' she enquired. I confirmed we indeed were, whereupon she picked up a phone, dialed a number, and babbled a jumble of Spanish bracketed by the words 'toothache' and 'English.' Just then a door swung open and a whiskery old man popped his head out. 'Come, please!' I had to stifle the urge to burst out laughing. His sudden appearance was so dramatic, it reminded me of a Monty Python sketch, and if John Cleese had appeared that would have been curtains, for me. *Blimey, what is it with these old people in these jobs? Are there no youngsters working anywhere? This fellow has to be well past his retirement date, white coat hanging from his bony frame, and I daren't look down in case he is wearing carpet slippers.*

Indicating us to sit, he proceeded to ignore his patient, and addressed his questions to me. 'Where does your woman have her pain?' *Oooo, you are on dodgy ground here, grandad. I can feel Chrissie bridling. Not right, is it 'your woman' in the twenty-first century? Still, other countries, and all that.* I smiled sweetly, indicating my top gum, and left cheek, in a *I think that might be where the pain is but she is only a chattel, after all,* kind of gesture. He nodded, gravely. 'And how long has she had the pain?' *Well why don't you ask her, she is sitting right next to you, and you are actually talking across her.* Suddenly I was struck by a thought. Is this actually a hospital, or a Vet? Does he think Chrissie is my companion-animal? Surely Eric Idle will walk in any minute, and start talking in a high, squeaky voice?

Exaggeratedly, I turned towards my wife. 'And how long have you had the pain, woman?'

She was shaking, but whether with rage or subterranean mirth it was impossible to tell. 'Since last night.'

I inclined my head and looked the vintage Vet squarely in the eye. 'She says, since last night' I confirmed, resisting the urge to add *stop asking me questions, she is only a servant.* Not a flicker. I was half-expecting him to smile and go *all right, all right, I know they're supposed to be equal, nowadays, but what can you do?* No.

He delved into his antique leather briefcase, rummaged around for a few seconds and with a flourish produced a foil-wrapped strip of a dozen tablets. 'Tell your woman to take one, three times a day.' And he stood up, opening the door, to indicate the end of the consultation, adding 'Have a good holiday!' Through gritted teeth, even though they were presumably hurting like hell, Chrissie managed a half-smile, I gave him a full 'gracias', more from the point of view of the entertainment value than his bedside manner, and we shuffled out into the corridor. Presumably now we have to give our details to cuticle-woman, but no. She had vanished. Disappeared from the face of the earth, seemingly. We were back on the Marie Celeste.

Stumbling into the blinding sunshine, my wife was scrabbling urgently at the foil to extract a tablet, then groped around in her bag to locate the small bottle of water she usually carries, glugging gratefully. I turned to face her. 'So tell me, woman, in the interests of customer satisfaction, on a scale of one to ten, how likely are you to recommend us to your friends?'

'One to ten?' she choked, coughing violently. 'One to bloody ten? If we were in the sixteenth century, probably an eight.' She took another swig, then started grinning. 'Mind you, think about this morning. An unidentifiable building, a woman who might have been a cleaner, a doctor older than Hippocrates himself, free tablets, and we were in and out in ten minutes flat. And, I was so angry in there that my toothache has gone, more or less. I call that a result, don't you?'

Sunday evening Chrissie, feeling much better after taking the course of tablets, calls Marie, who in turn calls her dentist cousin, Alphonso, and arranges for an emergency appointment at eight-thirty on the Monday, where we duly present ourselves at the allotted hour. Strange sort of place for a surgery, being more like a huge private house, massive wooden double doors, and a traditional bell-pull, which my wife tugs, having beaten me to it. Must have been an olive-oil baron's residence, I imagine, back in the day. A distant chiming is audible from within, and after a discrete period the door is opened by a young teenage girl, followed by a powerful blast of stale cigarette smoke. Blimey, is this a dentist, or a nightclub from about the end of the last century? Smoking is of course prohibited in Spain, same as the UK, and by and large the locals seem to obey, although there can be the odd bit of crafty lighting-up, towards closing time, but I haven't sniffed anything remotely approaching this for over a decade.

It seems however we are expected. 'Plees, thees way' giggles the girl, 'my father she expect you!' And into the poisonous atmosphere we step. I glance at Chrissie in a *bloody hell, how do they allow this in a public place* kind of way, and I thought we were supposed to have the first appointment? Some inconsiderate Spaniard has clearly been puffing away in the waiting room, and I feel overwhelmingly sorry for the girl having to put up with this, and why didn't her father, a medical professional for pity's sake, turf the miscreant out?

Suddenly a door opens and out steps a tall, distinguished-looking man, sixties easily, mass of wavy grey hair, the image of that opera singer, what was his name, I always forget, one of the Three Tenors, but not *that* one, exquisitely-tailored white coat hanging majestically from his elegant frame, a piano-player's hands with long, slim fingers, all the better for manipulating dental instruments, and a fug of dense smoke wafting behind him. Placido Domingo, that was it. *Or was it Jose Carreras?* 'Greeting!' he smiles. 'I Alphonso, cow-seen Marie. You Cristina and Juanee? Come, plees.' And he leads us into the surgery, where amongst the dental chair, the ceiling light, the drills and a tray of implements, is an ash-tray where a half-smoked cigarette lies smoldering. Oh. My. Actual. God. He is *smoking,* in the surgery. Never in my lifetime... I glance at Chrissie, stifling the urge to cough, theatrically, like someone caught downwind on a bonfire night, and through the haze I can just about make out she is blinking, rapidly, with a *bloody hell I am going to have to put all our clothes in the wash as soon as we get home* kind of look on here face. Now don't misunderstand me, Alphonso has every right to do whatever he likes in the privacy of his own home, and this *does* appear to be his own home, but in the *surgery?*

He takes me gently by the arm, and steers me towards the chair. 'Sit, plees.'

WHAT? I start to protest. 'No no, it is Cristina with toothache, not me! My teeth are perfectly in order!'

He smiles, sweetly. 'No, plees, you first, two minutos only!' Oh well, it seems as if I am getting a check-up as well as my wife. Just as well I suppose, as neither of us has had one, since moving here, one of the many things we just haven't got around to, what with all the lying around we seem to do. Now, I know that many people, Chrissie included, have a dread of the dentist. Luckily, however, I am not of that number, and when I was working, used to positively look forward to a thorough examination, with a bit of drilling thrown in for good measure. Am I a masochist? Not a bit of it. No, I am sure I read somewhere, years ago, that the dental profession in general were overwhelmingly in agreement that the best antidote to the taste of antiseptic, numb gums and general fiddling with the old molars was a Littlewood's 'Big Eight' breakfast, with free fried bread. I therefore arranged my appointments for first thing in the morning, nine-ish, to enable me to get into said breakfast emporium before the crowds of old folks descended. 'Ooh, what do I fancy?' 'What are you having, Mavis?' 'Well the bacon looks nice!' 'No I can't eat bacon, gets under me plate!' 'Think I might have beans on toast!' 'What about scrambled eggs?' No. In and out by half nine, avoid all that. Eight items, plus fried bread, some ridiculously low price. *No wonder they went bust.* My work colleagues knew what I was up to, of course. 'Funny dentist you have, J-A, there are baked beans on your chin!' 'Don't think much of that bloke, you have bits of sausage between your teeth!' Our receptionist, Sarah, was the worst. 'I see you have a dental appointment at eight-forty-five. Does that mean you will be visiting your special client, Mr Littlewood, on the way back to the office?'

Alphonso steps to the side of the room, retrieves his ciggy, and draws a luxurious lung-full, before exhaling pleasurably, like the Flying Scotsman pulling into King's Cross. He then rummages among his equipment, bringing forward a metal plate, which he gestures for me to hold between my teeth, pushing it into place with his nicotine-stained fingers. *Blimey, I am partial to oak-smoked pork and leek chipolatas, of course, although usually I prefer them fried...* He pulls a camera into place, then retreats behind a screen. It appears I am having an x-ray, although sadly, zero chance of a good old-fashioned fry-up afterwards. He repeats the operation on the opposite side, then gestures to Chrissie, who all this time has been standing as close to the window as possible, without actually sticking her head out, that it is her turn. *And she doesn't eat sausages…*

Eventually, we stumble gratefully onto the pavement, inhaling deeply, rubbing our eyes, my wife clutching an appointment slip for a filling on Friday. 'You don't need me to come with you, Friday, do you?' I splutter, wafting my hands dramatically. 'Do you have an old boiler-suit tucked away in your wardrobe somewhere?' Our first Spanish dental appointments, which, like everything else in this nutty country, were about as far removed from anything we ever experienced in the UK. Will there be a charge? Is this on the local NHS, or will someone shove a tatty yellow slip into our letterbox, addressed to Jose Ocana Pastor, in about three years time? Not the absolute foggiest.

There is just time to dash home, hot showers, throw our whiffy clothes into the wash-basket, before the conversation group at the library. To which Marie arrives a few minutes late, panting breathlessly, fanning her face with a large manila envelope, which she hands to Chrissie. 'Sorree I late! I see Alphonso thees day, he give me you raddyo-graffia. Take, plees. He say me, plees to give he you raddyo-graffia, from Eengland.'

There are nods around the table, and murmurs of 'yees,' 'raddyo-graffia,' 'much important,' whereas we are mystified, as always. Chrissie peers apprehensively into the package, and draws forth an x-ray, four x-rays in fact, two each I presume. She bursts out laughing. 'Well these are yours, look, like a row of condemned houses!' And she slides them across the table. Damn cheek! Condemned houses indeed? Lucky to have a single tooth in my head, quite honestly, after all the beer bottles I opened with them, as a callow youth, outside the Plough and Windmill, and the wallops I incurred, in the name of sport.

I throw Marie a puzzled look. 'Why do we need these? They are called *x-rays* in English. What are we supposed to do with them?'

There are incredulous gasps from the assembled Spaniards. Juan, as always, is the serious one. 'Ees much important, you must to keep you raddyo-graffia safety. Where you raddyo-graffia from Eengland, plees? You must to show Alphonso you raddyo-graffia from Eengland!'

Damn. I knew there was something we forgot to bring with us, when we moved. All those x-rays we had stored away in the loft. Never mind those Beatles albums we didn't have room for. Rafi senses our confusion. 'You no have raddyo-graffia from Eengland? I no understand.'

*She doesn't understand? How does she think we feel?* Got to be careful here, of course, they have their systems, however ridiculous they might seem to us, and we don't want to upset local sensibilities, a fact Chrissie recognises, to avoid me jumping in with both feet. 'We do things slightly differently in Britain' she smiles. 'Usually the dentist keeps the x-rays, so we don't have to. Can you imagine John here, losing his? You know what he is like!' *Oh yeah, knew it would be my fault.* She is correct, of course. Can you picture me, leaving my x-rays in Littlewood's cafe? Or turning up at the dentist the next time with bits of fried egg stuck to them?

'So what you call you different teeth in Eengliss, plees?' Teri enquires. 'In Espain we say incisivos, muela, canino, pre-muela, like thees. And why you laughing me, Jonneee?'

'Sorry!' I smile, 'I was not laughing at you, Teri, but in Britain we do not generally use the technical words, incisors, molars, canines. Dentists do, of course, but the public usually just say 'teeth.' Top teeth, bottom teeth, front teeth, back teeth. If you ever go to England, and need to visit the dentist with a toothache, just point to it, you will be fine!' *I was going to add that she should pop in Littlewood's afterwards, but sadly that option no longer exists.*

So there you have it. Another top tip. For anyone planning on buying a house over here, don't forget your x-rays!

A couple of weeks later, I return from my pre-breakfast jog to find Chrissie in the bathroom, slumped over the sink, in floods of tears. Gently, I place a supportive arm around her. 'What is it, what is wrong?'

She is inconsolable, however. 'I have a lump, inside my nose. You know, I told you, I have been having trouble breathing lately, I have just had a look, but I cannot see properly, but there is something up there, a growth of some kind……. here, take this torch…. I cannot see properly…. you look.'

My stomach lurches. In cold dread, I hold her in my arms. 'OK, it will be fine, don't worry, we will get it sorted, whatever it is. Just put your head back, and let me see.' I am terrified, quite honestly, what I might find, but have to stay strong. I flick on the torch and begin my examination, first one side, then the other. Oh my God. Slowly, I pull her upright, and grab a tissue. 'All right, dry your eyes, there is a small blockage, looks like bone, or cartilage to me, but is it painful, can you feel it?'

She wipes her tear-stained face. 'No, it doesn't hurt at all, I am not aware of it, but it felt blocked, so I just thought I would see if there was anything……'

The elephant in the room, of course. That dreaded word. I take a deep breath. 'So you have never had a peek up there before, in the past?'

'NO. Of course not' she sniffles. 'Why would I?'

'So think about it' I whisper. 'You might have had that bone, or cartilage or whatever it is, for years. Since you were young. You might even have been born with it. Do you see what I mean?'

Her face softens, visibly. 'Do you really think so?'

I smile, reassuringly. 'I am no doctor, of course, and we will get straight down there, get it checked out, but it doesn't look angry, or inflamed, or recent, to me.'

She perches herself on the bath. 'Oh my God, I was so worried….. yes, I think you might be right, I do vaguely recall, when I was a little kid, I had a similar problem, my mum took me to the doctor….' And she stands, and envelops me in a huge hug. 'Sorry to get so emotional.'

I have tears in my eyes, but blink them away. 'Well, we had the pleasure of the dentist a few weeks ago, today I guess we will find out what the doctors are like in this town! And heaven alone knows how you go about getting an appointment. Go down there and queue up for about a hundred years, I imagine?'

'Ah, well that is where you are wrong!' she giggles. 'Marie was telling me, when you were explaining the laws of cricket, or some other man-crap, to Jose and Juan, she said one of her boys was sick recently, and that they have a new online booking system now, at the doctors. So let's fire up the internet, and find out!' *And it is true!* 'Look at this!' she giggles, clearly feeling much happier. 'Appointments at three-minute intervals! Can you believe it? Look, eleven-oh-oh, eleven-oh-three, eleven-oh-six, oh-nine, and so on. Can you imagine a Spaniard having a three-minute medical appointment? Blimey, it would take that long for just the kissing! Then another three minutes shouting, and flapping their arms, another three telling about what happened in the street last night, then their life stories. Hell, they'd need a half-hour, minimum!'

'Perhaps you need to block-book!' I giggle. 'Although how long will we actually need? Better look up the Spanish word for nose, before we go, however!'

She claims what appears to be one of the last available appointments, at the remarkably un-Spanish time of eleven thirty-six, and, leaving plenty of time, we head down there, the same grand street as the dentist, a similar palatial four-storey building, thankfully on this occasion with the distinct absence of tobacco fumes. The massive wooden doors are wide open, leading to what appears to be a reception area, with typical medical posters lining the walls, a reception desk, but sadly no receptionist. Not a single soul, filing their nails. We stand around for a few minutes, unsure of what to do next, before an old man shuffles in from the street, although whether he has a medical complaint, or just needs a quick sit down, is unclear. I indicate the empty desk, and shrug, in a *what is supposed to be happening* fashion. 'Breakfast!' he hollers. 'The bastardos have gone for breakfast. Follow me, please.' And turning, he heads painfully up a flight of elegant marble stairs.

What is it with these locals and their breakfasts? Is there no concept of having it before they start work? And the lack of any form of consideration for customers, or patients in this case, is staggering, to my mind. OK, so if the receptionist is due a statutory break, and I don't actually believe they should be, having only opened half an hour ago, here's an idea. Why not arrange someone to cover, at a time when patients are booked in? Don't they need to check us off the list, so that the doctor can access our notes? Not that Chrissie has any previous notes, of course, but that will be most of the three minutes gone before we even start. 'Sorree, I not to find you raddyo-graffia. You must to go, plees.'

Wheezing mightily, the old fellow reaches a landing on the first floor, then barges unceremoniously into a small room which could comfortably hold five people, at a push, but into which around a dozen pensioners are crammed. 'ULTIMO?' he bellows. Ah yes, the famous *ultimo*. You hear it anywhere a queue has formed, and it translates as something like 'who is next before me?' And it always provokes the same response. 'I am next.' 'She was before me.' 'That man came in after her.' 'I think I was after her.' 'How's your Bert's lumbago?' 'Ooh, mustn't grumble!' OK, so I made one of those up, but you get the picture. The other day, I was standing patiently in the queue at the greengrocers, minding my own business, when an old woman came up behind me. 'Ultimo?' *Well actually I was thinking of firing this cauliflower into that imaginary basketball hoop up there on the wall……….* 'Si.'

So what is actually happening? Is there a doctor in the house? Is there a doctor in the province, given this apparent absence of any medical staff whatsoever? *Surely not?* Twelve people, three minutes each, that's thirty-six minutes, or it was when I was at school, appointments should have started at eleven, it is now gone half-past, all this lot are before us, none of them have been seen yet…. *surely not?* Looking around the room, I can almost mind-read. Everyone is thinking the same thing….. Suddenly the old fellow staggers to his feet, and flings open a door to another room, the surgery possibly, which anyone might reasonably assume to contain a medical professional. 'BASTARDO! He's gone for his breakfast!' *Yep. The room is empty.*

Suddenly, everyone is talking at once, although above the hullabaloo, I can hear footsteps on the stairs, slow, steady, heavy, laborious, and a what appears to be a paramedic materialises breathlessly in the doorway, an ambulance-woman in fact, mid-forties maybe, blonde pony-tail, dressed in dark-green scrubs and a huge florescent jacket, from which I swear she is brushing toast-crumbs…. So what is she doing here? Has there been a critical injury we haven't noticed? Is she here in case a fight breaks out, after all this time-wasting? Does she suspect the old chap might, I dunno, knee the doctor in the goolies, when he actually deigns to turn up? Wouldn't blame him, to be honest. Regaining her breath, slowly, she turns to face the room. 'Buenas dias. How are we all today?'

*How are we… oh we are all absolutely fine, thank you, there is not a single thing wrong with any of us, we just popped in to check you enjoyed your coffee and tostada, did you have it with olive oil, a few slices of jamon maybe….. how the bloody hell do you think we are? We are all sick. Sick of waiting for this cursed doctor, if you must know, so stagger your way back downstairs, get the doors of the ambulance open and the blue light flashing, because this thrice-damned quack is gonna need it….*

She turns towards the surgery door, then barges it open with her meaty hip. 'Ultimo?' The effect is exactly like firing a starting pistol. Everyone, excluding us but including the formerly hobbling old man, leaps to their feet and charges towards the surgery, like a savage pack of dohhs weeld. 'I am ultimo' 'you were after me' 'she was before you' 'get off my toes' 'what is that sticking in my back?' With a deftness belying her age, and size, the startled paramedic steps rapidly into the room, and bangs the door, leaving the baying Spaniards in her wake.

'Bloody hell!' I whisper, although I might as well have shouted it from the rooftops, the row this lot are making, 'so much for your precious appointment system! Quick, dial nine nine nine! Get reinforcements!'

She is shaking with laughter. 'It definitely said, on the website, that you have to make appointments online, or with the receptionist. You cannot just turn up on-spec, and if you do, you have to wait. Marie was saying this, there was hell-up when she came here, loads of old duffers trying to jump the queue!'

'Well anyway' I frown, surveying the chaos, 'all this lot are before us, aren't they? You got the last available appointment, you said, so we will just have to wait. Did you bring a book? Sadly I forgot my copy of *War and Peace!*'

'I'm not so sure now, actually. I booked it on my Kindle, so the script was a little small, clicking the time-slot. It looked like the last one, but maybe…..'

Suddenly the door of the surgery opens a crack and ambulance-woman pokes her head out. 'Reechard Cristina, plees.'

And the room goes berserk. 'I am ultimo!' 'No I was before you!' 'She is next!' 'Who is Reechard Cristina?' Everyone is hollering and bawling at the same time, whereas we sink lower in our seats, in total embarrassment.

The beleaguered paramedic holds up her hands, placatingly, although she might as well have fired a pea-shooter at a charging rhino, for all the good it does. 'LOOK!' she bellows. 'We have a new system. You must book online.'

Like poking a stick in a hornets nest. 'I don't have a computer!' 'Do I look like a little kid?' 'I am eighty, not eighteen!' 'I don't even have a phone, you tonta!'

Which doesn't go down well. 'Then you must telephone the receptionist. This is not my fault. Who is Reechard Cristina, plees?'

'WHAT PUTA RECEPTIONIST?' 'THERE IS NO RECEPTIONIST!' 'SHE IS HAVING HER EFFING BREAKFAST!' 'YOU ARE ALL TONTAS!'

Toes curling, we slink across the room, like a pair of whipped mongrels, shoulders hunched, avoiding eye-contact, slalom our way around the outraged oldies and slip gratefully into the surgery, closing the door silently behind us. Slumped in her chair, ambulance-woman rolls her eyes in a *Spaniards, eh, what are they like* gesture, although she might actually be thinking *how the bloody hell did you English jump the queue*. 'Dee-may?'

Ah yes, the famous *dee-may.* Literally 'tell me.' The universal greeting of any waiter, shopkeeper, and, it would appear, pretend-doctor. Not 'good morning what can I do for you?' Very direct, the Spanish language, but then again, we have just jumped an unruly queue and almost caused a riot, judging by the noise outside. So where is this elusive quack, anyway? Is this woman some sort of triage? Is she going to waste several of our precious three minutes discovering what is wrong, before passing us on to the actual doctor, who is, what, hiding in a broom cupboard somewhere, in a vain attempt to rid his white coat of traces of chopped tomato?

'I have a blockage inside my nose' Chrissie smiles, word-perfectly. Remarkable, I would have forgotten my lines by now, after the morning we've just had. *But she does have a Spanish 'O' level of course.*

Now you would have thought, wouldn't you, that upon hearing the symptoms so described, our unfriendly medico might whip out a pen-light, ask the patient to tilt back her head, and, here's a suggestion, take a quick peek? No. She reaches forward, taps disinterestedly at a keyboard, then straining her tired back in the direction of a printer, extracts the single sheet and passes it across with two fingers. 'Take this, come back next week.' Dismissed.

Stunned, we slowly turn, as strictly we still have almost two minutes left of our allotted time, and with a muted *gracias,* we fight our way through the milling, shouting herd, slope off down the stairs, and stumble into the bright sunshine. Chrissie examines her prescription, giggling. 'What do you suppose this is? Ointment?'

'Wouldn't surprise me if it was a stick of dynamite, knowing this lot!' I chuckle. 'That would clear your blockage! Anyway, here's the pharmacy, up the hill on the left. I guess you are about to find out. Light the blue touch-paper, and stand well back!'

The pharmacist is the model of politeness and efficiency. Chrissie hands her the prescription, she disappears into the storeroom, returning a few seconds later with a paper bag, stapled at the top. 'Take tree times day' she smiles. 'Seven euros plees.'

Oh, hell. *Forgot my wallet.* I turn to my wife, but she has anticipated the next question, and is already extracting the coins from her purse. Stepping outside, she eagerly tears open the package, when her face suddenly falls. 'Nasal spray. I've paid over six quid for bloody nasal spray, which I could have got in Poundland. For the sake of all….'

'Well how much is it in Poundland, then?' I enquire, all serious-face.

My intended joke falls flat, of course, she's heard it all before. 'Oh six hundred and fifty quid, how much do you think? Honestly, nasal spray, can you believe it?'

'Ah, but it's special Spanish nasal spray, for Spanish nasals!' I smile. 'You know, like the honking nasals we hear each morning, from the direction of Fernando and his sisters. Like the phlegmy nasals coming down the street, each morning. The Spanish nasal chorus! Just poke it up your hooter, and within the week you will sound exactly like......'

Nursing painful ribs, I unlock our front door, and usher the patient inside. 'Would you like me to administer the treatment, dearest?' I enquire.

'Not ruddy likely!' she exclaims, ungratefully, I feel. 'I need a little puff, not Niagara Falls. And stop flapping your wrist like that. I said PUFF. Your jokes are getting so old. For pity's sake go and lie in the garden, I will get lunch ready.' Thus dismissed, abruptly I feel, I turn to go, when suddenly she grabs my arm, and plants a wet slobbery kiss on my cheek. 'Thanks for your support, this morning.'


Over the next five days, she duly applies the spray as directed, and I am on hand with the torch to supply progress reports, which are sparse to say the least, as nothing whatsoever appears to be happening. The lump is getting no bigger, which is a blessing, but neither is it shrinking, although I do my best to sound encouraging. That evening, as I drain my final glass of wine, she slips her hand in mine. 'Now, please don't be offended, or get upset, but I've asked Rafi to come with me the day after tomorrow, for my next appointment. You don't mind do you, only I realised at the first appointment that our Spanish was not really good enough, for something like this. I was talking to her, and she actually suggested it. She said we should have insisted on seeing a proper doctor instead of that auxiliary, as she called her, and she knows her way around the system and all that.

I smile sweetly. 'I think you are right, we are completely out of our depth for something as important as this. Of course I am not offended, I can get on with the next level of the garden, and be here when you return.

So on the day in question I am laying out a few blocks, trying to picture what might go where, when my mobile rings. Chrissie sounds somewhat breathless.

'I have to go to hospital! The doctor didn't know what the lump was, he didn't think it was anything sinister but said it should be checked-out by a specialist.'

My heart lurches but she sounds relatively upbeat about the whole thing, even though this inevitably means a further delay in a final diagnosis. 'So did he give you any idea how long the appointment might take to come through? Months, I suppose?'

'Now!' she cries. 'We have to go now! Rafi's husband Pablo has gone to get the car, so can you meet us outside her house in about five minutes?'

My heart lurches for the second time. Bloody hell, it must be serious, surely, getting an appointment on the same day? 'Where do you have to go?' I croak, mouth having gone dry, but trying to keep the mounting panic out of my voice.

'Jaen .' she confirms. 'Rafi knows where the hospital is there, and which department we have to go to.'

'Jaen?' I splutter, 'blimey, isn't there anywhere nearer than that?'

'I don't know, it's where the consultant or specialist or whatever is, today, apparently. Anyway, see you in five, OK?'

After a quick swill, and, quite remarkably for me, remembering to grab some petrol-money, a few minutes later I am puffing my way up the stone steps to the street above, where a battered, dusty, war-torn Ford Sierra, with non-matching body panels, comes wheezing into view, driven by the diminutive figure of Pablo, mid-thirties maybe, dark, shoulder-length hair, straggly beard, intense, hypnotic eyes, faded Pink Floyd tee-shirt, a far-away look on his face as if he has just been beamed in from a Tibetan retreat. Chrissie is ensconced in the back with Rafi, who I can always imagine with a daisy-chain in her long, glossy chestnut hair, dressed in Woodstock-inspired hippy-chic, but who in reality is an unemployed primary school teacher, subsisting on short-term supply work, in this train-wreck of an economy. A tragedy, and such a waste of talent. Not sure what Pablo's background is, as we know Rafi far better from the library group, of course, although invariably, when we call in on them, he is upstairs 'meditating', which might or might not translate as 'having a bit of a kip'.

Unable to give my somewhat bewildered-looking spouse a comforting hug, I slide into the front passenger seat and flash her what I hope is a reassuring smile, before turning to Rafi, then Pablo. 'Thank you so much, both of you, for helping us out like this. You are such good friends to us!'

'Ah no to worry!' Pablo grins, scraping a battered wing-mirror along a cottage wall. 'I speak you of Peterrr Pan.' *Riiiight. Not the first clue.*

'How you say otto rhino in Eengliss, plees?' Rafi enquires. *Otto the rhino? Was he a character in the story? Been a long time since I read the book, admittedly, but I only remember the crocodile. Oh yes, and the dog. Nana, was it?*

'ENT.' Chrissie confirms. 'Ear, nose and throat, that is what we say.' *Otto the rhino. Oh my God, get a grip, Richards.*

Pablo manages to negotiate the narrow streets without further damage, and soon we are speeding along the main road. Chrissie and her friend are nattering away contentedly in the back, and as a passenger I can start to admire the stunning scenery, huge craggy mountains surrounded by a sea of olive trees, and allow myself a wry chuckle, bearing in mind my last trip along this road I was a pent-up ball of anger and frustration, on my way back to sort out that thieving tyre-dealer. 'Yees' Pablo continues. 'Lass jeer, Rafi and me we visit Lon-Donn. We take tooor see Peterrr Pan, in the night. Beeg Bens. Ees ver good. We take brax-fass Eengliss, een Lon-Donn. Oh my Gaad! Rafi she say me, I eaty brax-fass Eengliss, I must to die!'

His wife pipes up from the back seat. 'I never see brax-fass like thees! Bay-Conn, eghhs, shosh-shage, beeens, po-tayto fry, bread-th fry, I say Pablo, I no understand peoples Eenglees eaty thees!'

'Anyway,' I smile, trying to steer the conversation back to matters in hand, 'was the doctor helpful? Did you have all that aggro with the locals pushing in, and the online booking? Was there a receptionist this time, or was she on her break? Did he give you any idea what it might be?'

Before Chrissie can frame a reply, however, Pablo is off again. 'Thees jeer, we want visit Stonn-henhh, and Glass-tonn-booor. Joo visit thees place, plees? Harry Potterrrr. Lass jeer we see Harry Potterrrr. Thees jeer, we see Merr-leen. How you say, Merr-leen, magico?'

'How you say tranny-via in Eengliss?' Rafi enquires, before I have time to advise Pablo that Harry Potter is all grown-up now, and that Merlin the magician has been dead for quite a few years. 'Tranny-via. I so embarrass-ed. Gobby-Enry, he fixy tranny-via, een HH-ayen, he fixy the via, but no have tranny.'

Less than one iota, clearly, but while we are still digesting that news, and please let it be lost in translation, her husband is still in holiday mode. 'Sallis-booor. Cathedral much high. Batt. City of Romano. Hot Batt. Stonn-henhh. Glass-tonn-booor. Problem is mooch expensive, travel from Lon-Donn.'

The real problem at this precise moment is, actually, for the British contingent in this car, that we are approaching the outskirts of Jaen and I for one can feel, not panic, certainly, but rising tension, for sure, and I know my wife will be of similar mind. No, scrub that. She will be panicking. And the last thing she needs to hear is about Glass-tonn-bloody-booor. I turn to face our friends. 'Why don't we come to your house over the weekend, say Sunday evening, and we can help you with the various options, make some suggestions, work out what is best for your trip, when we have a bit more time, and can relax?'

Rafi claps her hands, bouncing in her seat. 'Fantastic! Thank you ver much. Now please shut-up about holly-day, Pablo!' *Amen to that....*

We leave the motorway and take a dual carriageway into town, and I notice what appears to be a tram-track down the middle of the road, complete with a huge 'park and ride' car park, little stations, crossing points with fully functioning lights, a massive warehouse bearing the legend Tran-via, but with a complete absence of actual trams, or passengers. The famous tranny, hopefully. No wonder she is embarrass-ed. 'So nothing is happen here, I say you,' she continues, 'Gobby-Enry pay for thees, but no money for tranny. *Elephante Blanco.* Was choice, thees tranny-via, or university hospital. Imagine, hospital of study, how you say, research, similar Granada, peoples want thees, no peoples want estupid tranny-via. I embarrass-ed my countree.'

Before I can frame a suitable reply, however, my heart takes another lurch, as up ahead is a hospital, a grey, forbidding structure, five stories maybe but who is counting, and a sign announcing *Hospital,* which is usually a good thing, although not today, actually, as we would have preferred to remain in the dark. *This is it.* Pablo steers expertly around the triple-parked melee, avoiding collateral damage, while I fish around in my pocket for change for the ticket machine, which causes massive hilarity on account of there being no charge whatsoever. *Embarrass-ed you countree, Rafi? Come to a British hospital, see how much they stiff you for, and don't even think about transgressing for more than thirty seconds, otherwise you will have bailiffs knocking on your door. Now THAT is embarrass-ed.*

We follow our friends into the building, Rafi checks her directions with a receptionist, and we head up to the first floor and a huge waiting room, maybe half-filled with patients, the majority of whom are clutching manila envelopes. *So you have to take your x-rays to hospital too? Who knew?* I feel conspicuous, somehow, an impostor, without any, as if the locals are whispering behind their hands, *look at those English people, with those hippies, and no raddyo-graffico.* Pablo and I slump into the uncomfortable plastic chairs, clearly designed for snake-hipped matadors, while Rafi guides the English patient to the corner of the room where a brief consultation takes place, then the pair of them disappear behind a curtain, my wife managing a brief, desperate, backwards glance in my direction. I turn to our friend, head in hands. 'I should be with her, Pablo.'

He fixes me with a deep, hypnotic stare, like Kaa the snake in the *Jungle Book*, although if his eyes start swirling in a *go to sleep, man-cub* sort of way, I am off. 'Ahh, no to worry, Rafi weeth she. Now, tell me, airporto, Lon-Donn. Soutt-end. Ees Soutt-end much distance Glass-ton-boor?'

*God I hope she will be OK. I am worried sick.* WHAT? Southend? My wife is stuck here in a foreign hospital and he is rattling on about bloody Southend? 'Why are you talking about Southend airport, Pablo? That is completely the wrong side of London, for the south-west. Do you want to visit the east coast, or London?'

*I wonder what they are doing in there?* 'No, lass jeer we visit Lon-Donn, we fly Soutt-end, ees much cheap. Thees jeer, I not know airporto Stonn-henhh, Sallis-booor. We no want visit Lon-Donn thees jeer.'

*Must be seeing the consultant, I imagine.* 'How much distance Glass-ton-boor to Sallis-booor?'

*Incredible service, though, isn't it? She only saw the GP this morning, and here we are, just a few hours later, with the consultant.* 'Ees possible walking Glass-ton-boor city to top of Glass-ton-boor Tooor?'

*Bloody hell though, the GP must have thought it was serious, to get in that quick?* 'You know King Artooor? Table round? Where city of he, plees?'

I glance down at the diminutive Spaniard, as if seeing him for the first time. 'Sorry Pablo, I'm finding it difficult to concentrate. The best airport for that area is Bournemouth, and you can fly there direct from Malaga. Bournemouth is a seaside town, so you can stay there for a ….HERE THEY ARE!' And I jump up, narrowly avoiding scattering half a dozen locals in my wake, and fling my arms around my approaching spouse. 'Oh my God, where have you been? I was getting so worried!'

Fanning her flushed cheeks, and returning, literally, to earth, she perches herself on a chair. 'Three consultants! I saw three consultants. The Three Amigos! The first one didn't know what it was, he called a second who wasn't sure, so they had to get the top guy, who luckily was here today, and he said it was nothing, just a bone deformity, I've probably had it all my life, but it's most likely  the dry atmosphere here, which I'm not used to of course, after humid old Britain…..but hold on! Whoa, boy!..' I am just about to perform back flips…. 'The camera revealed something on my throat, polyps they think, so I have to go for an MRI scan, downstairs, now. That is correct, Rafi?'

Our friend nods in agreement and seems about to comment, but her husband, who is bubbling with excitement, dives in ahead. *Bless him, he was worried all along, just trying to take my mind off everything.* Or not. 'Rafi! Jonneee say me no es necessary  travel Soutt-end Lon-Don! We must to travel Booorn-mooot! Es seaside! Eengliss seaside! Like we school books! Fees and cheeps! Donkeys! Pier! Fees and cheeps on pier! How you say, man-zanna caramelo?'

*Did I say there were donkeys?* 'Toffee apples.'

'Yees, toffee apples! Hot dohhs!'

His wife, becoming increasingly agitated, has clearly heard enough. 'Pablo. SHUT THE FOX!' She turns to Chrissie, head in hands. 'I sorree, Amador teach me thees! My hoos-ban, he so excity! Pablo! Jonneee say we, he come our house Sunday, talk about holly-day. Plees. Cristina have three doc-tor poky camera up nose of she! Not want listen you fees and cheeps! SEET DOWN!' And she grabs my startled wife by the arm and whisks her away, back down the stairs towards the MRI department, I assume.

*Blimey, she might be only five-foot, but these Latin types ain't half fierce, when they get fired up.* Actually, we are making a right spectacle of ourselves, and were this the UK, security would undoubtedly have been alerted by now. Here? Entirely normal. No one is batting an eyelid. A few old ladies are fanning themselves with their x-rays, and an old man is grinning widely, no doubt storing up the memories for out in his street tonight, but the rest are gazing disinterestedly at the Spanish soap opera playing at maximum volume on the giant TV screen on the far wall.

*Hell, an MRI scan? Didn't I see a picture of one once, a woman disappearing into a giant, shiny tube? Didn't I know someone who had one? I bury my head in my hands. I am hopeless at this stuff. Clueless. I could tell you the spark-plug gap on a 1200cc Harley Davidson, .038 of an inch, I usually set mine at .040, in case you were wondering, but medical matters?* 'Jonneee, what distance Stonn-henhh to Booorn-mooot, plees?'

*And they must think it is serious, getting her in straight away?* 'Ees easy get Sallis-booor?'

*Although maybe as she was already here, they managed to squeeze her in?* 'How we travel Glass-ton-boor, plees?'

*Very claustrophobic, MRI scans, aren't they? She is going to hate that.* 'What name city of King Artooor?

FOR THE LOVE OF MIKE. 'Right, Pablo, you fly Malaga to Bournemouth, on Ryanair, have a couple of days at the seaside, then train to Salisbury, two hours maximum. You change trains at Southampton but it's easy. Have a couple of days in Salisbury, tallest spire in England I think on the cathedral, lovely historic buildings, and there are local buses to Stonehenge. From Salisbury it is under an hour on the train to Bath, stay there, say, two nights, beautiful stone buildings from the Georgian period, Jane Austen, Roman baths. Then half an hour on the train to Bristol, huge waterfront, many bars and restaurants, an historic iron ship and suspension bridge. There are buses direct to Glastonbury from outside Bristol station, takes around an hour, but you can stop in Wells, England's smallest city, beautiful cathedral and architecture, on the way. Then in Glastonbury you have the ruined abbey, destroyed in the time of Henry the Eighth, the tor, of course, and a thorn tree planted by Joseph of Arimathea, who legend has it brought the infant Christ to Britain. Fantastic ancient pub in the High Street too, one of my favourites, and you can get a world-class giant pasty in a little cafe around the corner so you won't need to eat again for about a week! The train and bus tickets for all this maybe cost around fifty pounds each if you get them in advance. The seat of King Arthur was called Camelot, but there are several different locations for this, the most famous is a place called Tintagel, which is way down in the south west, you can get a train down there but would need a local bus to get to the village, not sure about that, but we can look it up ON SUNDAY WHEN WE COME ROUND!' *God, my head is banging. I wonder how she is? I should have gone down there with her, not stayed up here. Would they have let me in? Doubt it actually.* 'Pablo, I'm just off to the bathroom a minute, I won't be long.'

I prise my crippled posterior out of this relic of the Spanish Inquisition and am heading across the room when I am summoned again. 'Jonneee! What thees giant pasty, plees?'

I stagger towards the Gents, after which I find myself on the stairwell, staring, unseeing, out over the car-park, and with eyes closed, I rest my head on the glass. *Why couldn't it be me in there? Poor love, she must be scared to death. Polyps? I imagine them as small, white warty things. Do they need to be removed?*

Suddenly I feel a hand on my shoulder. 'Jonneee. I have mesh-age from Rafi. Cristina fin-ees now. We can to go home. Plees, thees way.' And he leads me downstairs, into another, smaller waiting room, containing an elderly couple, seated patiently, and my wife, pale as a ghost, supported by a nurse on one side, Rafi on the other.

At that precise split second, a number of different events occur. Chrissie appears light-headed, momentarily, and stumbles.

The nurse, all five-foot-nothing, grapples ineffectually with her patient.

Rafi, similarly vertically challenged, is pulled to one side and is heading for the floor.

I leap to my feet, dash the five yards to the tumbling trio, and wrap my arms around them, keeping my body weight low, just about managing to prevent the four of us ending up in an ungainly heap.

Rafi, arms flailing, catches me a stinging blow to the side of my head, narrowly avoiding gouging out an eye.

Chrissie retches, but mercifully, having been nil-by-mouth since last night, has nothing to bring up, and instead emits those grotesque heaving noises as practiced by Callers For God On The Big White Telephone everywhere. HUEYYYYY! BIIIIILLLLLLL!

The nurse detaches herself from the scrum but trips, staggering backwards onto Pablo's lap.

I half-drag, half-steer my barfing beauty towards a chair, and ignoring the stabbing pain in my shoulder-blade, lower her to relative safety.

Pablo is grinning, like all his Christmasses have arrived at once.

Rafi, confronted by the pornographic image of a blonde in a crisp white uniform and stockings straddling her errant husband, steps angrily forward as if to slap the startled professional painfully across the cheeks, but at the last second grabs her by the arm, and hauls her upright.

The old man, hitherto looking extremely green about the gills, staggers manfully to his feet, and with a cry of 'I am off' heads rapidly, for an octogenarian, towards the door.

His wife lunges desperately for his coat-tails, scattering her x-rays, which the nurse, scrabbling picturesquely on all-fours, is hurriedly attempting to gather.

Pablo is still grinning.

I am struggling to avert my gaze, but fail.

Chrissie stretches out a leg and boots me distressingly on the shin.

I step backwards onto a fugitive raddyo-graffico, my foot slips, and narrowly avoiding falling face-first onto the nurse, which could only have ended badly for my marriage, and immediate future, wrench myself to an upright position, at great cost to my spine, and slump gratefully into a chair.

And, breathe.

The nurse grabs the remaining x-rays, flaps them in the air to remove the dust and foreign bodies, stares angrily at the one bearing the imprint of an espadrille, stuffs them impatiently into the manila envelope, smooths down her uniform, fastens the top button which must have come undone in the melee, although I can't say I noticed personally, and smiles sweetly at the old lady in a *where's your husband gone* kind of way. The show is over.

Rafi takes Chrissie by the hand. 'Plees, you feely better?'

She lifts her head out of her hands and stretches, blowing out her cheeks, which are already regaining some element of colour. 'I am, thank you. In fact I have a craving for a Coke, and maybe a bite to eat. Does anyone fancy some lunch? My treat!'

'Rafi!' cries her husband. 'Jonneee say me, must to eaty giant pasty, een Glass-ton-boor! Ees similar empanada, more biggy, meeet, po-tayto, ony-on, toor-neep, but no bloody carrots, he say. Know you what ees bloody carrots? I not know bloody carrots! Come on, we take they our favourite restaurant! No have giant pasty weeth no bloody carrots, but we have good eaty, thees place! Yees.'

Light-headed, we stumble gratefully into the warm sunshine, and avoiding much in the way of collateral damage, Pablo guides us through the hospital car park, which thankfully features nothing in the way of barriers or number-plate recognition cameras, out onto the road, and down a hill towards a giant shopping centre. 'Thees our favourite restaurant, in HH-ayen' Rafi confirms. 'I think you enjoy. Follow, plees!' She leads us into a massive, domed space, complete with a kiddies funfair, shops dotted around the edge, and, as predicted, the tables and chairs of a cafe-bar. Just as we are taking our seats however comes the vaguely familiar sound of someone bellowing into a microphone. 'MARIA, POR FAVOR! ALICIA, POR FAVOR! JOSE, POR FAVOR!'

A HUNDRED MONTADITOS!  So it must be a chain restaurant, we suspected as much. Therefore, I know which one out of the hundred I am having. Not a giant pasty, either with or without carrots, and don't mention anything to my Cornish relatives, if you bump into them, but I've eaten both varieties. No, the *christorra,* of course. And we know what that is, don't we? Correct. Shoshage!

Three weeks later we are off to HH-ayen hospital again, for the polyp-removing appointment, this time on our own, as Rafi and Pablo have finally decided to embark on their summer holiday. *And they say the south of France is very pleasant this time of year, don't they? Grrrr.* Still, we know the way, and Chrissie is clutching her appointment letter, which arrived around five days after the MRI session, which I thought was pretty damned impressive, considering the water bills take twice that long, from walking-distance, so surely all we have to do is wave it under the nose of the first *medico* we encounter, and hey presto, we will be in. *Ever the optimist.*

Now, don't laugh, please, but in the boot is an overnight bag. For both of us. Even though, as far as I am aware, I will be a mere spectator, a visitor, a person who is planning on nipping down to Hundred Montaditos, providing I can find it, while my wife is undergoing treatment. Hospitals, like dental surgeries, always leave me feeling a little faint, and in the absence of a branch of Littlewood's in this neck of the woods, a Spanish Shoshage will be just what the doctor ordered. *Gotta follow medical advice, right?*

The explanation of this frankly bizarre arrangement was, as always, at the library group, with Marie on translation duties. 'Thees letter say plees to remember you hygiene personal productos and interior clothes, in casey you must to pass the night in hospital.' And she gazed across the table and smiled. At me.

I turned to Chrissie on my left, grinning. 'There you are, don't forget your toiletries bag and a change of knickers! Don't want to get caught short, do you!'

'No no no' Teri cried, wagging her finger in my direction. 'you must to take these things.'

I frowned. 'But I am only a visitor. Cristina is the patient, having the operation. If she has to stay overnight, the hospital will kick me out at the end of visiting time, and I will come home, then return in the morning when visiting starts again.' I didn't mention Hundred Montaditos. *Probably best keeping that to myself.*

There were sharp intakes of breath across the table. 'What thees kick me out, plees?' 'Visiting time, what ees thees?'

'Sorry' I giggled. 'Kick me out is to ask me to leave. At the end of visiting time, when visitors must go home, in the evening, so that patients can get some peace and quiet.' As soon as I said it, the penny dropped. *Peace and quiet? In this country?* I flapped my hands in a *sorry I have misunderstood* way. 'In Britain, there are usually visiting hours, times during the day when visitors are allowed to come in. And they have to leave at, I don't know, eight, eight-thirty in the evening.' And a vision of Hattie Jacques, as a battleaxe matron in *Carry On Doctor* ordering out the relatives, flashed through my mind.

'Oh my GAAD! Amador spluttered. 'You must to LEAVE? In Eengland you visity no sleepy in HOSPITAL?'

Next to me, Chrissie was shaking with subterranean mirth, no doubt having made the connection to Doctor Tinkle. Kenneth Williams, of course. Ooohhh, Matron! Classic. She regained her composure. 'So are you telling me that if I have to stay in overnight, John will sleep in the hospital too? Where, exactly?'

'In the BED!' replied an incredulous Doctor Tinkle.

'Yes but what bed? My bed?' enquired his perplexed patient. *Not sure I like the sound of this. I can just imagine Hattie Jacques ripping back the sheets in the morning and jabbing a ruddy great hypodermic up my back-side.*

'In a bed TEMPORARY!' chuckled Kenneth. 'In you ROOM! Jonneee must to sleep in bed temporary weeth YOU. Een Eengland you no doo THEES? Fox ME!'

So there you have it. If you are hospital-visiting in this country, plees to remember you hygiene personal productos and interior clothes. Mine are in the boot right now, although we still don't know whether or not this is actually true. We were expecting them to burst out laughing in a gigantic *APRIL FOOL!*

even though it is July. All will be revealed, very shortly, as here is the hospital, coming up on the left, so I need to concentrate, find somewhere to park, without involving shunting, and all will be well. Or not. Because we cannot find the hospital entrance door. Rafi and Pablo must have taken us in the back way, and there are at least three back doors, one of which turns out to be the boiler house. My wife is, understandably, somewhat tense. 'For pity's sake, can't you remember the way in? And please don't say you have slept since then.'

*Well it's true, I have, but probably best not to mention it, today.* I smile reassuringly. 'Don't worry, we have plenty of time, we are half an hour early, the appointment is not until nine-thirty, and it's barely nine. Let's go round the front, there is a massive set of steps, that must be the main entrance, so that must be where reception is. Follow me, please!' It seems however that my optimism is misplaced. There is indeed a massive set of steps, at the top of which is a huge glass entrance foyer, inside of which is….. nothing. Just a corridor, several corridors in fact, leading who knows where. But of reception, even an empty reception where the usual incumbent has gone for breakfast, there is no sign.

Just then a lift door opens and out steps a woman in a white coat. I wave the appointment letter under her nose, she studies it carefully, and smiles. 'Otto Rhino. First floor. You can use the lift.' I express my thanks, but honestly, why are there never any signs in this country? I am not panicking, yet, we still have twenty-five minutes, but we just don't need this. The place is a labyrinth, how is anyone expected to find... the lift pings and we step out onto the first floor, which is exactly the same as the ground. A MAZE OF CORRIDORS. I am starting to become agitated. We step one way, and another, then spot a group of around a dozen people, seated outside a door, which upon closer inspection bears the legend *Otto Rhino*, in letters about an inch high. Is this it? Must be. Everyone is staring at us so we grin, as if wandering around a strange hospital is an everyday event in our country, and take our seats, although something is clearly amiss here. 'Tell you what' I whisper, 'I remembered my clean pants, but you forgot your x-rays!'

She checks her watch. 'This isn't right. We didn't come here, before. Look, we only have fifteen minutes, what the hell are we going to do?'

Inwardly seething at the disorganisation, I nevertheless manage a smile. 'Look, you stay here, I will go back downstairs and have a good look round. There has to be a reception or enquires desk somewhere. If not I will strip off naked and run down the corridors! That will get us some attention!'

'Arrested more like!' she giggles. *But this is no laughing matter, is it?*

Back at the lift, I spot a stairwell in the corner, so decide to walk down to the ground floor, where in front of me, as plain as the nose on my face, is a reception. *The* reception. *What the hell?* Fixing the location in my mind, I turn a corner to find…. the main entrance, where we came in. *They hid the reception around a corner, and didn't bother to put up a sign? I don't believe this country sometimes…* I dash back upstairs, two at a time, *gonna need those clean pants any time now,* arriving breathlessly at the *Otto Rhino* door, where Chrissie is still sitting, nervously checking her watch. 'Downstairs' I pant. 'Reception, downstairs, quick, this way!' A dozen blank faces are staring at us so I grin, manically, as if dashing breathlessly down hospital corridors is entirely normal, where we come from, bid them a cheerful *adios*, and we scarper. *Five minutes.*

Miraculously, there is no-one waiting at the counter so Chrissie presents her letter to the smiling, helpful receptionist, who has not a trace of toast crumbs on her blouse. She reaches behind her and brings forth a clear plastic wallet containing several wrist bands and half a dozen or so sticky-backed labels, all bearing my wife's name, and medical number, which she passes across. 'Into the lift, first floor, turn right, fifty metres, on the left is a small reception. They are expecting you. Adios!' We follow her directions, and arrive at our destination, exactly as described, at the stroke of nine-thirty. Phew!

So, what are we expecting here this morning? Well, bearing in mind my BUPA subscription lapsed the day I retired, I am guessing that a private room and five-star service will be out of the question. And we have been gently cautioned by our friends at the library that when the locals have hospital appointments, however minor, the whole family usually accompany them, not just spouses or partners, but aunties, uncles, cousins, parents, children, nieces, nephews, with a few in-laws thrown in for good measure. And as we all know, Andalucian people are known to be prone to occasional bouts of mild excitement, so we were rather hoping for a smallish ward, populated by an even smaller number of elderly people, in the vain hope that we might avoid raucous Spanish shouting. *Fingers crossed….*

Actually, all joking aside, the safe removal of the polyps, and a subsequent biopsy report confirming they were benign, would be the best result of all, and to achieve this happy outcome I am sure Chrissie would be willing to undergo her treatment in the car-park, standing up. Anything else will be a bonus. And it appears we are about to find out, as down the corridor strides a Ronnie Corbett lookalike, a tiny, dapper man, sixties easily, rectangular-framed glasses, collar and tie covered by a spotless white medical coat. 'A cement mixer collided with a prison van earlier today' I whisper. 'Motorists are asked to keep a lookout for fifteen hardened criminals!'

Chrissie is holding on to the counter, giggling helplessly, as Ronnie approaches. 'Buenas dias' he smiles, taking her plastic wallet and checking the name with a list on his clipboard. 'Follow me please.' And he leads us down the hallway, towards….. a huge ward at the end…. no! He throws open a door on the left, peeks inside to check it if empty, and gestures us inside. A private room! Not five-star, admittedly, as the decor is minimalist, to say the least, but one hospital bed, two visitors' chairs, various medical paraphernalia… and what appears to be a tubular-framed camp bed. So it was true! Looks a bit small for my ample frame, mind you, but still, I've slept on worse, and the floor is tiled so there will be no squelchy, lagery carpet to negotiate. *And maybe I can persuade Chrissie to swap beds…*

'Make yourselves at home' Ronnie beams, 'I will be back soon.'

'And it's good night from him!' my wife titters, perching herself on the edge of her bed.

'And it's good night from me!' I cackle, dropping the bag, kicking off my espadrilles, and climbing onto my sleeping arrangements. *Blimey, mattress is a bit thin, probably designed for diminutive, ten-stone Spaniards.* I haul myself to my feet. 'Anyway, you will be very comfortable on that. Now, shift off my bed, will you, I had an early start this morning, I need a lie down!'

'On your bike, sunsh…'

Suddenly there is a knock at the door and Ronnie appears again, catching us laughing. *Blimey* he must be thinking, *what wonderful, easy patients these British are. No kissing, arm-flapping, hand-waving, standing around arguing, no mothers-in-law giving out orders...* He walks over to a cupboard in the corner, and extracts a hospital gown. 'Take off all your clothes please' he instructs me, 'put them in the wardrobe there, and get yourself into bed. I will be back in a couple of minutes.'

Now, no sniggering at the back, please. We're in a foreign country here. Things are different. They've provided me with accommodation for the night, maybe they need me to shed my street clothes, to avoid contamination? Chrissie is in stitches. 'Are you going commando? You will need to maintain your dignity, if you do, you know, man-spreading and all that. Keep your knees together at all times, please! Do you need me to tie you up, at the back? Just hold on while I get a photo!'

'I'll give you man-spreading!' I frown, puffing, mock-serious, stripping down to my underwear and hauling the gown, seams groaning, down over my shoulders. 'I...can...hardly...get...the...bloody...thing...over...my...gut!'

Another knock at the door and in pops Ronnie again. *Lovely people, these English. Always laughing.* He extracts a wrist-band from the plastic wallet and places it over my arm. The wrist-band bearing the legend Richards Cristina. 'No No No!' cries the person who actually goes by that name. 'That is me! I am having the operation, not him!'

Ronnie looks poleaxed for a split second, then bursts out laughing. *Stupid people, these English. Look at him, bulging out of that gown, and he's not even having a bloody operation...* 'Sorry' he giggles. 'I didn't recognise your British name. 'YOU take of all your clothes please, put them in the wardrobe there, and get yourself into bed. I will be back in a couple of minutes.'

My wife can barely stand. 'Come on Richards Cristina, give me my gown please! Ohh look, you've busted the seams, squeezing your great fat corpse into it. Damaging hospital property indeed. Still, I will have air-vents in the sides I suppose, in case it gets hot in the operating theatre!'

Niftily, with the utmost decorum, she slips the gown over her head, then manages to undress from the inside, a feat of endeavour beyond my wildest imagination, being someone who often manages to get two feet into the same trouser-leg. Now, of course, it is my turn to extract the Michael. 'Bloody hell, you look like a bell-tent! How many Wolf-Cubs do you have under there? Will we be sitting round a camp-fire later, eating burned sausages, singing Ging-Gang-Goolie-Goolie!?'

'Yeah, well at least we won't have to see your burned sausage and your Ging-Gang-Goolie, will we? I told you to keep your leg…..'

A rat-a-tat-tat at the door and in slips Ronnie, followed by a nurse, although sadly not the same one last seen sprawled across Pablo, which is probably just as well. This one means business, clearly, bearing a saline bag which she hooks up to a stand, while Ronnie attaches the wrist-band to the correct patient. The nurse then produces a cellophane package which looks suspiciously like something which might contain a needle, involving blood, and I just about manage to stagger to the window and fix my gaze on the far side of the car-park, and very interesting it is too, lots of cars, all different colours, many displaying the usual Spanish battle-damage, and ooh look there is that tranny-via thing, with no tranny, which Gobby-Enry he fixy, apparently, much embarrass-ed, and will you look at all those olive trees stretching to the horizon, I wonder if there are any dohhs weeld out there today, jumping into the branches.

The closing of the door announces that we are alone again, and I turn, ashen-faced, in severe need of a Spanish shoshage, to see my wife sat up in bed, draped in tubes, involving needles, I assume, although I cannot bear to look, which causes my stomach to lurch, although she seems extremely relaxed about the whole thing, surprisingly. 'Looks like I'm on the way, shortly' she smiles, brightly. 'Try not to faint, while I am gone, you poor chap. Best have a lie down, we don't want you falling over, causing any more damage to hospital property, do we? Would you like a quick peek at my NEEDLE before they take me down?'

SHUT UP, OK! Suddenly there is another tap on the door and in strides the nurse. 'Follow me, plees.' Suddenly she glances at my wife's lack of footwear, as presumably barefoot-Chrissie was under the impression they would wheel her down to the theatre. Or not, then. 'WHERE ARE YOUR SLIPPERS?'

*Er, at home?* Nobody said anything about slippers. The letter didn't mention anything, did it? A change of interior clothes yes, footwear, no. Anyway, what does it matter? She has her trainers, so I cross to the wardrobe, where they have been safely stored, as instructed by Ronnie, and hand them to my puzzled-looking wife. The nurse is not happy, however. 'No, not trainers. You must have slippers?' What is this? What difference does it make? Is the operating theatre fitted-out with ruinously expensive shag-pile, or magic carpets, woven by nomadic tribesmen from the fleeces of rare Himalayan mountain goats? Priceless Roman mosaics? Chrissie has a pair of slippers, of course, mules I think they would be called, but she wears them into the street, in the mornings, gathering her daily bread from Jose the Pan, and into the garden in the afternoons. So they are hardly sterile. Is that what all this is about? Undoubtedly, had she known, she would have bought a box-fresh pair, removed the tissue under the nose of old Hattie Jacques here, who, incredibly, appears to be refusing to budge.

Bloody hell, does this mean the operation is canceled? Do I need to dash off somewhere and buy a pair? Where? Is there a hospital shop? A retail outlet, like in the UK, an over-priced rip-off emporium, where the same stuff is half as much again as in the equivalent high-street store? Didn't see one, on the way in, although we didn't spot the reception either, did we? Suddenly, there is another tap on the door and in pops Ronnie, with a *what the hell is keeping you* look on his face. 'She has no slippers!' Hattie cries, accusingly.

Mr Corbett is dumbfounded. 'You have no slippers? Why do you have no slippers please?'

I have had just about enough of this. Inwardly raging, but nevertheless maintaining a sunny demeanour as the last thing we want is to jeopardise the whole operation over a stupid pair of footwear, I cross the room, extract the letter from Chrissie's bag, point to the bit about the change of pants and the after-shave, and swallow my pride. 'Sorry, we are English. We didn't know.'

Ronnie smiles. *Oh what a store of tales he has for out in his street, tonight.* 'OK, don't worry, but next time please remember to bring your slippers.' And he turns to Hattie. 'OK you can take her down, now.'

Hattie hasn't finished yet, however. 'OK, you can wear the trainers, but don't tie the laces, please. Just tuck the laces in.' And she mimics this action, in a *well you're too stupid to remember your slippers so here we are on the first day at primary school* kind of way. *Grrrr. How did we possibly make it to the grand old age of nearly sixty without this woman?* 'Follow me, please.'

*Blimey, this is it! She is off.* Got to give her a quick kiss, for luck, Chrissie I mean, not Hattie, or, heaven forbid, Ronnie, so without looking down, in case I spot something sharp and awful, and placing my hands on her shoulders to avoid ripping out any important tubing, I do just that, and the three of them file out into the corridor, closing the door behind them. I slump flat-out onto my camp-bed and close my eyes. Been a hell of a morning so far, all this hospital business. I mean, it's fine for my wife, she used to work in one, two actually, so she is used to this stuff, whereas me? Someone who gave their first pint of blood back when *Bohemian Rhapsody* was number-one, then promptly collapsed? Still, got a restorative pint of Guinness out of it from my concerned colleagues that day, thus setting the standard for every subsequent donation, but I'm just not good with matters medical. Gonna need that shoshage soon, but I'll just close my eyes for a few minutes…. actually, why am I scrunched up on this contraption, when there's a perfectly good hospital bed across the room? Who's going to know? Not coming back any time soon, are they? Closing the curtains, I hop up, adjust the pillows, stretch out luxuriously, and……. gone.

…... Suddenly I am running down a hospital corridor, pursued by the Two Ronnies, Freddy Mercury dressed in a blood transfusion uniform, and the entire cast of *Carry On Matron,* all of whom are shouting *slippers, don't forget your slippers, tuck in your laces, JONNEEE POR FAVOR! Cornish pasty, no bloody carrots, JONNEE POR FAVOR! Just gotta get out, just gotta get right out of he-re, which way Glass-ton-boor plees, where you raddyo-graffia from Eengland, take her to the oor-hen-thee-ya, neighbour, tell your woman to take one, three times a day….* Frantically, I crash round a corner to be confronted by Peter Pan and a huge great jaw-snapping crocodile, hollering *Soutt-end, Lon-Donn Soutt-*

*end, fees and cheep,* then Tinkerbell is hovering above me, laughing, laughing…. I open my eyes to find Chrissie, hand over her mouth, tittering helplessly, and Ronnie, who is also finding it funny. *Well, sleeping is a national pastime in this country.. but thank God Hattie is nowhere to be seen….*

My wife is still attached to her drip, so Ronnie plumps up her pillows, ostentatiously brushing down the blanket, thus removing all traces of large Englishmen, and helps her up. 'Relax now, please. I will return in two hours. Enjoy your siesta!'

Chrissie is clearly flagging, eyelids drooping, mouth numb from the anaesthetic. 'I need to sthleep!' she smiles, 'buth everythingth wath fine. There were three polypths, they removth them all, and the biopthy report will be…. a…. couple…. oth…. weekths……' Away to the land of nod.

Still haven't had my Hundred Montaditos yet, or even a single one, come to that, but I can hardly pop out now, can I, in case she wakes and needs something. *Just have to pray that my rumbling stomach doesn't wake her….* I climb aboard my camp-bed, wince painfully as my hip-bone jars against the frame, close my eyes…..

Several minutes, or it could have been several hours, later, comes another knock on the door and a tiny, smiley nurse enters the room. 'Time to have the saline removed! Then you can have a drink!' *Thank God, I am parched.* Or maybe she means Chrissie. Hang on, saline? Needles? I scrabble to my feet and dash to the window. Ooh look at that, a Chinese restaurant across the road. *Iron Wok, buffet libre* it says. Libre? Free? Surely not, they must mean *eat all you like.* This is torture, as I am absolutely ravenous, probably better off watching the needle removal, actually, but there is the tranny-via, still no tranny, mind you, wonder how much the Chinese buffet is? I could kill for a spring roll. NO don't think of that, has she finished yet? It appears she has. 'The doctor will be round in half an hour, then you can go home' she confirms, to my evidently-relieved spouse, who I have to say is looking vastly improved, having been relieved of her pipework.

Smiley departs, then immediately another tap on the door heralds the arrival of a trolley, a food trolley, pushed by a saviour, a Goddess, a bringer of nourishment to famished visitors, sorry, patients. *But what if it is meat?*

Shoshage, even. A repast entirely unsuitable for vegetarians? Couldn't let it go to waste, could I? Would be rude, wouldn't it? Ungrateful, even. *Fingers crossed...* Our good shepherdess places a large tray, easily two feet wide, onto the bed-table, grins, knowingly, and departs. Blimey, looks big enough for two, this tray, covered as it is by a molded plastic top, in the shape of a cup and at least three plates and dishes. *She can have the dessert.* I reach across, and start to prise off the lid. 'Oi, hands off, fatty. Oww! Yes I am feeling much better. Oww! Thank you for asking. Oww! The anaesthetic has worn off. Oww! But my throat is really sore, and it hurts to swallow. Oww!'

'Sorry!' I giggle. 'It is so long since I last ate, I have become delirious. Who are you again? Is this an oasis? Are there camels, lapping contentedly from a palm-fringed watering-hole? Anyway, you are off solids, for a few days surely? Bread and milk, like a hedgehog. Which is there, look.' And I tap the dish-shape. 'So get the lid off, and let me get at it!'

'No! Oww! This is mine. Ahh! You had the chance to go down Hundred Montaditos, while I was gone. But what did you do? Ahh! You fell asleep. So get back on your camp bed.' She narrows her eyes, and cackles, like some demented old witch. 'This is mine, all mine! Oww!' Slowly, she peels of the lid, and bursts out laughing. 'Oww oww oww!' She throws the cover across the bed, in disgust, to reveal a plastic mug sitting forlornly in the middle of the tray, and a cellophane pack containing two cheap, plain biscuits. 'Milk. Hot milk. I hate hot milk. Oww! Can you believe this? I don't think I've ever been so disappointed in my life. Apart from our wedding-night, of course. Oww! Why did they need this damn great tray for a stupid little cup of milk? Oww! My mouth feels like the armpit of one of those camels you just mentioned, and they give me bloody milk. OWW!'

I am slumped on my camp-bed, tears streaming down my face. 'Told you, didn't I? Bread and milk. Biscuits and milk. Just dunk your Rich Tea, and suck! But could you let me have one of your biscuits, please?' Absolutely priceless, her face was a picture, although that wedding-night jibe will be a discussion for another day. I thought it was a fantastic evening, actually. What was it, fourteen or fifteen pints of McEwen's Export I drank? Anyway, I still have one last surprise up my sleeve. Been a difficult day for her, hasn't it? A difficult few weeks, all in all. 'Listen' I smile. 'Tonight, when we finally get home, I will be serving *salmorejo,* you know, that chilled, thick, spicy, tomato, *gazpacho* soup. We had some in Cordoba, remember? You loved it, and it will be easy on the old tonsils, for you. Rick Stein has a recipe for it, in his book.'

She reaches across and squeezes my arm, although sadly not to pass me her remaining Rich Tea. 'That sounds great, and thank you for today. Oww!'

My eyes crinkle. 'Me? What have I done, today? Been asleep for most of it! Couldn't find the way in, or the reception, ripped your gown and wrinkled up your sheets, told a few Two Ronnies jokes, almost got naked and exposed my Ging-Gang-Goolie. Great help, wasn't I? And I have no idea where I left the car!' *Still, I know what she means. I think.*

The doctor duly arrives, discharges his patient, I manage to locate the car, and before we know it we are approaching home, just as dusk is falling. 'Tell you what' I smile. 'I will try to find a parking space on the zigzag, to save you walking. I am dead on my feet, so I can only imagine how you are feeling!' And by a miracle, there is just enough space to squeeze a little white SEAT in, although sadly I fail to factor in the possibility that one or two locals might be sprawled on cane chairs, clinging to the rocky hillside, enjoying the cool of the evening. Pirate Pete. *Oh no.* 'Where you been, neighbour?' he cries, spotting the overnight bag. 'Your caravan? Loli didn't say you were going to your caravan. Did you know they were in their caravan, Antonia? Manuela? Did anyone know? Nobody told me! Why did nobody tell me?'

Wearily, Chrissie explains that she has had a small operation on her throat, her *garganta,* to remove a few polyps. *Why did she say that? Why didn't she just agree with him. None the wiser. Gonna take the next hundred years to get home, now.*

'Poly-pus, neighbour? You don't get poly-pus down the *garganta!* I had poly-pus, neighbour. Up the arse! You hear that, up the ARSE! Isn't that right, Antonia, tell the English, I had poly-pus up the ARSE!' *There might be one or two people on the Costa del Sol who didn't get that, but I doubt it.*

'You disgusting old man!' Auntie Vera groans. 'Who cares about your ARSE? Cristina here has been to HH-ayen for an operation on her *garganta,* today. Shut up and go to bed!' And she envelops my wife in a massive bear-hug.

Pedro the pirate is not letting it go, however. 'Manuela! Where did I have my poly-pus, eh?' And he extends his middle finger, jabbing it in the direction of where the sun don't shine.

Leopard-skin Woman regards him distastefully, extends her own middle finger, and cackling manically, waves it under his nose. Antonia joins her, digit duly extended, and for a few seconds we relish in the spectacle of a Spanish finger-fight, like the Three Musketeers on their way home from the pub, after a skinful of beer. We finally make it home, mentally and physically exhausted. Wear you out, the Spanish neighbours, don't they? The hospital was a doddle, compared to running the gauntlet of that lot. *Bless them, though. We wouldn't have it any other way…...* Chrissie slumps on the sofa, I pour us a restorative glass of red each, then head out to the kitchen and start work on my creation, which I have to tell you goes down an absolute treat. Chrissie is in raptures, although bearing in mind she has only eaten two biscuits and drunk a half-cup of tepid milk in the last twenty-six hours, she damn well ought to be.

Insisting she is feeling very much better, she offers to take care of the washing-up, what little there is. *Oh hell, I forgot… I'm for it now.* Suddenly, comes the sound of agitated bellowing. 'You cheating swine! What is this? A carton? An empty carton of supermarket salmorejo? And you pretended to make it yourself! Oww! I can't believe you lied to me like that!'

I am rocking with laughter, tears in my eyes. 'Au contraire, my sweetness! I merely said there was a recipe, in Mr Stein's book, I didn't say I was actually following it, did I? Is it my fault, if you failed to pay attent….**OWW!**'


**THE FINAL CHAPTER. WASHING THE MONEY.**


It is with such overwhelming relief that I splutter down the final hill into Cherbourg, northern France, navigate the last few nondescript roundabouts, following the signs for *Poole Ferry,* and bring the bike to a juddering halt next to a half-dozen hairy, pierced and tattooed bikers slouched over a few scruffy benches outside a run-down chip van. Journeys end, for now at least. Relief for my aching torso, and soft bodily tissue, after two whole days in the saddle, over eleven-hundred miles across Spain and France, staying last night in Bayonne, in one of those French chain-hotels which bizarrely only sell overpriced beer, if you are prepared to buy overpriced food. *Une biere et une bag of Planters, s'il vous plaît? Non.* Relief too for my poor Harley, front brake having given up the ghost, the side-stand spring broken, held up temporarily by a bungee hook to avoid it dragging on the road, and unforgivably, bald patches showing in places on the back tyre. I deserve to be taken out and publicly shot, letting it get in that state, and I don't even have the excuse of the bike being a fifteen minute walk away on a dusty side street. No, it lives in our hallway, and I pass it dozens of times a day. In my defence, there was tread visible when I left home yesterday, *so it was five-hundred miles of rough French tarmac wot did it, officer.* That's my story, and I'm sticking to it. Anyway, all this, together with a brand-new MOT, will be sorted by my old mate Anton, in his excellent bike shop, two days hence, provided I can avoid any broken glass on the A35 that is. Chrissie will then fly over and we will have a holiday, visiting her mother, our girls, old friends, same as we did last year, only without the stress of petty parking regulations, and jobsworths, hopefully.

Wincing painfully, all the while grinning at my fellow road-warriors, I un-clip the bungee, allowing the side-stand to drop into position, and ease my right leg, which is numb from the waist down, over the saddle, and stagger to my full height, more or less. 'Anything in there worth eating?' I enquire of the hirsute horde, nodding at the kiosk. Christ, you should see the beards on these fellas, like a *ZZ Top* reunion gig, with extra hair. The one nearest me is ginger, half a dozen shades of, and he reminds me of a toddler who has just consumed a Cow & Gate peach dessert, then vomited the lot down his bib. His mate must be twenty-five stone, easily, face the size of a shovel onto which eyes, a nose and a pair of rubbery lips has been painted, with a forty-eight inch waist crammed optimistically into a pair of thirty-six inch leather trousers, the resulting muffin-top resembling a kiddies rubber ring stuffed under his bulging *Iron Maiden* tee-shirt. Or perhaps I am doing the guy a disservice. Maybe he is actually the size of Twiggy, but a nervous sailor, bearing in mind we are about to cross the busiest shipping lane in the world, in the dark, and has brought his own life-belt, which he is already wearing, in case, I dunno, unable to see his feet, he topples into the turgid waters of the dock?

'Nah' chuckles vomit-bib, 'unless you fancy eating the runners from the two-fifteen at Kempton Park, last Boxing Day. Ain't that right, Gnasher?', addressing another of the group, who, demolishing the remains of what might once have been a bacon-quadruple-cheese-burger, with extra fries and a tub of coleslaw, mouth crammed to the brim, is only able to nod, enthusiastically. His mates however start whinnying convincingly, and the whole bunch burst out laughing.

'Eat the horse, the rider and his bloody saddle, our Gnasher, wouldn't you, mate?' cries a multi-pierced specimen, with more metal attached to various parts of his head than you'd find in a Russian scrap-yard.

Boggle-eyed, old Gnash swallows painfully. 'If you ain't careful, Nobber, I'll eat your bloody saddle. Then you'd look great, wouldn't you, riding along with your battery up yer arse!'

'Give him extra sparks, to his plugs, though, wouldn't it!' chuckles Twiggy. Make him go a bit, you know, faster?'

With no visible markings of any description, and only a single day's growth on my chin, I am beginning to feel somewhat out of place among this lot, like a vicar in a lap-dancing club. 'Reckon I'll give it a miss, then' I grin, warily eyeing Gnasher's road-accident on a plate. 'Not that hungry, any more, actually! Think I'll just head inside the terminal, point Percy, wash this French dust out of my eyes.'

'He's enough to put a condemned man off his last meal, is Gnasher!' shouts scrap-yard, as I shuffle painfully across the car park. 'Don't be too long, though, they'll have us boarding, in about ten minutes.'

Chrissie and I have a system in place regarding communications, when I am on these bike trips. Basically, she doesn't bother, on the grounds that I would be unable to hear the phone ringing, or a message arriving, over the noise of the engine. So at the end of the day, or when I have arrived, I will give her a call. Inside the terminal, I check my phone, and see she has sent me a message.

'Give me a ring, as soon as you get this.' Oh blimey. Sounds serious, whatever it is that has happened.

Quick as a flash I dial her number, and she answers almost immediately, in a small, frightened voice, almost as if she has been crying. 'It's our Spanish bank account' she sniffs. 'They have frozen it, completely.'

This sounds ridiculous. 'What? Why in the hell would they do that? Are you sure?'

'If you would let me finish' she shouts, clearly in some distress, 'I went down there today, tried to pay in a hundred euros, to cover any water or electric bills while we are away, and they wouldn't let me. No paying in, no withdrawals. Account suspended. I had to go to see the manager, it was so embarrassing, frogmarched almost, I was so scared, he was babbling away but I was so flustered I couldn't take anything in.'

'Did you manage to catch anything else he said?' I enquire, somewhat aggrieved to hear about this officious jobsworth banker, when I am over a thousand miles away, with a ferry to catch.

'Oh, I don't know' she wails, '*limpiar dinero,* cleaning money, was what he said, God knows what that is supposed to mean, but that is it. We have been sussed, they have caught up with us. Rumbled. Without a bank account, we are finished, here.'

Suddenly I am gripped by panic, sick to the very depths of my stomach. Somehow, however, I manage to retain a sense of normality, in my voice. 'Oh, don't worry. You know what the Spanish are like. It will be something and nothing, just some ridiculous bureaucracy, a few forms to fill in. Forget it, and when we get back from the UK we will nip down there and get it all sorted. How much was in the account, anyway?'

She brightens, considerably. 'Well, there was about a hundred in there, but there might have been an electricity bill come out recently, I was going to get the passbook written up, but of course he wouldn't do that, either. But eighty euros, definitely.'

'So there you are then' I reply, reassuringly, 'that is plenty to cover any bills while we are away. We can go down there next month, and tell him to stuff his useless bank where the sun don't shine! Forget all about it. So, are you all ready for the bus ride to the airport tomorrow? Got your boarding pass all sorted out? Have you given Lydia the key, so she can pop in and water your plants? Looking forward to that lumpy old spare bed in your mother's?'

She laughs, and we discuss the various details of our journeys, and when we will finally meet up, but I cannot help wondering; *was I wrong to have lied to her?*

Stomach clenched with an icy grip of fear, I stumble, unseeingly, around the terminal, my mind a jumble of thoughts, all of them negative. *Why did this have to happen now, when everything was going so well?* The result of the biopsy on the polyps came through just a few days ago, the burden of the past month suddenly lifted from our shoulders, such overwhelming relief. Suddenly, I become aware of a voice, calling out, and I turn to see the girl behind the ticket desk, gesturing frantically in the direction of the ferry. Time to board, presumably. I wave vaguely, forcing a smile, but really all I want to do is head straight back to Santa Marta, and get this hideous mess sorted. How can I possibly enjoy a holiday, with the sword of Damocles hanging over us? I stumble outside, and see that the car park is in darkness. The bikers have departed, the chip van shuttered, and the guy on the customs post is waving irritably for me to get a move on. Instant decision time. Chrissie will not be there, by the time I get back, if I go back, and I have no idea where the bank book, or account details, are kept anyway. I have no choice but to continue with this pretence, this ridiculous charade of normality, for the next three weeks in the UK. Slinging my leg over the saddle, I straighten the bike, haul up the bungee to retract the stand, fire up the engine, and after a cursory glance at my passport, I am allowed to board.

Following the directions of the yellow-jacketed stewards, I park the bike in the depths of the ferry, stuff the key in my pocket then head straight out onto the deck, where I slump against the railing, staring blindly at the murky water of the harbour. *Cleaning money?* Money Laundering, of course. A serious criminal offence. Taking the proceeds of crime, and by a series of financial transactions, eventually obtaining 'clean' money. In my former life, in the accountants office, we were required, by law, to nominate a Money Laundering Reporting Officer, in our case the senior partner of the firm, to whom even the slightest suspicions, however trivial, had to be notified. It was then the duty of the MLRO to investigate, and if justified, report the findings to the Serious Organised Crime Agency I think it was, if memory serves.

So how in the name of all things holy have we been accused, or suspected, of this grave matter? On an account containing less than a hundred quid? In Spain, of all places, where a healthy disregard for the law seems like an everyday pastime? The rules are Europe-wide of course, although my memory is hazy, having promptly forgotten most of what I had learned, over the course of my career, the day I retired, but wasn't the cash limit fifteen thousand? Euros or sterling, I cannot remember, but clearly we have nothing to worry about. A storm in a teacup, and for the first time in what seems ages, I start to breathe easier. All of a sudden I am starving hungry. Time to investigate what they have to eat, on this boat. Not gristly ram, with rice and gravy, hopefully.

*Hang on a minute.* The icy grip returns, with a vengeance. We transferred twenty-five thousand sterling, via a currency exchange, into this Spanish account, to buy the house, less than two years ago, and that must be what this is all about. A bank audit presumably picked it up. The funds came from my pension pot, my tax-free lump sum, and I imagine I could provide a paper-trail, to prove it. In English, of course, so would they understand it? And as residents of Spain, are pension lump-sums actually tax-free over here? Should I have declared it? My stomach is in knots.

Then again, couldn't we just walk away from the account? Less than a hundred? Go against the grain, of course, but it wouldn't be the end of the world, to write that amount off. We only use the account for the electric and water bills, and we could easily pay these in the respective offices. Just forget all about the stupid bank. Or could we? This *limpiar dinero* business was obviously flagged-up on their system, and they know where we live, of course. If we don't get it sorted, might they pass it on to a higher authority? *And they had our passports.* Took copies, when we opened the account. *Oh dear God in Heaven.*

Wracked with dread, I glance mournfully at the outline of the French coast, disappearing into the dusk, lights of the little town twinkling. Is this really it? Is this the beginning of the end, of our lives in the land of sunsets, and olives?